Oracle 11g New Features
Get Started Fast with Oracle 11g Enhancements

Oracle In-Focus Series

Brian Carr
John Garmany
Lutz Hartmann
V. J. Jain
Steve Karam

RAMPANT
TECHPRESS

This book is dedicated to my amazing wife Toni and my three beautiful children Alex, Olivia and Adam. Toni, thank you for always believing in me. To all the wonderful people at Rampant TechPress, I thank you.

-Brian Carr

I dedicate my work in this book to my lovely wife Kristina, who has been and always will be my motivation to excel. I would also like to thank Robin Rademacher for her outstanding work managing the production of this book.

- Steve Karam

Oracle 11g New Features
Get Started Fast with Oracle 11g Enhancements

By Brian Carr, John Garmany, Lutz Hartmann, V. J. Jain, and Steve Karam

Copyright © 2008 by Rampant TechPress. All rights reserved.

Printed in the United States of America.

Published in Kittrell, North Carolina, USA.

Oracle In-focus Series: Book #30

Series Editor: Donald K. Burleson

Production Manager: Robin Rademacher

Editor: Valerre Aquitaine and Stephanie Filio

Production Editor: Teri Wade

Cover Design: Janet Burleson

Printing History: September 2008 for First Edition

ISBN: 978-0-9797951-0-7

Library of Congress Control Number: 2008936207

Table of Contents

Using the Online Code Depot

Purchase of this book provides complete access to the online code depot that contains sample code scripts. Any code depot scripts in this book are located at the following URL in zip format and ready to load and use:

rampant.cc/oracle_11g.htm

If technical assistance is needed with downloading or accessing the scripts, please contact Rampant TechPress at rtp@rampant.cc.

Conventions Used in this Book

It is critical for any technical publication to follow rigorous standards and employ consistent punctuation conventions to make the text easy to read. However, this is not an easy task. Within database terminology, there are many types of notation that can confuse a reader. For example, some Oracle utilities such as STATSPACK and TKPROF are always spelled in CAPITAL letters, while Oracle parameters and procedures have varying naming conventions in the database documentation. It is also important to remember that many database commands are case sensitive, and are always left in their original executable form, and never altered with italics or capitalization.

Hence, all Rampant TechPress books follow these conventions:

Parameters – All database parameters will be *lowercase italics*. Exceptions to this rule are parameter arguments that are commonly capitalized (KEEP pool, TKPROF), these will be left in ALL CAPS.

Variables – All procedural language (e.g. PL/SQL) program variables and arguments will also remain in *lowercase italics* (*dbms_job, dbms_utility*).

Tables & dictionary objects – All data dictionary objects are referenced in lowercase italics (*dba_indexes, v$sql*). This includes all *v$* and *x$* views (*x$kcbcbh, v$parameter*) and dictionary views (*dba_tables, user_indexes*).

SQL – All SQL is formatted for easy use in the code depot, and all SQL is displayed in lowercase. The main SQL terms (select, from, where, group by, order by, having) will always appear on a separate line.

Programs & Products – All products and programs that are known to the author are capitalized according to the vendor

---

specifications (CentOS, VMware, Oracle, etc). All names known by Rampant TechPress to be trademark names appear in this text as initial caps. References to UNIX are always made in uppercase.

Acknowledgements

This type of highly technical reference book requires the dedicated efforts of many people. Even though we are the authors, our work ends when we deliver the content. After each chapter is delivered, several Oracle DBAs carefully review and correct the technical content. After the technical review, experienced copy editors polish the grammar and syntax.

The finished work is then reviewed as page proofs and turned over to the production manager, who arranges the creation of the online code depot and manages the cover art, printing distribution, and warehousing.

In short, the authors play a small role in the development of this book, and we need to thank and acknowledge everyone who helped bring this book to fruition:

Robin Rademacher, for the production management, including the coordination of the cover art, page proofing, printing, and distribution.

Teri Wade, for help in the production of the page proofs.

Janet Burleson, for exceptional cover design and graphics.

John Lavender, for assistance with the web site, and for creating the code depot and the online shopping cart for this book.

With our sincerest thanks,

John Garmany
Steve Karam
Lutz Hartmann
V. J. Jain
Brian Carr

Credits

It is always difficult to write about features included in a brand new release since there are almost no references other than the online documentation available, no notes in metalink and only a few white papers in OTN. I was very lucky to get hold of the beta software very early and could start testing already half a year before the final release was published and was in direct contact with a number of Beta Testers in Switzerland

It was a great opportunity to take part in the pilot course for the 11g New Features for Administrators Course which was run in San Francisco in May 2007 even before the final release was published. This was a test run and was running on the last beta version and was attended by a handful of internal Oracle trainers from all over the world and I am very proud that I was one of the very few externals who were allowed into the class. Jean-Francois Verrier, Oracle's courseware developer for all New Features and RAC courses was our trainer in this course. It is always a great experience to have Jean-Francois delivering since he is one of the very few people in the world who are very close to Oracle Server Technologies and the developers and a t the same time is a highly skilled trainer. I could not imagine any better introduction and Jean-Francois did not leave any question unanswered although I had a lot of questions. He was wearing a t-shirt that showed that he had successfully challenged the Oak Table Network, this group of experts who claim that they can answer any Oracle question within 24 hours.

The second source for in depth answers were the information booths at the Oracle Open World Conference in September 2007 also in San Francisco where I had the chance to talk directly to a couple of the developers and designers of the New Features themselves. This is like drinking from the source.

But big challenge was to find qualified technical reviewers who were able to prove the contents of my chapters. I found them in four former colleagues working for Oracle University. Without them I would have not been able to deliver my chapters in time.

So I want to take this opportunity to thank Dr. Gerlinde Frenzen, Michael Cebulla and Roman Niehoff who are all trainers working for Oracle University in Duesseldorf in Germany as well as Jan van Stappen who is the lead trainer in Oracle's training Center in Brussels, Belguim. All of them were among the first to deliver 11g New Features Courses for Oracle Education. They all spent a great deal of their valuable free time even on public holidays to make it possible that I did not cross the publisher's delivery deadlines too much. We were all working under high pressure. I hope that I can pay this back to all of them some day.

Furthermore I want to than my father Walter Hartmann, who encouraged me a lot all the time to keep on going and even hosted me and Michael's entire family in his flat for a weekend.

Lutz Hartmann

Introduction to 11g New Features

CHAPTER

Inside 11g New Features

At Oracle Openworld 2006, Oracle announced some exciting new features of Oracle 11g, and they promise 482 new Oracle 11g features. Here is a list of some of the new Oracle 11g features:

- 11g SQL new features
- 11g language support new features
- 11g PL/SQL new features
- 11g DBA features
- 11g RAC new features & enhancements
- 11g performance features
- 11g security new features
- 11g Enterprise Manager new features
- 11g RMAN features
- 11g data mining

In this chapter, the new features in Oracle Database 11g that are the most important to the DBA and developer staff will be covered in more detail.

Oracle 11g DBA New Features

Partitioning in Oracle has played a key role in the support of very large databases and data warehousing requirements. One of the shortcomings of its use is that partition management has traditionally been assigned as a routine DBA task. Oracle 11g has introduced a new partitioning enhancement called Interval Partitioning that allows for the automatic creation of partitions based on a predefined interval of the partition key. This new feature is an extension to range partitioning and will likely prove to be a godsend for many DBAs that are responsible for the manual creation of new range partitions.

System Partitioning is a new feature that allows application level control for partitioning a table and indexes. The table or index is defined with partitions but does not contain a partition key. All operations on system partitioned objects need to explicitly state the partition.

When tables contain a clear parent-child relationship, reference partitioning allows the partitioning scheme of the child table to be inherited from the parent table based on a referential constraint. This eliminates the need to include duplicate columns in the child table. Since partition operations on the parent table automatically cascade to the child table, it also removes the need to manage partitions for the child table.

When the optimal partition key is derived from the values of other columns, Virtual Column-Based Partitioning supports partitioning based on that expression (virtual column). This eliminates the need for inefficient workarounds to achieve the same functionality such as including an additional physical column in the table and using triggers or additional application code to populate the additional column.

Composite Partitioning Enhancements – Prior to 11g, composite partitioning was limited to range-list and range-hash. With this release, all composite partitioning options are now available including range-range, list-range, list-list, and list-hash. These partitioning strategies are also accessible with interval and virtual column-based partitioning.

Partition Pruning Enhancements – The performance of partition pruning has been enhanced by the use of bloom filtering instead of subquery pruning. Partition pruning is now activated for any join involving a partitioned object.

Information Lifecycle Management (ILM) has been around for decades and has become a more important issue as the volume of data has historically grown with each passing year. Most companies regard their data storage as one of the most valuable assets in an organization. Oracle 11g is an ideal solution for enhanced ILM since the Oracle database is able to store all different data formats in a single location. This is advantageous since having all of the data in one database allows for simple implementation of an organization's ILM policy as well as a significant cost savings.

To meet the growing needs of organizations for better data retention policies, Oracle 11g features the ILM Assistant, a GUI designed to help users determine the best ILM policies. This GUI can help determine when it is appropriate to purge or move qualifying data to less expensive storage devices. The 11g ILM assistant is also capable of simulating different data storage models to help the user determine the most appropriate ILM solution. By leveraging Oracle's existing architecture with new data management features in Oracle 11g, such as enhanced partitioning and advanced data compression, the ILM assistant provides a simple tool for the management of multi-tiered data.

Invisible indexes are a new 11g feature that allow an index to be maintained by the database but ignored by the optimizer unless explicitly specified. Invisible indexes are useful for testing the removal of an index and for online application upgrades.

Table compression has been useful for DBAs in a data warehousing environment where bulk loads are common. This feature offers significant savings in disk storage, I/O, and redo. Oracle 11g has enhanced this feature for use in OLTP environments by introducing the option to use compression for all DML operations including inserts, updates, and deletes.

Oracle 11g has introduced a new method for accessing NFS V3 servers directly using an internal Direct NFS Client as part of the Oracle Database kernel. This improves performance and manageability by allowing Oracle-specific optimizations to be utilized. The direct NFS client eliminates the dependency on the operating system cache and allows for asynchronous I/O. Additionally, it removes the need to manually configure and tune most of the NFS client parameters.

Oracle 11g has introduced Database Resident Connection Pooling (DRCP) to support server-side connection pooling. Prior to this feature, only multithreaded applications were eligible to take advantage of session sharing capability. With DRCP, different application processes can share sessions on the same machine and also across a multitude of machines. This feature greatly increases the scalability of applications that cannot be deployed as multithreaded, such as PHP applications. This feature also benefits multi-threaded applications by relieving the overhead of maintaining a persistent connection to the database during idle periods.

Oracle Call Interface (OCI) Consistent Client Cache is a new caching feature that is complementary to the server result cache. The client result cache allows OCI clients to fetch result sets directly from a cache stored in the client's process memory instead of having the server execute queries repeatedly. This feature is enabled at the database level and since it is an inherent mechanism, it is transparently available to all OCI-based clients without requiring any changes to the application. This can provide significant improvements in response times, scalability, and the consumption of database resources.

Oracle 11g also introduces a new feature that allows virtual columns to be used in database tables. A virtual column is a column that is actually an expression stored in the table's metadata, such as "create table v1 (d1 number, d2 number, d3 as (d1+d2) virtual)" where column d3 appears to be a normal column in the table v1 but does not use disk space since it exists only in metadata. Virtual columns can be indexed, used as a partitioning key, and can contain optimizer statistics.

Prior to 11g, XML storage was limited to being either CLOB (unstructured) or schema-based (structured). CLOB storage consumes large amounts of disk space and has poor relational data access. Schema-based storage is efficient for disk space and relational access but requires substantial overhead for schema registration, schema changes, and file ingestion. Oracle 11g introduces a new storage option called Binary XML that combines the benefits from both CLOB and schema-based storage. Binary XML offers fast file ingestion, efficient disk space and relational access, and ease of maintenance for schema changes.

In order to improve the process of receiving help from Oracle Support, Oracle 11g introduces a new feature called Incident Package Service (IPS) that provides a tool to extract information about incidents (exceptions) from the Automatic Diagnostic Repository (ADR). This utility can be used to gather and submit all of the information about an incident to Oracle support. IPS is available from both a command line utility and the Enterprise Manager.

In some situations, it is necessary to restrict changes to a table without exception. Prior to 11g, a read-only table could be achieved by creating a table under a restricted account and granting select privileges to the appropriate users. Using this method, it is still possible for the owner of the table to unintentionally modify the table. 11g has introduced a much simpler method for enabling read only tables called Enhanced Read Only tables that protects the table from unintentional DML by the table's owner.

Oracle 11g High Availability & RAC new features

Oracle continues to enhance Real Application Clusters (RAC) in Oracle 11g and listed below are some exciting new features in RAC manageability and enhanced performance:

Hangman Utility – the Hang Manager (hangman) utility is a new 11g tool to detect database bottlenecks. An extension of the dba_waiters and dba_blockers views, the hangman tables have a hang chain that allow the DBA to find the source of hangs such as the deadly embrace, where mutually blocking locks or latches hang a process. In 11g, the hangman utility is installed on all RAC nodes by default, allowing for easier inter-node hang diagnostics.

New load balancing utilities – There have been several enhancements to load balancing utilities first introduced in Oracle 10g including RAC instance, ASM, Data Guard, and Listener load balancing. These will be covered in more depth in later chapters.

RAC instance load balancing - Starting in Oracle 10g release 2, Oracle JDBC and ODP.NET provide connection pool load balancing facilities through integration with the new load balancing advisory tool. This replaces the more cumbersome listener-based load balancing technique. Details on other RAC enhancements are provided in Chapter 3.

Oracle 11g RAC parallel upgrades - Oracle 11g promises to have a rolling upgrade feature whereby RAC database can be upgraded without any downtime. This is a very challenging and complex 11g new feature.

Oracle RAC load balancing advisor - Starting in 10gr2, there is a RAC load balancing advisor utility. The 11g RAC load balancing advisor is only available for clients who use .NET, ODBC, or the Oracle Call Interface (OCI).

ADDM for RAC is incorporated into the automatic database diagnostic monitor for cross-node advisories.

Optimized RAC cache fusion protocols go beyond the general cache fusion protocols in 10g to address specific scenarios where the protocols could be further optimized.

Oracle 11g RAC Grid provisioning - The Oracle grid control provisioning pack allows the ability to blow-out a RAC node without the time-consuming install by using a pre-installed footprint. Oracle 11g OEM has had easy server blade installs where a binary footprint is Tar'ed to the server blade and configured without a cumbersome install process.

Hot patching - Zero downtime patch application.

Data Guard Load Balancing – Oracle Data Guard allows for load balancing between standby databases. Data Guard new features are covered in more depth in Chapter 9.

Data Guard standby snapshot - The new standby snapshot feature enables a DBA to encapsulate a snapshot for regression testing. A standby snapshot can be collected and moved into a QA database, ensuring that the regression test uses real production data.

Quick Fault Resolution - Automatic capture of diagnostics (dumps) for a fault.

OEM - Enterprise Manager Oracle 11g new features

This section describes some of the new OEM features in 11g.

Feature Based Patching – All one-off patches are classified by which feature they affect. Therefore, it is now easy to identify which patches are necessary for the features that are being used. EM allows a subscription to a feature based patching service, so EM automatically scans for available patches for the features that are being used. Chapter 4 describes more OEM enhancements.

Interfaces to Applications (including foreign) - Extending Enterprise Manager's capabilities are part of Oracle's promise to seamlessly integrate the spoils of its many acquisitions, including the purchases of Siebel Systems and PeopleSoft Corp., into a single platform.

OEM Easy de-install - This uninstalls both successful and unsuccessful Oracle installs.

Database repair wizard – This is a GUI to guide beginners through the steps to diagnose and repair Oracle issues.

Better OEM Grid tools - Another new Oracle 11g feature may be improved RAC and Grid monitoring, especially on the cache fusion interconnect.

OEM Support workbench - Once the ADR has detected and reported a critical problem, the DBA can interrogate the ADR, report on the source of the problem, and, in some cases, even implement repairs.

Oracle 11g New Features Programming Language Support

There have been various programming enhancements in 11g.

PHP - Improved PHP driver for Oracle.

Compilers - Improved native Java & PL/SQL compilers.

Oracle 11g XML Enhancements - Oracle 11g also supports Content Repository API for Java Technology (JSR 170). Oracle 11g has XML duality, meaning that XML directives can be embedded inside PL/SQL and PL/SQL can be embedded inside XML code. Oracle 11g XML also supports schema-based document Type Definitions (DTDs) to describe internal structure of the XML document.

Scalable Java - The scalable execution feature is automatic creation of native Java code with just one parameter for each type with an on/off value. This provides a 100% performance boost for pure Java code and a 10%-30% boost for code containing SQL.

Improved sequence management - This new feature bypasses DML (sequence.nextval) and allows normal assignments on sequence values.

Intra-unit inlining - In the C language, a macro that gets inlined when called is able to be written. Now any stored procedure is eligible for inlining if Oracle thinks it will improve performance. No change to the code is required.

Oracle 11g PL/SQL New Features

Chapter 5 goes into more detail on enhancements involving PL/SQL, but here are a few highlights.

New PL/SQL Data Type SIMPLE_INTEGER – Oracle 11g has introduced a new data type called SIMPLE_INTEGER for improving performance when using native compilation. This data type is similar to PLS_INTEGER except that it is not checked for null or overflow values. When appropriate, using SIMPLE_INTEGER instead of PLS_INTEGER can yield significant performance improvements.

Faster DML triggers – One transparent improvement in Oracle 11g is faster execution of DML triggers when a row-level trigger performs DML on another table. Testing shows up to a 25% improvement in execution time (think audit trigger).

A super object-oriented DDL keyword – Oracle 11g introduces a new feature to support the use of supertypes using a simple syntax. This feature is an important step to bringing object-oriented programming to the Oracle Database. Prior to 11g, object-oriented programmers had to use a challenging workaround. Super is not a keyword, it is a syntax feature for creating subtypes in PL/SQL feature OO programming.

New Trigger features – A new type of compound trigger will have sections for BEFORE, ROW and AFTER processing. This is very helpful for avoiding errors and maintaining states between each section.

Table trigger firing order - Oracle 11g PL/SQL allows the DBA to specify trigger firing order.

PL/SQL continue keyword - This allows a C-Like continue in a loop that bypasses any ELSE Boolean conditions. A PL/SQL GOTO is no longer required to exit a Boolean within a loop.

Disabled state for PL/SQL - Another 11g new feature is a disabled state for PL/SQL (as opposed to enabled and invalid in dba_objects).

Easy PL/SQL compiling - Native Compilation no longer requires a C compiler to compile the PL/SQL. The code goes directly to a shared library.

Improved PL/SQL stored procedure invalidation mechanism - A new 11g feature is fine grained dependency tracking, reducing the number of objects which become invalid as a result of DDL.

Scalable PL/SQL - The scalable execution feature is automatic creation of native PL/SQL with just one parameter for each type with an on/off value. This provides a 100% performance boost for pure PL/SQL code, and a 10%-30% performance boost for code containing SQL.

Enhanced PL/SQL warnings - The 11g PL/SQL compiler issues a warning for a when others with no raise.

Stored Procedure named notation - Named notation is now supported when calling a stored procedure from SQL.

Oracle SQL optimizer (CBO) Improvements

Oracle has made a number of significant improvements to the 11g optimizer which improves the efficiency of SQL:

Improved optimizer statistics collection speed - Oracle 11g has improved the dbms_stats performance, allowing for faster CBO statistics creation.

Execution plan retention – In addition to storing execution plans inside AWR tables (dba_hist_sql_plan), Oracle11g now keeps a history of execution plans for any given SQL statement. Upon a re-parse of any SQL statement, the CBO will be able to compare a new execution plan against the original plan and choose the most optimal execution plan. Oracle 11g SQL will also allow a DBA to lock-in execution plans for specific SQL statements, (like the optimizer plan stability utility) and the plan will remain unchanged, regardless of statistics or database version changes.

Multi-column CBO statistics - Oracle 11g introduces multi-column statistics to give the CBO the ability to more accurately select rows when the WHERE clause contains multi-column conditions or joins.

Table-level control of CBO statistics refresh threshold - When Oracle automatically enables statistics collection, the default staleness threshold of 10% can now be changed with the dbms_stats.set_table_prefs procedure:

```
exec dbms_stats.set_table_prefs ('HR', EMPS', 'STALE_PERCENT', '15')
```

There are three new arguments to the set_table_prefs procedure designed to allow the DBA more control over the freshness of their statistics:

- *stale_percent* - overrides the one-size-fits-all value of 10%

- incremental - Incremental statistics gathering for partitions

- publish - Allows the DBA to test new statistics before publishing them to the data dictionary

This is an important 11g new feature because the DBA can now control the quality of optimizer statistics at the table level, thereby improving the behavior of the SQL optimizer to always choose the best execution plan for any query. Oracle 11g has also separated out the gather and publish operations, allowing CBO statistics to be retained for later use.

Oracle 11g SQL New Features

Chapter 6 provides more details on various SQL enhancements. The following is a brief description of some of those SQL improvements.

New PIVOT SQL clause - The new PIVOT SQL clause allows quick rollup, similar to an MS-Excel pivot table, where multiple rows can be displayed on one column with SQL. MS SQL Server 2005 also introduced a pivot clause. Laurent Schneider notes that the new SQL pivot syntax is great for converting rows-to-columns and columns-to-rows.

The /*+result_cache*/ SQL hint – The resulting data will be cached in the data buffers and not the intermediate data blocks that were accessed to obtain the query results. Both SQL and PL/SQL results can be cached for superior performance on subsequent retrievals. This relates to the scalable execution concept. The result cache has three areas:

- The SQL query result cache - This is an area of SGA memory for storing query results.

- The PL/SQL function result cache - This result cache can store the results from a PL/SQL function call.

- The OCI client result cache - This cache retains results from OCI calls, both for SQL queries or PL/SQL functions.

XML SQL queries – Oracle 11g supports query mechanisms for XML including XQuery and SQL XML with emerging standards for querying XML data stored inside tables.

SQL Replay - Similar to the previous feature, but this only captures and applies the SQL workload, not total workload.

SQL execution Plan Management

Oracle 11g SQL permits execution plans (explain plans) to be fixed for specific statements, regardless of statistics or database version changes. (Source: Dr. Tim Hall)

Dynamic SQL - DBMS_SQL is here to stay. It is faster and is being enhanced. DBMS_SQL and NDS can now accept

CLOBs (no more 32k limit on NDS). A ref cursor can become a DBMS_SQL cursor and vice versa. DBMS_SQL now supports user defined types and bulk operations. (Source: Lewis Cunningham)

Fully Automatic SQL Tuning - The 10g automatic tuning advisor makes tuning suggestions in the form of SQL profiles that will improve performance. 11g can be told to automatically apply SQL profiles for statements where the suggested profile gives three times better performance than the existing statement. The performance comparisons are done by a new administrative task during a user-specified maintenance window.

Improved SQL Access Advisor - The 11g SQL Access Advisor gives partitioning advice, including advice on the new interval partitioning. Interval partitioning is an automated version of range partitioning where new equally-sized partitions are automatically created when needed. Both range and interval partitions can exist for a single table, and range partitioned tables can be converted to interval partitioned tables.

11g Performance Tuning Optimization New Features

Oracle continues to improve the automation of the RAM regions used by the SGA and PGA regions. Chapter 7 also goes into more detail on performance enhancements.

Automatic Diagnostic Repository (ADR) - When critical errors are detected, they automatically create an "incident". Information relating to the incident is automatically captured, the DBA is notified and certain health checks are run automatically. This information can be packaged to be sent to Oracle technical support.

Health Monitor (HM) Utility – Oracle 11g includes a built-in framework called Health Monitor. The Health Monitor utility is an automation of the *dbms_repair* corruption detection utility. When a corruption-like problem happens, the HR utility will check for possible corruption within database blocks, redo log blocks, undo segments, or dictionary table blocks.

11g Oracle Streams Performance Advisor and Partitioning Advisor – The SQL Access advisor has also been enhanced to recommend partitioning in addition to its existing recommendations for missing indexes and materialized views.

Automated Storage Load Balancing - Oracle's Automatic Storage Management (ASM) now enables a single storage pool to be shared by multiple databases for optimal load balancing. Shared disk storage resources can alternatively be assigned to individual databases and easily moved from one database to another as processing requirements change. Additional ASM enhancements are covered in Chapter 12.

Automatic Memory Tuning - Automatic PGA tuning was introduced in Oracle 9i. Automatic SGA tuning was introduced in Oracle 10g. In 11g, all memory can be tuned automatically by setting one parameter. Tell Oracle how much memory it has and it determines how much to use for PGA, SGA and OS Processes. Maximum and minimum thresholds can be set.

The *memory_target* parameter - 11g automatic memory tuning is controlled by two new Oracle 11g parameters, *memory_target* and *memory_max_target*. Prior to Oracle 11g, the DBA set the *sga_target* and *sga_max_size* parameters, allowing Oracle to reallocate RAM within the SGA. The PGA was independent, as governed by the *pga_aggregate_target* parameter.

Now in Oracle 11g the *memory_max_target* parameter governs the total maximum RAM for both the PGA and SGA regions and the *memory_target* parameter governs the existing sizes. This allows RAM to be de-allocated from the SGA and transferred to the PGA.

This is an important Oracle11g new feature because it lays the foundation for inter-instance RAM memory sharing. As of 2008, the second age of mainframe computing is now evident as is server consolidation where it is not uncommon to find a dozen instances on a single large server.

In Oracle 10g, Automatic Memory Management (AMM) only allowed shifting of RAM within the confines of *sga_max_size*. Oracle 11g introduces Automatic Shared Memory Management (ASMM). The *memory_target* parameter is dynamic, meaning it can be changed using the alter system commands, and it allows RAM to be de-allocated from one instance re-allocated to another.

The Oracle 11g documentation notes that *memory_target* specifies the Oracle system-wide usable memory. The database tunes memory to the *memory_target* value, reducing or enlarging the SGA and PGA as needed. In a text initialization parameter file, if the line for *memory_max_target* is omitted and a value for *memory_target* is included, the database automatically sets *memory_max_target* to the value of *memory_target*.

If the line for *memory_target* is omitted and a value for *memory_max_target* is included, the *memory_target* parameter defaults to zero.

After startup, dynamically change *memory_target* to a non-zero value, provided that it does not exceed the value of *memory_max_target*.

Resource Manager - The 11g Resource Manager manages I/O, not just CPU. The priority associated with specific files, file types or ASM disk groups can be set.

ADDM - The ADDM in 11g can give advice on the whole RAC (database level), not just at the instance level. Directives have been added to ADDM so it can ignore issues that are of no concern. For example, if more memory is needed, set ADDM to not report those messages anymore.

Faster sorting - Starting in 10gr2, there is an improved sort algorithm that uses less memory and CPU resources. A hidden parameter *_newsort_enabled* = {TRUE|FALSE} governs whether the new sort algorithm will be used.

AWR Baselines - The AWR baselines have been extended to allow automatic creation of baselines for use in other features. A rolling week baseline is created by default.

Adaptive Metric Baselines - Notification thresholds in 10g were based on a fixed point. In 11g, notification thresholds can be associated with a baseline, so the notification thresholds vary throughout the day in line with the baseline.

Oracle 11g Security & Auditing New Features

Capture/Replay Database Workloads - The workload in production can be captured and applied in development. Oracle is moving toward more workload-based optimization by adjusting SQL execution plans based on existing server-side stress. This can be very useful for Oracle regression testing.

RMAN UNDO Bypass – Oracle 11g has optimized the backup process by selectively backing up the UNDO data that is necessary for the database recovery. Prior to this release, Oracle backed up all the UNDO data, including data for transactions that were already committed. This enhancement improves backup times and reduces the backup storage.

Enhanced Password Management - Pete Finnigan, noted Oracle security consultant, comments that 11g security has been enhanced with case sensitive passwords and also that the password algorithm has changed to SHA-1 instead of the old DES based hashing used.

Oracle SecureFiles – Mark Rittman, founder of Rittman Mead Consulting, noted that the SecureFiles replacement for large objects (LOBs) will be faster than UNIX files to read/write. There is great potential benefit for OLAP analytic workspaces (AW) as the LOBs used to hold AWs have historically been slower to write to than the old Express .db files.

Oracle 11g Audit Vault - Oracle Audit Vault is a new feature that will provide a solution to help customers address the most difficult security problems remaining today, protecting against insider threat and meeting regulatory compliance requirements.

Proxy Connect for SQL*Plus - New with 10r2 proxy identification in SQL*Plus, the connect command has been enhanced to allow for a proxy to aid applications that always connect with the same user ID:

```
connect sapr3[scott]/tiger
```

FGAC for UTL_SMTP, UTL_TCP and UTL_HTTP - Security on ports and URLs can now be defined.

Fine Grained Dependency Tracking (FGDT) – Prevents dependent objects from being invalidated when a column is added to a table or a cursor to a package spec.

Database Workload Replay - Oracle Replay allows the total database workload to be captured, transferred to a test database created from a backup or standby database, then replayed to test the affects of an upgrade or system change. To do the capture, specify the SQL tuning sets similar to the 10g offering and use the *dbms_sqlpa* package (SQL performance analyzer) to manage the SQL analyzer task with *dbms_sqlpa* procedures (*create_analysis_task*, *cancel_analysis_task*, *drop_analysis_task*, *reset_analysis_task*, *report_analysis_task*, *resume_analysis_task*, *interrupt_analysis_task*).

With a capture performance overhead of 5%, it could be possible to capture real production workloads.

Oracle 11g New RMAN Features

George Trujillo, Oracle DBA and blogger, notes many new 11g features:

- A Virtual Private Catalog can now make sure an RMAN user can only see databases they are authorized to use.

- Archive log management for Streams and Data Guard

- Network aware DUPLICATE

- Optimized undo backup

- Improved corrupt block detection

- Java, PL/SQL, XML, .NET, PHP, APEX

- PL/SQL Native Compilation without needing a Third-Party C Compiler

- Native PL/SQL use of *Seq.Nextval* in a PL/SQL program

- PL/SQL can use CLOBs to get around 32KB limitation of SQL character strings.

- Enhanced PL/SQL warnings and error messages

- PLSTIMER identifies hotspots and performance tuning opportunities in PL/SQL.

- New package *DBMS_HPROF* controls the recording of raw PLSTIMER data.

- Continued support of standards with JDBC 4.0 and JVM 5.0. Capability to upgrade to JVM 6.0 will be available in the future.

- Oracle JVM JIT supports transparent native Java compilation without a C Compiler.

- Significant performance improvements with JDBC performance, especially with Advanced Queuing.

- JDBC supports server side result cache along with OCI client side result cache. Also included are big improvements in the JIT and RAC support for JDBC.

- New command line interface to OracleJVM, thereby making it much easier to work with the JDK in the database.

- Support for database resident JARs

- JDBC support for starting and shutting down the database

- Performance enhancements to XPath query for Java

- XML applications can now process larger XML documents by loading and saving.

- DOM nodes in memory and using a page manager for physical binary data management

- Unified Java API for XML allows mid-tier Java programs to leverage lazy loading by allowing a disconnected mode of operation that allows an XMLType to be used with a session pool model of connection management.

HTML-DB 11g Enhancements

- APEX will be standard with an embedded PL/SQL gateway.

- APEX will have an application packager for packing and deployment of APEX applications.

- Data Pump Enhancements to use when moving data

- Compression and encryption enhancements

- Support for XML Schemas and schema-based tables

- Transportable partitions

- Change assurance (important for saving money during testing and migration) - Change assurance new features of Database Replay and SQL Replay can play a large role in reducing costs, testing and issues when migrating to Oracle Database 11g. This is one of the best new features in this release.

- Database replay - captures actual production workload and replays it on a separate system.

- SQL performance analyzer - finds and fixes SQL performance degradations. 10gR2 has a patch set that allows the replay to occur.

- Secure Files (Next generation LOBS) - Eliminates need for file systems. Very fast access of files. Just as fast as file systems with all the capabilities of the Oracle database since it is a new LOB type. It is very fast at accessing the files from a file system.

- Store all the data in the database with one consistent: Security and auditing model

- Backup and recovery mechanism

- Storage management (ASM)

- Transaction and concurrency model

- Interface and protocol

- Value-added services like encryption, compression, and de-duplication

Oracle 11g Business Intelligence & OLAP

Oracle warehouse guru Mark Rittman notes some of the upcoming features with Oracle 11g Business Intelligence suite and OLAP such as integration of materialized view query rewrite with OLAP:

However, in 10g OLAP although (one) could register a view over aggregated data in an analytic workspace with query rewrite, "normal" queries that used SUM(), AVG() and other aggregation functions, together with GROUP BY, wouldn't get rewritten as the SQL views used over analytic workspaces were based on fully-solved cubes, i.e. the view contained all levels of aggregation and measures were already aggregated.

With this forthcoming release of Oracle OLAP, just check a box in Analytic Workspace Manager to enable queries against the source tables for the analytic workspace to be re-written against the summary data in the analytic workspace, and the OLAP cube will then act in the same way as a regular materialized view, meaning the two technologies (in theory) will be interchangeable as a way of summarizing warehouse data.

Oracle 11g data mining

With the release of the first book on Oracle Data Mining (ODM), there is an increased interest in data mining within 11g and there are rumors that ODM will be greatly enhanced by moving data mining objects into the dictionary and improving the interface for complex analytics.

Conclusion

There are an abundance of new features in Oracle's 11g that will be covered in this book. This chapter is a synopsis of many of the features that are considered the most important to a DBA and are broken down by categories such as DBA, RAC, PL/SQL and RMAN new features. Each subsequent chapter will discuss these categories in greater detail and provide answers to the changes that are evident in 11g.

11g New DBA Features

11g for the DBA

This chapter examines the new features in Oracle Database 11g that are the most important to the DBA and developer staff.

Partitioning Enhancements

Interval Partitioning

Partitioning in Oracle is instrumental in supporting large databases and data warehousing requirements. While this feature dramatically improves manageability, performance, and availability, Oracle relies on the DBA to manually define each partition. In data warehousing environments, the creation of new partitions is a monotonous but necessary element of scheduled maintenance.

Oracle 11g has introduced a new partitioning feature, called Interval Partitioning, that allows Oracle to automatically create new partitions as data is inserted. While there are certain limitations to using interval partitioning, it has proven to be a very effective feature when used in the appropriate context. This section will demonstrate how to use this feature, look at its limitations, and provide recommendations for making the most of this exciting enhancement.

Partitioning is the division of tables, indexes, or index-organized tables into smaller pieces. These smaller pieces are called partitions which can be managed and accessed independently. This concept is commonly characterized as a divide-and-conquer approach to managing large tables and indexes. When defining a partitioned table, one or more columns are used as keys to match the row into the appropriate partition. Data loads in partitioned tables will fail if one or more records cannot be matched to an existing partition.

Interval partitioning is an enhancement to range partitioning. Range partitioning allows an object to be partitioned by a specified range on the partitioning key. For example, if a table was used to store sales data, it might be range partitioned by a DATE column, with each month in a different partition. Therefore, each month a new partition would need to be defined to store rows for that month. If a row was inserted for a new month before a partition was defined for that month, the following error would result:

```
ORA-14400: inserted partition key does not map to any partition
```

If this situation occurs, data loading will fail until the new partitions are created. This can cause serious problems in larger data warehouses where complex reporting has many steps and dependencies in a batch process. Mission critical reports might be delayed or incorrect due to this problem.

Interval partitioning can simplify the data manageability by automatically creating the new partitions as needed. Interval partitioning is enabled in the table's definition by defining one or more range partitions and including a specified interval. For example, consider the following table:

```
create table
pos_data (
   start_date        DATE,
   store_id          NUMBER,
   inventory_id      NUMBER(6),
   qty_sold          NUMBER(3),
)
PARTITION BY RANGE (start_date)
INTERVAL(NUMTOYMINTERVAL(1, 'MONTH'))
(
   PARTITION pos_data_p2 VALUES LESS THAN (TO_DATE('1-7-2007', 'DD-
MM-YYYY')),
   PARTITION pos_data_p3 VALUES LESS THAN (TO_DATE('1-8-2007', 'DD-
MM-YYYY'))
);
```

Here, two partitions have been defined and an interval of one month has been specified. If data is loaded into this table with a later date than the greatest defined partition, Oracle will automatically create a new partition for the new month. In the table above, the greatest defined interval is between July 1, 2007 and August 1, 2007. Inserting a row that has a date later than August 1, 2007 would raise an error with normal range partitioning. However, with interval partitioning, Oracle determines the high value of the defined range partitions, called the transition point, and creates new partitions for data that is beyond that high value.

```
insert into pos_data (start_date, store_id, inventory_id, qty_sold)
values ( '15-AUG-07', 1, 1, 1);
```

```
SELECT
   TABLE_NAME,
   PARTITION_NAME,
   PARTITION_POSITION,
   HIGH_VALUE
FROM
   DBA_TAB_PARTITIONS
WHERE
   TABLE_NAME='POS_DATA'
ORDER BY
   PARTITION_NAME;

PARTITION_NAME        HIGH_VALUE
```

```
POS_DATA_P0 TO_DATE(' 2007-07-01 00:00:00', 'SYYYY-MM-DD
HH24:MI:SS', 'NLS_CALENDAR=GREGORIAN')
POS_DATA_P1 TO_DATE(' 2007-08-01 00:00:00', 'SYYYY-MM-DD
HH24:MI:SS', 'NLS_CALENDAR=GREGORIAN')
SYS_P81     TO_DATE(' 2007-09-01 00:00:00', 'SYYYY-MM-DD
HH24:MI:SS', 'NLS_CALENDAR=GREGORIAN')
```

Notice that a system generated partition named SYS_P81 has been created upon inserting a row with a partition key greater than the transition point. Oracle will manage the creation of new partitions for any value beyond the high value. Therefore, the values do not need to be inserted in sequence.

Since the partitions are named automatically, Oracle has added a new syntax in order to reference specific partitions effectively. The normal way to reference a specific partition is to use the partition *(partition_name)* in the query:

```
select
   *
from
   pos_data partition (SYS_P81);
```

However, it would be cumbersome to look up the system generated partition name each time. Therefore, the new syntax to specify a partition is by using the *partition for (DATE)* clause in the query:

```
select
   *
from
   pos_data partition for (to_date('15-AUG-2007','dd-mon-yyyy'));
```

Another useful feature of partitioning is the ability to distribute partitions across different tablespaces. With interval partitioning, this can be accomplished by naming all of the tablespaces in the table definition's store in clause. The system created partitions are then assigned to different tablespaces in a round-robin manner. For example, if the choice was to distribute the table

---

across three tablespaces - tablespaceA, tablespaceB, and tablespaceC - use the following clause in the table definition.

```
INTERVAL(NUMTOYMINTERVAL(1, 'MONTH'))
STORE IN (tablespaceA, tablespaceB, tablespaceC)
```

There are a few restrictions on interval partitioning that must be taken into consideration before deciding if it is appropriate for the business requirement:

- Interval partitioning cannot be used for index organized tables

- Only one partitioning key column may be used and it must be a DATE or NUMBER

- Domain indexes cannot be created on interval partitioned tables

- Interval partitioning is not supported at the sub-partition level

This feature should be used as an enhancement to range partitioning when uniform distribution of range intervals for new partitions is acceptable. If the requirement demands the use of uneven intervals when adding new partitions, then interval partitioning would not be the best solution.

If interval partitioning is a feature that fits the requirement, there are a few new commands available to manage interval partitioning. First, convert a range partitioned table to use interval partitioning by using ALTER TABLE <table_name> SET INTERVAL(expr).

Consider this range partitioned table:

```
create table
pos_data_range (
    start_date      DATE,
    store_id        NUMBER,
    inventory_id    NUMBER(6),
    qty_sold        NUMBER(3)
```

```
)
   PARTITION BY RANGE (start_date)
(
   PARTITION pos_data_p0 VALUES LESS THAN (TO_DATE('1-7-2007', 'DD-
MM-YYYY')),
   PARTITION pos_data_p1 VALUES LESS THAN (TO_DATE('1-8-2007', 'DD-
MM-YYYY'))
);
```

If a row with a date of August 15, 2007 is inserted into the table, it will cause an error.

```
SQL> insert into pos_data_range (start_date, store_id, inventory_id,
qty_sold)
   2  values ( '15-AUG-07', 1, 1, 1);
insert into pos_data_range (start_date, store_id, inventory_id,
qty_sold)
       *
ERROR at line 1:
ORA-14400: inserted partition key does not map to any partition
```

This range partitioned table can easily be converted to use interval partitioning by using the following command:

```
alter table pos_data_range set INTERVAL(NUMTOYMINTERVAL(1,
'MONTH'));
```

Interval partitioning is now enabled, and the row with 15-AUG-07 can be inserted without error since Oracle will automatically create the new partition. To convert the table back to only range partitioning, use the following command:

```
alter table pos_data_range set INTERVAL();
```

The table is converted back to a range partitioned table and the boundaries for the interval partitions are set to the boundaries for the range partitions.

Using the same syntax, the interval can also be changed for existing interval partitioned tables. If changing the original table to be partitioned every three months instead of monthly, use the following command:

```
alter table pos_data set INTERVAL(NUMTOYMINTERVAL(3, 'MONTH'));
```

After inserting a row with the date of 15-NOV-07, a new partition is automatically generated with a high value of 01-DEC-07.

```
insert into
   pos_data (start_date, store_id, inventory_id, qty_sold)
values
   ('15-NOV-07', 1, 1, 1);

SELECT
   TABLE_NAME, PARTITION_NAME, PARTITION_POSITION, HIGH_VALUE
FROM
   DBA_TAB_PARTITIONS
WHERE
   TABLE_NAME='POS_DATA'
ORDER BY
   PARTITION_NAME;

PARTITION_NAME      HIGH_VALUE

POS_DATA_P0 TO_DATE(' 2007-07-01 00:00:00', 'SYYYY-MM-DD
HH24:MI:SS', 'NLS_CALENDAR=GREGORIAN')
POS_DATA_P1 TO_DATE(' 2007-08-01 00:00:00', 'SYYYY-MM-DD
HH24:MI:SS', 'NLS_CALENDAR=GREGORIAN')
SYS_P81     TO_DATE(' 2007-09-01 00:00:00', 'SYYYY-MM-DD
HH24:MI:SS', 'NLS_CALENDAR=GREGORIAN')
SYS_P84     TO_DATE(' 2007-12-01 00:00:00', 'SYYYY-MM-DD
HH24:MI:SS', 'NLS_CALENDAR=GREGORIAN')
```

The tablespace storage of the interval partitioned table can also be changed using a similar syntax. For example, when using a round-robin tablespace assignment for the table between tablespace1 to tablespace3, issue the following command:

```
alter table pos_data set STORE IN(tablespace1, tablespace2,
tablespace3);
```

Oracle interval partitioning offers a very useful extension to range partitioning. This greatly improves the manageability of range partitioned tables. In addition to providing system generated new

---

partitions, Oracle has provided a new syntax to simplify the reference of specific partitions. Furthermore, Oracle offers a group of commands to manage the new partitioning option.

System Partitioning

System partitioning allows application level control for partitioning a table or index. This partitioning option offers the same benefits as other methods of partitioning. However, the partitions are completely controlled by the application without partition keys or boundaries. This option should be used carefully, and all references to a system partitioned table must include extended partition syntax to specify a partition. Also, for inserts into a system partitioned table, the partition must be specified to avoid receiving an error. For all other operations, omitting the partition will cause all partitions to be scanned.

An example of a table that might benefit from system partitioning is a large lookup table owned by the development group. Consider the following table:

```
create table
misc_lookups (
    lookup_name varchar2(30),
    lookup_meaning varchar2(30)
);
```

If this table is very large and there is no obvious way to partition it, system partitioning might be a practical option. This option would be suitable if the table was primarily used in automated processes, such as PL/SQL packages. In either case, the developers would need to determine the rules for deciding how to choose which partitions to use for all operations on this table. In order to enable system partitioning with three partitions in different tablespaces, the table is created using the following syntax:

```
create table
misc_lookups (
    lookup_name varchar2(30),
    lookup_meaning varchar2(30)
)
partition by system
(
    partition misc_lookups_p0 tablespace tablespaceA,
    partition misc_lookups_p1 tablespace tablespaceB,
    partition misc_lookups_p2 tablespace tablespaceC
);
```

It is the developer's responsibility to use the extended partition syntax to specify the partition when using the table. This is a requirement when inserting a row into a system partitioned table since the database has no means for choosing which partition to store new rows. Failing to specify a partition when inserting a row will raise an error:

```
SQL> insert into misc_lookups values ('test', 'test meaning')
  2  /
insert into misc_lookups values ('test', 'test meaning')
            *
ERROR at line 1:
ORA-14701: partition-extended name or bind variable must be used for
DMLs on tables partitioned by the System method
```

Therefore, a partition must be specified when inserting data into a system partitioned table:

```
SQL> insert into misc_lookups partition (misc_lookups_p0) values
('test', 'test meaning')
  2  /

1 row created.
```

When selecting, updating, or deleting data from a system partitioned object, the best practice is to always specify the partition to avoid scanning all partitions. The use of system partitioning should be viewed with scrutiny by a DBA since it transfers responsibility of optimal use of partitions away from the DBA and to the developers and applications. Nevertheless, the

---

introduction of this new feature helps to extend the use of partitioning for any business situation.

Reference Partitioning

Reference partitioning is a new partitioning option in Oracle 11g that allows the partitioning of two related tables to be based on a referential constraint. In other words, when there is a parent-child relationship between two tables, the parent table can be defined with its partitions. Subsequently, the child table can be partitioned by defining the child table to inherit the partitioning key from the parent table, without the need to duplicate the partition key columns. This logical partitioning is achieved by the inheritance of the parent's partitioning scheme through a referential constraint in the child table. This feature enhances the manageability of the child table because all partition maintenance operations on the parent table automatically cascade to the child table. Additionally, this relieves the DBA of the responsibility of maintaining duplicate columns, and partitions in the child table, in order to achieve the same objective.

Using Reference Partitioning

In a relational database, there are countless numbers of situations where parent-child relationships exist. Consider the abundance of parent-child table relationships in Oracle schemas that support online transaction processing or data warehousing. For example, consider the following two tables based on an order management schema.

The table ORDER_HEADERS is a parent table that stores the header level information about a sales order. The business has made the decision to partition this table by sales regions North, East, South, and West. The table is created with the following statement:

```
create table
order_headers (
   header_id number primary key,
   order_date date,
   sales_region varchar2(1) not null
)
partition by
   list (sales_region)
(
   partition pN values ('N'),
   partition pE values ('E'),
   partition pS values ('S'),
   partition pW values ('W')
);
```

The table ORDER_LINES is a child table of the ORDER_HEADERS table and has a foreign key constraint *fk_lines_0* on *header_id* with its parent table. The ORDER_LINES table is defined as:

```
create table
order_lines (
   line_id number primary key,
   header_id number not null,
   customer_id number,
   product_id number,
   quantity number,
   price number,
   constraint  fk_lines_0
     foreign key (header_id)
     references order_headers
);
```

Given the child-parent relationship of ORDER_LINES with ORDER_HEADERS, it would be best to partition ORDER_LINES by SALES_REGION in order to take full advantage of partition-wise joins and enhance the manageability of these tables. However, this column is not included in the child table. Prior to 11g, this would be accomplished by duplicating the SALES_REGION column in the ORDER_LINES table. The DBA would then be forced to define and manage the partitions from both tables independently. However, by using reference partitioning in Oracle 11g, it is easy to partition

ORDER_LINES with its parent by using the foreign key constraint:

```
create table
order_lines (
   line_id number primary key,
   header_id number not null,
   customer_id number,
   product_id number,
   quantity number,
   price number,
   constraint  fk_lines_0
    foreign key (header_id)
    references order_headers
)
partition by
   reference (fk_lines_0);
```

This table now inherits the partitioning scheme from its parent table by reference without needing to include SALES_REGION in the ORDER_LINES table. The partitions for ORDER_LINES are created identical to its parent. ORDER_HEADERS, and any maintenance operations on the partitions of ORDER_HEADERS, will automatically cascade to its child table, ORDER_LINES. To view the partitions created for ORDER_LINES, use the dictionary views *dba_part_tables* and *dba_tab_partitions*:

```
select
   table_name,
   partition_count,
   ref_ptn_constraint_name
from
   dba_part_tables
where
   table_name = 'ORDER_LINES';
```

```
TABLE_NAME      PARTITION_COUNT    REF_PTN_CONSTRAINT_NAME
-------------   ------------------  -----------------------
ORDER_LINES     4                   FK_LINES_0
```

```
select
   partition_name
from
   dba_tab_partitions
where
   table_name = 'ORDER_LINES';
```

```
PARTITION_NAME
--------------
PE
PS
PW
PN
```

Reference partitioning cannot be used when the parent table uses interval partitioning. Referential constraint on the child table must be defined on a NOT NULL parent column and a virtual column cannot be part of the partitioning foreign key. Violating any of these limitations will cause the following error:

```
ORA-14652: reference partitioning foreign key is not supported
```

Reference partitioning improves and simplifies the partitioning of tables that have a parent-child relationship. It also allows the DBA to maintain both sets of partitions by only managing partitions on the parent table. This removes the necessity for managing the partitions on the child table. Similarly, reference partitioning also eliminates the need to include unnecessary duplicate columns from the parent table to enable partitioning of the child table.

Virtual Column-Based Partitioning

A virtual column is an expression based on one or more existing columns in the table. While a virtual column is only stored as metadata and does not consume physical space, it can be indexed and also contain optimizer statistics and histograms. Oracle 11g has included the support for partitioning a table using a partitioning key on a virtual column. Prior to 11g, the partitioning key was limited to using physical columns.

Therefore, in order to partition a table by using a derived value, a DBA would have been required to create and populate an additional physical column in order to achieve the same result. The derived value would then either need to be populated by the application or by a trigger that evaluates the expression before insertion. In either case, achieving this goal in 10g required additional overhead and increased disk space for the physical column.

The ability to use an expression as a partitioning key provides a more efficient way to meet comprehensive business requirements without incurring unnecessary overhead. This new feature can be very useful when a table cannot be partitioned by the existing data columns. Consider the following table that contains a list of accounts:

```
desc accounts
Name                            Null?    Type
------------------------------------------------------------------
ACCOUNT_NUMBER                           VARCHAR2(30)
ACCOUNT_NAME                             VARCHAR2(30)
CONTACT_PERSON                           VARCHAR2(30)


select
   *
from
   accounts;
```

```
ACCOUNT_NUMBER          ACCOUNT_NAME          CONTACT_PERSON
-------------------     --------------------  ----------------
3983-9339-1232-1292     N-JOHNS-INDUSTRIALS    JOHN
8778-5435-5345-5223     E-MATTEL-AUTOMOTIVE    MIKE
2432-6543-2244-0877     S-SOUTHERN-TRANSPORTS  DOUG
4333-3424-6564-1322     W-GLOBAL-DISTRUBTION   GERRY
```

Consider also that the business requires this table be partitioned by region. The ACCOUNT_NAME column in this table is prefixed by a single character representing the account's region, followed by a dash and the account holder's name (i.e. N-JOHNS-INDUSTRIALS is North region). Prior to 11g, in order to partition this table by region, an additional physical column representing the region would need to be added to the table. However, in Oracle 11g, a virtual column can be used to create an expression that represents the region such as SUBSTR(account_name,1,1).

In order to partition this table by region, the table can be defined with region as a virtual column and partitioned by this derived column:

```
create table
accounts_v (
   account_number varchar2(30),
   account_name varchar2(30),
   contact_person varchar2(30),
   region AS (case
              when substr(account_name,1,1) = 'N' then 'NORTH'
              when substr(account_name,1,1) = 'E' then 'EAST'
              when substr(account_name,1,1) = 'S' then 'SOUTH'
              when substr(account_name,1,1) = 'W' then 'WEST'
              end)
)
partition by
   list (region)
(
   partition pN values ('NORTH'),
   partition pE values ('EAST'),
   partition pS values ('SOUTH'),
   partition pW values ('WEST')
);
```

After inserting the same four rows with values for the ACCOUNT_NUMBER, ACCOUNT_NAME, and CONTACT_PERSON, the virtual column region is automatically derived when querying the table.

```
insert all
into accounts_v (account_number, account_name, contact_person)
VALUES ('3983-9339-1232-1292', 'N-JOHNS-INDUSTRIALS', 'JOHN')
into accounts_v (account_number, account_name, contact_person)
VALUES ('8778-5435-5345-5223', 'E-MATTEL-AUTOMOTIVE', 'MIKE')
into accounts_v (account_number, account_name, contact_person)
VALUES ('2432-6543-2244-0877', 'S-SOUTHERN-TRANSPORTS', 'DOUG')
into accounts_v (account_number, account_name, contact_person)
VALUES ('4333-3424-6564-1322', 'W-GLOBAL-DISTRUBTION', 'GERRY')
select 1 from dual;

select
```

```
     *
from
   accounts_v;
```

```
ACCOUNT_NUMBER          ACCOUNT_NAME        CONTACT_PERSON   REGION
--------------------    ----------------    --------------   -------
3983-9339-1232-1292     N-JOHNS-INDUSTRIALS     JOHN         NORTH
8778-5435-5345-5223     E-MATTEL-AUTOMOTIVE     MIKE         EAST
2432-6543-2244-0877     S-SOUTHERN-TRANSPORTS   DOUG         SOUTH
4333-3424-6564-1322     W-GLOBAL-DISTRUBTION    GERRY        WEST
```

In order to verify the partitioning of this table, use the following query:

```
SELECT
   TABLE_NAME, PARTITION_NAME, PARTITION_POSITION, HIGH_VALUE
FROM
   DBA_TAB_PARTITIONS
WHERE
   TABLE_NAME='ACCOUNTS_V'
ORDER BY
   PARTITION_NAME;
```

```
TABLE_NAME      PARTITION_  PARTITION_POSITION HIGH_VALUE
--------------- ----------  ------------------ ----------
ACCOUNTS_V      PE                 2           'EAST'
ACCOUNTS_V      PN                 1           'NORTH'
ACCOUNTS_V      PS                 3           'SOUTH'
ACCOUNTS_V      PW                 4           'WEST'
```

To verify the placement of records in the appropriate partitions, query a specific partition. The following query is for the accounts in the east region:

```
select
   *
from
   accounts_v partition (PE);
```

```
ACCOUNT_NUMBER          ACCOUNT_NAME        CONTACT_PERSON   REGION
--------------------    --------------------   ---------------- -------
8778-5435-5345-5223     E-MATTEL-AUTOMOTIVE     MIKE         EAST
```

In order to demonstrate the disk space advantages of using a virtual column instead of a physical column, define a table that is synonymous to ACCOUNTS_V and uses a physical column for region:

```
create table
   accounts_p (
   account_number varchar2(30),
   account_name varchar2(30),
   contact_person varchar2(30),
   region varchar2(5)
)
partition by
   list (region)
(
   partition pN values ('NORTH'),
   partition pE values ('EAST'),
   partition pS values ('SOUTH'),
   partition pW values ('WEST')
);
```

Notice that the region column has been changed from a virtual column to a varchar2(5) physical column. To compare the disk space consumption between ACCOUNTS_P and ACCOUNTS_V, populate each table with 100,000 rows. Before doing so, truncate ACCOUNTS_V to reset the high watermark.

```
truncate table accounts_v;

DECLARE
   i NUMBER := 1;
BEGIN
LOOP
 insert into accounts_v (account_number, account_name,
contact_person)
 VALUES ('3983-9339-1232-1292', 'N-JOHNS-INDUSTRIALS', 'JOHN');
 insert into accounts_p (account_number, account_name,
contact_person, region)
 VALUES ('3983-9339-1232-1292', 'N-JOHNS-INDUSTRIALS', 'JOHN',
'NORTH');
 i := i+1;
 EXIT WHEN i>100000;
END LOOP;
COMMIT;
END;
```

In order to compare disk space consumption, gather statistics on both of these tables:

```
exec dbms_stats.gather_table_stats('VJ', 'ACCOUNTS_V');

exec dbms_stats.gather_table_stats('VJ', 'ACCOUNTS_P');
```

Now, query the data dictionary to compare how many blocks each table is using:

```
select
   table_name,
   num_rows,
   blocks
from
   dba_tables
where
   table_name in ('ACCOUNTS_V', 'ACCOUNTS_P');
```

```
TABLE_NAME      NUM_ROWS BLOCKS
--------------- -------- ------
ACCOUNTS_V        100000    748
ACCOUNTS_P        100000    874
```

Notice that both tables have identical data and partitions. However, the table using a virtual column to derive the region column consumes significantly less disk space than the table that uses a physical column for storing the region. This is attributed to the fact that virtual columns are part of the metadata and do not consume disk space.

Virtual column-based partitioning improves a DBA's capability to partition tables that do not have an obvious partition key. This new feature avoids suboptimal alternatives to derive the partition key, such as using triggers or modifying application code to evaluate and insert additional physical columns. Use of virtual columns, instead of physical columns, also improves disk space efficiency.

Composite Partitioning Enhancements

With each subsequent release of the Oracle database, additional composite partitioning, or subpartitioning, options have been made available. Partitioning data with finer granularity provides substantial advantages in database manageability and performance. Composite partitioning involves the partitioning of data using a primary criterion and then subpartitioning each partition based on a secondary criterion. In Oracle 10g, the available composite partitioning choices were range-hash and range-list. Oracle 11g introduces a number of new composite partitioning strategies including: range-range, list-list, list-hash, and list-range. These partitioning strategies are also available with interval partitioning and the use of virtual columns in the partitioning key.

	Range	List	Hash
Range	11g	10g	10g
Interval	11g	11g	11g
List	11g	11g	11g

Table 2.1: *Composite Partitioning Options*

As the chart above exhibits, in Oracle 11g there are many more composite partitioning strategies available allowing data to be divided to its finest possible granularity.

Enhanced Partition Pruning Capabilities

Partition pruning occurs when an SQL statement involving a partitioned object is executed and the database recognizes that the selection criteria are only specific partitions. This allows the database to access only the relevant partitions and ignore all partitions that are not necessary for the SQL statement. In other words, partition pruning is the act of eliminating or ignoring partitions that are irrelevant to the SQL statement's selection criteria.

Beginning with Oracle 11g, partition pruning uses bloom filtering instead of subquery pruning. A bloom filter essentially tests if an element is a member of a set or not. In deciding whether to use partition pruning, a bloom filter uses partition pruning whenever a partitioned object is detected in the SQL statement. This enhances the performance of partition pruning because bloom filtering does not require additional resources. Also, it is not evaluated as a cost based decision. Instead, bloom filtering is constantly active as well as automatically activated for any join with a partitioned object. This transparent enhancement improves the performance of partition pruning.

Enhanced Information Lifecycle Management

The concept of Information Lifecycle Management (ILM) has been around for many decades. In a nutshell, ILM is the intelligent archiving of historical Oracle data on cheaper tertiary media, like inexpensive disks, optical jukeboxes, and magnetic tape.

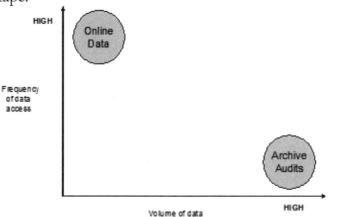

Figure 2.1: *ILM - It's all about the cost of storage*

In a perfect world, with negligible-cost fast storage, ILM would be unnecessary because offloading and storing historical data would not be driven by economics. However, even though disk and SSD is now cheaper than ever before, archiving historical data remains problematic, especially within the realm of Oracle auditing for regulatory compliance.

Government regulations such as SOX, GLBA and HIPAA require auditing of updates (DML) and disclosure (SQL selects). According to the law, organizations must provide complete audit trails for all DDL (i.e., schema changes), DML (e.g., updates, insert, deletes), and select confidential patient information.

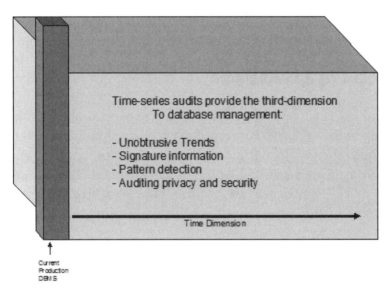

Figure 2.2: *Time-Series Audit Chart*

As highly active data ages out and becomes low-activity, ILM allows the DBA to easily move it away from the high-cost storage onto cheaper media.

The basic idea of ILM is to develop a hierarchy of storage based upon storage cost and data activity. ILM leaves highly active current data on high-speed solid-state disk (e.g. SSD which can be 300x faster than platter disks) and archives low-activity historical data to cheaper platter disk and tertiary media (tape)

Oracle introduced an ILM assistant in Oracle 9i, an Apex (HTML-DB) application, to offload and archive large volumes of historical database information. Oracle notes that as long as Oracle Application Express is used in Databases 9i and up, Apex is useful for the following reasons:

- ILM environments are managed via a GUI interface

- Lifecycle definitions are defined

- Security and compliance are managed

- It advises when data needs to be moved and generates scripts

The Oracle 11g ILM Assistant

In Oracle 11g, ILM has been enhanced to incorporate Oracle partitioning to allow easy data movement at the partition level. This includes the all-important exchange partition syntax. As highly-active data ages out and becomes low-activity, ILM allows the DBA to easily move it away from high-cost storage onto cheaper media. Oracle says that the basic ILM steps include the following:

- Define the data classes

- Create storage tiers for the data classes

- Create data access and migration policies

- Define and enforce compliance policies

To allow for easy data movement within ILM, Oracle leverages their Automatic Storage Management (ASM) and partitioning features. These features are offered within an 11g ILM assistant, which is a GUI designed to remove the tedium from managing many layers of storage. Oracle 11g introduces these new additions within ILM:

- Oracle advanced data compression for tables, LOBs and partitions

    - Interval, Ref and virtual column partitioning methods

    - 11g partitioning methods (list-list, list-range, list-hash and range-range)

In summary, ILM is more of a collection and integration of existing tools, such as ASM and partitioning, than a separate product. Furthermore, the Apex front-end ILM assistant provides an easy interface to the management of multi-tiered data.

New Index Features

Invisible indexes

Invisible indexes are a new feature of Oracle 11g that are useful in several different situations. An invisible index is an index that is maintained by the database but ignored by the optimizer unless explicitly specified. The invisible index is an alternative to dropping or making an index unusable. This feature is also functional when certain modules of an application require a specific index without affecting the rest of the application.

One use of the invisible index feature is to test the removal of an index before dropping it. Prior to 11g, this was typically achieved by making an index unusable during a set period of time. During this observation period, the DBA would monitor the database performance to determine whether or not to drop the index. If performance was negatively affected, the index would need to be rebuilt before it could be used again. Beginning with Oracle 11g, the DBA has the option of making the index invisible as opposed to unusable during this observation period. If performance degradation is observed, the index can be made visible again without having to rebuild the index. This can minimize the period of performance degradation, while also preventing an expensive operation to rebuild or recreate an index.

The syntax to change the visibility of an index is simple.

```
ALTER INDEX index_name INVISIBLE;
```

It is equally simple to make an index visible again.

```
ALTER INDEX index_name VISIBLE;
```

It is possible to query the column VISIBILITY from the data dictionary view *dba_indexes* to determine the current status of an index.

Another potential use for invisible indexes is in situations where specific applications require an index temporarily. An index can be created as invisible to allow specific SQL statements to use the index while leaving the rest of the database unaffected. Creating a visible index for this same purpose would cause the optimizer to consider the new index for all execution plans on that object.

Consider the introduction of a reporting application into a large production database. Shortly after the go-live, a query in the application is found to be running slow. The query is consuming excessive amounts of resources due to a full table scan on a large, highly referenced table, ORDER_LINES. After identifying this query, there is a realization that creating an index on column ORDER_LINES.ATTRIBUTE7 would immediately resolve this particular issue. This issue needs to be resolved as soon as possible without impacting any other processes that use this object. In this situation, creating an invisible index as a temporary solution until the application code can be reviewed would be an ideal solution. This method would alleviate the immediate problem without potentially affecting other users and processes that use the ORDER_LINES table.

Use the following code to create an invisible index on ORDER_LINES.ATTRIBUTE7:

```
create
    index order_lines_inv
on
    order_lines(ATTRIBUTE7) INVISIBLE;
```

This one query can be modified to explicitly use the invisible index with a hint:

```
select /*+ INDEX (order_lines ORDER_LINES_INV) */
    id
from
    order_lines
where
    attribute7 = 11001;
```

If the application code cannot be modified, it is possible to instruct the optimizer to include invisible indexes at the session level:

```
alter session set optimizer_use_invisible_indexes = true;
```

Keep in mind that rebuilding an invisible index will make it visible.

Invisible indexes are an attractive feature for the process of dropping an index. They are also useful when a specific application needs the benefit of a temporary index without impacting the database on a wider scale. Since the database must still maintain an invisible index for all DML operations, invisible indexes should not be used unless necessary. Though they should be removed once their purpose has been served, invisible indexes offer substantial advantages for short-term solutions.

Improved table compression

Oracle 11g extends the use of compressed tables to be used for all DML operations. Previous releases of Oracle only supported compression for direct-path inserts. Using compression saves disk space, reduces memory use in the buffer cache, and increases the speed of read operations. Compressed tables typically consume two to three times less disk space than uncompressed copies of the same data. The concept of data compression fits well with new technology trends such as larger and faster memory and the use of solid-state disks. While data compression has many benefits, note that it does incur CPU overhead when writing data.

Oracle 11g uses a table compression algorithm that minimizes the performance overhead of using compression for OLTP tables. The algorithm works by compressing a block in batch mode instead of each time a write operation takes place. A newly initialized block becomes compressed only after reaching an internally controlled threshold, at which time all data in the block is compressed. For an OLTP table, this guarantees a high level of compression and limits the performance overhead to only transactions that trigger the block compression. The frequency of triggering block compression will be affected by the block size and row length. In most cases, the overwhelming majority of transactions will have the same performance when writing to compressed blocks as uncompressed blocks. Once the blocks have been compressed, Oracle can read the compressed blocks directly without requiring the block to first be uncompressed.

This new enhancement for table compression allows data compression to be utilized in OLTP environments. By default, enabling compression by using COMPRESS in a table's DDL will be the same as specifying compress for DIRECT_LOAD operations. The syntax to enable compression for all DML operations is COMPRESS FOR ALL OPERATIONS in the compression portion of the table's DDL:

```
create table
    table_name ( ... )
compress
    for all operations;
```

To enable compression for all DML on an uncompressed table, the alter table syntax as follows:

```
alter table
    table_name
compress
    for all operations;
```

To disable compression for all DML operations and only use it for direct-path inserts, use this code:

```
alter table
    table_name
compress
    for direct_load operations;
```

To completely disable compression from a table, use these statements:

```
alter table
    table_name
nocompress;
```

For partitioned tables, compression can be controlled at the partition level. This allows the same table to have partitions that are compressed differently. Defining compression at the partition level overrides the compression settings at the table level, allowing for a finer level of control for compressing large tables based on specific business requirements.

Next to be covered is the impact of using compression in conjunction with DML operations on an OLTP table that might be found in a schema used to support order management. In order to perform an impact analysis, two versions of the table ORDER_LINES are defined, one without compression and one with compression for all DML.

```
create table
    order_lines_uncompressed (
    line_id number primary key,
    header_id number not null,
    customer_id number,
    customer_name varchar2(30),
    product_id number,
    quantity number,
    price number
);

create table
order_lines_compressed (
    line_id number primary key,
    header_id number not null,
    customer_id number,
    customer_name varchar2(30),
    product_id number,
    quantity number,
    price number
)
compress for all operations;
```

The data dictionary view *dba_tables* in 11g has an additional column, *compress_for*, to show the type of compression on a table. The query to show this information for the newly created tables is:

```
SELECT
    table_name, compression, compress_for
FROM
    dba_tables
where
    table_name in ('ORDER_LINES_UNCOMPRESSED',
'ORDER_LINES_COMPRESSED');
```

```
TABLE_NAME                         COMPRESS COMPRESS_FOR
------------------------------     -------- ------------------
ORDER_LINES_UNCOMPRESSED           DISABLED
ORDER_LINES_COMPRESSED             ENABLED  FOR ALL OPERATIONS
```

After both tables are created, a new session must be opened and a block of PL/SQL code should be run to insert 100,000 rows into each of the new tables. Since this is a simulation of an OLTP environment, a commit is issued after each insertion:

```
SQL> DECLARE
  2      i NUMBER := 1;
  3  BEGIN
  4  LOOP
  5   insert into ORDER_LINES_UNCOMPRESSED
  6   VALUES (i,i,12345,'TEST CUSTOMER',123,1,100);
  7   COMMIT;
  8   i := i+1;
  9   EXIT WHEN i>100000;
 10  END LOOP;
 11  END;
 12  /
```

PL/SQL procedure successfully completed.

Elapsed: 00:00:24.23

```
SQL> DECLARE
  2      i NUMBER := 1;
  3  BEGIN
  4  LOOP
  5   insert into ORDER_LINES_COMPRESSED
  6   VALUES (i,i,12345,'TEST CUSTOMER',123,1,100);
  7   COMMIT;
  8   i := i+1;
  9   EXIT WHEN i>100000;
 10  END LOOP;
 11  END;
 12  /
```

PL/SQL procedure successfully completed.

Elapsed: 00:00:29.39

Notice that the inserts into the compressed table take slightly longer than the uncompressed table. This is due to a slight CPU overhead for maintaining compression during DML operations. This occurs as the blocks reach an internally controlled threshold.

A comparison of the SQL Trace from each of these PL/SQL blocks can offer an explanation. These components show that the inserts to the compressed table consumed slightly more CPU and contained additional I/O wait events that totaled less than ½ of a second. The overhead for maintaining compression for all DML appears to be minimal. This will most likely prove acceptable for most database requirements, given the advantages that compression offers.

The most obvious benefit of compression is the reduction of disk space consumption. The following query shows that the compressed version of the table from the example above consumes substantially less disk space than the uncompressed version:

```
SQL> select
  2      segment_name, blocks, bytes
  3  from
  4      dba_segments
  5  where
  6      segment_name in
('ORDER_LINES_UNCOMPRESSED','ORDER_LINES_COMPRESSED');
```

```
SEGMENT_NAME                BLOCKS      BYTES
------------------------- ---------- ----------
ORDER_LINES_COMPRESSED         384    3145728
ORDER_LINES_UNCOMPRESSED       640    5242880
```

In addition to saving disk storage, the more important benefits of compression are arguably the extra savings in I/O and cache efficiency. Oracle operates directly on the compressed data without incurring the overhead required to uncompress the data. Since operations on the compressed version of the table must scan fewer blocks, physical I/O is reduced. The performance of table scans is then more efficient. By using the autotrace feature, the improvement can be demonstrated between querying the compressed and uncompressed versions of the table. The following query uses the uncompressed version and requires 627 consistent gets:

```
SQL> set autotrace traceonly
SQL> select
  2     *
  3  from
  4     order_lines_uncompressed
  5  where
  6     header_id = 50000;
```

```
Statistics
-----------------------------------------------------------
          0  recursive calls
          0  db block gets
        627  consistent gets
          0  physical reads
          0  redo size
```

The same query on the compressed version of the table uses 317 consistent gets:

```
SQL> select
  2     *
  3  from
  4     order_lines_compressed
  5  where
  6     header_id = 50000;
```

```
Statistics
-----------------------------------------------------------
          0  recursive calls
          0  db block gets
        317  consistent gets
          0  physical reads
          0  redo size
```

Further testing shows similar savings in I/O for update and delete operations. The new feature for enabling table compression for all DML operations extends the use of table compression to OLTP environments. While Oracle's compression algorithm does incur a slight CPU overhead when writing data, the benefits of compression are substantial and include a savings in disk storage, I/O, and cache efficiency. Furthermore, the ease of altering between the compression methods mitigates the risk of changing the compression method. Considering the significant savings with the use of compression,

---

at the minimal cost of a small performance overhead when inserting the data, this new feature is ideal for OLTP tables. This feature is a major advancement in the use of compression and one of the most exciting features of Oracle 11g.

Improved NFS Performance/Management

Oracle 11g has introduced a new method for directly accessing NFS V3 servers by using an internal Direct NFS Client as part of the Oracle Database kernel. This improves performance and manageability by allowing Oracle-specific optimizations to be utilized. Additionally, it removes the need to manually configure and tune most of the NFS client parameters.

The use of network attached storage (NAS) systems has become increasingly common in enterprise database environments. This is due to the growing need to consolidate data to a single point of access. NAS technology offers an ideal solution to this need by allowing access to network drives as if they were directly attached to the client. This allows the users, applications, or the database itself to access files stored on the network as if they were stored on local drives.

Files used by the database can be stored on the NFS drive, including data files. However, due to the performance limitations of NFS storage prior to Oracle 11g, many production databases opted to use network storage for files and processes. With these, the performance limitation was acceptable. Using NFS drives allows for scalability of disk space without requiring an upgrade of the existing architecture. Now the system administrator can attach a network drive and access the drive as if it was attached locally. Once the network drive is available, data files can be moved or created in the newly available drives.

NFS drives provide a common access point between multiple systems that are unable to directly connect to each other but can independently connect to the network file system. This is a common situation that can arise from a multitude of reasons. For example, security protocol on a server that supports an ERP database generally restricts other systems from direct access. However, the ERP database might have several dependencies on external systems, such as systems that support electronic data interchange (EDI). By utilizing a network drive, the data transmission can flow from the external systems into the ERP system without the two systems ever being directly connected. There are many other uses for NFS storage and as enterprise systems grow in size, the importance of this technology in a system's architecture will become increasingly important.

Prior to the 11g release of Oracle, the benefits of NFS and the database have been subject to certain drawbacks such as performance degradation and complex configuration requirements of the NFS client. These drawbacks have been minimized in Oracle 11g by the integration of a direct NFS client in the Oracle kernel. This client allows Oracle to optimize the I/O path between Oracle and the NFS server directly. Utilizing Oracle's direct NFS client is also automated and simplified in configuration to achieve optimal performance.

Benefits of Direct NFS

The direct NFS client has two fundamental optimizations that increase performance. First, the direct NFS client is capable of performing concurrent direct I/O. This removes the need to utilize the operating system's cache and bypassing limitations which are imposed by the operating system configuration. Using the operating system to configure the NFS client, and data written from the database to the NFS, requires that the data be read from Oracle's memory to the operating system cache. This is done before it is copied from the system cache to the NFS. By using the direct NFS client, the Oracle data no longer needs to be cached in the operating system. The process reduces the overall memory consumption and kernel CPU when writing to the network drive.

In addition to eliminating the dependency on the operating system cache, the second fundamental optimization is that the direct NFS client now supports asynchronous I/O on NFS file systems. Asynchronous I/O (AIO), also known as non-blocking I/O, allows I/O processing to continue independently from other I/O that has not yet completed. This setting makes a tremendous difference for read/write performance, whether using an NFS or a local drive. Many DBAs have experience enabling AIO on their local file systems and recall the performance improvement when switching from synchronous I/O to asynchronous I/O. As of Oracle 11.1, the direct NFS client supports up to four parallel network paths. The direct NFS client automatically performs load balancing across all specified paths.

Another advantage of the direct NFS client is that Oracle manages the configuration across different platforms. This greatly simplifies the task of administering NFS storage by allowing Oracle to internally manage the NFS configurations for all platforms. This eliminates the need to manage different configurations on each platform, or use storage-specific drivers. This feature also uses simple Ethernet for storage connectivity, eliminating the need for additional architecture components such as redundant host bus adaptors, Fibre Channel switches, or bonded network interfaces.

The direct NFS client supports both single instance databases as well as real application cluster (RAC) environments. The client recognizes when an instance is part of a RAC environment and automatically optimizes the NFS configuration accordingly.

Enable Direct NFS

The direct NFS client looks for mount settings in the following order:

- *$ORACLE_HOME/dbs/oranfstab* for settings on a single database

- */etc/oranfstab* for NFS mounts available to all Oracle databases on the host

- Lastly, the mount tab file (i.e. */etc/mtab* on Linux) to determine available NFS mounts

The oranfstab file should be created to include the server, path, export (path), and mount. For example, one possible content of this file could be the following:

```
server: MyServer
path: 135.34.28.11
path: 135.34.28.12
export: /vol/oradata mount: C:\oracle\11g\oradata\ora11gr1
```

Server = NFS server name
Path = Up to four network paths to the NFS server
Export = Exported path from the NFS server
Mount = Local mount point for NFS server

Prior to enabling the direct NFS client, the NFS file systems should already be mounted and available over regular NFS mounts. Once the NFS file systems are mounted, it is necessary to replace the standard Oracle Disk Manager (ODM) library with one that supports the direct NFS client. This can be accomplished by issuing the following commands on the server:

```
> cd $ORACLE_HOME/lib
> cp libodm11.so libodm11.so_stub
> ln -s libnfsodm11.so libodm11.so
```

These commands create a copy of the ODM library. They also create a symbolic link between the ODM library that supports the direct NFS client and old ODM library.

Monitor Direct NFS

Oracle 11g has introduced several new dynamic views to provide visibility on the configuration and performance of direct NFS in the database.

- *v$dnfs_servers* – View servers accessed using Direct NFS

- *v$dnfs_files* – View files currently open using Direct NFS

- *v$dnfs_channels* – View open network paths or channels to servers for which Direct NFS is providing files

- *v$dnfs_stats* – View performance statistics for Direct NFS

Direct NFS in OLTP and DSS

Case studies from Oracle demonstrate that the direct NFS client provides a significant improvement over the kernel NFS for throughput and CPU utilization in both DSS and OLTP environments. In DSS environments, the improvement increases dramatically as additional network interfaces are added. Oracle's case study shows an approximately 40% improvement in DSS environments and an 11% improvement in OLTP environments. These metrics are only one element of the full benefits of using the direct NFS client rather than the kernel NFS. Other factors that should be considered when evaluating this feature include the simplicity of setup, maintenance, and the reduced infrastructure requirements.

Database Resident Connection Pooling

Oracle 11g has introduced Database Resident Connection Pooling (DRCP) to support server-side connection pooling. With DRCP, different application processes can share sessions on the same machine and across a multitude of other machines. This new feature greatly increases the scalability of applications that cannot be deployed as multithreaded, such as PHP applications. DRCP is also useful in multi-threaded applications that frequently maintain idle connections.

Unlike some other databases, creating a new connection in Oracle requires a non-trivial amount of database resources. The Oracle database architecture is designed to create a connection that is capable of performing many concurrent operations using the same connection. Web-tier and middle-tier database applications generally require many threads during their execution. Each thread must take its turn to consume database resources. In order to build scalable applications, minimal connections should be used by the application. In order to support this practice, Oracle has provided connection-pooling options in all of their data access drivers such as OCI and ODP.NET. The use of connection-pooling in an application allows multiple threads to share resources. This reduces the number of sessions required to support multiple application end users and allows for very scalable applications.

The Growing Need for DRCP

Since its introduction in 1995, PHP has grown to be one of the most popular languages on the web. Other major database vendors have already taken steps to provide better support for PHP applications. As the use of this language becomes more common, it is no surprise that Oracle's customers have been eager to use PHP in their web-based applications. Until Oracle

11g, the major obstacle for using PHP to access Oracle databases was the inability of single-threaded PHP to use middle-tier connection pooling. The PHP architecture was not efficient with Oracle's connection architecture. Consequently, Oracle users who wanted PHP applications were forced to either use another language or another database. However, with the introduction of DRCP in Oracle 11g, this is no longer the case.

Database Resident Connection Pooling provides a connection pool within the database server. The DRCP supports situations where an application requires a database connection for a short amount of time before releasing the connection. DRCP works by creating a pool of dedicated servers which consist of a server foreground and a database session combined; a model that is referred to as pooled servers.

Prior to DRCP, only multithreaded applications were eligible to take advantage of the session sharing capability. By utilizing DRCP, the pooled servers are shared across middle-tier processes on the same host and across different middle-tier hosts. Additionally, DRCP complements middle-tier connection pools because it eliminates the need to maintain persistent database connections at the middle-tier in order to avoid the overhead of connection creation and termination.

About DRCP

The pooled servers are managed within the database by a process called the connection broker. Upon a client request, the connection broker hands the client off to an available pooled server. If no pooled servers are available, it creates one. If the pool has reached its defined maximum, the client request is placed on a queue until a pooled server is available. The client communicates directly with the assigned pooled server, which essentially behaves as a dedicated server. When the client releases it, the pooled server is returned to the connection broker.

The DRCP connection architecture might sound similar to Oracle's shared server model. However, there are some distinct differences between using shared servers and DRCP. Primarily, shared servers require the termination of a session when releasing database resources, whereas DRCP involves the release of the pooled server back to the pool. Therefore, the memory requirement for DRCP is fairly consistent and relative to the number of pooled servers. On the other hand, the memory requirement for shared servers is proportional to the sum of the shared servers since each client has a session. The result is that DRCP can scale much better than shared servers for applications that frequently require sessions for a short amount of time.

Using DRCP results in a significant reduction of database resources and memory required to support a large number of application end-users. This greatly increases the scalability of both the database tier and the middle-tiers. DRCP is designed to scale to tens of thousands of simultaneous connections.

DRCP should be used when a large number of client connections need to be supported, and the client applications are similar and can share sessions. The applications are similar if they connect to the database using the same credentials and the same schema. The client applications should require each database connection for a short duration before releasing the connection.

Configuring the Pool

Before starting DRCP, the pool settings can optionally be configured using the *dbms_connection_pool.configure_pool* procedure or the *dbms_connection_pool.alter_param* procedure. This is only necessary if the default settings need to be changed. Following are two important options that can be configured for the DRCP pool:

- *minsize* – Minimum number of pooled servers (default is 4).

- *maxsize* – Maximum number of pooled servers (default is 40).

Additional pool options that can be configured include the following:

- *inactivity_timeout* – Maximum time, in seconds, that a pooled server can stay idle in the pool before being terminated. Default is 300. This does not apply when the number of pooled servers equals the *minsize*.

- *incrsize* – Number of pooled servers by which the pool is incremented if a server is unavailable when a client request is received. Default is 3.

- *session_cached_cursors* – Number of cursors to cache for each pooled server session. Default is 20.

- *max_think_time* – Maximum time, in seconds, of inactivity for a client to hold a pooled server before the client connection is terminated (default is 30).

- *max_use_session* – Number of times a pooled server can be taken and released by the pool. Default is 5000.

- *max_lifetime_session* – Maximum time, in seconds, for a pooled server to live in the pool. Default 3600.

- *num_cbrok* – Number of connection brokers created to handle client requests. Default is 1.

- *maxconn_cbrok* – Maximum number of connections that each connection broker can handle. Default is 40000.

Since Oracle has provided default values for each of these options, it is recommended to not change these values unless necessary. If it happens that the customized configuration options are proving problematic, they can be restored using the defaults:

```
SQL> execute dbms_connection_pool.restore_defaults();
```

Enabling DRCP

In order to enable DRCP, the connection broker needs to be started. The following command starts the broker, which registers itself with the database listener from sys user:

```
SQL> execute dbms_connection_pool.start_pool();
```

Once the pool is started, it remains in this state until it is explicitly stopped. The pool is automatically restarted if it is active when the database instance is restarted.

In order for the client connections to use the connection pool, the connect string must specify the connect type as POOLED. For example, the TNS connect descriptor to use DRCP for client connections could be:

```
(DESCRIPTION=(ADDRESS=(PROTOCOL=tcp) (HOST=databasehost)
    (PORT=1521))(CONNECT_DATA=(SERVICE_NAME=ora11gr1)
    (SERVER=POOLED)))
```

The DRCP pool can be stopped when all client requests managed by DRCP have completed using the following command from sys user:

```
SQL> execute dbms_connection_pool.stop_pool();
```

Considerations with DRCP

Since the pooled servers are essentially a pool of preserved dedicated servers, there are certain special considerations that apply to the use of DRCP in the database:

- **Modifying database users of DRCP** – Since pooled servers are dedicated servers owned by the user, it is not possible to change the password of a user while that user is connected. Also, when dropping a user, make sure that no sessions authenticated by that user are in the pool.

- **Shutting down the database** – When client connections are actively being handled by DRCP, the database needs to wait until all pooled servers are returned to the connection broker before stopping the pool and shutting down the database.

- **Advanced Security Option** (ASO) – ASO options are not available for pooled servers.

Monitoring DRCP

Oracle 11g has provided several dynamic views for monitoring database resident connection pooling including:

- *dba_cpool_info* - Contains information about the connection pool including the maximum and minimum number of connections, pool status, and timeout for idle sessions.

- *v$cpool_stats* - Contains pool statistics including the number of session requests, the total wait time for a session request, and the number of times a session that matches the request was found in the pool.

- *v$cpool_cc_stats* - Contains connection-class level statistics for the pool.

Oracle Call Interface (OCI) Consistent Client Cache

Oracle 11g introduces a number of features to expand the use of memory caching in order to improve query performance. These features also decrease the overall memory requirements of queries and applications. In addition to the features that support server-side caching, there is also a new feature to support a client-side result cache that allows OCI clients to fetch result sets stored in process memory instead of requiring access to the server's memory. The Client Result Cache is enabled and configured at the database level and available to all OCI-based clients.

Using the client's memory to cache query result sets significantly improves the performance of repetitive queries by OCI-based clients that would otherwise require a cache hit on the server-side. The client cache utilizes per-process memory on the OCI client and its contents can be shared across multiple sessions and threads. When executing repetitive queries, the clients fetch results directly from the client cache rather than having the server execute the query. In certain situations, this will greatly reduce the number of round-trips between the client and the database server. This also reduces CPU consumption on the server and greatly increases the query response times. Situations that will benefit most from the client cache are queries that use small lookup tables or mostly read-only tables.

The consistency between the client cache and the database server is managed internally by the database, and is a feature available to all OCI clients.

Configuring the Client Cache from the Database

The current client cache initialization parameters can be viewed by issuing the following statement:

```
SQL> show parameter client_result

NAME                                 TYPE        VALUE
------------------------------------ ----------- -----
client_result_cache_lag              big integer 3000
client_result_cache_size             big integer 0
SQL>
```

To enable the client cache, the initialization parameter *client_result_cache_size* must be set to a value greater than zero since the value of zero disables the client cache. This parameter is the maximum size of the client-per-process result set cache. All OCI client processes get this maximum size.

The *client_result_cache_lag* parameter specifies the maximum amount of time, in milliseconds, that the client result cache can lag behind any changes in the database that affect the result sets. By default, the value is 3000ms (or three seconds). Since ideally this feature is used for read-only tables, this setting should not have a significant impact on the consistency of the cached results.

Both of these initialization parameters are static parameters. This being, changing their values should be done with SCOPE=SPFILE and any new values will not become effective until the database is restarted. For example, to enable the client cache with a value of 2M for the client cache, issue the following command:

```
SQL> alter system set client_result_cache_size=2M scope=SPFILE;
System altered.
```

After restarting the database, the new settings have taken effect:

```
SQL> show parameter client_result

NAME                                 TYPE        VALUE
------------------------------------ ----------- -----
client_result_cache_lag              big integer 3000
client_result_cache_size             big integer 2M
SQL>
```

Override Client Cache Configuration from the Client

The client can optionally override the database settings by maintaining a client configuration file. However, if the client cache is disabled at the server level, the client configuration settings will be ignored.

The following settings can be overridden by the client using the *sqlnet.ora*:

- *oci_result_cache_max_size* - maximum size of the result cache
- *oci_result_cache_max_rset_size* - maximum size of any result set
- *oci_result_cache_max_rset_rows* - maximum number of rows in any result set

The server settings are able to be overridden by managing the client cache on the database level. However, the settings are controlled for all OCI clients in a centralized manner. These settings should only be overridden after consulting with the DBA.

Using the Client Cache

The client cache can be utilized from the OCI client application by using the hint *result_cache* in the query. Alternatively, the *result_cache_mode* initialization parameter can be set to FORCE in order to force the use of the result cache whenever possible. When the client cache has been enabled, using the result cache hint will store the query results in the client's process memory upon the first query on the table. Subsequent executions of that query will return the results using the client cache. Consider a table STATIC_LOOKUPS that contains a listing of lookup names and values. If the OCI client uses this table to retrieve values of a multi-user application, the client cache can improve the efficiency and speed of querying this table. The following is the autotrace output for a query without using the client cache:

```
SQL> select lookup_value from static_lookups where lookup_name =
'CA';

Execution Plan
----------------------------------------------------------
Plan hash value: 53038468
```

```
------------------------------------------------------------------------
----------------
| Id  | Operation           | Name            | Rows  | Bytes | Cost
(%CPU)| Time     |
------------------------------------------------------------------------
----------------
|   0 | SELECT STATEMENT    |                 |    2  |   38  |   22
(0)|  00:00:01 |
|*  1 |   TABLE ACCESS FULL | STATIC_LOOKUPS  |    2  |   38  |   22
(0)|  00:00:01 |
------------------------------------------------------------------------
----------------

Predicate Information (identified by operation id):
---------------------------------------------------

   1 - filter("LOOKUP_NAME"='CA')


Statistics
----------------------------------------------------------
          1  recursive calls
          0  db block gets
         77  consistent gets
          0  physical reads
          0  redo size
        497  bytes sent via SQL*Net to client
        434  bytes received via SQL*Net from client
          2  SQL*Net roundtrips to/from client
          0  sorts (memory)
          0  sorts (disk)
          1  rows processed

SQL>
```

By using the result cache hint, the query results are cached in the client's process memory on the first execution, and in subsequent executions, there is a significant reduction in resource consumption:

```
SQL> select /*+ result_cache */ lookup_value from static_lookups
where lookup_name = 'CA';
```

```
Execution Plan
----------------------------------------------------------
Plan hash value: 53038468


------------------------------------------------------------------------
----------------------------
| Id  | Operation           | Name                    | Rows  |
Bytes | Cost (%CPU)| Time     |
```

```
------------------------------------------------------------------------
----------------------------
|   0 | SELECT STATEMENT    |                                  |    2 |
38 |    22    (0)| 00:00:01 |
|   1 |   RESULT CACHE      | f1bdppb5chzgtaxuxw70nq49hz |        |
|        |              |
|*  2 |    TABLE ACCESS FULL| STATIC_LOOKUPS                   |    2 |
38 |    22    (0)| 00:00:01 |
------------------------------------------------------------------------
----------------------------

Predicate Information (identified by operation id):
---------------------------------------------------

   2 - filter("LOOKUP_NAME"='CA')

Result Cache Information (identified by operation id):
-----------------------------------------------------

   1 - column-count=1; dependencies=(VJ.STATIC_LOOKUPS);
parameters=(nls); name="select
   /*+ result_cache */ lookup_value from static_lookups where
lookup_name = 'CA'"

Statistics
----------------------------------------------------------
          2  recursive calls
          0  db block gets
          2  consistent gets
          0  physical reads
          0  redo size
        514  bytes sent via SQL*Net to client
        434  bytes received via SQL*Net from client
          2  SQL*Net roundtrips to/from client
          0  sorts (memory)
          0  sorts (disk)
          1  rows processed

SQL>
```

The result cache is utilized to return the results with minimal overhead. Even in a brand new session, the client result cache is used to return results for the same query. This improvement can also be observed for operations on larger tables. Consider a query that computes a count of ORDER_LINES_NOV07, which has about one million rows and is used for mostly read-only reporting purposes:

```
SQL> select count(*) from ORDER_LINES_NOV07;
```

```
   COUNT(*)
----------
  1000000


Execution Plan
----------------------------------------------------------
Plan hash value: 336444469


----------------------------------------------------------------------
----------
| Id  | Operation             | Name         | Rows  | Cost (%CPU)|
Time    |
----------------------------------------------------------------------
----------
|   0 | SELECT STATEMENT      |              |     1 |   512   (1)|
00:00:07 |
|   1 |  SORT AGGREGATE       |              |     1 |            |
|
|   2 |   INDEX FAST FULL SCAN| SYS_C0010418 | 1162K|   512   (1)|
00:00:07 |
----------------------------------------------------------------------
----------

Note
-----
   - dynamic sampling used for this statement


Statistics
----------------------------------------------------------
          0  recursive calls
          0  db block gets
       1898  consistent gets
          0  physical reads
          0  redo size
        510  bytes sent via SQL*Net to client
        434  bytes received via SQL*Net from client
          2  SQL*Net roundtrips to/from client
          0  sorts (memory)
          0  sorts (disk)
          1  rows processed

SQL>
```

In a reporting application, this count might be continually recalculated even though the result will not change since it is used for historical information. By using the client cache, this query can be greatly improved:

```
SQL> select /*+ result_cache */ count(*) from ORDER_LINES_NOV07;
```

```
  COUNT(*)
----------
   1000000

Execution Plan
----------------------------------------------------------
Plan hash value: 336444469
-----------------------------------------------------------------------
-------------------------
| Id  | Operation               | Name                       | Rows
|  Cost (%CPU)| Time     |
-----------------------------------------------------------------------
-------------------------
|   0 | SELECT STATEMENT        |                            |      1
|   512    (1)| 00:00:07 |
|   1 |  RESULT CACHE           | 072j3kqba3bwb91a78u11zj2tn |
|        |          |
|   2 |   SORT AGGREGATE        |                            |      1
|        |          |
|   3 |    INDEX FAST FULL SCAN| SYS_C0010418                |
1162K|   512    (1)| 00:00:07 |
-----------------------------------------------------------------------
-------------------------

Result Cache Information (identified by operation id):
--------------------------------------------------------

   1 - column-count=1; dependencies=(VJ.ORDER_LINES_NOV07);
attributes=(single-row); name="select /*+ result_cache */ count(*)
from ORDER_LINES_NOV07"

Note
-----
   - dynamic sampling used for this statement


Statistics
----------------------------------------------------------
          2  recursive calls
          0  db block gets
          2  consistent gets
          0  physical reads
          0  redo size
        502  bytes sent via SQL*Net to client
        434  bytes received via SQL*Net from client
          2  SQL*Net roundtrips to/from client
          0  sorts (memory)
          0  sorts (disk)
          1  rows processed

SQL>
```

The improvement for this query, by using the result cache, is very
significant. This reduction in resources to return the results

improves the response time and greatly reduces the CPU and I/O on the server.

Viewing Client Cache Statistics

The client cache statistics are available from a dynamic view called *client_result_cache_stats$*. This view includes information such as the number of result sets cached, number of cached result sets that were invalidated, and the number of cache hits.

```
SQL> select cache_id, name, value from client_result_cache_stats$;
```

```
CACHE_ID NAME                                VALUE
-------- ------------------------------- --------
      55 Block Size                           256
      55 Block Count Max                     8192
      55 Block Count Current                  128
      55 Hash Bucket Count                   1024
      55 Create Count Success                   2
      55 Create Count Failure                   0
      55 Find Count                             0
      55 Invalidation Count                     1
      55 Delete Count Invalid                   0
      55 Delete Count Valid                     0
```

A few important values to monitor in this dynamic view are as follows:

- **Block Count Max** - a computed value that shows the maximum number of blocks that can be allocated in the result cache. This is based on the configuration parameters.

- **Block Count Current** - the number of blocks currently being used by the client result cache. The ratio of Block Count Max to Block Count Current shows the utilization of the result cache.

- **Create Count Success** - the number of cached result sets that did not get invalidated prior to caching the result set.

- **Invalidation Count** - the number of cached result sets that got invalidated due to database changes that could affect the result set. The ratio of Create Count Success to Invalidation Count will provide a metric which determines if the use of the result cache is inefficient due to frequent changes on the database object. As mentioned previously, the client cache should be used for tables that are either read-only or near read-only. If the result cache is used for tables which have frequent changes like inserts, updates and deletes, it will force the database to spend resources to ensure consistency between the client cache and the database object.

Further detail about this dynamic view can be found in the documentation for Oracle Database Reference.

Virtual columns

A virtual column is an expression based on one or more existing columns in the table. As previously covered in the section for Virtual Column-Based Partitioning, using a virtual column in a table provides advantages in disk space utilization. While a virtual column is only stored as metadata, and does not consume physical space, it can be indexed. The virtual column also contains optimizer statistics and histograms.

Using a virtual column also simplifies the use of derived columns. This is done by transparently deriving the values instead of requiring the application to calculate and insert an additional value. It also prevents the need to use a trigger on the table to provide an alternate implementation of this functionality. Another benefit of using virtual columns in tables is eliminating the need to use views to display derived column values.

To define a new table with a virtual column, use the following syntax:

```
create table <table_name>(
   <column_name> <data_type>,
   …
```

```
    <column_name> [<data_type>] [generated always] as
(<column_expression>) [virtual]
);
```

In order to add a virtual column to an existing table, use the alter table syntax:

```
alter table <table_name>
add (<column_name> [<data_type>] [generated always] as
(<column_expression>) [virtual]);
```

When defining a virtual column in a table, a DBA could either include the datatype or let the database determine the datatype based on the expression. The phrases *generated always* and *virtual* can be optionally used for syntactic clarity. Keep in mind that the column expression must reference columns defined on the same table. However, the column expression can refer to a PL/SQL function if the function is designated DETERMINISTIC during its creation.

As an example, a virtual column might be helpful in a table that stores employee information:

```
SQL> create table employees(
  2      employee_name varchar2(30),
  3      start_date date,
  4      end_date date,
  5      hourly_rate generated always as (annual_salary/2080),
  6      annual_salary number,
  7      active as (case when end_date is null then 'Y' else 'N'
end));

Table created.

SQL> insert into employees
  2      (employee_name,
  3      start_date,
  4      end_date,
  5      annual_salary)
  6  values
  7  ('V.J. JAIN', '01-AUG-2005', NULL, 100000);
1 row created.

SQL> select * from employees
  2  /
```

```
EMPLOYEE_NAME    START_DATE END_DATE  HOURLY_RATE ANNUAL_SALARY
ACTIVE
---------------  ---------- --------- ----------- ------------- -----
-----
V.J. JAIN        01-AUG-05               48.0769231      100000 Y

SQL>
```

While the insert statement required to create a new record in this table only requires four values, a query of this table displays all six values. This includes the two virtual columns derived from other columns. The first virtual column, hourly rate, is an expression of the annual salary divided by 2080 hours in a year. The second virtual column displays if the employee is active by examining the row's end date.

Virtual columns can be used for partitioning, indexing, constraints and foreign keys. However, virtual columns cannot be used for index-organized, external, object, cluster, or temporary tables.

Note that updates or deletes cannot be performed directly on virtual columns since they are expressions.

11g virtual columns only work within the specified table, and you cannot reference columns within other tables.

Oracle 11g Binary XML data storage

In previous versions of Oracle, two Extensible Markup Language (XML) storage options were available: unstructured or CLOB, and storage and structured, or schema-based. In Oracle 11g, binary XML has been added as a new storage option.

Unstructured storage treats an XML document as a large object and stores the file in the database without being aware of the content. This option has the best insertion and deletion performance, but the worst relational access and consumption of disk space.

Structured storage requires prior registration of the XML schema and inserts an XML document into an object-relational structure. This storage option has the best query performance and disk space consumption, but the highest cost during initial insertion. This high cost is caused because during insertion, the document is shredded and stored into database objects created during the registration of the XML schema.

Binary XML, the new storage option introduced in 11g, stores the document in a post-parse binary format designed specifically for XML. This option will likely be the best choice for most XML requirements. The additional binary storage offers insertion performance comparable to unstructured storage, yet query and disk space performance that is comparable to structured storage. Unlike structured storage, the benefits of binary XML are not dependent on schema registration. This is due to the option of registering a binary XML schema to have schema based binary XML tables. However, one limitation remains in that a registered XML schema cannot be shared between a binary XML and object relational table.

The best strategy when choosing how to manage XML content is to first try the binary storage option and evaluate whether the performance is acceptable. If the relational access performance is not acceptable, then try the structured storage option. The reason that binary storage is preferred is that it is easy to use and requires the least amount of maintenance because schema registration is not required. Binary XML type columns are also easier to use in non-XMLType tables since performance is not dependent on the creation of indexes.

To use binary storage, the XML table must be created with the following syntax:

```
SQL> CREATE TABLE BINARY_XML_TABLE OF XMLType XMLTYPE STORE AS
BINARY XML
  2  /

Table created.
```

Consider the following XML document for order transactions:

```
test_document.xml
<?xml version="1.0"?>
<order>
    <customer>
        <name>Customer ABC</name>
        <ccNum>1234123412341234</ccNum>
    </customer>
    <orderLines>
        <item>
          <item_id>108</item_id>
          <item_name>ORACLE 11G NEW FEATURES BOOK ED1.0</item_name>
          <quantity>1</quantity>
          <unitPrice>$38.00</unitPrice>
        </item>
        <item>
          <item_id>109</item_id>
          <item_name>ORACLE TUNING GUIDE ED1.0</item_name>
          <quantity>1</quantity>
          <unitPrice>$22.00</unitPrice>
        </item>
    </orderLines>
    <receipt>
        <subtotal>$60.00</subtotal>
        <salesTax>$4.80</salesTax>
        <total>$64.80</total>
    </receipt>
</order>
```

Insert this document into the binary XML table using the following syntax:

```
SQL> insert into BINARY_XML_TABLE values (XMLTYPE(BFILENAME
('XML_DIR','test_document.xml'),nls_charset_id('AL32UTF8')));

1 row created.
```

After insertion, the document is immediately available for relational access.

```
SELECT
    extractValue(value(b),'/order/customer/name')  customer_name,
    extractValue(value(d),'/item/item_id')  item_id,
    extractValue(value(d),'/item/quantity')  quantity,
    extractValue(value(d),'/item/unitPrice')  unit_price,
    extractValue(value(b),'/order/receipt/subtotal')  subtotal,
    extractValue(value(b),'/order/receipt/salesTax')  salesTax,
    extractValue(value(b),'/order/receipt/total')  total
from
BINARY_XML_TABLE a
,TABLE(XMLSequence(Extract(object_value,'/order'))) b
,TABLE(XMLSequence(Extract(value(b),'/order/orderLines'))) c
,TABLE(XMLSequence(Extract(value(c),'/orderLines/item'))) d;
```

```
CUSTOMER_NAME  ITEM_ID QUANTITY UNIT_PRICE SUBTOTAL SALESTAX TOTAL
-------------- ------- -------- ---------- -------- -------- ------
Customer ABC   108     1        $38.00     $60.00   $4.80    $64.80
Customer ABC   109     1        $22.00     $60.00   $4.80    $64.80
```

As demonstrated above, the syntax for relational access to a binary XML table does not change from other storage options.

Incident Packaging Service

In order to improve the process of receiving help from Oracle Support, Oracle 11g introduces a new feature called Incident Package Service (IPS) that provides a utility to extract information about incidents, or exceptions, from the Automatic Diagnostic Repository (ADR).

Obtaining Oracle Support

As any experienced Oracle professional knows, obtaining support from Oracle requires submitting a Service Request (SR), formerly known as a Technical Assistance Request, TAR, via a MetaLink account. Service Requests are assigned a severity depending on the impact of the incident. This is based on a set of rules that Oracle defines; the higher the severity, the higher the priority. The severity is generally assigned using the following criterion:

- Severity 1 – issue is critical to the business, impacting production, and requires immediate attention

- Severity 2 – issue causes a severe loss of service with no acceptable workaround; however, operation can continue

- Severity 3 – issue causes a minor loss of service that is inconvenient

- Severity 4 – issue causes no business impact

Severity 1 service requests are worked on around the clock 24/7 by Oracle support which passes the SR between support staff in centers around the world. Most SRs will be assigned a severity of either 2 or 3. In theory, this support paradigm should be effective and provide a great level of customer satisfaction.

The SR process from beginning to end is usually a time consuming process and often requires several follow ups before the issue is clearly identified. The majority of service requests involve the assigned Oracle support engineer requesting additional information, such as trace files, specific database settings, or the output from a provided script. Each time that additional information is requested, the SR is placed in a hold status until the customer replies. Since most of the Oracle support centers are located outside the U.S., the assigned engineer often does not respond during regular U.S. business hours. Depending on the severity of the SR, the replies from the assigned support representative can take a considerable amount of time.

In most cases, the main reason that the support process seems so inefficient is because the original SR was submitted without adequate information. This is necessary for the support engineer to accurately diagnose the root cause of the incident. In Oracle 11g, a new feature called the incident packaging service (IPS) can be used to gather and submit all of the information about an incident to Oracle support.

How IPS Works

The Incident Packaging Service is an extension of another new feature in Oracle 11g called the Automatic Diagnostic Repository. The ADR is a system managed repository for organizing and storing trace files and other diagnostic data and is discussed in greater detail in Chapter 7. When problems are detected in the database, they automatically create an incident in the ADR. A problem can have many incidents since the same problem might occur many times.

An incident package is a logical structure that contains a collection of metadata. This is stored in the ADR, and points to diagnostic data files both inside and outside of ADR. The incident package only exists as metadata and has no content until a physical package is generated from the logical package. IPS can be used to create packages based on a problem, an incident, a time interval, or an empty package.

- An IPS package based on an incident includes diagnostic data related to that incident. The data includes trace files, dumps, health monitor reports and such.

- A package based on a problem includes the diagnostic data for incidents that reference the problem.

- An incident package based on a time interval includes diagnostic data for incidents that occurred during the provided time interval.

Upon generating the physical incident package, all diagnostic and information files are placed into a zip file in a designated directory. Once the zip file has been created for a logical package, an incremental zip file can be created for the same logical package. This package contains all diagnostic files added or changed since the last zip file. There are several methods for using IPS including the Enterprise Manager's Support Workbench and the command line ADRCI (ADR Command Interpreter) utility.

Using ADRCI for IPS

From the command prompt, the ADRCI utility is entered by typing the following command:

```
C:\>adrci

ADRCI: Release 11.1.0.6.0 - Beta on Thu Nov 15 22:21:42 2007

Copyright (c) 1982, 2007, Oracle.  All rights reserved.

ADR base = "c:\oracle\11g"
adrci>
```

ADRCI commands are based on one or more base directories known as ADR homes. Before using the ADRCI commands, it is helpful to set an active ADR home to work with a single instance. The available homes can be seen by typing the following:

```
adrci> show homes
ADR Homes:
diag\clients\user_system\host_1475088825_11
diag\clients\user_varun jain\host_1475088825_11
diag\rdbms\ora11g4\ora11g4
diag\rdbms\ora11gr1\ora11gr1
diag\tnslsnr\dcfx7hb1\listener
adrci>
```

The output above shows that there are several available home directories on which ADR can operate. If a DBA wants to only access diagnostic data from one of the available homes, the active ADR home should be set appropriately. The active home can be set using the set homepath command:

```
adrci> set homepath diag\rdbms\ora11gr1\ora11gr1
adrci> show homes
ADR Homes:
diag\rdbms\ora11gr1\ora11gr1
adrci>
```

The output demonstrates that after setting the active ADR home, only the active home displays.

Creating Incident Packages

Once the incident or problem that should be included in the incident package is identified, two options remain. The DBA can then either create a physical package immediately or create a logical package to verify the package contents and customize the package to include the files that are needed.

Incidents in the ADR home can be viewed by using the SHOW INCIDENT command:

```
adrci> set homepath diag\rdbms\ora11gr1\ora11gr1
adrci> show incident

ADR Home = c:\oracle\11g\diag\rdbms\ora11gr1\ora11gr1:
*****************************************************************************
*****
INCIDENT_ID          PROBLEM_KEY
CREATE_TIME
-------------------- ---------------------------------------------------
---------------------------------
5138                 ORA 7445 [qmxarFindPartition()+15]       2007-
11-15 22:53:58.343000 -08:00
5137                 ORA 600 [qmxarElemAt2]                   2007-
11-15 22:53:40.859000 -08:00
2 rows fetched

adrci>
```

> Note: If an active ADR home has not been set, this will include incidents from all homes listed in the "show homes" command.

If the problem reported has not been captured as an incident in ADR, then it is best to create a logical package and add the necessary files before generating the zip file.

If the physical package needs to be generated immediately based on an incident, problem, problem key, or time interval without the opportunity to customize the logical package, the IPS PACK command can be used as follows:

```
ips pack [incident incident_id|problem problem_id|problemkey
prob_key|seconds secs|time start_time to end_time] [correlate
{basic|typical|all}] [in path]
```

Consider the following example:

```
adrci> ips pack incident 5137 in C:\tmp
Generated package 5 in file
C:\tmp\ORA600qmx_20071116175948_COM_1.zip, mode complete
adrci>
```

To create the logical incident package, use a variation of the IPS CREATE PACKATE command:

```
ips create package {incident incident_id|problem
problem_id|problemkey problem_key|seconds secs|time start_time to
end_time} [correlate basic|typical|all]
```

It is possible to create a logical package based on incident number such as the following:

```
adrci> ips create package incident 5138
Created package 1 based on incident id 5138, correlation level
typical
adrci>
```

New Index Features

To create an incident package based on a problem, it is necessary to find the *problem_id* by using the SHOW INCIDENT command:

```
show incident [-p predicate_string] [-mode {BASIC|BRIEF|DETAIL}]
```

For example:

```
adrci> show incident -mode brief -p "incident_id=5137"

ADR Home = c:\oracle\11g\diag\rdbms\ora11gr1\ora11gr1:
***********************************************************************
****

****************************************************************
INCIDENT INFO RECORD 1
****************************************************************
    INCIDENT_ID                 5137
    STATUS                      ready
    CREATE_TIME                 2007-11-15 22:53:40.859000 -08:00
    PROBLEM_ID                  1
    CLOSE_TIME                  <NULL>
    FLOOD_CONTROLLED            none
    ERROR_FACILITY              ORA
    ERROR_NUMBER                600
    ERROR_ARG1                  qmxarElemAt2
    ERROR_ARG2                  144
    ERROR_ARG3                  <NULL>
    ERROR_ARG4                  <NULL>
    ERROR_ARG5                  <NULL>
    ERROR_ARG6                  <NULL>
    ERROR_ARG7                  <NULL>
    ERROR_ARG8                  <NULL>
    SIGNALLING_COMPONENT        <NULL>
    SIGNALLING_SUBCOMPONENT     <NULL>
    SUSPECT_COMPONENT           <NULL>
    SUSPECT_SUBCOMPONENT        <NULL>
    ECID                        <NULL>
    IMPACTS                     0
1 rows fetched

adrci>
```

This shows that incident 5137 has been assigned the problem id of 1. Using this problem id, create the package for this problem with the following command:

```
adrci> ips create package problem 1
Created package 2 based on problem id 1, correlation level typical
adrci>
```

To create the package based on the problem key, use the *problem_key* value displayed in the show incident output. For example:

```
adrci> ips create package problemkey "ORA 7445
[qmxarFindPartition()+15]"
Created package 3 based on problem key ORA 7445
[qmxarFindPartition()+15], correlation level typical
adrci>
```

As previously stated, creating an incident package based on a problem includes diagnostic information for incidents associated with that problem. Since the same problem could potentially include many incidents, only the first and last three incidents associated with the problem will be included. This prevents the inclusion of superfluous information in the package. Additionally, incidents older than 90 days are excluded to prevent the inclusion of incidents that are no longer impacting the database. These settings apply to all generated incident packages except manually created packages. Both of these options are configurable by either using IPS set configuration or the Enterprise Manager Support Workbench.

When creating an incident package based on a time interval, the DBA can either include incidents that occurred relative to the current time, or inside of a specific time interval. To create a package based on incidents that occurred a certain time from the present, use IPS CREATE PACKAGE SECONDS [*seconds*]. This will include incidents that occurred within [*seconds*] from the time the command was run. For example, IPS CREATE PACKAGE SECONDS 600 will create a package including incidents that occurred within the last 10 minutes.

To use a time interval instead, use the command IPS CREATE PACKAGE TIME '*start_time*' TO '*end_time*'". The start and end times in the command must be in the time format 'YYYY-MM-DD HH24:MI:SS.FF TZR' or 'YYYY-MM-DD HH24:MI:SS TZR'. The colons in the 'HH24:MI:SS' can optionally be substituted with periods. To create the package based on the incidents that occurred between November 11, 2007 10PM and November 12, 2007 12AM (2 hour window), the command would be:

```
adrci> IPS CREATE PACKAGE TIME '2007-11-11 22:00:00 -08:00' to
'2007-11-12 00:00:00 -08:00'
Created package 4 based on time range 2007-11-11 22:00:00 -08:00 to
2007-11-12 00:00:00 -08:00, correlation level typical
adrci>
```

If the issue that is being reported to Oracle Support has not been captured as an incident, create an empty package using IPS CREATE PACKAGE without any options.

Modifying Existing Logical Packages

Once the logical package has been created, it is possible to add diagnostic information or additional files in ADR to the existing package. To add an incident to an existing package, the command is IPS ADD INCIDENT [*incident_number*] PACKAGE [*package_number*]. To add a file to an existing package, the command is IPS ADD FILE [*file_path*] PACKAGE [*package_number*], with [*file_path*] as a fully qualified path and file name. Only files within the ADR base directory can be added.

IPS SHOW INCIDENTS PACKAGE [*package_number*] can be used to view the incidents contained within the logical package:

```
adrci> ips show incidents package 1
*********************************************************
Main INCIDENTS
*********************************************************
```

```
------------------------------------------------------------
************************************************************
INCIDENT RECORD
************************************************************


------------------------------------------------------------
INCIDENT INFORMATION:
    INCIDENT_ID                   5138
    PROBLEM_ID                    2
    EXCLUDE                       0


------------------------------------------------------------
************************************************************
Correlated INCIDENTS
************************************************************


------------------------------------------------------------
************************************************************
INCIDENT RECORD
************************************************************


------------------------------------------------------------
INCIDENT INFORMATION:
    INCIDENT_ID                   5137
    PROBLEM_ID                    1
    EXCLUDE                       0

------------------------------------------------------------
adrci>
```

To view the files included in a package, use the command IPS
SHOW FILES PACKAGE [*package_number*]. The output of this
command will show all the files that will be included in the zip
file when the physical package is generated. Listed below is the
output generated from this command for 2/42 files in package 1.

```
************************************************************

------------------------------------------------------------
FILE INFORMATION:
    FILE_LOCATION
<ADR_HOME>/incpkg/pkg_1/seq_2/export!c:\oracle\11g\diag\rdbms\ora11g
r1\ora11gr1
    FILE_NAME                     HM_RUN.dmp
    LAST_SEQUENCE                 2
    EXCLUDE                       0


------------------------------------------------------------
************************************************************
FILE RECORD
************************************************************
```

```
---------------------------------------------------------------
FILE INFORMATION:
   FILE_LOCATION
<ADR_HOME>/incpkg/pkg_1/seq_2/export!c:\oracle\11g\diag\rdbms\oral1g
r1\oral1gr1
   FILE_NAME                          EM_USER_ACTIVITY.dmp
   LAST_SEQUENCE                      2
   EXCLUDE                            0

---------------------------------------------------------------
```

Viewing additional IPS commands available from ADRCI is done by typing HELP IPS [*topic*] from the adrci prompt. Detailed information for all available commands is available using the help option. A complete list of possible ADR operations is also available from Oracle's documentation library in Oracle Database Utilities ADRCI: ADR Command Interpreter.

Generating the Physical Incident Package

If this is the first time creating the zip file for the logical package, then a complete zip file will be created. However, if a zip file for the logical package has already been generated, then an incremental physical package can be generated to include only incidents or files that have been added since the last package generation. Once the logical package is satisfactory, the DBA can generate the zip file from the logical package by using the command IPS GENERATE PACKAGE *package_id* [*output_path*] [*complete | incremental*]

The output path is the path to the directory that the zip file will be placed. If this field is omitted, the package will be generated in the current working directory. For example, issue this command to generate the zip file for package 1 in C:\tmp:

```
adrci> ips generate package 1 in C:\tmp
Generated package 1 in file
C:\tmp\ORA7445qm_20071116141007_COM_1.zip, mode complete
adrci>
```

Zip files are named according to the following nomenclature: packageName_*mode_sequence.zip,* where packageName is the problem key concatenated with a timestamp; mode is either 'COM' for complete or 'INC' for incremental; and, sequence is an integer.

If a logical package has been modified and already generated a physical package, the zip file can be generated using an incremental mode:

```
adrci> ips generate package 1 in C:\tmp incremental
Generated package 1 in file
C:\tmp\ORA7445qm_20071116141007_INC_2.zip, mode incremental
adrci>
```

Using the Enterprise Manager for IPS

In order to view incidents captured by ADR, and to access the Incident Packaging Services through the Enterprise Manager, navigate to the Support Workbench by clicking on the Software and Support tab as shown below.

Figure 2.3: *Using the Software and Support tab*

From the Support Workbench, problems captured in the ADR are viewed. There is also a tab for accessing existing packages. To create a new package, select the checkbox for one or more problems to add to the package and click on the Package button.

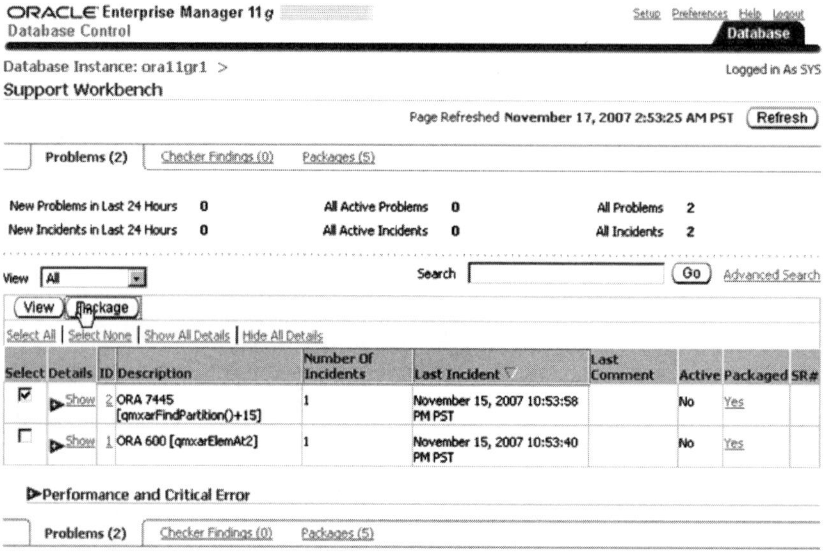

Figure 2.4: *Viewing Problems on the Support Workbench*

This menu offers choices to use the quick packaging or a custom package.

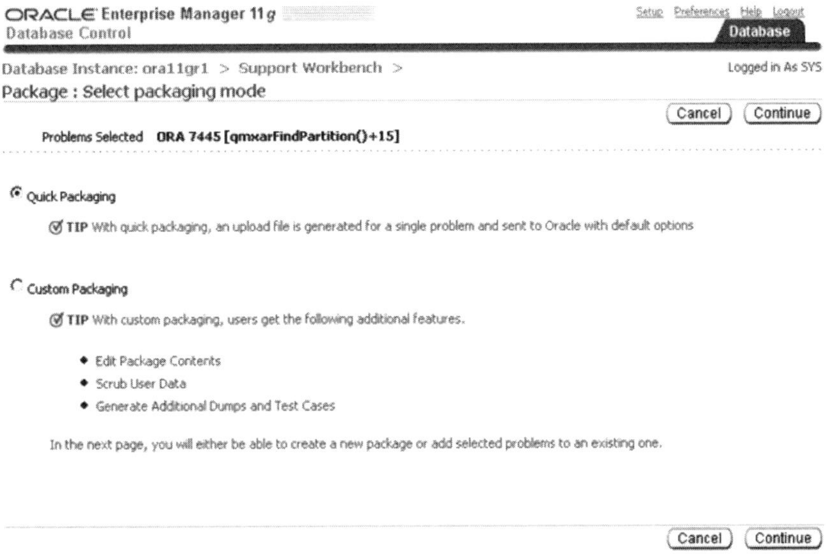

Figure 2.5: *The Quick Packaging or Custom Packaging Options*

Using Quick Packaging

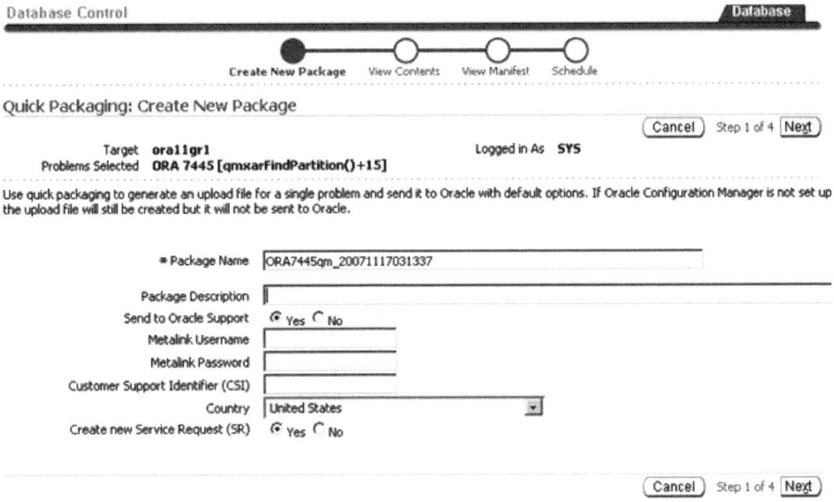

Figure 2.6: *Quick Packaging with Package Name*

From the first step of the quick packaging, it is possible to enter Metalink details to automatically send the zip file to Oracle Support. A new Service Request based on the package can also be created. Clicking on the next button generates the logical package and offers a view of the contents of the package.

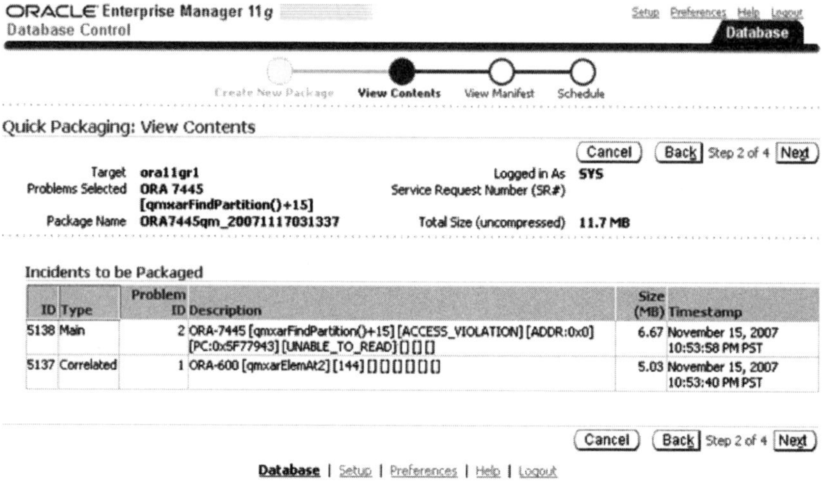

Figure 2.7: *Viewing the Package Contents*

The next step will display the package manifest. This includes information about the package, included problems and incidents, and a listing of the files that will be included.

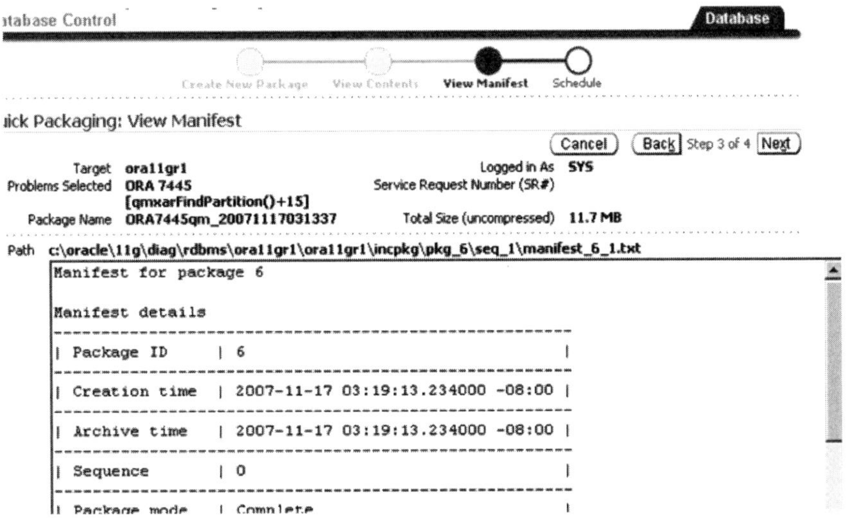

Figure 2.8: *Viewing the Package Manifest*

The final step allows the DBA to schedule the generation of the physical package.

Figure 2.9: *Scheduling the Generation of the Physical Package*

Clicking the submit button will generate the zip file and display a confirmation and location of the physical file on disk.

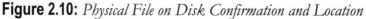

ORACLE Enterprise Manager 11g   Setup Preferences Help Logout
Database Control   Database

🔲 Confirmation
   Upload file for package: ORA7445qm_20071117031337 has been successfully generated. The upload file is located at
   C:\oracle\11g\product\11.1.0\db_4\dcfx7hb1.localhost_ora11gr1\sysman\emd\state\ORA7445qm_2007111703133
   Please send it manually to Oracle.

                                                                    OK

                     Database | **Setup** | Preferences | Help | Logout

Figure 2.10: *Physical File on Disk Confirmation and Location*

The problem information, incident information, trace files, and dumps associated with the selected problems are automatically added to the zip file. The zip file can either be uploaded manually on the MetaLink service request or uploaded through Oracle's Configuration Manager. To view all the files in the zip file, navigate to the Packages tab on the Support Workbench and click on the package.

Custom Package

If the choice is to create a custom package, the option of creating the package based on either an existing package or a new package is offered.

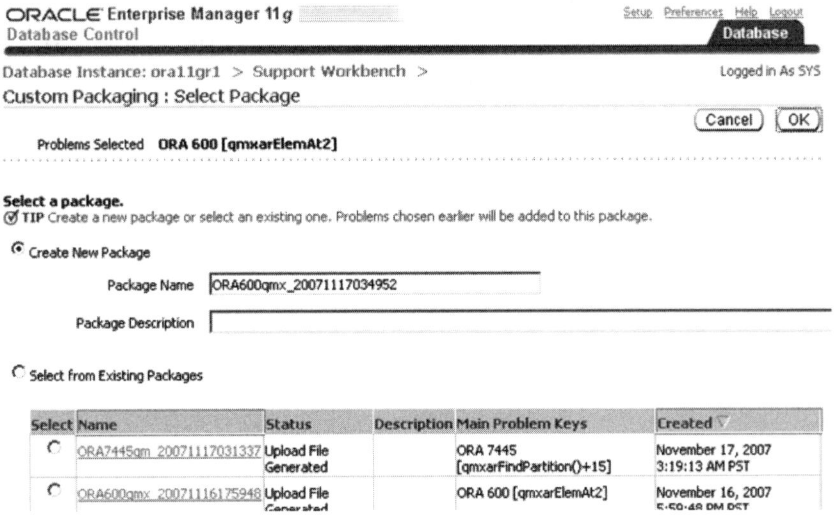

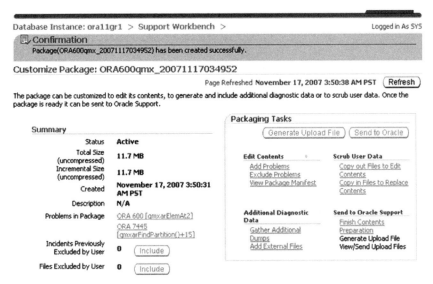

Figure 2.11: *Choosing Between an Existing or New Package*

From the next screen, it is possible to add or remove problems, incidents, and files. This gives a simple GUI for customizing the package before generating it.

Figure 2.12: *GUI for Package Customization*

Once the package is satisfactory, the next step is to click on Finish Contents Preparation and generate the upload file. If the package is chosen to be built on an existing package, there is the option to do an incremental generation. Otherwise, the full package will have to be generated.

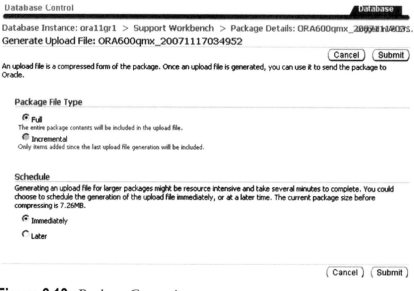

Figure 2.13: *Package Generation*

Once the package is created, external files can be added to the package. In addition, selected files will modify or be removed. From this view, it is also possible to view an activity log for the package that shows a history of the package's activity.

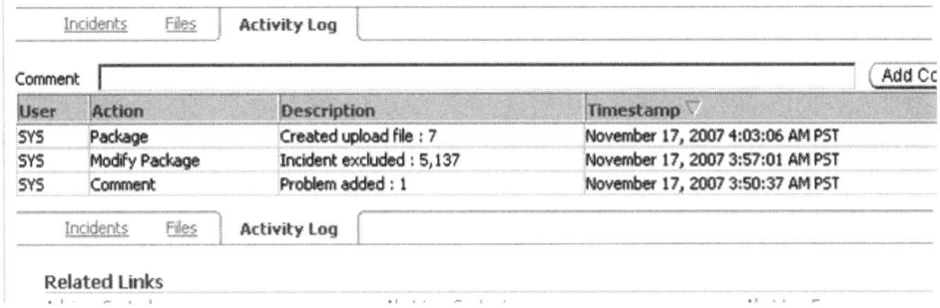

Figure 2.14: *Activity Log View*

The IPS functionality available from the Support Workbench is very similar to the interactive utility ADRCI. As demonstrated, either ADRCI or OEM can be used to achieve the same objectives. Regardless of personal preference, IPS provides a means to generate zip files that contain all the information necessary for Oracle to efficiently provide support for Service Requests when database issues arise.

Enhanced Read-only tables

Oracle 11g has introduced a much simpler method for enabling read-only tables that even protect the table from unintentional DML by the table's owner. Prior to 11g, a read-only table was achieved by creating a table under a restricted account and granting select privileges to the appropriate users. However, using this method, it is possible for the owner of the table to unintentionally modify the table.

Oracle Database 11g introduces new ALTER TABLE syntax. For example, a table can be set to read-only by issuing the following command:

```
ALTER TABLE <name> READ ONLY;
```

A table can be returned to read and write using the following command:

```
ALTER TABLE <name> READ WRITE;
```

In read-only mode, the following operations are permitted on the table:

- Select

- Management indexes, constraints, supplemental log

- Dropping and deallocation of unused columns

- Renaming and moving of the table

- Altering the table for physical property changes, row movement, and shrinking the segment

- Drop table

The following operations are disabled on a table in read-only mode:

- DML on table or any table partitions

- Truncation of table

- Select for update

- Adding, removing, renaming, dropping, or setting a column to unused

- Dropping a partition or sub partition belonging to the table

- Online redefinition

- Flashback on the table

For example, consider a transactional table that stores a customer's account, sales amount, and transaction date:

```
SQL> desc account_sales
```

```
Name                                            Null?    Type
----------------------------------------------- -------- ------

ACCOUNT_ID                                               NUMBER
SALES_AMOUNT                                             NUMBER
TRX_DATE                                                 DATE
```

The business might request that this table be used to keep a historical record of accounts that were active during each month. If it is November 1st, 2007, the DBA might run the following command to meet this requirement and then make the table read-only since the table is only for a historical record:

```
SQL> create table
  2     account_sales_october2007
  3  as
  4  select
  5     *
  6  from
  7     account_sales
  8  where
  9     trx_date between ('01-OCT-07') and ('31-OCT-07');

Table created.

SQL> alter table account_sales_october2007 read only;

Table altered.
```

A table's read-only status is available from the *read_only* column of the dictionary views for *[user | all | dba]_tables*. For example:

```
SQL> select
  2     table_name,
  3     read_only
  4  from
  5     user_tables
  6  where
  7     table_name = 'ACCOUNT_SALES_OCTOBER2007';

TABLE_NAME                      READ_ONLY
------------------------------- ----------
ACCOUNT_SALES_OCTOBER2007       YES
```

Any attempts to insert, delete, or update the data from this table while it is in read-only status results in the following error:

```
SQL> insert into
  2      account_sales_october2007
  3  values (3, 100, '31-OCT-2007');
    account_sales_october2007
    *
ERROR at line 2:
ORA-12081: update operation not allowed on table
"VJ"."ACCOUNT_SALES_OCTOBER2007"


SQL> delete from
  2      account_sales_october2007
  3  where
  4      account_id = 3;
    account_sales_october2007
    *
ERROR at line 2:
ORA-12081: update operation not allowed on table
"VJ"."ACCOUNT_SALES_OCTOBER2007"


SQL> update
  2      account_sales_october2007
  3  set
  4      sales_amount = 2*sales_amount
  5  where
  6      customer_id = 3;
    account_sales_october2007
    *
ERROR at line 2:
ORA-12081: update operation not allowed on table
"VJ"."ACCOUNT_SALES_OCTOBER2007"
```

While the example above has been simplified to focus on the new feature, there are many business cases where a read-only table is appropriate. Most of these business cases share the fact that the data is being stored for historical record or reference, and there is no reason that the table should need to be updated. In many cases, protecting the integrity of the data is a main priority. An example is an OLTP table with transactional data and sales compensation based on the table's monthly activity. It would be desirable to have each month's data stored in a read-only table that is protected from modification.

The need for read-only data has existed long before the new release of Oracle. However, this new feature greatly simplifies the process of enabling and disabling read-only status from a table with its simple syntax.

Faster DML triggers

Another transparent enhancement with Oracle 11g is quicker triggers, reported to be up to 25% faster when row-level triggers perform DML on other tables. While this improvement has not been widely publicized by Oracle in the 11g release, it offers a noticeable improvement in several business cases. For example, this improvement might show substantial benefits in triggers used for auditing.

To demonstrate the improvement, define a table for sensitive information such as CREDIT_CARD:

```
create table
   credit_cards (
   account_id number,
   credit_card_number varchar2(30),
   expiration_date date);
```

Next, create tables AUDIT_LOG and AUDIT_TABLES for storing audit information:

```
create table
   audit_log (
   username varchar2(30),
   table_name varchar2(30),
   user_operation varchar2(30),
   user_time date);

create table
   audit_tables (
   table_name varchar2(30),
   last_updated_by varchar2(30),
   last_update_time date);
```

Define a trigger on CREDIT_CARDS that inserts a record into AUDIT_LOG and updates AUDIT_TABLES whenever an insert occurs:

```
CREATE OR REPLACE TRIGGER credit_cards_tr1
BEFORE INSERT
ON VJ.CREDIT_CARDS
REFERENCING NEW AS New OLD AS Old
FOR EACH ROW
DECLARE
BEGIN
   INSERT INTO
      AUDIT_LOG (USERNAME, TABLE_NAME, USER_OPERATION, USER_TIME)
   VALUES
      (USER , 'CREDIT_CARDS', 'INSERT - ' || :NEW.ACCOUNT_ID,
SYSDATE );
   UPDATE
      audit_tables
   SET
      last_updated_by = USER,
      last_update_time = SYSDATE
   WHERE
      table_name = 'CREDIT_CARDS';
   EXCEPTION
     WHEN OTHERS THEN
       RAISE;
END credit_cards_tr1;
/
```

After completing the setup, in Oracle 10.2, the following PL/SQL block should be executed:

```
Connected to:
Oracle Database 10g Enterprise Edition Release 10.2.0.3.0 -
Production
With the Partitioning, OLAP and Data Mining options

SQL> set timing on
SQL> DECLARE
  2      i NUMBER := 1;
  3  BEGIN
  4  LOOP
  5  insert into
  6     credit_cards
  7  VALUES (i, '1234123412341234', '01-JAN-2009');
  8  COMMIT;
  9   i := i+1;
 10   EXIT WHEN i>10000;
 11  END LOOP;
 12  END;
 13  /

PL/SQL procedure successfully completed.

Elapsed: 00:00:04.57
```

Following the same steps on Oracle 11.1, the result is:

```
Connected to:
Oracle Database 11g Enterprise Edition Release 11.1.0.6.0 -
Production
With the Partitioning, OLAP, Data Mining and Real Application
Testing options

SQL> set timing on
SQL> DECLARE
  2      i NUMBER := 1;
  3  BEGIN
  4  LOOP
  5  insert into
  6     credit_cards
  7  VALUES (i, '1234123412341234', '01-JAN-2009');
  8  COMMIT;
  9   i := i+1;
 10   EXIT WHEN i>10000;
 11  END LOOP;
 12  END;
 13  /

PL/SQL procedure successfully completed.

Elapsed: 00:00:04.00
```

The improvement in trigger execution times appears to be more prevalent as the trigger performs DML on a larger number of tables. This enhancement should prove to be useful in many situations where triggers perform DML on other tables

Conclusion

Through partitioning and index enhancements, Oracle 11g offers many new tools to simplify the tasks of DBAs and developer staffs.

This includes:

- A new partitioning feature, Interval Partitioning to create new partitions

- System partitioning allowing application level control in tables or indexes

- Reference partitioning in Oracle 11g that allows the partitioning of two related tables to be partitioned based on a referential constraint

- Support for partitioning tables using a partitioning key on virtual columns

- New composite partitioning strategies

- Partition pruning utilizing bloom filtering

To compliment the new partitioning enhancements in Oracle 11g, ILM has also been enhanced allowing easier data movements.

This chapter also includes a review of new index enhancements and features in 11g:

- Invisible indexes useful in many diverse situations

- Extended features of compressed tables for all DML operations

- Improved direct path inserts through directly accessing NFS V3 servers, using an internal Direct NFS Client with the Oracle Database kernel.

- Another part of the new Oracle 11g enhancements is Database Resident Connection Pooling (DRCP) which supports server-side connection pooling.

- OCI in 11g then expands use of memory caching to improve query performance.

- Furthermore, a virtual column, an expression based on existing columns in the table, which in a table can provide advantages in disk space utilization.

- Additionally, binary XML has been added as a new option for storage.

Oracle 11g also offers a new feature to improve help requests from Oracle Support called Incident Package Service. Furthermore, enabling read-only tables now utilizes easier processes.

High Availability and RAC New Features

CHAPTER

3

Background of Oracle RAC

Adoption of high availability practices are quickly becoming one of the hottest trends in the Oracle field. As data becomes more and more crucial to millions of businesses worldwide, it is being found that enterprise business cannot tolerate downtime.

Thanks to advances in Business Intelligence (BI), many companies now employ vast networks of decision support systems, expert systems, and analytic databases to back their OLTP environments. These warehouses, which once could be taken offline for days at a time, are now expected to remain online with the same uptime as one would expect from an enterprise public-facing environment. In short, data rules the business world.

Unfortunately, servers, databases, and applications can go offline for a variety of reasons. Sometimes downtime is expected such as in the case of a planned outage for upgrades. Still more dangerous is unplanned downtime, such as when a component failure causes an outage, or worse, data loss.

Oracle has made great strides to keep enterprise systems online and operational at all times. Perhaps the largest advances came in Oracle 9i, when Oracle introduced Real Application Clusters (RAC) to replace Oracle Parallel Server (OPS). This move allowed more clients to take on a clustered Oracle environment without sacrificing performance and manageability. RAC allowed not only a better scalability model across multiple clustered nodes, but a transparent application layer, allowing any applications to connect to a RAC cluster without any extra consideration on the part of the application developer.

Oracle 10g enhanced the RAC product, introducing portable Oracle-driven Clusterware, new administrative tools, and performance enhancements. These new changes transformed the look of RAC to include such concepts as Virtual IPs (VIPs) and the Oracle Notification Server (ONS). Another important feature known as services were introduced, allowing a DBA to manage and use RAC connections while leaving a simple connection method for applications. These services allowed a DBA to manage resource use such as CPU and parallel processes on each node across the cluster, while also providing failover capabilities using Transparent Application Failover (TAF) on the backend.

Oracle 11g extends the 10g RAC framework with new features targeted towards providing optimal throughput while retaining total uptime. In addition, Oracle has expanded products such as Dataguard to provide additional fault prevention. All of this together forms the Maximum Availability Architecture (MAA). The MAA is an Oracle model for high uptime and complete disaster recovery. In this chapter, how Oracle 11g makes high availability a scalable, high performance, enterprise-ready model will be explored.

Scalability

Oracle RAC truly shines as a high availability solution, but it also allows a certain degree of scalability. Traditional monolithic computing architecture has always endorsed vertical scalability as the means to grow an enterprise. Therefore, when a business function has outgrown its server, more RAM, CPU, and disk resources could be added to the server to make it more powerful. When the server reached capacity, a new monolithic powerhouse would be required.

With RAC, companies are now able to grow their database environment horizontally. This means that instead of building their database hardware up, they expand out into multiple servers. Oracle RAC allows connections to all servers in a cluster simultaneously. Oracle 11g expands on this concept and allows more intelligent load balancing in order to improve scalability. In this section, these new scalability enhancements will be reviewed along with some 10g capabilities, most of which fall under the title of Automatic Workload Management (AWM).

Automatic Workload Repository

The Automatic Workload Repository (AWR) is covered in greater detail in other chapters. However, AWR is especially important for RAC in Oracle 11g as an aggregator of statistics that are important for horizontal scalability. AWR collects service level metrics and passes these metrics to the overall Workload Management framework, allowing Oracle to make proper suggestions for the cluster as a whole.

This usage should be equated to object level statistics. Without those statistics, Oracle cannot properly decide the best path to use when running your queries. With RAC, Oracle must maintain good statistics to decide the best path to use when making connections to Oracle.

Services

Services are the backbone behind the Workload Management framework in Oracle 11g. A service is a server-side component that acts as a connection target. This means that client-side connections to the cluster can connect to a service, which can then be configured across the cluster. For instance, in a four node RAC cluster, a service can be configured to use nodes 1 and 2 as the primary connection nodes, node 3 as a backup node, and node 4 as an unusable node. Connections to this service will use the service rules as defined by the DBA.

In addition, services could be used with the Resource Manager, allowing a DBA to decide the level of CPU resources each connection will be allowed. In Oracle 11g, services work as the backend to the new Connection Load Balancing features.

Fast Application Notification

Fast Application Notification (FAN) is simply a series of published events by Oracle Notification Service (ONS). ONS publishes events as a RAC service, including UP and DOWN events in the case of server failure. FAN is built into Oracle's integrated client protocols, such as JDBC, ODP.NET, and OCI, so that programs written to connect with these protocols can subscribe to FAN events and use them to make cluster-wide decisions. For example, several programs can be run against a two node RAC cluster, including batch processes. The batch applications can be programmed to respond to a FAN DOWN event so that if a node fails, the batch process pauses until the node comes back online.

Another feature, Fast Connection Failover (FCF), allows clients to respond to FAN events with quick failover to other nodes in the event of an outage.

Load Balancing Advisory (LBA)

The Load Balancing Advisory was introduced in Oracle 10gR2. It monitors the load across clustered nodes and calculates percentages of incoming load for services. Percentage values are, for each instance, configured as part of a service and are published via FAN events and put into the AWR. This advisory can be used with supported connection pools to make intelligent connection decisions.

OCI Runtime Connection Load Balancing

Any Oracle 11.1 or higher client connecting to an Oracle 10gR2 database or higher will have OCI Runtime Connection Load Balancing enabled by default. OCI Session Pools will connect to an Oracle Service, and the Service will provide event notifications to the client containing information published by the Load Balancing Advisory. To use this feature, Oracle services must be configured with load balancing goals. Services, the Load Balancing Advisory, AWR, and FAN come together to provide this capability.

Putting Load Balancing into Action

Bringing all these features together primarily involves configuration of services to interact with the Load Balancing Advisory. One of the great features of Oracle 11g is that many clients (JDBC, ODP.NET, OCI) are now fully integrated with FAN and FCF through connection pools. In order to configure services to work with the Load Balancing Advisory, first a Load Balancing Goal (CLB_GOAL) must be set.

CLB_GOAL = LONG: A LONG load balancing goal is primarily for connections that will remain connected for long periods of time. Batch jobs, dedicated applications, and client-side connection pools are good examples of this category. By default, LONG is the load balancing goal. However, it can be configured for a service specifically with the following code:

```
exec dbms_service.modify_service (service_name =>
'example_service', clb_goal => dbms_service.clb_goal_long);
```

CLB_GOAL = SHORT: A goal of SHORT is appropriate for short lived connections. Examples include standard OLTP applications that connect directly to Oracle. In order to configure a service to a goal of "short," the following code can be used:

```
exec dbms_service.modify_service(service_name =>
'example_service', clb_goal => dbms_service.clb_goal_short);
```

Another important goal is the way that services would be measured. The Load Balancing Advisory can be configured to respond based upon THROUGHPUT or SERVICE TIME.

GOAL = THROUGHPUT: When the service-level goal is set to THROUGHPUT, Oracle will attempt to direct the request to the proper node based upon the rate at which work is completed on that node and the available bandwidth of the service. This goal is best used in batch environments where jobs require a large amount of resources in order to succeed. This goal can be set for a service with the following code:

```
exec dbms_service.modify_service(service_name =>
'example_service', goal => dbms_service.goal_throughput);
```

GOAL = SERVICE TIME: A service-level goal of SERVICE TIME will produce load balancing recommendations based on response time. This is perfect for OLTP applications where connections seek a quick result. This goal can be set for a service with this code:

```
exec dbms_service.modify_service(service_name =>
'example_service', goal => dbms_service.goal_throughput);
```

GOAL = NONE: To disable load balancing for services completely, the load balancing goal can be set to NONE. This is done with the following code:

```
exec dbms_service.modify_service(service_name =>
'example_service', goal => dbms_service.goal_none);
```

Cloning a Cluster to another Cluster

Once a RAC cluster with ASM is successfully installed, the ASM and RAC setup can now be cloned to a new cluster. While it was possible before 11g to clone RAC and ASM to a new node in the same cluster, there is now the capability to clone entire clusters for easy deployment. This is a scripted method of quickly deploying RAC clusters across the grid.

In order to clone ASM and RAC configurations, a new script called *clone.pl* is used along with pre-scripted silent runs of NetCA and DBCA. The Perl script *clone.pl* can be used to clone both ASM homes and Oracle Database homes. Software is deployed between nodes using the standard tar and gzip commands.

Here are the steps involved in cloning RAC instances with ASM to another cluster:

1. Install Oracle Clusterware on the new nodes

2. Take a tar backup of the Oracle 11g software

3. Backup the ASM Home

4. Backup the DB Home

5. Restore the ASM tar backup onto the new cluster nodes

6. Run the *clone.pl* Perl script on each node for ASM

7. Run the root.sh script on each node as root for ASM

8. Run NetCA in silent mode to create listeners on each node

---

9. Run DBCA in silent mode to create the ASM instance on each node

10. Restore the DB tar backup onto the new cluster nodes

11. Run the *clone.pl* Perl script on each node for the DB Home

12. Run the root.sh script as root on each node for the DB Home

13. Run DBCA to create the RAC instances

Full instructions on how to do this can be found in Oracle's documentation at the following URL:

http://download.oracle.com/docs/cd/B28359_01/rac.111/b282 54/clonerac.htm

Scalability Conclusion

Oracle 11g's new scalability features extend those given in Oracle 10g and 10gR2, allowing Oracle to properly balance connections across multiple instances. In addition, true grid environments can be created by cloning the clusters.

Cluster Performance

Oracle RAC carries the promise of better performance through horizontal scalability. With proper load balancing, dividing the work among multiple nodes allows for greater throughput overall. For instance, if a single instance is highly I/O bound, the CPU may be wasted due to the physical I/O bottleneck. With RAC and services, the load can be distributed to multiple servers, allowing more resources to be used across the board.

In order to monitor and tune the system, Oracle introduced the AWR and Automatic Database Diagnostic Monitor ADDM in Oracle 10g. The AWR is not only responsible for storing database snapshot statistics for automatic tuning, but also for producing reports that are useable by a DBA to further tune their system. ADDM creates human readable suggestions on ways to optimize the performance by eliminating bottlenecks based on information from the AWR. In Oracle 11g, ADDM reports have been extended to also provide diagnostic information about RAC clusters.

ADDM for RAC

The Automatic Database Diagnostic Monitor (ADDM) was introduced in Oracle 10g. Using information from the AWR, ADDM would provide plain English solutions to the DBA in the form of findings. The report would show the impact of issues on a database instance and offer solutions to fix the problem.

In Oracle 11g, ADDM has been extended to include RAC, and provides information on the entire cluster including latency issues on the cluster interconnect, global cache hot blocks (blocks with concurrency issues across multiple nodes), and general object usage information across multiple nodes.

The key to using ADDM for RAC is running the tool in database mode. Remember that a RAC cluster is a single database with multiple instances; normally ADDM is run against an instance. In database mode, a single instance system will run the same; however, a RAC cluster will report on multiple nodes.

Creating an ADDM Task

If the object is to run in database mode, the following syntax can be used:

```
exec dbms_addm.analyze_db( -
task_name => 'name for your task', -
begin_snapshot => begin_snapshot_num, -
end_snapshot => end_snapshot_num, -
db_id => db_id_optional -
);
```

For example, a call to the report may look like the following:

```
exec dbms_addm.analyze_db('My ADDM Task', 100, 102);
```

Note that an ADDM report can also be run for RAC across a subset of instances in the cluster using *dbms_addm.analyze_partial*. For instance:

```
exec dbms_addm.analyze_partial ('My Partial ADDM Task', '1,2', 100,
102);
```

The second parameter (with value '1,2') represents the instance numbers that should be analyzed ADDM report.

Gathering the Report

The report can be gathered via a function called *dbms_addm.get_report*. The task name that was assigned the ADDM run will be needed.

```
set long 9999999
set pages 0
select dbms_addm.get_report ('My ADDM Task') from dual;
```

The reports in Database Control can also be viewed on the Cluster Database home page. The report is found under the Diagnostic Summary area by clicking the link next to ADDM Findings. Doing so will allow a graphical version of the ADDM report to be viewed.

High Availability

The high availability enhancements to Oracle 11g primarily focus on upgrading, which is considered planned downtime. However, there are times when planning downtime is difficult. Oracle 11g alleviates this issue by allowing cluster nodes to be patched to the latest release one node at a time, allowing the entire cluster to remain online longer.

Please note that it is always advisable to perform a backup before attempting any upgrade, rolling or otherwise. In addition, rolling upgrades are not possible if a shared home is used for the Clusterware, ASM, or Oracle Database.

Clusterware Rolling Upgrades

Oracle Clusterware can now be upgraded in a rolling fashion, with only one node going down at a time. Performing a rolling Clusterware upgrade is much like performing a standard upgrade, except that only services on the nodes will be stopped that are needed to be patched. For instance, in a four node cluster, the nodes can be upgraded two at a time, with the first iteration of the rolling process taking down nodes 1 and 2.

In this situation, first stop all services on the nodes that need to be taken offline. This can be done using the *srvctl* utility.

```
srvctl stop instance -d dbname -i instance_name
srvctl stop asm -n nodename
srvctl stop nodeapps -n nodename
```

Run these commands to stop all instances, ASM, and Clusterware on the nodes that are desired to be upgraded. For example, for a node called *dbprod1* with a database named *dbp*:

```
srvctl stop instance -d dbp -i dbp1
srvctl stop asm -n dbprod1
srvctl stop nodeapps -n dbprod1
```

Once the nodes that are to be upgraded have all Oracle services halted, proceed with the upgrade process. On each node being upgraded, it is important to run the *preupdate.sh* script as the root user:

```
$ORA_CRS_HOME/upgrade/preupdate.sh -crshome $ORA_CRS_HOME -crsuser
crs
```

> Note: In this example, the environment variable $ora_crs_home must be set to the Clusterware install directory. The example also assumes Clusterware has been installed under the 'crs' user.

Once the *preupdate.sh* script has been completed, invoke the Oracle Universal Installer (OUI) to upgrade Clusterware on the prepared nodes. When prompted, choose only the nodes that have been prepared for the rolling upgrade, and follow all on-screen directions to complete the patch. This includes running *$ora_crs_home/install/rootupgrade.sh* once the software update has completed.

ASM Rolling Upgrades

Beginning in Oracle 11gR1, ASM versions can differ for the purpose of rolling upgrades (version greater than or equal to 11.1). Note that this is meant to be a temporary state, and all nodes should be upgraded to the latest release as quickly as possible.

First, fully upgrade the Clusterware to the new release on all nodes before attempting to perform a rolling upgrade of ASM. Once the Clusterware has been upgraded, place the ASM instance into rolling upgrade mode with the following command:

```
alter system start rolling migration to x.x.x.x.x;
```

Replace 'x.x.x.x.x' with the version to which the ASM instance will be migrating:

```
alter system start rolling migration to 11.2.0.0.0;
```

At this point, it is best to shut down each individual ASM instance, upgrade to the latest version, and start the ASM instance to rejoin the cluster. Do this for each node in the cluster.

It is important to note that the upgrade will fail if there are any rebalance operations currently being performed. This means avoiding adding or removing disks from the ASM disk groups before performing a rolling upgrade of ASM software.

Once the rolling upgrade is finished, stop the rolling upgrade process with the following command:

```
alter system stop rolling migration;
```

If, for any reason ASM must be downgraded, it can be done in a rolling fashion with the same commands. Downgrade to the lowest version currently in use in the cluster.

Example: There is a three node RAC cluster. Two nodes have been upgraded to Oracle 11.2.0.0.0. One node remains on Oracle 11.1.0.0.0. Issue the following command on the upgraded nodes:

```
alter system start rolling migration to 11.1.0.0.0;
```

Once this command has been run, downgrade the patch and rejoin the cluster. End the rolling migration with the same command previously mentioned:

```
alter system stop rolling migration;
```

Conclusion

Oracle 11g's new features for high availability make RAC a more manageable solution. A DBA can now properly manage connections across their RAC instances from a multitude of client sources, clone entire RAC configurations, and upgrade with ease.

In addition, with tools like ADDM extending their use to include RAC, a DBA will not be in the dark when trying to locate and fix issues that could be affecting the entire cluster as a whole. Coupled with other new features available in Oracle 11g, Oracle's high availability offering can be a very powerful addition to the database architecture.

OEM Oracle 11g new features

Introduction to OEM

Oracle Enterprise Manager was originally introduced in 1996 as a database management tool. OEM version 1.0 billed itself as allowing the DBA to quickly and easily administer database. Earlier versions were cast off by veteran Oracle professionals, favoring to instead execute commands directly from SQL*Plus. As stated by Oracle, OEM is the foundation on which management for Oracle's Fusion Applications are being built. With this future goal in mind, it is well advised that users should become familiar with this powerful management tool.

OEM improved over the years however, with new enhancements and greater integration of third party applications. Consequently, OEM 10g took a massive leap from a tool at which many DBAs turned their noses to a powerful management tool. OEM 10g also became known as Oracle Enterprise Manager Database Control or simply DBConsole, and was no longer just a database management tool. It went beyond the database to include management capabilities for Fusion Middleware, Oracle Applications, and other applications. This improvement was driven primarily due to Oracle's acquisitions over the past few years, as many of the acquired products do not run solely on the Oracle stack.

In general, the OEM screens are better organized in 11g and lead to a better tool with greater ease-of-use. Oracle has built upon the success of the previous version with several new enhancements:

- Improved Database Home Page and Performance changes

- Integrated Interface for LogMiner

- Advanced Replication Interface

- Wait Activity Detail Enhancement

- Easy Oracle Text Management

- Better OEM Grid Tools

- Clone Database Enhancements

- Migrate Database (and more!) to ASM

- Workspace Manager

Improved Database Home Page and Performance changes

The Database home page gives a general overview of the status of the database. Although the Database home page is not unlike the previous database home page that DBAs are familiar with, it does have a few new advantages. The first noticeable layout change is more tabs. Figure 4.1 shows the additional available tabs. The tabbed links across the top of the page offer access to performance, availability, and additional administration pages for managing the database.

ORACLE Enterprise Manager 11*g*
Database Control

Database

Logged in As SYS

Database Instance: dev11

| Home | Performance | Availability | Server | Schema | Data Movement | Software and Support |

Latest Data Collected From Target Oct 18, 2007 11:27:14 AM EDT (Refresh) View Data Automatically (60 sec) ▼

General

Status Up
Up Since Oct 15, 2007 12:09:57 PM EDT
Instance Name dev11
Version 11.1.0.6.0
Host orcldev
Listener LISTENER_akr-orcldev

(Shutdown) (Black Out)

View All Properties

Host CPU

100%
75
50   Other
25   dev11
0

Load 0.10 Paging 0.00

Active Sessions

2.0
1.5
1.0   Wait
0.5   User I/O
0.0   CPU

Maximum CPU 2

SQL Response Time

1.0
        Latest
0.5   Collection
        (seconds)
        Reference
0.0   Collection
        (seconds)

SQL Response Time (%) 104.96
(Edit Reference Collection)

Diagnostic Summary

ADDM Findings 0
Alert Log No ORA- errors
Active Incidents 0

Database Instance Health

Space Summary

Database Size (GB) 1.339
Problem Tablespaces 0
Segment Advisor Recommendations 0
Policy Violations ✔ 0
Dump Area Used (%) 40

High Availability

Instance Recovery Time (sec) 6
Last Backup n/a
Usable Flash Recovery Area (%) 100
Flashback Database Logging Disabled

▶Alerts

▶Related Alerts

Policy Violations

All 11   Critical Rules Violated 8   Critical Security Patches 0   Compliance Score (%) 94

Job Activity

Jobs scheduled to start no more than 7 days ago

Scheduled Executions 0Running Executions 0Suspended Executions ✔ 0Problem Executions ✔ 0

| Home | Performance | Availability | Server | Schema | Data Movement | Software and Support |

Figure 4.1: *New Database Home Page*

As seen in Figure 4.1, 11g also added a new button to the Database home page labeled "Blackout." Previously, 10g required the DBA to drill into the Administration tab to set Blackouts.

As noted in Oracle documentation, there are also new charts in 11g to more easily access database performance information. Figure 4.2 shows the changes to the Performance Page in DBConsole.

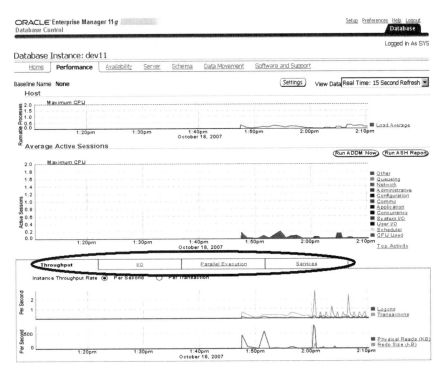

Figure 4.2: *Performance Page in DBConsole*

Though the throughput of the database was present in 10g, the new tabs for I/O, Parallel Execution, and Services are offered in 11g. These allow performance issues to more quickly be identified.

Integrated Interface for LogMiner

LogMiner has also been an important tool in the DBA's arsenal. However, due to the lack of a simpler interface, this tool was often overlooked. Previously, DBAs would use a standalone interface for LogMiner, which even Oracle noted as "cumbersome to install."

A new feature of 11g OEM provides an integrated interface for the DBA to use for LogMiner. The graphical interface allows the

---

DBA to extract transactions from the redo logs to examine and flashback a transaction if desired. The LogMiner interface in OEM provides DBAs with an intuitive and easy to use tool for several purposes:

- to isolate transactions by time or SCN

- to isolate transactions by table or database user

- an advanced option for further filtering transactions

- to establish the appropriate steps needed for the recovery of unintentional changes, including dependent transactions

To access LogMiner, first click the Availability tab, then View and Manage Transactions, as shown in Figure 4.3.

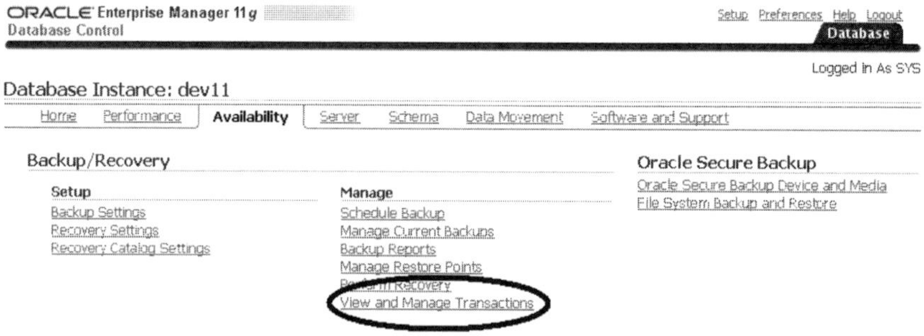

Figure 4.3: *Accessing LogMiner*

The LogMiner interface is shown in Figure 4.4.

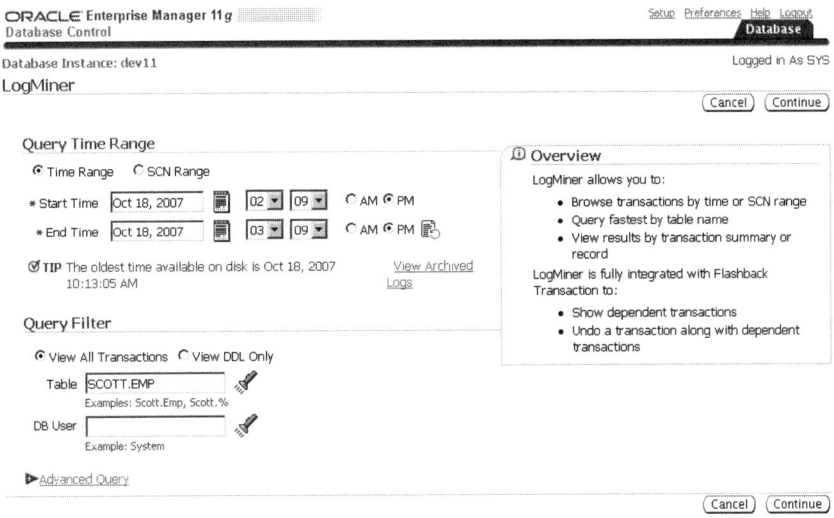

Figure 4.4: *LogMiner interface*

Advanced Replication Interface

To assist with the setup and management of replication environments, the Advanced Replication interface in Oracle Enterprise Manager can now be used. In previous releases, Advanced Replication was a trigger-based process of replication. With 11*g*, this feature is now built-in to Enterprise Manager Database Control. Figure 4.5 shows this Advanced Replication interface, which allows replications to be managed from within OEM.

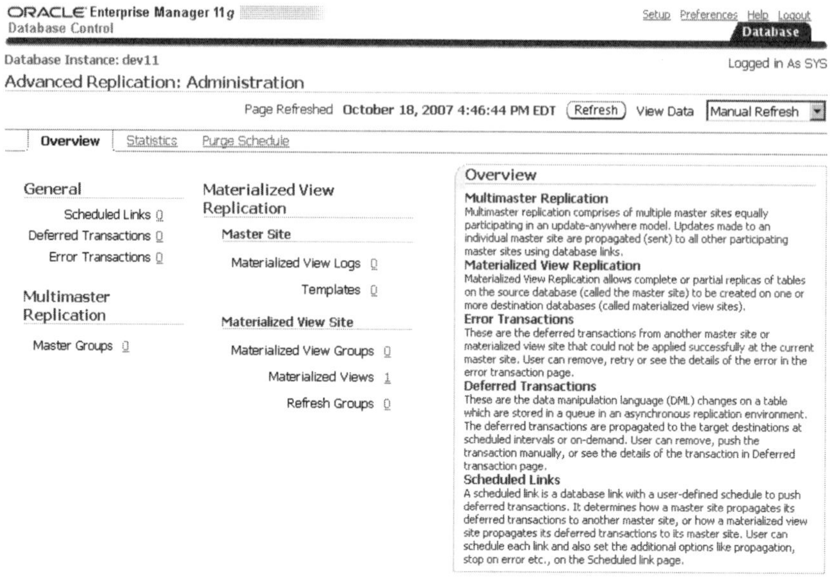

ORACLE Enterprise Manager 11*g*

Database Control

Setup   Preferences   Help   Logout

Database

Database Instance: dev11

Logged in As SYS

Advanced Replication: Administration

Page Refreshed   October 18, 2007 4:46:44 PM EDT   (Refresh)   View Data   Manual Refresh ▾

Overview   Statistics   Purge Schedule

General

Scheduled Links 0

Deferred Transactions 0

Error Transactions 0

Multimaster Replication

Master Groups 0

Materialized View Replication

Master Site

Materialized View Logs 0

Templates 0

Materialized View Site

Materialized View Groups 0

Materialized Views 1

Refresh Groups 0

Overview

Multimaster Replication
Multimaster replication comprises of multiple master sites equally participating in an update-anywhere model. Updates made to an individual master site are propagated (sent) to all other participating master sites using database links.

Materialized View Replication
Materialized View Replication allows complete or partial replicas of tables on the source database (called the master site) to be created on one or more destination databases (called materialized view sites).

Error Transactions
These are the deferred transactions from another master site or materialized view site that could not be applied successfully at the current master site. User can remove, retry or see the details of the error in the error transaction page.

Deferred Transactions
These are the data manipulation language (DML) changes on a table which are stored in a queue in an asynchronous replication environment. The deferred transactions are propagated to the target destinations at scheduled intervals or on-demand. User can remove, push the transaction manually, or see the details of the transaction in Deferred transaction page.

Scheduled Links
A scheduled link is a database link with a user-defined schedule to push deferred transactions. It determines how a master site propagates its deferred transactions to another master site, or how a materialized view site propagates its deferred transactions to its master site. User can schedule each link and also set the additional options like propagation, stop on error etc., on the Scheduled link page.

Figure 4.5: *Advanced Replication interface*

Wait Activity Detail Enhancement

In previous versions, such as in OEM 10g, Oracle Enterprise Manager displayed the Wait Activity Drilldown detail in chart format as shown in Figure 4.6:

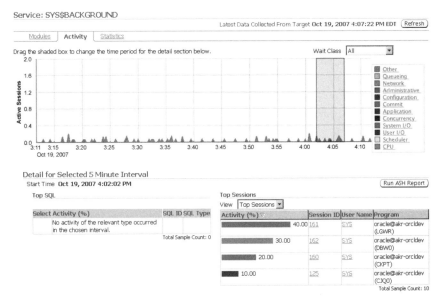

Service: SYS$BACKGROUND

Page Refreshed Oct 19, 2007 4:07:48 PM (Refresh)

Modules | Statistics

Top Modules

■ Unnamed(100%)

Active Modules

View | Active Modules ▼

Module	Activity (% for the last 5 minutes) ▽	Aggregation Enabled	SQL Trace Enabled	Delta Elapsed Time (seconds)	Cumulative Elapsed Time (seconds)	Delta CPU Time (seconds)	Cumulative CPU Time (seconds)	Delta Physical I/O (blocks)	Cumulative Physical I/O (blocks)
Unnamed	100.0	FALSE	FALSE						

Figure 4.6: *Chart format of the Wait Activity Drilldown detail*

The best way to identify constraints and bottlenecks within the database is to analyze wait events. 11g OEM offers this ability with less effort. OEM 11g provides more detail for Wait Activity information such as the enhanced drilldown detail, and ability to quickly select the Wait Class, as shown in Figure 4.7.

Service: SYS$BACKGROUND

Latest Data Collected From Target Oct 19, 2007 4:07:22 PM EDT (Refresh)

Modules | **Activity** | Statistics

Drag the shaded box to change the time period for the detail section below.   Wait Class | All ▼

Active Sessions

2.0, 1.6, 1.2, 0.8, 0.4, 0.0

3:11 3:15 3:20 3:25 3:30 3:35 3:40 3:45 3:50 3:55 4:00 4:05 4:10
Oct 19, 2007

■ Other
■ Queueing
■ Network
■ Administrative
■ Configuration
■ Commit
■ Application
■ Concurrency
■ System I/O
■ User I/O
■ Scheduler
■ CPU

Detail for Selected 5 Minute Interval

Start Time Oct 19, 2007 4:02:02 PM   (Run ASH Report)

Top SQL

Select	Activity (%)	SQL ID	SQL Type
	No activity of the relevant type occurred in the chosen interval.		
	Total Sample Count: 0		

Top Sessions

View | Top Sessions ▼

Activity (%) ▽	Session ID	User Name	Program
40.00	161	SYS	oracle@akr-orcldev (LGWR)
30.00	162	SYS	oracle@akr-orcldev (DBW0)
20.00	160	SYS	oracle@akr-orcldev (CKPT)
10.00	125	SYS	oracle@akr-orcldev (CJQ0)

Total Sample Count: 10

Figure 4.7: *Wait Activity information page*

Easy Oracle Text Management

Among many other advances, Oracle offers several improvements to Oracle Text in 11g. These new Oracle Text enhancements are broken down into four categories:

- Performance

- Minimization of application downtime

- Internationalization

- Ease of Maintenance

From the improvements listed above, 11g OEM provides ease of maintenance with a powerful integrated Oracle Text interface. Oracle Enterprise Manager supplies an interface, as shown in Figure 4.8, for configuration, maintenance, and administration of Oracle Text which include:

- Viewing details of Oracle Text indexes

- Synchronizing Oracle Text indexes

- Optimizing Oracle Text indexes

- Rebuilding indexes

- Editing Oracle Text indexes

- Querying log analysis

Database Instance: dev11

Text Indexes

Oracle Text is a technology that enables you to build text query applications and document classification applications. Oracle Text provides indexing, word and theme searching, and viewing capabilities for text.

Page Refreshed Oct 19, 2007 4:44:38 PM EDT

Indexes	
Invalid	0
Partition Invalid	0
In Progress	0
Partition In Progress	0
Valid	2
Total	2

Job Activity

Status of Text Index related Jobs scheduled to start no more than 7 days ago.

Scheduled Executions 0   Problem Executions 0
Running Executions 0

View Edit   Actions Synchronize ▼ Go

Select	Index Name	Index Type	Owner	Status	Total Documents	Failed Documents	Unsynchronized Documents	Partitioned
⦿	IDXSCOTTEMP	CONTEXT	SYSTEM	Valid	14	0	0	No
○	WK$DOC_PATH_IDX	CONTEXT	WK_TEST	Valid	0	0	0	No

Figure 4.8: *Oracle Enterprise Manager interface*

In the past, DBAs would query the *ctx_user_index_errors* table for errors that were generated for an Oracle Text index. Now the OEM Text Manager interface can be used as shown in Figure 4.9

Text Index Errors:SYSTEM.IDXSCOTTEMP
The table below has all the errors that were generated for this Index.

Cancel

Purge Criteria
To 'Purge' errors between a specific period, select the Begin Date and End Date and click 'Purge'. Use 'Purge All' to delete all errors for this index.

Start Date [   ] 🗓 Time [0 ▼] : [00 ▼] ○ AM ○ PM
(example: Oct 19, 2007)

End Date [   ] 🗓 Time [0 ▼] : [00 ▼] ○ AM ○ PM

Purge

Purge Selected Errors   Purge All Errors

Select	Timestamp	Row ID or Operation Error Description
	No Items Found	

Figure 4.9: *Using OEM Text Manager interface for errors generated for Oracle Text*

Better OEM Grid Tools

In previous releases, Database Configuration Assistant was used to configure a database with either Database Control or Grid Control. This could be done while creating the database or later by reconfiguring the database. As noted by Oracle, this reconfiguring required considerable manual effort.

Luckily, making the transition from Database Control to Grid Control is now much easier with 11g. After making sure there is a central agent installed, migrating to Grid Control consists of the following steps:

14. Create a database with Database Control

15. Invoke DBCA in configure mode and select the database

16. In Management options page, select "Switch to grid control to manage the database"

Note: The agent needs to be installed for this to be an option in DBCA!

Clone Database Enhancements

Database cloning is a process by which the DBA can update TEST or DEV databases from PROD. Cloning the production instance is especially useful for providing developers full-scale TEST or DEV databases. In the past the DBA would run the command, ALTER DATABASE BACKUP CONTROLFILE TO TRACE, shutdown production, copy files to the new server, copy and edit the controlfile, etc. Over the years, Oracle has been adding tools to help with these cloning operations. 11g offers improvements which allow database cloning within Oracle Enterprise Manager.

These new features provide the following enhancements to the OEM cloning pages:

- Removes the requirement for source and destination stage area

- Supports cloning from a generic RMAN backup set

- Enhanced job summary

To access the Clone Database interface, click the Data Movement tab, then Clone Database. Figure 4.10 illustrates this improved interface for database cloning. Here, it is possible to create a clone from an existing RMAN backup.

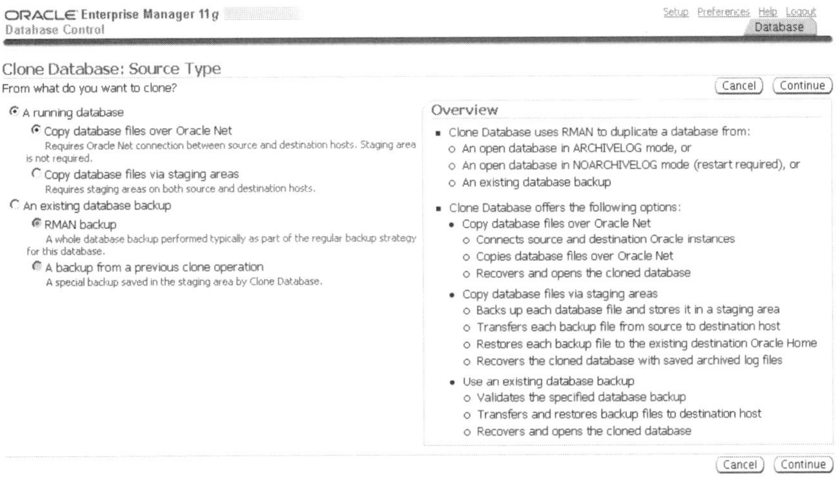

Figure 4.10: *Interface used for Database Cloning*

Migrate Database (and more!) to ASM

The OEM page for Migrate Database to ASM makes it easier to use Enterprise Manager to migrate non-ASM databases.

Automatic Storage Management (ASM) was a new feature in Oracle 10g that freed the DBA from managing files and disk drives, which eliminated the need for third-party volume managers. Later, Oracle 10gR2 introduced the ability to migrate an entire database to ASM. Finally, 11g now supports the capability to migrate tablespaces to ASM with a Tablespace Migration Wizard in OEM.

Initially, migrating a tablespace to ASM may be a little tricky. The process is begun by first clicking the Server tab, then Migrate to ASM. Next is a prompt to enter host credentials, followed by the migration options screen. The next screen presented is the Disk Group Options, as shown in Figure 4.11.

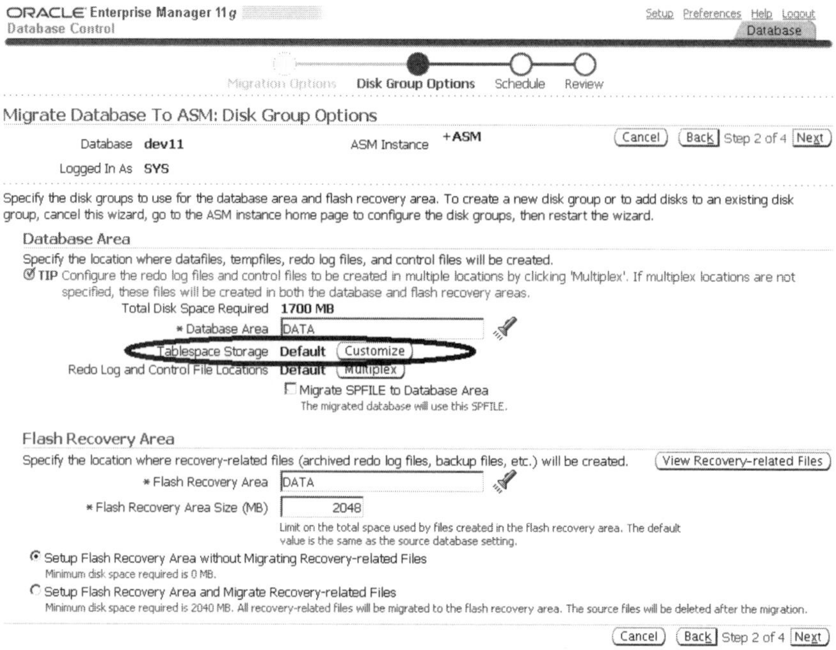

Figure 4.11: *Using the Customize button within the Disk Group Options page*

Click the Customize button, as noted in Figure 4.11 above, and the next screen allows the selection of specific tablespaces to migrate over to ASM, as shown in Figure 4.12.

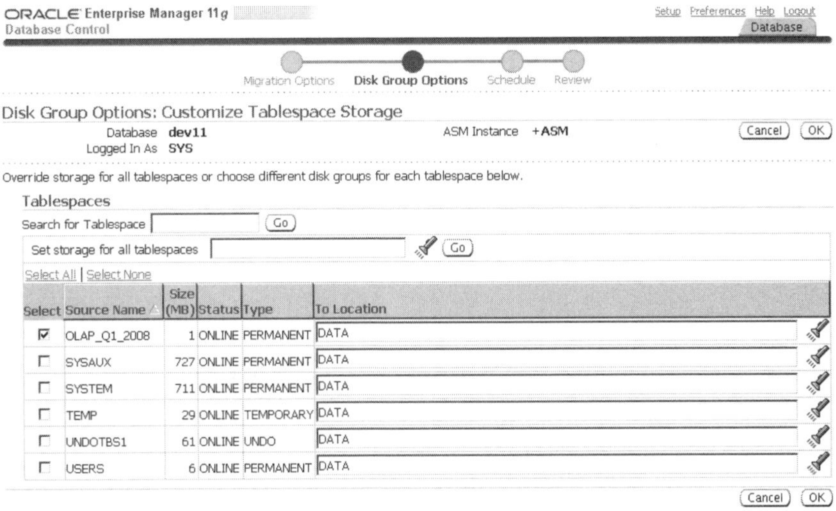

Figure 4.12: *Selecting tablespaces for migration to ASM*

Workspace Manager

Version 10g required DBAs to use the Enterprise Manager 10g
Java Console to manage Advanced Replication and Workspace.
However, in 11g DBAs can access the Workspace Manager
within OEM. To access the Workspace Manager interface, click
the Schema tab, then Workspaces. The Workspace Manager has
been improved to include support for:

- Finding Referential Integrity Constraints

- Compressing a Workspace

- Managing System Parameters

- Privilege Management

Find Referential Integrity Constraints

Previously, DBAs would call the *DBMS_WM.FindRICSet*
procedure to find tables that needed to be version-enabled due to

referential integrity constraints. 11g provides an interface for this, as shown in Figure 4.13.

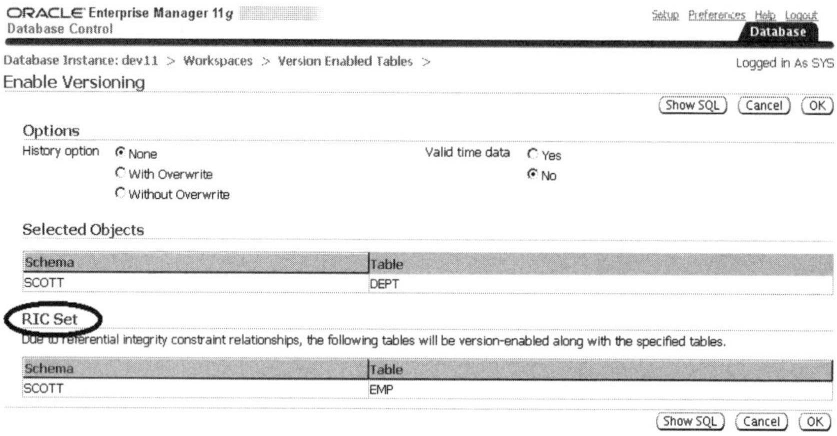

Figure 4.13: *Version-enabling tables in the new 11g interface*

Compress a Workspace

To compress a workspace within OEM, choose Compress from the Actions dropdown as shown in Figure 4.14.

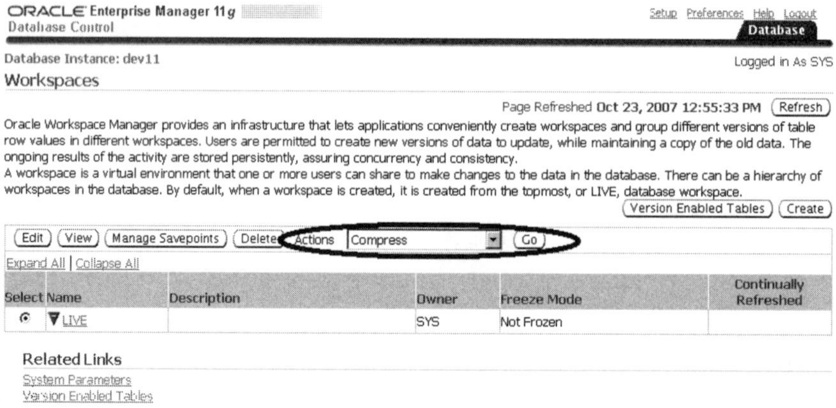

Figure 4.14: *Compressing workspaces*

Manage System Parameters

Figure 4.15 shows the system parameters that are available. To access the System Parameters interface click the Schema tab, then Workspaces. System Parameters are found under Related Links.

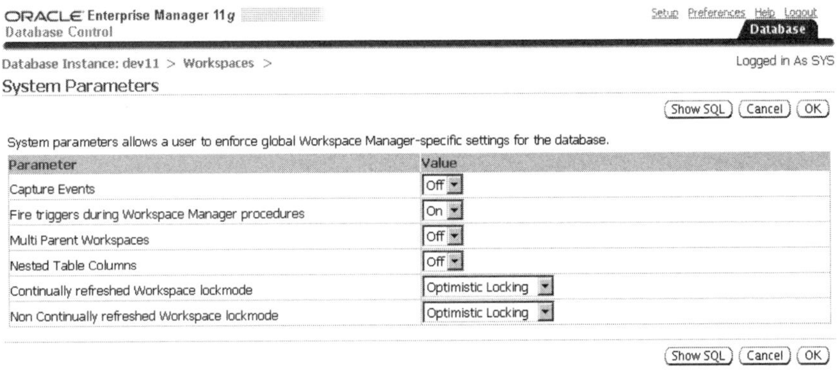

Figure 4.15 *System Parameters interface*

Privilege Management

Granting privileges on Workspaces can also be achieved within 11g OEM, as shown in Figure 4.16.

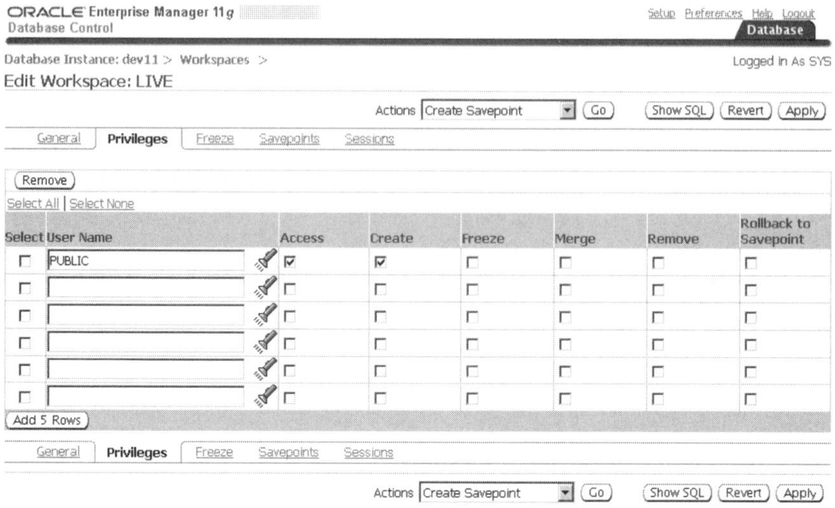

Figure 4.16: *Granting privileges on Workspaces in 11g OEM*

Conclusion

OEM is a management tool for DBAs that extends beyond the database. An academic definition of management includes the activities of planning, organizing, controlling and directing. OEM is able to provide the DBA with the ability to plan for growth, organize data, control access and data usage and direct the RDBMS through a fairly intuitive interface.

However, becoming familiar with Oracle Enterprise Manager requires an investment of time on the part of the DBA. This investment is well advised considering the benefits provided by this ever evolving tool.

E.F. Codd said that future users of large databases must be protected from having to know how the data is organized in the machine. OEM helps remove the DBA from having to know extensive operating system commands. OEM also provides a management interface between the DBA and the underlying database and operating system. This is significant because it nearly eliminates the need for experience with burdensome OS command line syntax that is required to display server-side information. These commands are obviously different between Windows, UNIX and Linux. They can also be slightly different between flavors of Linux.

Oracle Enterprise Manager gives a first glimpse of the 482 new features introduced in Oracle 11g. Many of these new features can be configured and taken advantage of within OEM.

The new features of OEM covered in this chapter were:

- Improved Database Home Page and Performance changes
- Integrated Interface for LogMiner
- Advanced Replication Interface
- Wait Activity Detail Enhancement
- Easy Oracle Text Management
- Better OEM Grid Tools
- Clone Database Enhancements
- Migrate Database (and more!) to ASM
- Workspace Manager

Oracle 11g PL/SQL New Features

11g PL/SQL New Features

Oracle has provided some powerful new capabilities to the PL/SQL language in the 11g database. Some are small changes that enhance the languages readability and usability. Others are full blown features that have a dramatic impact on the application performance. This chapter will introduce the new PL/SQL language features focusing on the powerful new language additions. The new features include:

- PL/SQL Sequence Access Enhancements

- New SIMPLE Number Types

- The CONTINUE Clause

- PL/SQL Code Inlining

- Compound Triggers and Trigger Enhancements

- The Cross-Session PL/SQL Result Cache

In the 11g database, the PL/SQL compiler will not compile native code directly. Prior versions of the database would compile the code in two steps, thus requiring a C compiler for the last step. This was problematic on systems that were not allowed to have a compiler present due to security requirements. Because the PL/SQL compiler now produces the native code itself, all users can take advantage of the performance increase provided by native code.

PL/SQL Sequence Access

Prior to the Oracle 11g database, the next sequence number could be grabbed using a SQL statement such as what is shown below.

```
declare
  n_num number;
begin
  select seq_1.nextval into n_num from dual;
  dbms_output.put_line('Seq: '||n_num);
end;
/
```

With 11g, a number can be assigned the NEXTVAL or CURRVAL directly. This results in easier to understand code and better performance.

```
declare
  n_num number;
begin
  n_num := seq_1.nextval;
  dbms_output.put_line('Seq: '||n_num);
  dbms_output.put_line('Cur: '||seq_1.currval
end;
/

Seq: 3
Cur: 3
```

The NEXTVAL and CURRVAL sequence functions can be used anywhere a number type would be used.

SIMPLE Number Types

Numbers are large and take extra processing to use. Oracle has provided the PLS_INTEGER as a more efficient number type for integer numbers. With 11g, Oracle provides an even more efficient number type called a SIMPLE_INTEGER.

A SIMPLE_INTEGER is a subtype of a PLS_INTEGER. Like the PLS_INTEGER, the SIMPLE_INTEGER has a range of 2147483648 to 2147483648; however, the SIMPLE_INTEGER has a NOT NULL constraint. The difference is that the SIMPLE_INTEGER does not check bounds nor does it check for a NULL value. What this means to the programmer is that a SIMPLE_INTEGER will wrap from positive to negative when the bounds are exceeded and not throw an error. A PLS_INTEGER will throw an error when the bounds are exceeded.

A SIMPLE_FLOAT is the same as a BINARY_FLOAT except that is has a NOT NULL constraint. A SIMPLE_DOUBLE is the same as a BINARY_DOUBLE except that it has a NOT NULL constraint.

So why use these SIMPLE number types? Because they do not check bounds or NULLs, so they are more efficient. If the PL/SQL code is natively compiled, the number computations on SIMPLE_INTEGERs can be performed in hardware, therefore making them substantially more efficient.

The CONTINUE Statement

The CONTINUE statement is used to control program flow within a loop. When the CONTINUE statement is executed, that loop interaction is stopped and flow continues at the top of the loop. Below are examples of using an IF/THEN statement, a CONTINUE statement and a CONTINUE WHEN statement.

```
declare
  n_num number := 0;
begin
  loop
    n_num := n_num + 1;
    if n_num < 5 then
      dbms_output.put_line('Num: '||n_num);
    end if;
```

```
      exit when n_num > 9;
   end loop;
end;
/

Num: 1
Num: 2
Num: 3
Num: 4

PL/SQL procedure successfully completed.
```

Using the CONTINUE statement:

```
declare
  n_num number := 0;
begin
  loop
    n_num := n_num + 1;
    if n_num => 5 then continue;
    end if;
    dbms_output.put_line('Num: '||n_num);
    exit when n_num > 9;
  end loop;
end;
/

Num: 1
Num: 2
Num: 3
Num: 4

PL/SQL procedure successfully completed.
```

Using the CONTINUE WHEN statement:

```
declare
  n_num number := 0;
begin
  loop
    n_num := n_num + 1;
    continue when n_num => 5;
    dbms_output.put_line('Num: '||n_num);
    exit when n_num > 9;
  end loop;
end;
/

Num: 1
Num: 2
```

```
Num: 3
Num: 4

PL/SQL procedure successfully completed.
```

If labels are used to identify loops, the CONTINUE statement can be used to stop the iteration of a specific labeled loop. Normally it stops the iteration of the current inner loop. If a label is used to stop the iteration of an outer loop, cursors opened in the inner loop will automatically be closed.

PL/SQL Subprogram Inlining

Subprogram inlining has been around in optimizing compilers for a long time. With the 11g database, Oracle has included this feature in PL/SQL. Basically, subprogram inlining is where the program calls a subprogram (procedure or function) and the compiler places the actual subprogram code in place of the call to that code. Since the subprogram code is in the main code (INLINE), the overhead of calling that subprogram is saved. This allows the ability to program using a modular method, and producing readable, maintainable source code while the compiler optimizes the code to make it more efficient.

If the *plsql_optimizer_level* is set to 3, the compiler will automatically try and inline subprograms. If the *plsql_optimizer_level* is set to 2 (the default), it will not automatically try and inline subprograms. So the PRAGMA INLINE is used to tell the optimizer to inline or not to inline depending on the setting of the optimizer level.

The PRAGMA INLINE statement is used to tell the optimizer if the following statement's subprograms should be placed inline or not.

In the example below, the PRAGMA INLINE is used to inline the first function call but not the second. The PRAGMA INLINE statement only effects the statement following the PARGMA INLINE statement.

```
create or replace package inline_demo is
  procedure runtest;
end;
/


create or replace package body inline_demo as

function newadd(n1 number) return number
as
 n11 number;
begin
  n11:= n1+n1;
  return n11;
end;

procedure runtest as
  n2 number := 0;
begin
  n2 := 3;
  dbms_output.put('Num: '||n2);
  PRAGMA INLINE (newadd,'YES');
  n2 := newadd(n2);
  dbms_output.put('  Num2: '||n2);
  PRAGMA INLINE (newadd,'NO');
  n2 := newadd(n2);
  dbms_output.put_line('  Num3: '||n2);
end;

end inline_demo;
/


SQL> exec inline_demo.runtest;
Num: 3  Num2: 6  Num3: 12

PL/SQL procedure successfully completed.
```

The PRAGMA INLINE impacts all calls in the statement that follows it. If the statement is a loop, then all calls to the subprogram in the loop are placed inline.

Inlining subprogram code is a common and powerful code optimization capability that should be used when possible.

Placing the *plsql_optimizer_level* parameter to 3 will automate the code inline process.

PL/SQL Compound Triggers

A compound trigger is a PL/SQL trigger that contains multiple actions that take place at different timing points. The timing points for a compound trigger on a table are:

- BEFORE STATEMENT   - before trigger statement executes.

- AFTER STATEMENT   - after the trigger statement executes.

- BEFORE EACH ROW   - before each row the statement impacts.

- AFTER EACH ROW   - after each row the statement impacts.

If the compound trigger is on a view, the only timing point is:

- INSTEAD OF EACH ROW

The real advantage of the compound trigger is that the trigger definition has a declaration section and variable state is maintained through each timing section from the firing of the trigger to completion. The statements at each timing point have some restrictions. The statement must be DML and can contain inserting, updating, deleting and applying. If the statement at the timing point does not impact any rows, the before statement and after statement do not fire. The compound trigger body does not have an initialization block and thus, no exception block. All exceptions must be handled in the section that raised the exception. Execution can not be passed from one section to another using an exception handler or a GOTO statement. The references to :OLD, :NEW or :PARENT cannot be used in the declaration section, BEFORE STATEMENT or AFTER

STATEMENT. Only the BEFORE EACH ROW section can change the :NEW value.

The order of firing within a compound trigger is defined; however, like simple triggers, the order of firing of multiple triggers (compound or simple) is not guaranteed. The order of firing multiple triggers can be defined using the FOLLOWS statement. The FOLLOWS option is explained in the next section.

Now, a compound triggerwill be examined more closely. The following code creates a test table and a compound trigger that fires for each timing point associated with INSERT, UPDATE and DELETE statements. The triggering actions are logged in a PL/SQL table defined in the global declaration section. The final timing point for each statement prints out the content of the PL/SQL table to show that the variable state has been maintained throughout the lifetime of the statement.

The example below is courtesy of Dr. Tim Hall (www.oracle-base.com):

```
CREATE TABLE compound_trigger_test (
  id           NUMBER,
  description  VARCHAR2(50)
);

CREATE OR REPLACE TRIGGER compound_trigger_test_trg
  FOR INSERT OR UPDATE OR DELETE ON compound_trigger_test
    COMPOUND TRIGGER

  -- Global declaration.
  TYPE t_tab IS TABLE OF VARCHAR2(50);
  l_tab t_tab := t_tab();

  BEFORE STATEMENT IS
  BEGIN
    l_tab.extend;
    CASE
      WHEN INSERTING THEN
        l_tab(l_tab.last) := 'BEFORE STATEMENT - INSERT';
      WHEN UPDATING THEN
        l_tab(l_tab.last) := 'BEFORE STATEMENT - UPDATE';
      WHEN DELETING THEN
```

```
          l_tab(l_tab.last) := 'BEFORE STATEMENT - DELETE';
      END CASE;
    END BEFORE STATEMENT;

    BEFORE EACH ROW IS
    BEGIN
      l_tab.extend;
      CASE
        WHEN INSERTING THEN
          l_tab(l_tab.last) := 'BEFORE EACH ROW - INSERT (new.id=' ||
:new.id || ')';
        WHEN UPDATING THEN
          l_tab(l_tab.last) := 'BEFORE EACH ROW - UPDATE (new.id=' ||
:new.id || ' old.id=' || :old.id || ')';
        WHEN DELETING THEN
          l_tab(l_tab.last) := 'BEFORE EACH ROW - DELETE (old.id=' ||
:old.id || ')';
      END CASE;
    END BEFORE EACH ROW;

    AFTER EACH ROW IS
    BEGIN
      l_tab.extend;
      CASE
        WHEN INSERTING THEN
          l_tab(l_tab.last) := 'AFTER EACH ROW - INSERT (new.id=' ||
:new.id || ')';
        WHEN UPDATING THEN
          l_tab(l_tab.last) := 'AFTER EACH ROW - UPDATE (new.id=' ||
:new.id || ' old.id=' || :old.id || ')';
        WHEN DELETING THEN
          l_tab(l_tab.last) := 'AFTER EACH ROW - DELETE (old.id=' ||
:old.id || ')';
      END CASE;
    END AFTER EACH ROW;

    AFTER STATEMENT IS
    BEGIN
      l_tab.extend;
      CASE
        WHEN INSERTING THEN
          l_tab(l_tab.last) := 'AFTER STATEMENT - INSERT';
        WHEN UPDATING THEN
          l_tab(l_tab.last) := 'AFTER STATEMENT - UPDATE';
        WHEN DELETING THEN
          l_tab(l_tab.last) := 'AFTER STATEMENT - DELETE';
      END CASE;

      FOR i IN l_tab.first .. l_tab.last LOOP
        DBMS_OUTPUT.put_line(l_tab(i));
      END LOOP;
      l_tab.delete;
    END AFTER STATEMENT;

END compound_trigger_test_trg;
/
```

By issuing several INSERT, UPDATE and DELETE statements against the test table, it is evident that the compound trigger is working as expected.

```
SQL> SET SERVEROUTPUT ON
SQL> INSERT INTO compound_trigger_test VALUES (1, 'ONE');
BEFORE STATEMENT - INSERT
BEFORE EACH ROW - INSERT (new.id=1)
AFTER EACH ROW - INSERT (new.id=1)
AFTER STATEMENT - INSERT

1 row created.

SQL> INSERT INTO compound_trigger_test VALUES (2, 'TWO');
BEFORE STATEMENT - INSERT
BEFORE EACH ROW - INSERT (new.id=2)
AFTER EACH ROW - INSERT (new.id=2)
AFTER STATEMENT - INSERT

1 row created.

SQL> UPDATE compound_trigger_test SET id = id;
BEFORE STATEMENT - UPDATE
BEFORE EACH ROW - UPDATE (new.id=2 old.id=2)
AFTER EACH ROW - UPDATE (new.id=2 old.id=2)
BEFORE EACH ROW - UPDATE (new.id=1 old.id=1)
AFTER EACH ROW - UPDATE (new.id=1 old.id=1)
AFTER STATEMENT - UPDATE

2 rows updated.

SQL> DELETE FROM compound_trigger_test;
BEFORE STATEMENT - DELETE
BEFORE EACH ROW - DELETE (old.id=2)
AFTER EACH ROW - DELETE (old.id=2)
BEFORE EACH ROW - DELETE (old.id=1)
AFTER EACH ROW - DELETE (old.id=1)
AFTER STATEMENT - DELETE

2 rows deleted.

SQL>
```

One of the real advantages of a compound trigger is to use the FOR EACH ROW statement to capture changes and load them into a PL/SQL table, then use AFTER STATEMENT to bulk load the changes into another table. Using simple triggers, a package would have to be referenced to load the data and then execute the bulk load. With a compound trigger, these operations are internal to the trigger.

PL/SQL Trigger Enhancements

One issue that triggers have always had is that if there are multiple triggers on a statement, the order in which they fire is not defined. The programmer had to place the trigger bodies in one trigger to insure the firing order. In 11g, Oracle has provided a FOLLOWS statement to allow multiple triggers of the same type on the same table to fire in a specified order:

```
create or replace trigger fist_fire_tr
before insert on table1 for each row
begin
  do something.
end;
/

create or replace trigger second_fire_tr
before insert on table1 for each row
follows first_fire_tr
begin
  do stuff
end;
/
```

The programmer can also create a trigger in a disabled state. This is useful to allow the trigger to be created and compiled without enabling it. Once the trigger compiles correctly, the programmer can enable it.

```
create or replace trigger disabled_tr
before insert on table1 for each row
disable
begin
  do something.
end;
/

alter trigger disabled_tr enable;

alter table table1 enable all triggers;
```

By creating a trigger in a disabled state, the programmer has the flexibility to add the trigger without having it immediately impact the table data.

Cross-Session PL/SQL Function Result Cache

The Result Cache is a powerful new feature that allows the programmer to specify that a function's results be stored in the SGA for future use. The use of the Result Cache with SQL statements is equally powerful and is covered in the next chapter. Basically, the 11g database has the ability to save the result of a PL/SQL function call in the SGA and reuse it if the same function is called with the same parameters. The capability is called cross-session because once the results are in the SGA, they are available for any session to reuse. The performance results come from the fact that once a function is executed, all future calls to that function with the same parameters will return the results stored in the SGA rather than execute the function call. For example, when a call to a function returns a value that executes in 10 seconds, future calls will execute immediately because the result has been saved. This is a two-edged performance sword. Once stored, the database will continue to serve the stored result even if the data changes and a new call to the function would return a different value. More on invalidating the result cache in a moment, but first look at how the result cache works.

In the following example, a DBA needs to know if a store has above average sales on books. Below is a function that is passed a *store_key* and returns true if the store has above average sales in the sales table.

```
create or replace function above_avg(str_ky in varchar2)
  return boolean
  result_cache
as
  n_avg number := 0;
```

```
  n_total number := 0;
begin
  select avg(st_total) into n_avg
  from (select    sum(quantity) st_total
        from sales
        group by store_key)
  ;

  select sum(quantity) into n_total
  from sales
  where sales.store_key = str_ky;

  if n_total > n_avg then return true;
  else return false;
  end if;
end;
/
```

Notice the result cache clause after the function signature. This tells the database to save the results for use in any session that calls this function with the same *store_key*.

Now use the below function to run through the ten stores and see which *store_key* represent above average sales.

```
declare
  t_begin number;
begin
  t_begin := DBMS_UTILITY.get_time;
  for r_cl in (select distinct(store_key)
              from sales
              order by store_key) loop
  if (above_avg(r_cl.store_key)) then
    dbms_output.put_line('Store_key: '||r_cl.store_key||
                         ' Above Average');
  else
    dbms_output.put_line('Store_key: '||r_cl.store_key||
                         ' Below Average');
  end if;
  end loop;
  dbms_output.put_line('Time: '||(DBMS_UTILITY.get_time - t_begin));
end;
/

Store_key: S101 Below Average
Store_key: S102 Above Average
Store_key: S103 Below Average
Store_key: S104 Above Average
Store_key: S105 Above Average
Store_key: S106 Below Average
Store_key: S107 Above Average
```

```
Store_key: S108 Below Average
Store_key: S109 Above Average
Store_key: S110 Below Average
Time: 1
```

The actual time was 0.14 seconds on average reported by SQL Developer 1.5. When the anonymous block is run again, time goes to 0. Because of running the function and calculating the results, the database is returning the result cached from the first run.

```
Store_key: S101 Below Average
Store_key: S102 Above Average
Store_key: S103 Below Average
Store_key: S104 Above Average
Store_key: S105 Above Average
Store_key: S106 Below Average
Store_key: S107 Above Average
Store_key: S108 Below Average
Store_key: S109 Above Average
Store_key: S110 Below Average
Time: 0
```

This is a real performance boost. Instead of calculating the average sale for each call to the function, the database simply checks to see if the result is cached and returns that cached result.

There is, however, a problem with the underlying data changes. The sales table has only 100 rows by default, so that number needs to be jumped up to see the impact. The code below adds rows to the sales table. Note, it only adds them to the S110 store_key.

```
begin
  for indx in 1..100 loop
    insert into sales (select * from sales
                        where store_key='S110');
    commit;
  end loop;
end;
/
```

When the anonymous block is run again, the results are the same as before.

```
Store_key: S101 Below Average
Store_key: S102 Above Average
Store_key: S103 Below Average
Store_key: S104 Above Average
Store_key: S105 Above Average
Store_key: S106 Below Average
Store_key: S107 Above Average
Store_key: S108 Below Average
Store_key: S109 Above Average
Store_key: S110 Below Average
Time: 0
```

The database again used the results cached from the first run. The issue is that the data has changed. The key S110 had below average sales before, but now has almost all the sales. The function can be told that it is dependent on a table's data and that it should not use the result cache if the table data has changed since the function was run to create that cache. To establish this dependency, add the *relies_on* clause to the function.

```
create or replace function above_avg(str_ky in varchar2)
  return boolean
  result_cache relies_on (pubs.sales)
as
  n_avg number := 0;
  n_total number := 0;
begin
  select avg(st_total) into n_avg
  from (select   sum(quantity) st_total
        from sales
        group by store_key)
  ;

  select sum(quantity) into n_total
  from sales
  where sales.store_key = str_ky;

  if n_total > n_avg then return true;
  else return false;
  end if;
end;
/
```

Now, before using the result cache, the depend table is checked and if the data in the table has changed, the database will execute the function and update the result cache. Below, the anonymous block is run twice, after reloading the function and reloading the addition rows into the sales table.

```
Store_key: S101 Below Average
Store_key: S102 Below Average
Store_key: S103 Below Average
Store_key: S104 Below Average
Store_key: S105 Below Average
Store_key: S106 Below Average
Store_key: S107 Below Average
Store_key: S108 Below Average
Store_key: S109 Below Average
Store_key: S110 Above Average
Time: 11


PL/SQL procedure successfully completed.


SQL> /
Store_key: S101 Below Average
Store_key: S102 Below Average
Store_key: S103 Below Average
Store_key: S104 Below Average
Store_key: S105 Below Average
Store_key: S106 Below Average
Store_key: S107 Below Average
Store_key: S108 Below Average
Store_key: S109 Below Average
Store_key: S110 Above Average
Time: 1

PL/SQL procedure successfully completed.
```

Note that this run took significantly more time to complete and S110 is now the only store with above average sales. Running the block a second time will show the result cache again being used. After entering another row into the sales table, the anonymous block is run to show that the result cache was invalidated.

```
SQL> INSERT INTO SALES VALUES ('S102', 'B115', 'O189',
  2  to_date('05-10-2004 16:30','MM-DD-YYYY HH24:MI'), 8800);
1 row created.

SQL> commit;
```

```
Commit complete.

SQL> declare
  2    t_begin number;
  3  begin
...
 17  end;
 18  /
Store_key: S101 Below Average
Store_key: S102 Below Average
Store_key: S103 Below Average
Store_key: S104 Below Average
Store_key: S105 Below Average
Store_key: S106 Below Average
Store_key: S107 Below Average
Store_key: S108 Below Average
Store_key: S109 Below Average
Store_key: S110 Above Average
Time: 12

PL/SQL procedure successfully completed.
```

The block ran in 12 hsec, showing that the result cache was properly invalidated.

As shown in the example, it is important to identify the dependencies for the result cache if the wish is to have current data. And since all sessions can and will utilize the result cache, keeping it current with the data is critical.

Because the result cache uses the PL/SQL signature (name, passed variables and return type) to uniquely identify cached result sets, there are some restrictions on what can be passed as variables:

- No *in-out* or *out* variable parameter

- No invoker rights or anonymous blocks

- No pipelined table functions

- No *in* variable parameters of type BLOB, CLOB,NCLOB, REF CURSOR, COLLECTION, OBJECT or RECORD

- No *return* type of BLOB, CLOB, NCLOB, REF CURSOR, OBJECT, COLLECTION or RECORD

The result cache will consider a request a cache hit if the function and all parameters are bit-wise identical. The characters 'AA' and 'AA ' are not bit-wise identical and will not result in a result cache hit. If the function throws an unhandled exception, the results are not stored.

In a RAC environment, each instance will maintain its own result cache, but cache invalidation will propagate to all instances. This allows for caching for applications affiliated with that instance but still invalidates that result cache if the dependent object is changed by any instance.

There are four new database initialization parameters that are used to support the result cache.

result_cache_max_size: This parameter will define the maximum amount of SGA memory the result cache can use. If set to 0, then the result cache is disabled.

result_cache_max_result: This parameter defines the maximum memory that one result set can access. It is a percentage of the result_cache_max_size.

***result_cache_mode* = FORCE|MANUAL**: This parameter works on SQL statements discussed in the next chapter. If set to FORCE, all valid SQL statement results are cached. If this parameter is set to MANUAL, only SQL containing the result cache hint will be cached.

result_cache_remote_expiration: This parameter defines the number of minutes that a result based on a remote object will remain valid. Since the remote object cannot be monitored for changes, this parameter is used to invalidate those cached objects.

There is a new PL/SQL package added to the database to support using the result cache called *dbms_result_cache*. Below is an edited description of the package.

```
SQL> desc DBMS_RESULT_CACHE
PROCEDURE BYPASS
FUNCTION FLUSH RETURNS BOOLEAN
PROCEDURE FLUSH
FUNCTION INVALIDATE RETURNS NUMBER
PROCEDURE INVALIDATE
FUNCTION INVALIDATE RETURNS NUMBER
PROCEDURE INVALIDATE
FUNCTION INVALIDATE_OBJECT RETURNS NUMBER
PROCEDURE INVALIDATE_OBJECT
FUNCTION INVALIDATE_OBJECT RETURNS NUMBER
PROCEDURE INVALIDATE_OBJECT
PROCEDURE MEMORY_REPORT
FUNCTION STATUS RETURNS VARCHAR2
```

The procedure BYPASS turns the result cache functionality on and off. If set to true, the result cache is turned off and not used. The cache is not flushed by using the procedure. The example shown below turns off the result cache.

```
SQL> exec dbms_result_cache.bypass (true);
```

Running this command with a false parameter will turn on the result cache and any previously cached data will be returned.

The *status* function will return the current status of the result cache functionality.

```
SQL> select dbms_result_cache.status from dual;
```

```
STATUS
------------------------------------------------

ENABLED
```

The *memory_report* procedure returns a report on the current memory use by the result cache.

```
SQL> set serveroutput on
SQL> exec dbms_result_cache.memory_report
Result   Cache   Memory   Report
[Parameters]
Block Size         = 1K bytes
Maximum Cache Size = 2112K bytes (2112 blocks)
Maximum Result Size = 105K bytes (105 blocks)
[Memory]
Total Memory = 103536 bytes [0.069% of the Shared Pool]
... Fixed Memory = 5140 bytes [0.003% of the Shared Pool]
... Dynamic Memory = 98396 bytes [0.065% of the Shared Pool]
....... Overhead = 65628 bytes
....... Cache Memory = 32K bytes (32 blocks)
.......... Unused Memory = 7 blocks
.......... Used Memory = 25 blocks
.............. Dependencies = 2 blocks (2 count)
.............. Results = 23 blocks
................ PLSQL    = 10 blocks (10 count)
................ Invalid = 13 blocks (13 count)

PL/SQL procedure successfully completed.
```

The report covers the functions covered earlier in the chapter which have a Boolean result so the memory use is very small. When functions return larger values, this report can assist with tuning memory allocations.

The above report is the normal or default report. A more detailed report is available by passing a TRUE parameter to the procedure.

The remaining functions and procedures in the package are used to invalidate results or flush the cache. The package provides a procedure and a function for each operation, and either can be used as they both execute with the same results.

The *flush* operation will remove all results from the cache. It has two Boolean parameters; the first determines if the memory is maintained in the cache or released to the system. The second parameter determines if the cache statistics are maintained or also flushed. The following example uses the defaults and will flush the cache, releasing the memory to the system and clearing the statistics.

```
SQL> exec dbms_result_cache.flush;
```

If the memory report is rerun, the dynamic memory will report 0, indicating that the cache released the memory.

```
Total Memory = 5140 bytes [0.003% of the Shared Pool]
... Fixed Memory = 5140 bytes [0.003% of the Shared Pool]
... Dynamic Memory = 0 bytes [0.000% of the Shared Pool]
```

The *invalidate* operation invalidates all results in the cache that are dependent on an object. These functions are overloaded so the object can be identified by owner and name or by *object_id*.

```
SQL> exec dbms_result_cache.invalidate('PUBS','SALES');
```

The function will return a number indicating the number of results invalidated by the command.

The *invalidate_object* operation invalidates specific result objects. Result objects from *v$result_cache_objects* are found in the dynamic performance view.

```
SQL> select id, name from v$result_cache_objects order by 1;

 ID  NAME
--- -------------------------------------------------------------
  0 PUBS.SALES
  1 PUBS.ABOVE_AVG
  2 "PUBS"."ABOVE_AVG"::8."ABOVE_AVG"#48348295b9e89e56 #1
  3 "PUBS"."ABOVE_AVG"::8."ABOVE_AVG"#48348295b9e89e56 #1
  4 "PUBS"."ABOVE_AVG"::8."ABOVE_AVG"#48348295b9e89e56 #1
  5 "PUBS"."ABOVE_AVG"::8."ABOVE_AVG"#48348295b9e89e56 #1
  6 "PUBS"."ABOVE_AVG"::8."ABOVE_AVG"#48348295b9e89e56 #1
  7 "PUBS"."ABOVE_AVG"::8."ABOVE_AVG"#48348295b9e89e56 #1
  8 "PUBS"."ABOVE_AVG"::8."ABOVE_AVG"#48348295b9e89e56 #1
  9 "PUBS"."ABOVE_AVG"::8."ABOVE_AVG"#48348295b9e89e56 #1
 10 "PUBS"."ABOVE_AVG"::8."ABOVE_AVG"#48348295b9e89e56 #1
 11 "PUBS"."ABOVE_AVG"::8."ABOVE_AVG"#48348295b9e89e56 #1

12 rows selected.
```

To invalidate object 11, use the command below.

```
SQL> exec dbms_result_cache.invalidate_object(11);
```

The cross-session result cache can provide an incredible performance boost by not constantly executing the same function again and again. Many times a batch job will execute hundreds of queries on each pass that execute the same function for each query. By adding the result cache, the function is executed once at the beginning of the run and the result will be used by all the other queries in that run. This can make a huge difference in execution performance. The result cache is also available to a SQL query using a hint. If there are a large number of queries that all execute the same subquery, placing the result of the subquery in the result cache can make the results available to all the other queries. This is covered in the next chapter on SQL.

Conclusion

In this chapter, the enhancements to the PL/SQL Language introduced in the 11g database have been covered. These included:

- PL/SQL - Sequence access enhancements allow a more efficient method to get the NEXTAL or CURRVAL of a sequence without using a query. This new format is also easier to read making the code more manageable.

- The SIMPLE number type is used when there is no need to check bounds or null values. The SIMPLE integer is more efficient to use and executes in the compiler.

- The CONTINUE clause provides a method to terminate the current iteration of a loop and start the next iteration.

- PL/SQL Code Inlining provides compile time code optimization.

- Compound Triggers provide the ability to perform multiple actions at different timing points in one trigger. This keeps the trigger code in the trigger and still provides modularity.

- The Cross-Session PL/SQL Result Cache is a powerful new feature that saves function results in a cache and will reuse the cached result if the function is called with the same parameters instead of repeatedly executing the function.

The next chapter will introduce some complementary SQL new features that integrate completely into PL/SQL.

Oracle 11g SQL New Features

11g SQL

This chapter examines the SQL enhancements in the 11g database, including a number of powerful new SQL features that can improve execution efficiency by 200% (Oracle's Results), along with needed additions to Regular Expressions. The new features include:

- PIVOT and UNPIVOT Operators

- Regular Expressions

- The /*+result_cache*/ SQL hint

- Added built-in functions to support advanced statistics added in 11g and are covered in detail in the documentation.

SQL PIVOT and UNPIVOT Operators

The new PIVOT SQL clause will allow quick rollup, similar to an MS-Excel pivot table, where you can display multiple rows on one column with SQL.

Pivoting databases consists of taking a result set and turning columns into rows. Spreadsheet users have long had the ability to PIVOT data with ease. Here is another example of PIVOT in use by displaying books sold by month:

```
SELECT
   EXTRACT(MONTH FROM order_date) Dates,
   book_key,
   sum(quantity)
FROM sales
where book_key in ('B101','B102')
group by EXTRACT(MONTH FROM order_date), book_key
order by EXTRACT(MONTH FROM order_date);
```

```
    DATES BOOK_K SUM(QUANTITY)
---------- ------ -------------
        1 B101            1000
        1 B102            2590
        2 B101             100
        2 B102             200
        3 B102             900
        4 B101             300
        4 B102            7100
        5 B101           16800
        5 B102            5500
```

While the needed data is returned, it may be more appropriate to have the *book_key* as columns rather than rows. In SQL, pivoting data used to entail a large, complicated SQL statement. This was made up of multiple DECODE/CASE operations. Luckily, Oracle has added the PIVOT and UNPIVOT operators to make this process less complicated, and less prone to error.

Using PIVOT will reorder the values of rows into columns, and execute the aggregate functions.

```
PIVOT (<aggregate function> (expression) [AS <alias>]
FOR (<column_list>)
IN <subquery>)
```

Here is the same query using the PIVOT operator to move the *book_key*s from rows to columns. Notice that the aggregate is moved into the PIVOT clause:

```
SELECT *
FROM (SELECT
        EXTRACT(MONTH FROM order_date) Dates,
        book_key,
        quantity
      FROM sales)
PIVOT (SUM(quantity)
```

```
FOR book_key
IN ('B101','B102'))
order by 1;
```

```
DATES     'B101'     'B102'
--------- --------- ---------
        1      1000      2590
        2       100       200
        3                 900
        4       300      7100
        5     16800      5500
```

The rows are still listed by month, but the summed quantities are now the data points with the *book_keys* columns.

While the PIVOT operator moves data from rows to columns, the UNPIVOT operator moves data in the opposite direction; from columns to rows.

```
UNPIVOT [<INCLUDE | EXCLUDE> NULLS] (<column_list>) FOR
(<column_list>) IN (<column_list>)
```

Here, the UNPIVOT defaults to exclude NULLS, but there is an option to include them. Furthermore, the first two-column list defines the names for the columns created by the data move from columns to rows. The example below selects data from the SALES table:

```
SELECT
  order_date,
  book_key,
  store_key,
  quantity
FROM sales
where book_key in ('B101','B102')
order by 1;
```

```
ORDER_DAT BOOK_K STOR   QUANTITY
--------- ------ ----  ---------
02-JAN-04 B102   S102         10
02-JAN-04 B101   S101       1000
02-JAN-04 B102   S103        200
03-JAN-04 B102   S104        400
03-JAN-04 B102   S105        800
04-JAN-04 B102   S110        160
04-JAN-04 B102   S109       1020
12-FEB-04 B102   S103        200
```

```
12-FEB-04 B101    S103         100
25-MAR-04 B102    S107         900
02-APR-04 B101    S110         300
02-APR-04 B102    S110        1900
26-APR-04 B102    S107        5200
17-MAY-04 B101    S105        8000
18-MAY-04 B102    S106        5500
20-MAY-04 B101    S104        8800
```

16 rows selected.

The Quantity column can be moved into the rows by using the UNPIVOT operator.

```
select *
FROM (SELECT
        order_date,
        book_key,
        store_key,
        quantity
      FROM sales
      where book_key in ('B101','B102'))
   UNPIVOT (Qty FOR Type IN (quantity))
 order by 1;
```

```
ORDER_DAT BOOK_K STOR TYPE            QTY
--------- ------ ---- -------- ----------
02-JAN-04 B102   S102 QUANTITY         10
02-JAN-04 B101   S101 QUANTITY       1000
02-JAN-04 B102   S103 QUANTITY        200
03-JAN-04 B102   S104 QUANTITY        400
03-JAN-04 B102   S105 QUANTITY        800
04-JAN-04 B102   S110 QUANTITY        160
04-JAN-04 B102   S109 QUANTITY       1020
12-FEB-04 B102   S103 QUANTITY        200
12-FEB-04 B101   S103 QUANTITY        100
25-MAR-04 B102   S107 QUANTITY        900
02-APR-04 B101   S110 QUANTITY        300
02-APR-04 B102   S110 QUANTITY       1900
26-APR-04 B102   S107 QUANTITY       5200
17-MAY-04 B101   S105 QUANTITY       8000
18-MAY-04 B102   S106 QUANTITY       5500
20-MAY-04 B101   S104 QUANTITY       8800
```

16 rows selected.

Using careful observation, it can be seen that the QUANTITY column has been moved into the TYPE column and added to each row. Subsequently, the quantity values have been moved to the QTY column. This operator becomes even more useful when the UNPIVOT operation is performed on multiple columns. Each column generates another row in the result set. In the example below, the usefulness of this function in analyzing data is seen by adding an additional constant column to the example queries above.

```
SELECT
   order_date,
   book_key,
   store_key,
   quantity,
   5 as OddNumber
FROM sales
where book_key in ('B101','B102')
order by 1;
```

```
ORDER_DAT BOOK_K STOR   QUANTITY  ODDNUMBER
--------- ------ ---- ---------- ----------
02-JAN-04 B102   S102         10          5
02-JAN-04 B101   S101       1000          5
02-JAN-04 B102   S103        200          5
03-JAN-04 B102   S104        400          5
03-JAN-04 B102   S105        800          5
04-JAN-04 B102   S110        160          5
04-JAN-04 B102   S109       1020          5
12-FEB-04 B102   S103        200          5
12-FEB-04 B101   S103        100          5
25-MAR-04 B102   S107        900          5
02-APR-04 B101   S110        300          5
02-APR-04 B102   S110       1900          5
26-APR-04 B102   S107       5200          5
17-MAY-04 B101   S105       8000          5
18-MAY-04 B102   S106       5500          5
20-MAY-04 B101   S104       8800          5

16 rows selected.
```

Now the UNPIVOT operator can be used to move the QUANTITY and ODDNUMBER columns into data rows.

```
select *
FROM (SELECT
        order_date,
        book_key,
        store_key,
        quantity,
        5 as num
     FROM sales
     where book_key in ('B101','B102'))
```

```
    UNPIVOT (Num FOR Type IN (quantity, num))
  order by 1;
```

```
ORDER_DAT BOOK_K STOR TYPE            NUM
--------- ------ ---- -------- ----------
02-JAN-04 B102   S102 NUM               5
02-JAN-04 B102   S102 QUANTITY         10
02-JAN-04 B101   S101 NUM               5
02-JAN-04 B101   S101 QUANTITY       1000
02-JAN-04 B102   S103 QUANTITY        200
02-JAN-04 B102   S103 NUM               5
03-JAN-04 B102   S104 QUANTITY        400
03-JAN-04 B102   S104 NUM               5
03-JAN-04 B102   S105 QUANTITY        800
03-JAN-04 B102   S105 NUM               5
04-JAN-04 B102   S110 QUANTITY        160
04-JAN-04 B102   S110 NUM               5
04-JAN-04 B102   S109 QUANTITY       1020
04-JAN-04 B102   S109 NUM               5
12-FEB-04 B102   S103 QUANTITY        200
12-FEB-04 B102   S103 NUM               5
12-FEB-04 B101   S103 QUANTITY        100
12-FEB-04 B101   S103 NUM               5
25-MAR-04 B102   S107 QUANTITY        900
25-MAR-04 B102   S107 NUM               5
02-APR-04 B101   S110 QUANTITY        300
02-APR-04 B101   S110 NUM               5
02-APR-04 B102   S110 QUANTITY       1900
02-APR-04 B102   S110 NUM               5
26-APR-04 B102   S107 QUANTITY       5200
26-APR-04 B102   S107 NUM               5
17-MAY-04 B101   S105 QUANTITY       8000
17-MAY-04 B101   S105 NUM               5
18-MAY-04 B102   S106 QUANTITY       5500
18-MAY-04 B102   S106 NUM               5
20-MAY-04 B101   S104 QUANTITY       8800
20-MAY-04 B101   S104 NUM               5

32 rows selected.
```

Once the data is organized for easy manipulation, queries can be run against the results of the UNPIVOT.

```
select book_key, store_key, sum(Num)
FROM (SELECT
        order_date,
        book_key,
        store_key,
        quantity,
        5 as num
     FROM sales
     where book_key in ('B101','B102'))
   UNPIVOT (Num FOR Type IN (quantity, num))
where type = 'NUM'
```

```
group by book_key, store_key
order by 1;
```

```
BOOK_K  STOR   SUM(NUM)
------  ----   ----------
B101    S101          5
B101    S103          5
B101    S104          5
B101    S105          5
B101    S110          5
B102    S102          5
B102    S103         10
B102    S104          5
B102    S105          5
B102    S106          5
B102    S107         10
B102    S109          5
B102    S110         10

13 rows selected.
```

Both the PIVOT and UNPIVOT operators can be used to organize data for further analysis, or to generate reports that are easier to read and understand. The PIVOT and UNPIVOT operators are typically more efficient at generating a result set than the same query using the traditional DECODE/CASE operators.

Regular Expressions Enhancements

The use of Regular Expressions for pattern matching was introduced in Oracle 10g. Oracle 10g included four expression matching functions:

- *regexp_like* - Returns true if the pattern is matched; otherwise it is false.

- *regexp_instr* - Returns the position of the start or end of the matching string. Returns zero if the pattern does not match.

- *regexp_replace* - Returns a string where each matching string is replaced with the text specified.

- *regexp_substr* - Returns the matching string or NULL if no match is found.

Oracle 11g adds functionality to use sub patterns in *regexp_instr* and *regexp_substr*. The new release also adds a new function called *regexp_count*:

- *regexp_count* - Returns the number of occurrences of an expression in a string.

All five functions can be used in SQL statements or PL/SQL. They operate on the database character datatypes to include VARCHAR2, CHAR, CLOB, NVARCHAR2, NCHAR, and NCLOB.

regexp_instr

Syntax: *regexp_instr*(source, pattern, position, occurrence, begin_end, options, subexp)

The source of *regexp_instr* can be a string literal, variable, or column, and the pattern is the expression to be replaced. The optional position is the location to begin the search, which defaults to 1. Occurrence defines the occurrence you are looking for, and *begin_end* defines whether the position of beginning of the occurrence or the position of the end of the occurrence is being sought. The default is 0, which is the beginning of the occurrence. One the other hand, to get the end position, 1 is used. The matching options are:

- i = case insensitive

- c = case sensitive

- n = the period will match a new line character

- m = allows the ^ and $ to match the beginning and end of lines contained in the source.

New to 11g is the subexpression parameter. The subexpression parameter identifies the sub expression of the pattern that is the actual match. Furthermore, this parameter is an integer that identifies the sub expression of the pattern. If subexpression is not included or defined as 0, the entire pattern is used. If a subexpression is used, but the pattern does not have that subexpression, the function returns a zero. It is important to note that if the subexpression is defined as NULL, the function returns NULL.

```
select
  regexp_instr ('We are driving south by south east','south')
from dual;
```

16

```
select
  regexp_instr ('We are driving south by south east',
                'south', 1, 2, 1)
from dual;
```

30

Here is a look at the sub expression, first using the entire pattern.

```
select
  regexp_instr ('We are driving south by south east',
                '((sou)(th))', 1, 2, 1,null,0)
from dual;
```

30

Next, the first subexpression, which in this instance is the pattern, needs to be used

```
select
  regexp_instr ('We are driving south by south east',
                '((sou)(th))', 1, 2, 1,null,1)
from dual;
```

30

At this point, the query can be executed using the second subexpression. The result is a different answer.

```
select
  regexp_instr ('We are driving south by south east',
   '((sou)(th))', 1, 2, 1,null,2)
from dual;
```

28

Finally, the function below will always return a NULL since the subexpression is defined as NULL.

```
select
  regexp_instr ('We are driving south by south east',
                '((sou)(th))', 1, 2, 1,null,null)
from dual;
```

```
Nothing was returned => NULL.
```

regexp_substr

Syntax: *regexp_substr*(source,   pattern,   position,   occurrence, options, subexp)

The source for *regexp_substr* can be a string literal, variable, or column, and the pattern is the expression to be replaced. Again, the optional position is the location to begin the search, and defaults to 1. Optional occurrence define the occurrence that is being sought. The matching options are the same as with *regexp_instr*. Again, as with *regexp_instr*, 11g adds the ability to use a subexpression for the actual match.

```
select
  regexp_substr ('We are driving south by south east',
   '((sou)(th))',1,1,null,0)
from dual;
```

```
south
```

The same query is executed using the second subexpression.

```
select
  regexp_substr ('We are driving south by south east',
   '((sou)(th))',1,1,null,2)
from dual;
```

```
sou
```

regexp_count

Syntax: *regexp_count*(source, pattern, position, options)

As with the other REGEXP functions, in *regexp_count* the source can be a string literal, variable, or column. The pattern is the regular expression, and the position indicates the character in the source where the search begins. The default is 1, or the first character. The matching options are the same as the other REGEXP functions.

```
select
  regexp_count ('We are driving south by south east', 'south')
from dual;
```

2

Using what Oracle refers to as the Perl-influenced patterns, the number of words can be counted.

```
select
  regexp_count ('We are driving south by south east', '\w+')
from dual;
```

7

It is important to mention that the *regexp_count* function ignores subexpression.

Using Regular Expressions can add a powerful pattern-matching capability to the SQL and PL/SQL toolbox. However, Regular Expressions should not be used when a simple LIKE clause will work. This is because there is much more overhead to matching a pattern using Regular Expressions, as opposed to character wild cards. If all rows where *last_name* starts with 'GAR' is being sought, the LIKE clause (where xxx like 'GAR%') will perform better than using a Regular Expression. But as searches become more complicated, pattern matching with Regular Expressions can be very powerful.

Result Cache Hint

The result cache is a powerful new feature that caches a result set in the SGA for a specified period of time. The first query will create the result set and subsequent queries will use the cached result set instead of creating their own result set. Basically, the Result Cache hint tells Oracle to check the SGA for a copy of the result set, if found use it, if not, create the result set and cache it.

Using the result cache can impact a database differently based on the database configuration. Like a materialized view, the result cache can be used to eliminate the overhead of repeatedly joining multiple tables in a highly normalized schema. Using prejoined data from the result cache will reduce physical I/O on uncached table blocks and reduce consistent gets and CPU usage on fully cached systems. The result cache does have a cost in the additional contention for space in the SGA.

Below are some result cache details:

- The result cache is stored in the SGA and is available across sessions. This is in contrast to a PL/SQL collection, which is stored in PGA and normally only available to the session that created it.

- The result cache can be implemented by using the *result_cache* hint in PL/SQL and at the session level.

The *result_cache* SQL hint suggests that the result data will be cached in the data buffers, and not the intermediate data blocks that were accessed to obtain the query results. You can cache SQL and PL/SQL results for super-fast subsequent retrieval. The result cache ties into the scalable execution concept. There are three areas of the result cache:

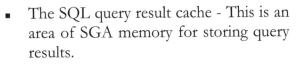

- The SQL query result cache - This is an area of SGA memory for storing query results.

- The PL/SQL function result cache - This result cache can store the results from a PL/SQL function call.

- The OCI client result cache - This cache retains results from OCI calls, both for SQL queries or PL/SQL functions.

- The result cache will remain in use until it times out or is invalidated by changes to the dependent objects. Invalidating a result cache set can be done using a PL/SQL procedure but not using SQL.

- The result cache space in the SGA is available to age out. If space is needed in the SGA, the LRU algorithm can age out a low use result cache set. On first execution, the cached result set will be recreated in the SGA. On an SGA sized constrained system, this can add considerably to SGA contention.

- Result Cache sets are managed with two new latches and latch contention appears to increase exponentially as concurrency increases. This is in addition to the SGA contention that can result from caching large numbers of result sets in a memory constrained SGA.

- Result Cache can not be used on Dictionary or temporary tables, sequence pseudo columns, non-deterministic functions, and SQL select date functions such as SELECT *current_date*, xxx,yyy...

- If the SQL contains bind variables, the bind variables are stored with the result set and the cached result set can be used if the SQL statements are the same or use the same bind variables. Different bind variables will produce new result sets.

Using the Result Cache in PL/SQL provides much more flexibility, including the ability to manage cached sets and dependencies to invalidate cached sets. The PL/SQL implementation of the result cache will be covered in the PL/SQL Chapter.

There are three parameters supporting the new result cache feature:

```
RESULT_CACHE_MAX_SIZE = integer [K | M | G]
```

result_cache_max_size defines the maximum amount of SGA memory available to the result cache feature. Setting this parameter to 0 will disable the result cache. The default value is derived form the *shared_pool_size, sga_target*, or *memory_target*, depending on which is currently in use. The ALTER SYSTEM command can be used to dynamically change the value of this parameter.

```
RESULT_CACHE_MAX_RESULT = integer
```

Result_cache_max_result defines the maximum percentage of the *result_cache_max_size* that any one result set can use. This

parameter defaults to 5% and can be changed using the ALTER
SYSTEM command.

```
RESULT_CACHE_MODE = { MANUAL | FORCE }
```

Result_cache_max_mode defines how the result cache is applied to
the SQL statement. When set to MANUAL, only SQL with the
result_cache hint will use the result cache feature. When set to
FORCE, the operator is applied to the root of all SELECT
statements. The default value is MANUAL, and the parameter
can be modified by ALTER SYSTEM and ALTER SESSION
commands.

In the example below, the SQL query returns the stores that have
above average sales. Here, the execution plan and 18 consistent
gets can be seen:

```
column c1 heading "Store Name" format a30
column c2 heading Total        format 999,999
select
  initcap(store_name)  c1,
  total                c2
from
  (select
     store_name,
     sum(quantity) total
   from store join sales using (store_key)
   group by store_name)
where
  total > (select avg(total)
           from (select
                    sum(quantity) total
                 from store join sales using (store_key)
                 group by store_name))
;
```

```
Store Name                      Total
------------------------------  --------
Borders                         21,860
Books For Dummies               13,000
Wee Bee Books                   13,700
Wild And Lively Books           24,700
Eaton Books                     12,120
```

Regular Expressions Enhancements

181

```
-----------------------------------------
| Id  | Operation                        |
-----------------------------------------
|   0 | SELECT STATEMENT                 |
|*  1 |  FILTER                          |
|   2 |   HASH GROUP BY                  |
|   3 |    MERGE JOIN                    |
|   4 |     TABLE ACCESS BY INDEX ROWID  |
|   5 |      INDEX FULL SCAN             |
|*  6 |     SORT JOIN                    |
|   7 |      TABLE ACCESS FULL           |
|   8 |   SORT AGGREGATE                 |
|   9 |    VIEW                          |
|  10 |     SORT GROUP BY                |
|  11 |      MERGE JOIN                  |
|  12 |       TABLE ACCESS BY INDEX ROWID|
|  13 |        INDEX FULL SCAN           |
|* 14 |        SORT JOIN                 |
|  15 |         TABLE ACCESS FULL        |
-----------------------------------------
Statistics
----------------------------------------------------------
          1  recursive calls
          0  db block gets
         18  consistent gets
          0  physical reads
          0  redo size
        608  bytes sent via SQL*Net to client
        420  bytes received via SQL*Net from client
          2  SQL*Net roundtrips to/from client
          3  sorts (memory)
          0  sorts (disk)
          5  rows processed
```

The first time the same query is run using the *result_cache* hint, the statistics are the same.

```
select /*+ RESULT_CACHE */
  initcap(store_name)   c1,
  total                 c2
from
  (select
     store_name,
     sum(quantity) total
   from store join sales using (store_key)
   group by store_name)
where
  total > (select avg(total)
           from (select
                   sum(quantity) total
                 from store join sales using (store_key)
                 group by store_name))
;
```

```
Statistics
------------------------------------------------------------
          1  recursive calls
          0  db block gets
         18  consistent gets
          0  physical reads
          0  redo size
        608  bytes sent via SQL*Net to client
        420  bytes received via SQL*Net from client
          2  SQL*Net roundtrips to/from client
          3  sorts (memory)
          0  sorts (disk)
          5  rows processed
```

Following this, each subsequent execution of the query with the hint will use the cached results set. This can be seen in both the execution plan, which includes the execution plan for the result set, and in the statistics, which show that there were no block gets.

```
select /*+ RESULT_CACHE */
  initcap(store_name)  c1,
  total                c2
from
  (select
     store_name,
     sum(quantity) total
   from store join sales using (store_key)
   group by store_name)
where
  total > (select avg(total)
           from (select
                   sum(quantity) total
                 from store join sales using (store_key)
                 group by store_name))
;
```

```
Store Name                        Total
---------------------------  --------
Borders                        21,860
Books For Dummies              13,000
Wee Bee Books                  13,700
Wild And Lively Books          24,700
Eaton Books                    12,120


-------------------------------------------
| Id  | Operation                         |
-------------------------------------------
|   0 | SELECT STATEMENT                  |
|   1 |  RESULT CACHE                     |
|*  2 |   FILTER                          |
|   3 |    HASH GROUP BY                  |
```

```
|   4 |    MERGE JOIN                         |
|   5 |     TABLE ACCESS BY INDEX ROWID       |
|   6 |      INDEX FULL SCAN                   |
|*  7 |     SORT JOIN                         |
|   8 |      TABLE ACCESS FULL                |
|   9 |   SORT AGGREGATE                      |
|  10 |   VIEW                                |
|  11 |    SORT GROUP BY                      |
|  12 |     MERGE JOIN                        |
|  13 |      TABLE ACCESS BY INDEX ROWID|
|  14 |       INDEX FULL SCAN                 |
|* 15 |      SORT JOIN                        |
|  16 |       TABLE ACCESS FULL               |
-------------------------------------------
```

```
Statistics
-----------------------------------------------------------
        0   recursive calls
        0   db block gets
        0   consistent gets
        0   physical reads
        0   redo size
      608   bytes sent via SQL*Net to client
      420   bytes received via SQL*Net from client
        2   SQL*Net roundtrips to/from client
        0   sorts (memory)
        0   sorts (disk)
        5   rows processed
```

The example above illustrates how powerful this feature is, but the hint does not have to only be in the root of the SQL statement. In the next example, the subqueries are removed and placed in a view. Though it is common to find poorly performing SQL statements based on views, this view will really benefit from the performance of Result Cache.

To begin, the view should be created and the query needs to be run to get a base line.

```
create view v1 as
select
     store_name,
     sum(quantity) total
   from store join sales using (store_key)
   group by store_name;


select
  initcap(store_name)   c1,
  total                 c2
```

```
from v1
where
  total > (select avg(total)
          from v1);
```

```
Statistics
----------------------------------------------------------
         15  recursive calls
          0  db block gets
         22  consistent gets
          0  physical reads
          0  redo size
        608  bytes sent via SQL*Net to client
        420  bytes received via SQL*Net from client
          2  SQL*Net roundtrips to/from client
          3  sorts (memory)
          0  sorts (disk)
          5  rows processed
```

Here, there are 22 consistent gets. Next, the current view must be dropped and replaced with a view containing the hint.

```
drop view v1;

create view v1 as
select /*+ RESULT_CACHE */
    store_name,
    sum(quantity) total
  from store join sales using (store_key)
  group by store_name;
```

The query next must be run twice to show the result cache impact:

```
select
  initcap(store_name)  c1,
  total                c2
from v1
where
  total > (select avg(total)
          from v1);
```

```
Statistics
----------------------------------------------------------
        135  recursive calls
          8  db block gets
         68  consistent gets
          0  physical reads
          0  redo size
        608  bytes sent via SQL*Net to client
        420  bytes received via SQL*Net from client
```

```
        2   SQL*Net roundtrips to/from client
       10   sorts (memory)
        0   sorts (disk)
        5   rows processed
```

```
select
  initcap(store_name)  c1,
  total                c2
from v1
where
  total > (select avg(total)
           from v1);
```

```
-------------------------------------------
| Id  | Operation                         |
-------------------------------------------
|   0 | SELECT STATEMENT                  |
|*  1 |  VIEW                             |
|   2 |   RESULT CACHE                    |
|   3 |    HASH GROUP BY                  |
|   4 |     MERGE JOIN                    |
|   5 |      TABLE ACCESS BY INDEX ROWID  |
|   6 |       INDEX FULL SCAN             |
|*  7 |      SORT JOIN                    |
|   8 |       TABLE ACCESS FULL           |
|   9 |  SORT AGGREGATE                   |
|  10 |   VIEW                            |
|  11 |    RESULT CACHE                   |
|  12 |     SORT GROUP BY                 |
|  13 |      MERGE JOIN                   |
|  14 |       TABLE ACCESS BY INDEX ROWID |
|  15 |        INDEX FULL SCAN            |
|* 16 |       SORT JOIN                   |
|  17 |        TABLE ACCESS FULL          |
-------------------------------------------
```

```
Statistics
-------------------------------------------------------------
        0   recursive calls
        0   db block gets
        0   consistent gets
        0   physical reads
        0   redo size
      608   bytes sent via SQL*Net to client
      420   bytes received via SQL*Net from client
        2   SQL*Net roundtrips to/from client
        0   sorts (memory)
        0   sorts (disk)
        5   rows processed
```

Notice in the execution plan that the cached result set was utilized twice and the statistics show no consistent gets.

Oracle provides a number of views and packages to look into the cached and cleared objects in the Result Cache for optimal monitoring. To list the objects in the result cache, *v$result_cache_objects* is used.

```
select cache_id,name from v$result_cache_objects;

CACHE_ID                          NAME
------------------------------------------------------------
PUBS.STORE                        PUBS.STORE

PUBS.SALES                        PUBS.SALES

cqdxahmy5120z7s0wjs4wwuvfy        PUBS.V1

5qbrt9zvmpruh3an1mwq1wg9zf        select /*+ RESULT_CACHE */
                                    initcap(store_name)  c1,
                                    total                c2
                                  from
                                    (select
                                        store_name,
                                        sum(quantit
```

Invalidating the cached objects can be done by flushing the Result Cache, as seen below:

```
select count(*) from v$result_cache_objects;

  COUNT(*)
----------
        5

exec dbms_result_cache.flush;

select count(*) from v$result_cache_objects;

  COUNT(*)
----------
        0
```

Additional packages used to maintain and invalidate the Result Cache will be covered in the PL/SQL Chapter.

From the examples covered, the impact of using the Result Cache hint with SQL can be seen. Being able to cache the results of expensive SQL, such as constantly used views, can have a

---

dramatic impact on SQL performance. However, there is a price to be paid in the additional memory, contention, and latching in the SGA.

HASH OUTER JOINS

A new capability of the optimizer is to use a hash algorithm to execute outer joins. Using this new hash outer join can result in a 50% reduction in logical I/O. An outer join returns the rows that match plus the rows that do not match from one or both tables. Using the PUBS schema, the following example shows the HASH OUTER JOIN at work.

Below, a FULL OUTER JOIN is used with the AUTHOR and BOOK_AUTHOR tables. This will return all matching rows and the non-matching rows in both the AUTHOR table, which contains a list of authors that have no books, and the BOOK_AUTHOR table, which contains planned books that do not have authors.

```
select
  author_last_name,
  book_key
from
  author full outer join book_author using (author_key)
order by 1;
```

```
---------------------------------
| Id  | Operation               |
---------------------------------
|   0 | SELECT STATEMENT        |
|   1 |  SORT ORDER BY          |
|   2 |   VIEW                  |
|*  3 |    HASH JOIN FULL OUTER |
|   4 |     TABLE ACCESS FULL   |
|   5 |     INDEX FAST FULL SCAN|
---------------------------------
```

Notice the HASH JOIN FULL OUTER step in the execution plan. There is no hint to force the optimizer to use or not to use the HASH OUTER JOIN method.

Notice the HASH JOIN FULL OUTER step in the execution plan. There is no hint to force the optimizer to use or not to use the HASH OUTER JOIN method.

Conclusion

In this chapter, the enhancements to SQL introduced in 11g have been explored. First, the PIVOT and UNPIVOT operators are used to shift data in a result set from rows to columns and columns to rows. Regular Expressions were also covered, which allow DBAs to pattern match both a pattern and a sub pattern. Additionally, the *regexp_count* function returns the number of matches found, and the *result_cache* hint caches a query result set in the SGA for use by multiple sessions. These provide a significant performance boost to query execution time and resources. Also in 11g, the new HASH OUTER JOIN optimizer access method can significantly reduce logical I/O. All of these new SQL features enhance the DBA's ability to efficiently interact with the database.

New features of 11g SQL covered in this chapter were:

- Pivot and Unpivot
- Regular expressions
- Hash outer joins

11g Performance Tuning Features

New Performance Tuning Features

Oracle 10g introduced several major performance enhancements, many of them in the form of advisors and automatic features. The new analysis available with 10g allowed a DBA to locate the root cause of their performance issues and drill down into waits and bottlenecks. Those abilities have been enhanced in Oracle 11g using analytic data built into the AWR in new ways.

For instance, many of the performance features of Oracle 10g allowed reactive analysis, limited forecasting, and proactive tuning. Oracle 11g introduces new tools that allow full-scale proactive tuning, maintenance, and testing. One of the most comprehensive tools available for 11g that assists with all three of these goals is the SQL Performance Analyzer.

A trip to the SPA – Inside the 11g SQL Performance Analyzer

The declarative nature of the SQL syntax has always made it difficult to perform SQL tuning. The basic tenet of cost-based SQL optimization is that the person who writes a SQL query simply declares what columns they want to see (the SELECT clause), the tables where the columns reside (the FROM clause), and the filtering conditions (the WHERE clause). It is up to the SQL optimizer to determine the optimal execution plan. This is a formidable challenge, especially in a dynamic environment, which is why Oracle introduced the 10g new feature of CBO dynamic sampling.

Oracle tuning consultants have known for many years that the best way to tune an Oracle system is to take a top-down approach. This involves finding the optimal configuration for external factors such as OS kernel settings and disk I/O subsystem, and then determining the best overall setting for the Oracle instance (i.e. *init.ora* parameters).

Holistic tuning involves tuning a representative workload, then adjusting global parameters in order to optimize as much SQL as possible. Only then is it prudent to start tuning individual SQL statements. Many Oracle professionals who adopt a bottom-up approach by tuning the SQL first find all of their hard work undone when a change is made to a global setting, such as to one of the SQL optimizer parameters or by recomputing optimizer statistics.

Oracle's holistic SQL tuning approach is new and given the misleading marketing name of Fully Automated SQL Tuning. Holistic tuning is well known to working DBAs that have been doing manual workload-based optimization since Oracle 6. Now in 11g, Oracle gives DBAs an automated method.

 **The main benefit to holistic SQL tuning is that the DBA can now test changes to global parameters against a real-world workload, using a SQL Tuning Set (STS).**

The Oracle 11g SQL Performance Analyzer (SPA) is primarily designed to speed up the holistic SQL tuning process, automating much of the tedium. Once a workload is created, called a SQL Tuning Set or STS, Oracle will repeatedly execute the workload using sophisticated predictive models like using a regression testing approach to accurately identify the salient changes to execution plans based on the environmental changes.

Using SPA, the impact of system changes on a workload can be calculated and changes in response times can be predicted for SQL after making any change like parameter changes, schema changes, hardware changes, OS changes, or Oracle upgrades. Any change that influence SQL plans is a good candidate for SPA.

Decision Support and Expert Systems Technology

Oracle had made a commitment to Decision Support Systems (DSS) Technology starting in Oracle 9i when they started to publish advisory utilities. This was the result of monitoring the Oracle instance and coming up with estimated benefits for making a change to the database configuration. In the world of applied artificial intelligence, an expert system such as AMM or ASM solves a well-structured problem for the DBA, while a decision support system solves a semi-structured problem with the DBA who supplies the human intuition required to solve a complex problem.

Oracle has made a commitment to distinguishing themselves in the database marketplace and this is one of the major reasons that they command a major market share. One of the most exciting areas of Oracle technology is automation, especially the self-management features. Oracle has now automated many critical components including memory advisors (AMM) and automated storage management (ASM). They are now working to enhance more intelligent utilities including ADDM, the Automated Database Diagnostic Monitor, and the brand new 11g SQL Performance Analyzer (SPA).

The Oracle 11g SPA functions as a DSS and this helps the DBA by automating the well-structured components of a complex tuning task such as hypothesis testing. In SPA, the DBA defines a representative workload and then tests this workload empirically, running the actual queries against the database and collecting performance metrics. SPA allows the DBA to obtain real-world performance results for several types of environmental changes:

- Optimizer software levels – compare SQL execution between different releases of the cost-based optimizer (CBO)

- Initialization parameters – pre-test changes to global parameters, most often the Oracle optimizer parameters (*optimizer_mode, optimizer_index_cost_adj, optimizer_index_caching*). Prior to Oracle 10g, adjusting these optimizer parameters was the only way to compensate for sample size issues with *dbms_stats*.

- Guided workflow – This is a hypothesis testing option that allows the DBA to create customized experiments and validate their hypotheses using empirical methods.

Instead of using theory and mathematical calculations, Oracle SPA tests the SQL Tuning Set (STS) workload in a real-world environment, running the workload repeatedly while using heuristic methods to tally the optimal execution plan for the SQL. The DBA can then review the changes to execution plans and tune the SQL using the SQL Tuning Advisor to lock in the execution plans using SQL profiles.

The next part of this chapter will review SPA and see how holistic SQL tuning can remove the tedium of tuning SQL statements.

Inside the Oracle 11g SQL Performance Analyzer

The Oracle 11g SQL Performance Analyzer is a step in the direction of fully automated SQL tuning, allowing the database administrator to create an STS workload, which is a unified set of SQL which comes from either the cursor cache (Shared Pool) or from the Automated Workload Repository (AWR). The DBA can use exception thresholds to select the SQL for each STS based on execution criteria such as disk reads, consistent gets, executions and the like. Once the DBA has chosen the STS, SPA allows them to run the workload while changing Oracle environmental factors, namely the CBO release level, *init.ora* parameters and customized hypothesis testing using the guided workflow option.

The central question becomes which Oracle initialization parameters would be the most appropriate within the SQL performance analyzer? Because the SPA is used to measure changes in SQL execution plans, it only makes sense that those Oracle parameters would be chosen that will influence the behavior of the Oracle optimizer. These would include the basic Oracle optimizer parameters, including *optimizer_index_cost_adj*, *optimizer_mode*, *optimizer_index_caching*, as well as other important initialization parameters. There are also non-optimizer parameters which effect SQL execution plan decisions:

- *db_file_multiblock_read_count* - When this parameter is set to a high value, the Oracle cost-based optimizer recognizes that scattered multiblock reads may be less expensive than sequential reads (i.e. full table scans and full index scans).

> 10gr2 Note: Starting in Oracle 10g release2, Oracle recommends not setting the *db_file_multiblock_read_count* parameter, allowing them to empirically determine the optimal setting.

- *parallel_automatic_tuning* - When *parallel_automatic_tuning* is set to "on," the Oracle optimizer will parallelize legitimate full table scans. Because Oracle has been told that parallel full table scans can be done very quickly using parallel query, Oracle's cost-based optimizer will assign a higher cost index access; therefore, making the optimizer friendlier to full table scans.

- *hash_area_size* (if not overridden by *pga_aggregate_target*) - The setting for *hash_area_size* governs the propensity of Oracle's optimizer to favor hash joins over nested loops and merge joins. This makes it an ideal testing parameter for changes to Oracle memory regions so that one can see how they would be affected within a production environment.

- *pga_aggregate_target* - The settings for *pga_aggregate_target* have a profound impact on the behavior of Oracle SQL statements, making this an interesting test case for the SQL performance analyzer, especially with regard to the propensity of the Oracle optimizer in memory sorts and hash joins.

- *sort_area_size* (if not overridden by *pga_aggregate_target*) - The *sort_area_size* parameter influences the cost-based optimizer when deciding whether or not to perform index access or to perform a sort of the ultimate results set from the SQL query. The higher the value for *sort_area_size*, the more likely it will be that the Oracle 11g optimizer will invoke a backend sort because it knows that the sort can be performed in memory. Of course, this depends on the Oracle optimizers estimated cardinality for the results set of the SQL query.

Naturally, any parameters can be changed as desired. The next issue is to see how the SPA captures changes in SQL execution plans.

A trip to the SPA

Until there were the Oracle 10g intelligent SQL tuning advisors, SQL Access Advisor, and SQL Tuning Advisor, SQL tuning was a time-consuming and tedious task. That all started to change in Oracle 10g and it is even more exciting in Oracle 11g, where Oracle has promised fully automated SQL tuning via the new SQL Performance Analyzer and improvements in the SQL advisories.

The Oracle 10g automatic tuning advisor allowed the DBA to implement tuning suggestions in the form of SQL profiles that would improve performance. Now with Oracle 11g, the DBA can tell Oracle to automatically apply SQL profiles for statements whenever the suggested profile gives three times better performance than the existing statement. These performance comparisons are done by a new 11g administrative task that is executed during a user-specified maintenance window. In a nutshell, the 11g fully automated SQL tuning works like this:

- Define the SQL workload - The DBA defines a set of problematic SQL statements using exception thresholds (e.g. all SQL with > 100,000 disk reads) selected from the cursor cache or the AWR. This is called the SQL Tuning set, or STS.

- Set-up a changed environment - Here the DBA can choose to change the initialization parameters, test the performance against a previous release of the CBO or conduct custom experiments on the effect of environmental changes on the SQL tuning set.

- Schedule and run the tests - The workload is scheduled for execution during low usage periods so that an empirical sample of real-world execution times can be collected and compared using different execution plans.

- Implement the changes – SQL statements can be flagged for changes and tuned with the SQL Tuning advisor.

> 🔔 Tip: Also related is the Oracle 11g automated SQL Tuning Advisor, whereby changes can be automatically implemented that cause the SQL to run more than 3x faster.

The Oracle 11g automated SQL tuning advisor will implement all execution plan changes via SQL Profiles, a tool that is conceptually similar to stored outlines and is a method to bypass the generation of execution plans for incoming SQL, replacing it with a pre-tuned access plan.

The automatic SQL tuning advisor also recommends restructuring badly formed SQL and adding missing indexes and materialized views, but these require a manual decision. Before the nuances of the 11g fully automated SQL tuning features are examined, a review of the goals of SQL tuning will be covered briefly.

 **If your shop has relatively static tables and indexes, you may want to adopt the persistent SQL philosophy that states that there exists only one optimal execution plan for any SQL statement. Shops that subscribe to this philosophy are characterized by stable OLTP applications that have been tuned to use host variables (instead of literal values) in all SQL queries.**

The goals of holistic SQL tuning

Holistic tuning in Oracle 11g is a broad-brush approach that can save thousands of hours of tedious manual SQL tuning. By applying global changes, the DBA can tune hundreds of queries at once and implement them via SQL profiles. DBAs who fail to do holistic SQL tuning first, especially those who tune SQL with optimizer directives, may find that subsequent global changes (e.g. optimizer parameter change) may detune their SQL. By starting with system-level tuning, the DBA can establish an optimal baseline before diving into the tuning of individual SQL statements:

- Optimize the server kernel - Always tune the disk and network I/O subsystem (RAID, DASD bandwidth, network) to optimize the I/O time, network packet size and dispatching frequency. Kernel settings have an indirect effect on SQL performance. For example, a kernel setting may speed up I/O, a change which is noted by the CBO workload statistics using *dbms_stats.gather_workload_stats*. This, in turn, directly influences the optimizer's access decisions.

- Adjusting the optimizer statistics - Always collect and store optimizer statistics to allow the optimizer to learn more about the distribution of the data to make more intelligent execution plans. Histograms can hypercharge SQL in cases of determining optimal table join order and when making access decisions on skewed WHERE clause predicates. Also new with 11g is that multi-column statistics can be gathered for use by the optimizer to determine optimal ways to run queries based upon multiple column criteria.

- Adjust optimizer parameters - *optimizer_mode*, *optimizer_index_caching*, and o*ptimizer_index_cost_adj*.

- Optimize the instance - The choice of *db_block_size*, *db_cache_size*, and OS parameters (*db_file_multiblock_read_count*, *cpu_count*, &c), can influence SQL performance.

- Tune the SQL Access workload with physical indexes and materialized views - Just as the 10g SQL Access Advisor recommends missing indexes and missing materialized views, a DBA should always optimize the SQL workload with indexes, especially function-based indexes.

 **By capturing and replaying a representative SQL workload, you can verify many holistic settings, before diving into the tuning of specific SQL statements. Full workload tuning is essential because you want to tune as much SQL as possible at the system level.**

Oracle 11g does not have all of the intelligence of a human SQL tuning expert, but the 11g SQL Performance Analyzer is a great way to test for the effect of environmental changes to the Oracle environment. Next is a more detailed look at how Oracle has automated the SQL tuning process with SPA.

The SPA treatment

The SQL performance analyzer allows the DBA to define the SQL Tuning set (STS) as a source for the test, usually using historical SQL from the AWR tables.

The SPA receives one or more SQL statements as input and provides advice on which tuning conditions have the best execution plans. It then gives the proof for the advice, shows an estimated performance benefit, and allegedly has a facility to automatically implement changes that are more than 3x faster than the before condition.

Gathering the SQL Tuning set

The SQL workload (STS) can be thought of as a container for conducting and analyzing many SQL statements. The STS is fed to the SPA for real-world execution with before-and-after

---

comparisons of changes to holistic environmental conditions, specifically CBO levels or changed *init.ora* parameters.

Internally, SPA is stored as a database object that contains one or more SQL statements combined with their execution statistics and context such as particular schema, application module name, a list of bind variables and such. The STS also includes a set of basic execution statistics such as CPU and elapsed times, disk reads and buffer gets, number of executions and more.

When creating a STS, the SQL statements can be filtered by different patterns such as application module name or by execution statistics like high disk reads. Once created, STS can be an input source for the SQL Tuning Advisor.

Typically, the following steps are used to define the STS using the *dbms_sqltune* package. The steps within the new 11g OEM screen for guided workflow are simple and straightforward and serve as an online interface to the *dbms_sqltune.create_sqlset* procedure:

1. Options – Choose a name for the SQL tuning set (STS). This encapsulated SQL workload is created using the *dbms_sqltune.create_sqlset* procedure. For example, the following script can be used to create a STS called SQLSET1:

```
Exec dbms_sqltune.create_sqlset ('MYSET1');
```

2. Load methods - Here is where the source for the SQL workload can be chosen and where historical SQL statements from AWR can be taken.

3. Filter options - Filtering conditions can be chosen based on the specific tuning needs. For example, if the database is disk I/O bound, it is possible to choose only SQL statements that have more than 100k disk reads.

4. Schedule – This is an interface to the *dbms_scheduler* package allowing a job to be scheduled and defined.

5. Review – This is where the actual source calls to *dbms_sqltune.create_sqlset* can be seen and the *dbms_scheduler.create_job* procedure calls syntax.

There is an interface to the SQL Performance Analyzer in the enterprise manager of the OEM Advisor Central area and a number of new *dba_advisor* views have been added in 11g which will display information from the SQL Performance Advisor.

The technology behind SPA is encapsulated inside a new package called *dbms_sqlpa*. Here is an overview for the procedures of the *dbms_sqlpa* package:

- *cancel_analysis_task* – This procedure cancels the currently executing task analysis of one or more SQL statements.

- *create_analysis_task* – This function creates an advisor task to process and analyze one or more SQL statements.

- *drop_analysis_task* - This procedure drops a SQL analysis task.

- *execute_analysis_task* – This function and procedure executes a previously created analysis task.

- *interrupt_anaylsis_task* - This procedure interrupts the currently executing analysis task.

- *report_analysis_task* – This function displays the results of an analysis task.

- *reset_analysis_task* – This procedure resets the currently executing analysis task to its initial state.

- *resume_analysis_task* – This procedure resumes a previously interrupted analysis task that was created to process a SQL tuning set.

- *set_analysis_task_parameter* – This procedure sets the SQL analysis task parameter value.

- *set_analysis_default_parameter* – This procedure sets the SQL analysis task parameter default value.

In sum, the new 11g SQL Performance Analyzer is a great way to test for holistic tuning changes. Remember, the savvy Oracle DBA will always adjust their Oracle initialization parameters to optimize as much of the workload as possible before diving into the tuning of specific SQL statements.

Oracle 11g guided workflow screen

The OEM screen for the SPA guided workflow contains a pre-defined set of steps for holistic SQL workload tuning:

1. Create SQL Performance Analyzer Task, based on SQL Tuning Set
2. Replay SQL Tuning Set in initial environment
3. Create replay trial using changed environment
4. Create replay trial comparison (using trials from step 2 and step 3)
5. View trial comparison report

Using the guided workflow functionality, take the SQL tuning set and execute it twice, before and after, and save the SQL execution results, like disk reads and buffer gets, using some of the common SQL execution metrics found in the *dba_hist_sqlstat* table:

FETCHES_TOTAL
END_OF_FETCH_COUNT_TOTAL
SORTS_TOTAL
EXECUTIONS_TOTAL
LOADS_TOTAL
INVALIDATIONS_TOTAL
PARSE_CALLS_TOTAL
DISK_READS_TOTAL

BUFFER_GETS_TOTAL
ROWS_PROCESSED_TOTAL
CPU_TIME_TOTAL
ELAPSED_TIME_TOTAL

Table 7.1: *dba_hist_sqlstat Columns*

EXECUTE_ELAPSED_TIME
ELAPSED_TIME
PARSE_TIME
EXECUTE_ELAPSED_TIME
EXECUTE_CPU_TIME
BUFFER_GETS
DISK_READS
DIRECT_WRITES
OPTIMIZER_COST

Table 7.2: *Guided Workflow Items*

It is important to note that the guided workflow does not measure these important SQL execution metrics such as sorts and fetches.

Comparing the SPA Results

The final step in SPA allows the DBA to quickly isolate sub-optimal SQL statements and tune them with the 11g SQL Tuning Advisor. When viewing the results, use OEM for a visual display of all delta values between the execution run and, most importantly, do a side-by-side comparison of the before-and-after execution plans.

Oracle has always been ahead of the curve in automating well-structured DBA tasks and SPA is just the latest incarnation in real-world SQL tuning tools. Tools such as SPA free up the DBA to pursue other important DBA tasks, relieving them of the tedium of individually tuning SQL statements.

Extended Optimizer Statistics

Another exciting feature of Oracle 11g is additional features built into the *dbms_stats* package, specifically the ability to aid complex queries by providing extended statistics to the cost-based optimizer (CBO). The 11g extended optimizer statistics are intended to improve the optimizer's guesses for the cardinality of combined columns and columns that are modified by a built-in or user-defined function.

In Oracle 10g, dynamic sampling is used to provide inter-table cardinality estimates, but dynamic sampling has significant limitations. However, the 11g extended statistics in *dbms_stats* relieves much of the problem of sub-optimal table join orders.

In the absence of column histograms and extended statistics, the Oracle cost-based optimizer must be able to guess the size of complex result sets information and it sometimes gets it wrong. This is one reason why the ORDERED and LEADING hints are two of the most popular SQL tuning hints; using the ORDERED hint allows one to specify that the tables be joined together in the same order that they appear in the FROM clause. The LEADING hint indicates the first table to use when deciding upon a join order.

In this example, the four-way table join only returns 18 rows, but the query carries 9,000 rows in intermediate result sets, slowing-down the SQL execution speed:

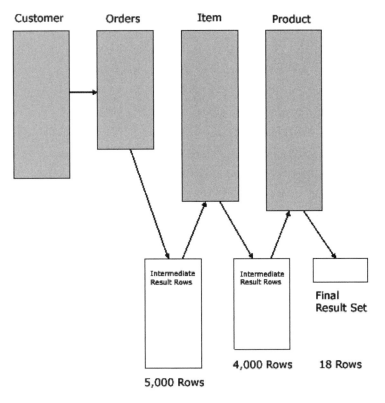

Figure 7.1: *A Suboptimal Table Join Order*

If the sizes of the intermediate results can be predicted, the table-join order can be re-sequenced to carry less intermediate baggage during the four-way table join. In the next example, only 3,000 intermediate rows between the table joins are carried:

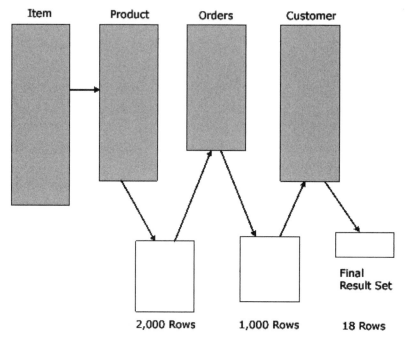

Figure 7.2: *3,000 Rows Between Table Joins*

The next topic to be covered is how the 11g extended *dbms_stats* data helps the optimizer make better guesses of result set sizes.

Inside Extended Optimizer Statistics

The purpose behind histograms is to allow Oracle's optimizer to make intelligent decisions regarding data that is skewed, meaning when one set of data is not necessarily representative of the rest of the data in the table. Histograms provide a remedy by allowing Oracle to capture metadata based upon the distribution of data in a particular column of a table. However, histogram gathering to this point has been guesswork at best unless a DBA has taken the time to perform proper data profiling.

Some data profiling is still necessary. Gathering histograms on all columns, including unnecessary ones, is a lengthy and time-consuming process. Oracle 11g provides the ability to gather better histograms when extended statistics are required.

The new 11g *dbms_stats* package has several new procedures to aid in supplementing histogram data:

```
dbms_stats.create_extended_stats
dbms_stats.show_extended_stats_name
dbms_stats.drop_extended_stats
```

Extended histograms can be seen in the *user_tab_col_statistics* view.

Gathering extended statistics allows histograms not only on one column, but multiple columns at a time. This is importable for both table joins as mentioned in the last section and for multi-column WHERE criteria. Columns generally are not used independently and better decision-making is imperative when queries are run with multiple criteria.

Extended statistics can also be generated on a function of a column; for instance, on *upper(column_name)*. In proper data profiling, it is necessary to account for possible changes in data, such as case changes, since queries may have different requirements for the presentation of data.

Oracle must also account for these changes; however, Oracle does not have the same decision making capabilities of a human sitting in front of a computer. Without information about different presentations of data or multiple column choices, Oracle cannot be expected to tune all queries as a human being could. As such, these extended statistics help Oracle make more intelligent decisions.

Automatic Diagnostic Repository

In Oracle 11g, there is a new ADR (Automatic Diagnostic Repository) and Incident Packaging System, all designed to allow quick access to alert and diagnostic information. The new $ADR_HOME directory is located by default at $ORACLE_BASE/diag, with the directories for each instance at $ORACLE_HOME/diag/$ORACLE_SID at the same level as the traditional bdump, udump and cdump directories.

Starting in Oracle11g, there are not as many of the original OFA file system structures and the ancient dump destination *init.ora* parameters (*core_dump_dest, background_dump_dest, user_dump_dest*) are replaced by a single *diagnostic_dest* parameter.

The new initialization parameter *diagnostic_dest* can be used to specify an alternative location for the diag directory contents.

Automatic Memory Tuning

Prior to Oracle 11g, the DBA set the *sga_target* and *sga_max_size* parameters, allowing Oracle to reallocate RAM within the SGA. The PGA was independent, as governed by the *pga_aggregate_target* parameter.

Now in Oracle 11g the *memory_max_target* parameter, which governs the total maximum RAM for both the PGA and SGA regions, is evident. Also evident is the new *memory_target* parameter which governs the existing sizes. This allows RAM to be de-allocated from the SGA and transferred to the PGA. This is an important Oracle 11g new feature because it lays the foundation for inter-instance RAM memory sharing.

The second age of mainframe computing is now here, as is server consolidation where it is not uncommon to find a dozen instances on a single large server.

As of Oracle 10g, Automatic Memory Management (AMM) only allows shifting of RAM within the confines of *sga_max_size*. Now in Oracle 11g, there is the new Automatic Shared Memory Management (ASMM). The *memory_target* parameter is dynamic (changeable with ALTER SYSTEM commands), whereby RAM can be deallocated from the instance SGA/PGA and reallocated to another instance.

Conclusion

Oracle 11g's new performance tuning features allow a DBA to be much more proactive, while at the same time taking some of the busy work from the DBA's day. By gathering statistics that are more meaningful for Oracle's optimizer, Oracle is able to produce better results when data skewing is involved. Automatic Memory Tuning enhances the previous Automatic Memory Management capabilities, thus allowing full instance RAM tuning in a single parameter. Testing can be more thoroughly accomplished for both reactive and proactive tuning with the SQL Performance Analyzer. Finally, using the Automatic Diagnostic Repository maintenance and diagnostic alerts and messages can be managed in one centralized location. Although not specifically performance related, this feature allows the DBA to analyze diagnostic data quickly and effectively, freeing up time for performance analysis instead of chasing rabbit hole issues.

Oracle 11g Security Enhancements

New Password Security Features

Oracle has taken a great number of steps towards a more secure database with 11g by introducing new anti-hacking features. In the following section the most important security improvements will be covered, beginning with the benefits of the enhanced password features.

Enhances hashing algorithm

Publication of the Oracle password hashing algorithm in October, 2005 by the SANS institute[1] started a new era of hacking attacks. If somebody could get hold of the hashes from the data dictionary and knew the hashing algorithm, they could reverse engineer passwords of Oracle users. Therefore, Oracle has changed the view *dba_users* in 11g as shown below. It can no longer be used to retrieve the hashed passwords.

```
LUTZ AS SYSDBA @ orcl SQL> SELECT username, password FROM dba_users;

USERNAME                          PASSWORD
-------------------------------   ------------------------------
MGMT_VIEW
SYS
SYSTEM
DBSNMP
SYSMAN
LUTZ1
```

---

[1] "An Assessment of the Oracle Password Hashing Algorithm", SANS Institute, http://www.sans.org/rr/special/index.php?id=oracle_pass

---

```
LUTZ
L_SEC
LUT
OUTLN
FLOWS_FILES
ANONYMOUS
EXFSYS
WMSYS
XDB
FLOWS_030000
DIP
APEX_PUBLIC_USER
ORACLE_OCM
TSMSYS
XS$NULL
```

However, there is still the threat of a passive attack where the username and hashes from outside the database can be retrieved by sniffing network packages. Such attacks are very difficult to detect.

In March 2007, two hackers published a paper with detailed information on how a passive attack could be launched and how to crack passwords for Oracle user accounts on a hacker site called THC[1]. They claimed to be able to crack any eight digit Oracle password with a normal PC within a maximum of 41 days or even minutes if the password did not exceed a length of six characters.

> 🔔 Oracle strongly recommends customers to use passwords with a minimum length of 10 characters!

In 10g and before, Oracle used a hashing algorithm to create passwords which converted the password string to uppercase and then encrypted it. It used the username as a seed for the encryption. This made it easy for somebody who knew how to

---

[2]The hackers choice: http://www.thc.org/thc-orakel/
Paper by vonJeek & RevMoon: "The next level of Oracle attacks" , March 2007

---

reverse engineer to discover a password if they could get hold of a list with the usernames and the encrypted password strings

Starting with the version 11g, Oracle uses the more secure 160-bit hashing algorithm SHA-1 to encrypt a password that does not use the username for hashing. Passwords are salted, which means that identical usernames and passwords create different hashes. The encrypted password is sent through the network.   The column spare4 in the view *sys.user$* returns the enhanced hashes.

```
LUTZ AS SYSDBA @ orcl SQL> SELECT name, SPARE4 FROM sys.user$;

NAME                            SPARE4
------------------------------  --------------------------------
SYS S:4C2155AAA66F2360470789ED3371EC6D7E677A21739DA379376573ADA06E
PUBLIC
CONNECT
RESOURCE
DBA
SYSTEM
S:287AB640295568BC2A68038DE0E72495D86AF48A0C29ACCBA1F8148080F7
SELECT_CATALOG_ROLE
EXECUTE_CATALOG_ROLE
DELETE_CATALOG_ROLE
OUTLN
S:3D4AE339C6E34FBFD59671A5BE9456E8D36EC9C05F94FF09799B44F0DDDA
EXP_FULL_DATABASE
IMP_FULL_DATABASE
LOGSTDBY_ADMINISTRATOR
DIP S:09737BB5C3C953E97FC66EA76E1219AA4ABC1D8929804B6A136E7257509C
TSMSYS
S:7ADDA4A0404C5FC5C868CAD4251B0DD5F08833E1342B514DFB5AC5DD6BA0
AQ_ADMINISTRATOR_ROLE
AQ_USER_ROLE
DATAPUMP_EXP_FULL_DATABASE
DATAPUMP_IMP_FULL_DATABASE
GATHER_SYSTEM_STATISTICS
ORACLE_OCM
S:B99DA77F6710001D1B3681DD1E3DB68A8E78C924985AF6278DEF7DA93572
XDBADMIN
RECOVERY_CATALOG_OWNER
SCHEDULER_ADMIN
HS_ADMIN_ROLE
GLOBAL_AQ_USER_ROLE
OEM_ADVISOR
OEM_MONITOR
DBSNMP
S:B29CB866BF7A73B0C74B70DF09DAF4B462D1AD4445118962BBDA96550161
WMSYS
S:15BDF5FE5FFE5DB12158AACE20681A568B251BFA01E07B91BFF1B76DEF74
```

```
WM_ADMIN_ROLE
JAVAUSERPRIV
JAVAIDPRIV
JAVASYSPRIV
JAVADEBUGPRIV
EJBCLIENT
JMXSERVER
JAVA_ADMIN
JAVA_DEPLOY
EXFSYS
S:7DCF3854E05D331F84F4656330AADFFCF7CD3E5C62822D943D9C52C29B7D
XDB
S:5F0CE0691D0049201DBA7AFE207401BCA921A32E8BD4349A57EEA5DEB747
ANONYMOUS
XS$NULL
S:540B7513773DCA68ABE9E14E8DBC6CB03DC89C005C4B0844D655E69E442C
XDB_SET_INVOKER
AUTHENTICATEDUSER
XDB_WEBSERVICES
XDB_WEBSERVICES_WITH_PUBLIC
XDB_WEBSERVICES_OVER_HTTP
_NEXT_USER
SYSMAN
S:B9E055880876E2758725EBA09D350720B896E2C554225979A7145B77B7B7
MGMT_USER
MGMT_VIEW
S:39689CD0FB2793A01E9E70377BFA36E1FB4C8F240516AB1851840D4018DC
FLOWS_FILES
S:54340332D71F4E3644D5CA2214277AD7DF2144405D2550D99ABB433F6495
APEX_PUBLIC_USER
S:62326448860BEBC08BEDBABF051DE1A0994DC85A20331EE64242E2247C65
FLOWS_030000
S:BF187319591F4C1D5D6AEEEE17CB39C9F805EF2A3BFB400EF3CD04F47943
LUTZ
S:F2DFB72CB8966B0D5357A2306F3F8F6CE51DC63A6B93AE3B292A91940408
```

Passwords with symbols in 11g

In previous releases, an Oracle password could have a maximum length of 30 characters. This has not changed. A password is an identifier like any other identifier in the database and identifiers are still limited to a maximum length of 30 characters. 30 character Oracle passwords can now contain a mix of symbols and multi-byte characters. Prior to 11g, Oracle only allowed the _, $ and # symbols.

When trying to create a password with symbols:

```
SYS AS SYSDBA @ orcl SQL> alter user lutz identified by _#new%&;
```

```
SP2-0317: expected symbol name is missing
alter user lutz identified by _#new%&
                                      *

ERROR at line 1:
ORA-00911: invalid character
```

It does not work. So try again, this time with single quotes:

```
SYS AS SYSDBA @ orcl SQL> alter user lutz identified by '_#new%&';
```

```
alter user lutz identified by '_#new%&'
                                      *
ERROR at line 1:
ORA-00988: missing or invalid password(s)
```

Therefore, use double quotes for passwords with symbols other than _, # or $.

```
SYS AS SYSDBA @ orcl SQL> alter user lutz identified by "_#new%&";
```

```
User altered.
```

Not all symbols can be used in 11g passwords without special care, not even when using double quotes. What happens if an ampersand (&) is used?

```
SYS AS SYSDBA @ orcl SQL> alter user lutz identified by
"_#new%&1234567890";
```

```
    Enter value for 1234567890:
    old  1: alter user lutz identified by "_#new%&1234567890"
    new  1: alter user lutz identified by "_#new%"

    User altered.
```

This works like an exchange variable and is caused by the default setting for *DEFINE* in *SQL*PLUS*:

```
SYS AS SYSDBA @ orcl SQL> show define
```

```
define "&" (hex 26)
```

Beware of ampersands (&) in passwords. Commas, backslashes, double quotes and the *DEFINE* symbol are not allowed in passwords. It is strongly recommended to use the pls*sql command password in order to change the password and use an ampersand (&) as a symbol in a password.

Now check the maximum length of passwords:

```
SYS AS SYSDBA @ orcl SQL> alter user lutz identified by
"_#new%1234567890%123454667890%1";
```

```
alter user lutz identified by
"_#new%1234567890%123454667890%1234567890"
                                         *
ERROR at line 1:
ORA-00972: identifier is too long
```

```
[oracle@rhas4 ~]$ oerr ora 972
```

```
00972, 00000, "identifier is too long"
// *Cause:  An identifier with more than 30 characters was
specified.
// *Action:  Specify at most 30 characters.
```

So this shows that the password must be kept to no more than 30 characters.

Case sensitive passwords

A new 11g database uses case sensitive passwords by default if they were created with the database configuration assistant (DBCA). This is implemented through the new initialization parameter *sec_case_sensitive_login*.

A 10g database which is upgraded with the database upgrade assistant (DBUA) also uses case sensitive passwords by default but only for newly created user accounts. If an 11g database is created manually with a create database command, case sensitive passwords are not used by default.

```
SYSTEM   @ orcl111 SQL> show parameter sec_case

NAME                                TYPE         VALUE
----------------------------------- ------------ --------------------
sec_case_sensitive_logon            boolean      TRUE
```

The default for the parameter *sec_case_sensitive_login* is FALSE.

An Oracle 11g password file can also store case sensitive passwords. The password file creation utility evaluates the new parameter *ignorecase* to allow case sensitive passwords or restrict passwords to case insensitivity.

> 🔔In order to create a password file with orapwd, which disallows case sensitive passwords, set *ignorecase* to N.

```
[oracle@rhas4 ~]$ orapwd help=y
```

Usage: orapwd file=<fname> password=<password> entries=<users>
force=<y/n> ignorecase=<y/n> nosysdba=<y/n>

- Where file - name of password file (required)
- password - password for SYS (optional)
- entries - maximum number of distinct DBA (required)
- force - whether to overwrite existing file (optional)
- ignorecase - passwords are case-insensitive (optional)
- nosysdba - whether to shut out the SYSDBA logon (optional Database vault only.)

There must be no spaces around the equal-to (=) character.

Case sensitive passwords and database upgrade to 11g

An upgrade to a new release always makes a lot of testing necessary. This is especially the case if one upgrades to 11g and wants to use the case sensitive passwords feature. The parameter *sec_case_sensitive_login* must be set to TRUE explicitly to enable the feature after a manual upgrade.

When upgrading from 10g to 11g with the upgrade assistant (DBUA), the passwords of all user accounts are case insensitive until they are changed the next time.

DBCA as well as DBUA allow the choice of enabling the new security features or starting with the pre-11g functionalities and enabling the new 11g security features later on as shown in Figure 8.1:

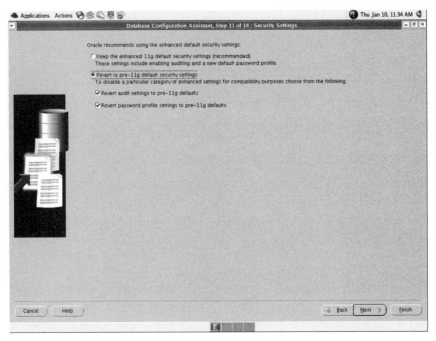

Figure 8.1: *Database Configuration Assistant Security Settings*

How to enable the Oracle 11g EXCLUSIVE MODE

Oracle 10g utilities, which use the OCI drivers including SQL*PLUS, Forms, and ODBC, .NET are compatible with Oracle 11g EXCLUSIVE MODE. This mode can be enabled after making an upgrade to 11g database.

```
sqlnet.allowed_logon_versions=11
```

This parameter defines the minimum client versions that are allowed to connect to the database instance.

Before enabling EXCLUSIVE MODE after upgrading to 11g, make sure that all clients are compatible with this mode. The default for *sqlnet.allowed_logon_versions* is eight.

After this, it is necessary to remove all old password hashes from the database. Be connected as SYSDBA:

```
LUTZ AS SYSDBA @ orcl SQL> UPDATE sys.user$ SET password=NULL;
LUTZ AS SYSDBA @ orcl SQL> DELETE FROM user_history$;
LUTZ AS SYSDBA @ orcl SQL> COMMIT;
```

> ⌨JDBC (thin) versions prior to Oracle 11g cannot use the enhanced 11g Oracle password algorithm or the Oracle Call Interface (OCI) driver prior to Oracle 10g.

Test carefully before using case sensitive passwords in production. There might be a number of pitfalls waiting with hard coded passwords for logons. Case sensitive passwords are a very good feature but, on the other hand, they can also cause a lot of problems - especially if upgrading to 11g since many applications use hard coded passwords in scripts and routines which cannot be easily changed.

Specifically, take care of database links in pre-11g databases which log on to release 11g databases with case sensitive passwords. The passwords for those database links must be recreated in uppercase because Oracle stores these passwords in uppercase even if the original password in the 11g database is created in lower or mixed case.

It might be necessary to disable case sensitive passwords if it is not possible to modify scripts and routines which log on to an 11g database or use database links until all necessary changes to all scripts have been applied. Keep in mind that the parameter *sec_case_sensitive_login* is a dynamic parameter and that it is possible to change it to TRUE any time with an ALTER SYSTEM command.

In 11g, it is possible to check if a password is case sensitive. The new column *password_versions* has been added to data dictionary view *dba_users*. The value "10g" indicates a user account which still uses the old case insensitive password. The value "10g 11g" indicates a user account with a case sensitive password.

```
SYSTEM @ orcl111 SQL> SELECT username, password_versions AS
versions,
                FROM dba_users;
```

```
USERNAME                         VERSIONS
------------------------------   --------
MGMT_VIEW                        10G 11G
SYS                              10G 11G
SYSTEM                           10G 11G
DBSNMP                           10G 11G
SYSMAN                           10G 11G
LUTZ                             10G
OUTLN                            10G 11G
FLOWS_FILES                      10G 11G
ANONYMOUS
EXFSYS                           10G 11G
WMSYS                            10G 11G
XDB                              10G 11G
FLOWS_030000                     10G 11G
DIP                              10G 11G
APEX_PUBLIC_USER                 10G 11G
ORACLE_OCM                       10G 11G
TSMSYS                           10G 11G
XS$NULL                          10G 11G
```

Enforcing complex passwords

Case sensitive passwords improve the security for the database greatly so it is strongly recommended to use them because this feature makes it much more difficult for a potential hacker to break into the system. There are a number of additional rules that apply to secure passwords that make the hacker's life more difficult. A secure password is always a complex password and Oracle strongly recommends the use of secure passwords.

A complex password contains:

- At least 10 characters

- A mixture of letters and numbers

- Mixed case letters (11g)

- Symbols (11g)

- Little or no relation to an actual word

Oracle recommends customers enforce checks and response actions for failed logins, password complexity, password expiration and password reuse. Password complexity can be implemented through profiles.

The script for password management implementation *utlpwdmg.sql* has been modified in 11g. It can be used to create a new function to verify password complexity rules. This function is an enhanced version of the *verify_function* from pre-11g versions.

The default settings in the *verify_function_11g* for password complexity are:

- minimum length of eight characters
- the password must not be the reverse username
- the password must not be the username with a numeric suffix of 1-100
- the password must not be oracle with a numeric suffix of 1-100
- the password must not be the database's name
- the password must not be the database's name with a numeric suffix of 1-100
- the password must contain at least one digit and one character
- a new password must differ in at least three positions from the old password
- the password must not be a string from a predefined list (this list has also been adjusted in the 11g function)

The defaults for the default profile have also been modified in the script *utlpwdmg.sql*. Some limits are automatically set if an 11g database is created using DBCA:

```
LUTZ AS SYSDBA @ orcl SQL> SELECT * FROM user_password_limits;
```

```
RESOURCE_NAME                     LIMIT
------------------------------    --------------------------------
FAILED_LOGIN_ATTEMPTS             10
PASSWORD_LIFE_TIME                180
PASSWORD_REUSE_TIME               UNLIMITED
PASSWORD_REUSE_MAX                UNLIMITED
PASSWORD_VERIFY_FUNCTION          NULL
PASSWORD_LOCK_TIME                1
PASSWORD_GRACE_TIME               7
```

Password complexity check is not enabled by default. The verify function must be created and the default profile manually altered to enable it.

How to find accounts with default passwords in 11g

Oracle 11g comes with a great number of automatically created user accounts. The following table, Table 8.1, lists all default accounts of Oracle 11g Enterprise Edition:

User_name	Account_Status
ANONYMOUS	EXPIRED&LOCKED
APEX_PUBLIC_USER	EXPIRED&LOCKED
CTXSYS	EXPIRED&LOCKED
DBSNMP	EXPIRED&LOCKED
DIP	OPEN
DMSYS	EXPIRED&LOCKED
EXFSYS	EXPIRED&LOCKED
FLOWS_3000	EXPIRED&LOCKED
FLOWS_FILES	EXPIRED&LOCKED
HR	EXPIRED&LOCKED
LBACSYS	EXPIRED&LOCKED
MDDATA	EXPIRED&LOCKED
MDSYS	EXPIRED&LOCKED
MGMT_VIEW	OPEN
ODM	EXPIRED&LOCKED
ODM_MTR	EXPIRED&LOCKED
OE	EXPIRED&LOCKED
OLAPSYS	EXPIRED&LOCKED
ORACLE_OCM	EXPIRED&LOCKED

ORDPLUGINS	EXPIRED&LOCKED
ORDSYS	EXPIRED&LOCKED
OUTLN	EXPIRED&LOCKED
OWBSY	EXPIRED&LOCKED
PM	EXPIRED&LOCKED
PUBLIC	EXPIRED&LOCKED
QS	EXPIRED&LOCKED
QS_ADM	EXPIRED&LOCKED
QS_CS	EXPIRED&LOCKED
QS_ES	EXPIRED&LOCKED
QS_OS	EXPIRED&LOCKED
QS_WS	EXPIRED&LOCKED
RMAN	EXPIRED&LOCKED
SCOTT	EXPIRED&LOCKED
SH	EXPIRED&LOCKED
SI_INFORMTN_SCHEMA	EXPIRED&LOCKED
SPATIAL_CSW_ADMIN_USR	EXPIRED&LOCKED
SPATIAL_WFS_ADMIN_USR	EXPIRED&LOCKED
SYS	OPEN
SYSMAN	OPEN
SYSTEM	OPEN
TSMSYS	EXPIRED&LOCKED
WK_TEST	EXPIRED&LOCKED
WKPROXY	EXPIRED&LOCKED
WKSYS	EXPIRED&LOCKED
WMSYS	EXPIRED&LOCKED
XDB	EXPIRED&LOCKED

Table 8.1: *Default Accounts of Oracle 11g*

Default passwords are a serious threat and it is strongly recommended to change the passwords for all automatically created accounts right away after database creation. In previous releases, it was necessary to use home grown code to find out which accounts still used the default password. The data dictionary of an 11g database can be queried for user accounts which are still using the initial default password. The view *dba_users_with_defpwd* shows the DBA all accounts for which the password is still the default and thus should be changed immediately:

```
SYSTEM @ orcl111 SQL> SELECT * FROM dba_users_with_defpwd;

USERNAME
------------------------------
DIP
OUTLN
EXFSYS
XDB
WMSYS
```

Other Hacking Prevention Features

Oracle 11g automatically delays the logon prompt gradually after the third unsuccessful logon attempt for up to 10 seconds with each new attempt to logon with another password. Additionally, Oracle has introduced a number of new security parameters for the *spfile*, among others, to protect against denial of service and brute force attacks. Some of those parameters are covered next.

sec_max_failed_login_attempts specifies the number of unsuccessful authentication attempts from a client to the server before the client process is dropped. This parameter targets against brute force attacks with automated password crackers which try to attempt to create a server process in the first place and then issue an unlimited number of authentication requests by trying different user accounts and passwords in order to gain access to the database. The default value for this parameter is 10.

As an example, consider a logon script that has been created to try to logon as user lutz and uses different passwords one after the other. For the first 10 times, Oracle continues to throttle the logon prompt and after the 10th attempt, the account is automatically locked:

```
SQL> start logon
```

```
ERROR:
ORA-01017: invalid username/password; logon denied

Warning: You are no longer connected to ORACLE.
Elapsed: 00:00:00.10
ERROR:
ORA-01017: invalid username/password; logon denied

Elapsed: 00:00:00.19
ERROR:
ORA-01017: invalid username/password; logon denied

Elapsed: 00:00:00.28
ERROR:
ORA-01017: invalid username/password; logon denied
Elapsed: 00:00:01.39
ERROR:
ORA-01017: invalid username/password; logon denied

Elapsed: 00:00:03.49
ERROR:
ORA-01017: invalid username/password; logon denied

Elapsed: 00:00:06.58
ERROR:
ORA-01017: invalid username/password; logon denied

Elapsed: 00:00:10.68
ERROR:
ORA-01017: invalid username/password; logon denied

Elapsed: 00:00:15.79
ERROR:
ORA-01017: invalid username/password; logon denied

Elapsed: 00:00:21.95
ERROR:
ORA-01017: invalid username/password; logon denied

Elapsed: 00:00:29.13
ERROR:
ORA-28000: the account is locked

Elapsed: 00:00:29.47
ERROR:
ORA-28000: the account is locked

Elapsed: 00:00:29.83
ERROR:
ORA-28000: the account is locked
```

The parameters *sec_protocol_error_further_action* and *sec_protocol_error_trace_action* are parameters which specify how the database should react in case of denial of service attacks (DoS).

For those attacks, aggressive clients send packets through the Oracle Call Interface (OCI) which then causes very large dump files on the disk, leading to disk flooding and denial of service. *sec_protocol_error_further_action* defaults to CONTINUE.

> ● ※ With the default setting, the server is possibly subject to further attacks!

Sec_protocol_error_further_action can be set to:

- CONTINUE
- DELAY, n
- DROP, n .

With DELAY, n one can specify in seconds how long the server waits before it accepts further requests. This can prevent malicious clients from permanently consuming resources and, thus, slowing the system down. By setting the parameter to DROP, n, it specifies that the client connection will be dropped after the nth bad packet has been received.

Sec_protocol_error_trace_action defaults to TRACE. This is helpful for debugging if a client sends bad packets as the result of a bug because it creates the trace file on disk which can then be further analyzed. By setting this parameter to LOG, the creation of very large traces on disk can be prevented. The server then only creates a short message in the server trace file. Here, the danger of DoS is banned and the availability of the database server is protected. At the same time, a certain minimum amount of necessary auditing information is available. The setting ALERT causes a short message in the alert.logs in addition to the trace file created with *LOG*.

In order to reduce information about the database system a client receives as a banner when he logs on, it is possible to set *sec_return_server_release_banner* to TRUE. Then the Oracle server should not send information about the installed modules and the used version. This would make it more difficult to hack the database server because the aggressor cannot know the possible vulnerabilities. The default setting is FALSE and the instance must be restarted to make a change to this parameter effective.

With Release 11.1.0.6.0, this parameter does not really seem to work yet. There is not any visible difference in the returned banner on the system with either setting. For this test, REDHAT Advanced Server 4 was used with Oracle 11.1.0.6 Enterprise Edition. Also there is a misstatement in the server documentation for this parameter. It can only be set to TRUE or FALSE but not to YES or NO.

Auditing by DEFAULT in 11g

It is possible when creating a new 11g database with DBCA, as well as with DBUA, for a database upgrade to 11g to enable default security settings. These default settings include auditing settings for a number of system privileges. The parameter *audit_trail* is set to the value DB by default in 11g if the database was created with DBCA or upgraded to 11g with DBUA.

The table *aud$* is located in the system tablespace. The audit records should be archived and the table should be purged manually on a regular basis so it does not become too big because the system tablespace is auto extensible with an unlimited max size.

Here is a list of the privileges which are audited by access by default in 11g:

```
ALTER ANY PROCEDURE
ALTER ANY TABLE
ALTER DATABASE
ALTER PROFILE
AUDIT ROLE BY ACCESS
ALTER SYSTEM
ALTER USER
AUDIT SYSTEM
AUDIT SYSTEM BY ACCESS
CREATE ANY JOB
CREATE ANY LIBRARY
CREATE ANY PROCEDURE
CREATE ANY TABLE
CREATE EXTERNAL JOB
CREATE PUBLIC DATABASE LINK
CREATE SESSION
CREATE USER
DROP ANY PROCEDURE
DROP ANY TABLE
DROP PROFILE
DROP USER
EXEMPT ACCESS POLICY
GRANT ANY OBJECT PRIVILEGE
GRANT ANY PRIVILEGE
GRANT ANY ROLE
```

Strong Authentication for SYSDBA and SYSOPER in 11g

Connections with SYSDBA or SYSOPER privileges must always be authenticated. This is possible through OS authentication by assigning the appropriate OS group to the OS user. Another method is the use of a password file. If there is concern that the password file might be vulnerable, the following strong authentication methods can be used with Oracle database 11g:

- Oracle Internet Directory (OID) grants for SYSDBA and SYSOPER

- Kerberos ticket server

- Secure Socket Layer (SSL) certificates

In order to use OID, the parameter *ldap_directory_access* must be set to PASSWORD or SSL. If the intent is to use any of these strong authentication methods, the initialization parameter *ldap_directory_sysauth* must be set to YES. Its default is NO.

For strong authentication of SYSDBA and SYSOPER, a license is needed for the Advance Security Option.

Limiting Access to External Networking Services

It is possible to establish network connections from inside the database using TCP or higher network protocols. Oracle is shipped with a number of built-in packages for this such as UTL_TCP, UTL_HTTP, UTL_MAIL, UTL_INADDR, and UTL_SMTP.

In Oracle releases prior to 11g, the only way to limit access to the network via these packages was to restrict privileges on the packages. Since these packages are granted to PUBLIC by default, an intruder who gained access to the database could maliciously affect the network with them.

EXECUTE privileges on some of these packages are still granted to the user PUBLIC by default. This is no longer a serious security risk as it was in 10g and it does not create a violation of Oracle's built in policies in 11g.

With 11g, Oracle has introduced a more fine-grained control mechanism for outward bound network connections by restricting the hosts by which a database can connect. Oracle 11g database uses Access Control Lists (ACLs) to restrict the allowed target hosts. This feature greatly improves network security. Basically, there are two different ways to use this feature. Either method can be used to create and manage ACLs.

- using Oracle XML DB

- using the new packages *dbms_network_acl_admin* and *dbms_network_acl_utility*.

The application will encounter an ORA-24247 error if it relies on one of the network packages and no proper ACL has been created. For the use of the following packages, it is mandatory to have an ACL for the application user in place in 11g:

- UTL_TCP

- UTL_SMTP

- UTL_MAIL

- UTL_HTTP

- UTL_INADDR

These packages are running with invoker's privileges in 11g. The invoking user needs the connect privilege granted in the access control list assigned to the remote network host to which he wants to connect.

Figure 8.2 shows the page for security policies in the Enterprise Manager:

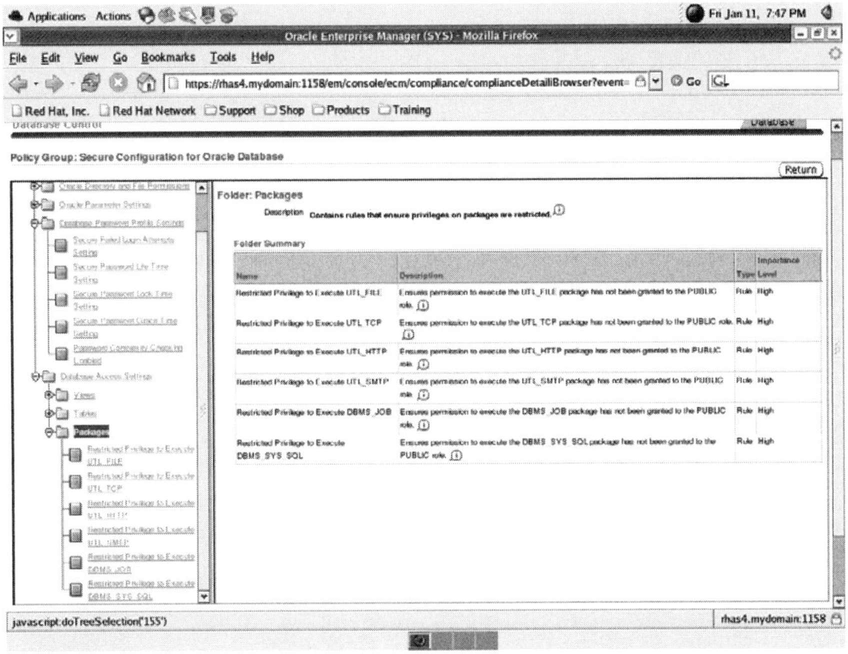

Figure 8.2: *Oracle Enterprise Manager Security Policies Screen*

> 🔔When upgrading a database to 11g and the application uses the ***UTL_TCP, UTL_SMTP, UTL_MAIL, UTL_HTTP,*** or ***UTL_INADDR*** packages, configure network access control lists (ACLs) in the database before these packages can work as they did in prior releases.

Following is the explanation for error ORA-24247:

```
[oracle@rhas4 ~]$ oerr ora 24247

24247, 00000, "network access denied by access control list (ACL)"
// *Cause:   No access control list (ACL) has been assigned to the
target
//          host or the privilege necessary to access the target
host has not
//          been granted to the user in the access control list.
// *Action: Ensure that an access control list (ACL) has been
assigned to
```

```
//              the target host and the privilege necessary to access
the target
//              host has been granted to the user.
```

How to create and manage ACLs with PL/SQL

ACLs are stored in XML DB. XML DB must be installed for the use of ACLs. The creation of ACLs is a two step procedure. The first step is to create the actual ACL and define the privileges for it. The general syntax is as follows.

```
BEGIN
DBMS_NETWORK_ACL_ADMIN.CREATE_ACL (
acl => 'file_name.xml',
description => 'file description',
principal => 'user_or_role',
is_grant => TRUE|FALSE,
privilege => 'connect|resolve',
start_date => null|timestamp_with_time_zone,
end_date => null|timestamp_with_time_zone);
END;
```

The value *connect* for the parameter *privilege* includes *resolve*. This is necessary for the package *UTL_INTADDR*. The parameter *principal* specifies the first username granted the ACL and is case sensitive. To grant multiple users, use the DBMS_NETWORK_ACL.ADD_PRIVILEGE procedure to add users. Here is an example for an ACL.

```
BEGIN
 DBMS_NETWORK_ACL_ADMIN.CREATE_ACL (
  acl => 'sysdba-ch-permissions.xml',
  description => 'Permissions for sysdba network',
  principal => 'LUTZ',
  is_grant => TRUE,
  privilege => 'connect');
END;
```

This creates an xml file which holds a list of users and privileges. This container is located under /sys/acl/ in the XML DB.

The second step is to assign network hosts to the ACL. After the creation of the ACL, hosts can be added to it. Below, again, is the general syntax.

```
BEGIN
DBMS_NETWORK_ACL_ADMIN.ASSIGN_ACL (
acl => 'file_name.xml',
host => 'network_host',
lower_port => null|port_number,
upper_port => null|port_number);
END;
```

And here is an example:

```
BEGIN
 DBMS_NETWORK_ACL_ADMIN.ASSIGN_ACL (
  acl => 'sysdba-ch-permissions.xml',
  host => '*.sysdba.ch',
  lower_port => 80,
  upper_port => null);
END;
```

There are also the DELETE_PRIVILEGE and DROP_ACL procedures in the package.

It is possible to use wildcards in the *hosts* parameter. This allows access to all hosts in the domain. Host names are case sensitive. An IP address as well as a DNS hostname can be used. Only one ACL can be assigned to a host or domain or IP subnet or port range, if specified. Multiple hosts can be assigned to the same ACL by calling DBMS_NETWORK_ACL_ADMIN.ASSIGN_ACL multiple times. Oracle evaluated ACLs in the following sequence:

- fully qualified hostnames are evaluated

- hostnames with ports

- partial domain names and sub-domains

> ☀ **Do not modify the xml files with a text editor!**

The data dictionary views related to ACLs are *dba_network_acls* and *dba_user_network_acl_privileges*:

```
LUTZ AS SYSDBA @ orcl SQL> DESC dba_network_acls

Name                           Null?     Type
---------------------------    --------  ----------------------------
HOST                           NOT NULL  VARCHAR2(1000)
LOWER_PORT                               NUMBER(5)
UPPER_PORT                               NUMBER(5)
ACL                                      VARCHAR2(4000)
ACLID                          NOT NULL  RAW(16)
```

```
LUTZ AS SYSDBA @ orcl SQL> DESC dba_network_acl_privileges

Name                           Null?     Type
---------------------------    --------  ----------------------------
ACL                                      VARCHAR2(4000)
ACLID                                    RAW(16)
PRINCIPAL                                VARCHAR2(4000)
PRIVILEGE                                VARCHAR2(7)
IS_GRANT                                 VARCHAR2(5)
INVERT                                   VARCHAR2(5)
START_DATE                               TIMESTAMP(9) WITH TIME ZONE
END_DATE                                 TIMESTAMP(9) WITH TIME ZONE
```

How to create and manage ACLs with OEM

The friends of graphical interfaces can also create and manage ACLs. There is an interface to the XML DB integrated into the Enterprise Manager. Access Control Lists are an XML DB functionality. The link for the ACLs is located in the SCHEMA pane in Database Control 11g in Figure 8.3:

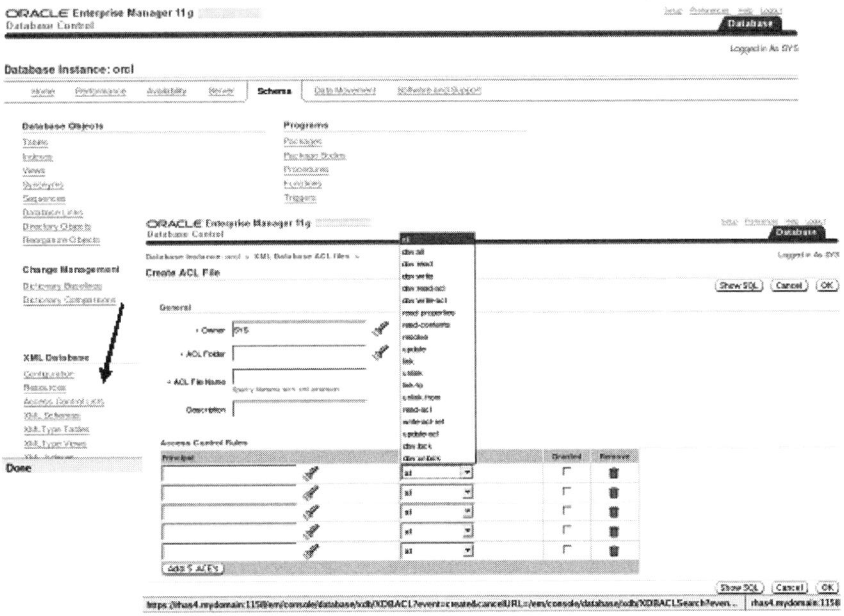

Figure 8.3: *SCHEMA Screen – Database Instance: orcl*

Other network security features

The listener is secured by default in 11g. It is not possible to manage the listener from remote any longer without a password or Class of Secure Transports (COST). Only the local user who started the listener can stop it in 11g.

```
STATUS of the LISTENER
-----------------------
Alias                    LISTENER
Version                  TNSLSNR for Linux: Version 11.1.0.6.0 - Production
Start Date               25-JAN-2008 05:57:03
Uptime                   0 days 0 hr. 0 min. 1 sec
Trace Level              off
Security                 ON: Local OS Authentication
SNMP                     OFF
Listener Parameter File  /u01/app/oracle/product/11.1.6/db_1/network/admin/list
ener.ora
Listener Log File        /u01/app/oracle/diag/tnslsnr/rhas4/listener/alert/log.
xml
Listening Endpoints Summary...
  (DESCRIPTION=(ADDRESS=(PROTOCOL=tcp)(HOST=rhas4.mydomain)(PORT=1521)))
Services Summary...
Service "orcl" has 1 instance(s).
  Instance "orcl", status UNKNOWN, has 1 handler(s) for this service...
```

> 🔔There is still a default listener with the name LISTENER and port 1521!

Transparent Data Encryption Features in 11g

External Master Key Storage using Hardware Security Module

Transparent Data Encryption (TDE) was introduced in release 10g. It can be used to encrypt column data inside the database. A wallet is used to store an encryption master key that is used to encrypt the keys and these are used to encrypt the actual data in the columns. The wallet can be located in a secure location on disk and Oracle Net Services can be used to determine the location of the wallet on disk. This configuration is secure enough for most environments. However, the master key must be kept in memory for the cryptographic operations such as encrypting and decrypting.

A potential hacker could use various methods to dump the memory buffers with the master key and retrieve the master key from the dump file. In order to further improve protection of the master key, Oracle has introduced the ability to store the master key on an external hardware module called Hardware Security Module (HSM). This is special hardware which is attached to the database server. The hardware vendor ships a shared library that functions as a plug-in and must be copied to the database server. The database uses a dedicated user account to communicate with the hardware module. The PKCS#11 library should be located for UNIX in:

- /opt/oracle/extapi/[32,64]/hsm/{VENDOR}/{VERSION}/libapiname.ext

For Windows in:

- %SYSTEM_DRIVE%\oracle\extapi\[32,64]\hsm\{VENDOR}\{VERSION}\libapiname.ext

  - [32, 64] here stands for the 32 bit resp. 64 bit version, the prefix lib is mandatory for the API-name.

The HSM provides storage for the master key as well as memory for cryptographic operations such as encryption and decryption. The use of Hardware Security Module needs the Advanced Security Option to be installed, which is an extra cost. In order to configure the usage of an HSM, you need to issue the following command:

```
ALTER SYSTEM SET ENCRYPTION KEY IDENTIFIED BY user_Id:password;
```

Here, *user_id* is the identifier for an already existing Oracle user account which is used especially for the communication between the database and the HSM. If there is an existing wallet, add the MIGRATE USING <wallet_password> syntax in order to decrypt the existing column keys and re-encrypt them with the newly created HSM related master key:

```
ALTER SYSTEM SET ENCRYPTION KEY IDENTIFIED BY user_Id:password
MIGRATE USING <wallet_password>;
```

All cryptographic operations are performed in the external hardware based storage and the master key is never located in the database server's memory. The HSM is only used to encrypt the column keys which are passed to the database afterwards. Oracle recommends using the Advanced Security Network Encryption Option to encrypt the traffic between the database server and the HSM. The use of a HSM makes it possible to use the same master key for multiple databases as well as for multiple instances in a Real Application Cluster (RAC).

A Hardware Security Module cannot be used for tablespace encryption, encrypted exports and encrypted RMAN backups. These functionalities need access to the software wallet.

TDE with Logminer and Logical Standby Database

With Oracle database 10g, TDE could not be used by Logminer. Since data gets encrypted in the datafiles, including the undo segments as well as the redo logs, it was not possible to use TDE for Logical Standby Database because log miner could not handle encrypted data in prior releases. Starting with release 11g, this functionality has been added to log miner. This makes it possible now to use TDE for a Logical Standby Database.

The wallet needs to be opened and reachable for Logminer to decrypt the column data. The wallet on the standby location is a copy of the wallet on the primary site. The passwords used to open the wallet can be different on the primary and standby sites. The master key is only changeable on the primary site. An attempt to change it on the standby site would raise an error. After changing the master key on the primary site, the wallet needs to be copied to the standby site.

It is possible to use different column keys and encryption algorithms on the standby and primary site. It could be changed with the following command:

```
SYSTEM @ orcl SQL> ALTER TABLE my_tab REKEY USING '3DES168';
```

There is no need to change the master key or the wallet password to re-key a table. To change the encryption algorithm for a table, set the Data Guard to NONE.

Logminer uses the dynamic view *v$logmnr_contents* to populate the decrypted data into it. This view is only accessible if the database is mounted.

```
LUTZ AS SYSDBA @ orcl SQL> desc v$logmnr_contents
```

Name	Null?	Type
SCN		NUMBER
START_SCN		NUMBER
COMMIT_SCN		NUMBER
TIMESTAMP		DATE
START_TIMESTAMP		DATE
COMMIT_TIMESTAMP		DATE
XIDUSN		NUMBER
XIDSLT		NUMBER
XIDSQN		NUMBER
XID		RAW(8)
PXIDUSN		NUMBER
PXIDSLT		NUMBER
PXIDSQN		NUMBER
PXID		RAW(8)
TX_NAME		VARCHAR2(256)
OPERATION		VARCHAR2(32)
OPERATION_CODE		NUMBER
ROLLBACK		NUMBER
SEG_OWNER		VARCHAR2(32)
SEG_NAME		VARCHAR2(256)
TABLE_NAME		VARCHAR2(32)
SEG_TYPE		NUMBER
SEG_TYPE_NAME		VARCHAR2(32)
TABLE_SPACE		VARCHAR2(32)
ROW_ID		VARCHAR2(18)
USERNAME		VARCHAR2(30)
OS_USERNAME		VARCHAR2(4000)
MACHINE_NAME		VARCHAR2(4000)
AUDIT_SESSIONID		NUMBER
SESSION#		NUMBER

```
SERIAL#                    NUMBER
SESSION_INFO               VARCHAR2(4000)
THREAD#                     NUMBER
SEQUENCE#                   NUMBER
RBASQN                      NUMBER
RBABLK                      NUMBER
RBABYTE                     NUMBER
UBAFIL                      NUMBER
UBABLK                      NUMBER
UBAREC                      NUMBER
UBASQN                      NUMBER
ABS_FILE#                   NUMBER
REL_FILE#                   NUMBER
DATA_BLK#                   NUMBER
DATA_OBJ#                   NUMBER
DATA_OBJV#                  NUMBER
DATA_OBJD#                  NUMBER
SQL_REDO                    VARCHAR2(4000)
SQL_UNDO                    VARCHAR2(4000)
RS_ID                       VARCHAR2(32)
SSN                         NUMBER
CSF                         NUMBER
INFO                        VARCHAR2(32)
STATUS                      NUMBER
REDO_VALUE                  NUMBER
UNDO_VALUE                  NUMBER
SAFE_RESUME_SCN             NUMBER
CSCN                        NUMBER
OBJECT_ID                   RAW(16)
```

> 🔔 The use of Hardware Security Modules is not supported for Logminer in 11g release 1!

TDE with Export Data Pump

Oracle 11g export data pump comes with a number of new parameters related to TDE. It is now possible to create entire dumpfile sets which are encrypted and compressed.

The parameter *encryption* can be used to encrypt the following:

- column data only
- metadata only
- both column data and metadata.

encryption_algorithm defaults to AES128. Possible values are AES192 or AES256. If one does not specify either the *encryption* or *encryption_password* parameter at the same time, an error is returned by expdp. *encryption_mode* defaults to DUAL if the wallet is open at export time. If the wallet is closed during the export, the parameter defaults to PASSWORD.

> 🔔These parameters are only available for Enterprise Edition and require the extra cost Advanced Security Option ($ 10'000/CPU)

Expdp can use a master key located in a secure wallet, a password, or use the dual mode. The value PASSWORD requires the specification of a password for the export and the same password must be used for the import. The encrypted export dumpfile set can be securely transported to a remote site with this mode. The value DUAL creates a dumpfile set which can be decrypted on the target site using either a password if there is no wallet available or with a wallet.

The DUAL mode comes in handy if the export dump set is created using a wallet and might be used for import on another site without a wallet in place. The value TRANSPARENT should only be used if the dump set is used for import into the same database which it was created from. Then no interaction of the DBA is required.

> 🔔The parameter *encryption_password* cannot be used in combination with TRANSPARENT.

Transparent Tablespace Encryption

In 10g, it is only possible to enable table TDE for particular columns in tables. This made it difficult to analyze an application and keep an overview of all relevant columns with sensitive personal data.

Transparent (Tablespace) Encryption is part of the extra cost Advanced Security Option. Starting with Oracle Database 11g, it is possible to encrypt entire tablespaces. This makes it much easier to see that all relevant data is encrypted because everything that is put into such a tablespace gets encrypted automatically.

In order to use encrypted tablespaces, create a master encryption key for tablespaces. This is a different master form the one used for TDE. The syntax to create the master key for tablespace encryption is the same as for the creation of the TDE master key:

```
LUTZ AS SYSDBA @ orcl SQL> ALTER SYSTEM SET ENCRYPTION KEY <my_key>;
```

This command creates a master key for column encryption with TDE as well as a master key for tablespace encryption in an external encrypted wallet. This wallet is the same wallet which is used for the TDE master keys. The location of the wallet is specified in the *sqlnet.ora* file with the parameters *encryption_wallen_location* or *wallet_location*

The status of the wallet can be viewed using the view *v$encryption_wallet*.

```
LUTZ AS SYSDBA @ orcl SQL> SELECT * FROM v$encryption_wallet;

WRL_TYPE    WRL_PARAMETER                STATUS
--------    -------------------------    ---------
file        /etc/ORACLE/WALLETS/oracle/  OPEN
```

If a 10g database that used TDE has been upgraded to 11g and a tablespace encryption needs to be used after the upgrade, reissue this command after setting the *compatible* parameter to 11.1. This will re-create the TDE master key and add the tablespace master key to the wallet.

For the use of a Hardware Security Module, the tablespace encryption master key must have been created first before the HSM is configured, as covered in the previous HSM section. Here is the syntax for encrypted tablespaces:

```
SQL> CREATE TABLESPACE encr_ts
    DATAFILE '/u01/app/oracle/oradata/orcl/encr_ts_01.dbf' SIZE 100M
    ENCRYPTION USING '3DES168'
    DEFAULT STORAGE (ENCRYPT);
```

In the encryption clause, the algorithm to use is specified. Valid values for the algorithms are 3DES168, AES128, AES192, and AES256. The default is AES128. The view *v$encrypted_tablespaces* show in detail information about the tablespace properties:

```
LUTZ AS SYSDBA @ orcl SQL> DESC v$encrypted_tablespaces;

Name                                     Null?    Type
---------------------------------------- -------- ----------------
TS#                                               NUMBER
ENCRYPTIONALG                                     VARCHAR2(7)
ENCRYPTEDTS                                       VARCHAR2(3)
```

Data from encrypted tablespaces is protected on the temporary tablespace during sort and join operations. This also applies to undo and redo information for encrypted data.

NOTE: It is not possible to transport an encrypted tablespace cross platform. Re-keying is not supported for encrypted tablespaces and only permanent tablespaces can be encrypted. Data stored outside the database, namely *BFILES* and *External Tables,* cannot be encrypted

Index range scans can be performed on data in encrypted tablespaces, but are not supported for single columns encrypted with TDE.

Encryption for tablespaces is always "salted".

Transparent Data Encryption Features in 11g   **243**

TDE with Enterprise Manager

TDE is now fully integrated into OEM. The interface to TDE is found in the SERVER pane. It is possible to change the wallet location and to recreate the master key. On the TDE page, find links to all related functionalities such as Export/Import, Tables, and Tablespaces at the bottom as shown in Figure 8.4.

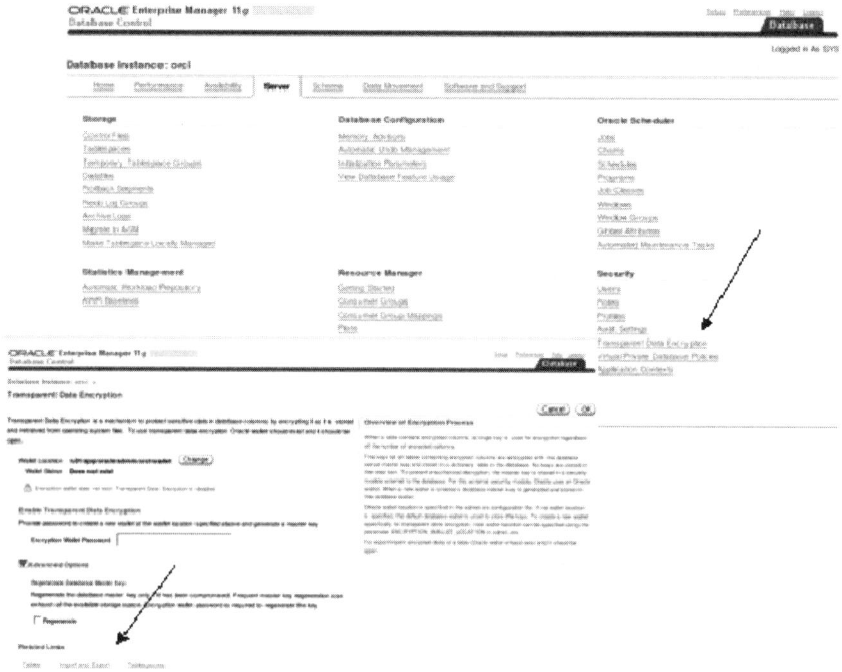

Figure 8.4: *Screen for Changing Wallet Location and Master Key*

Intelligent LOB Encryption with Secure File LOBs

Many applications need to store large amounts of unstructured data in the form of files such as images of checks and X-rays as well as other scanned documents like invoices, article drafts or satellite images. This is a big challenge in terms of performance and can be a severe security risk.

With Release 11g, Oracle has extended the TDE functionality for LOBs. Oracle has completely reinvented the LOB datatype to improve performance and security. This new LOB datatype data is always stored inside the database and it comes with benefits such as file system like logging.

Performance tests have shown that query read access is up to 2 times faster and inserting can even be up to 5 times faster compared with conventional LOBs, which are called basicfile LOBs. Securefile LOBs even outperform Linux NFS/EXT3 files system at all file sizes.

Securefiles are fully compatible with the traditional LOB interfaces such as JDBC (Java thick and thin clients), ODBC, OCI, and .NET. PL/SQL and applications can fully transparently take advantage of securefile LOBs.

It is possible to use operating system interfaces to access securefile LOBs through the WebDAV servers of Oracle XML DB or Oracle Content DB. Data can be accessed using protocols such as WebDAV, HTTP, NFS and FTP. The new securefile LOB columns can be compressed and they support de-duplication file systems like logging and encryption. For compression and de-duplication the Advanced Compression Option is needed at an added cost.

This chapter will go over the security aspects of securefile LOBs without going into detail about features like compression and de-duplication. The following Oracle products use securefile LOBs as underlying storage:

- XML DB

- Oracle Spatial

- Oracle Multimedia

- Content DB

For encrypted securefile LOBs, the Advanced Security Option is needed. The following encryption algorithms are supported for securefile LOBS:

- 3DES168:   Triple Data Encryption Standard with a 168-bit key size

- AES128:   Advanced Encryption Standard with a 128 bit key size

- AES192:   Advanced Encryption Standard with a 192-bit key size

- AES256:   Advanced Encryption Standard with a 256-bit key size

Securefile LOBs are fully capable of the following Oracle features:

- Transactions and Read Consistency

- Flashback

- Backward Compatibility with LOB Interfaces

- Readable Standby

- Consistent Backup

- Point in Time Recovery

- Fine Grained Auditing

- Label Security

- XML indexing, XML Queries, XPath

- Real Application Clusters (RAC)

- Automatic Storage Management (ASM)
- Partitioning

Securefile Lobs at work

The dynamic parameter *db_securefile* is used to specify how to store large objects by default. LOBs can now be stored as securefiles or basicfiles. By default, Oracle 11g allows for the use of both securefile and basicfile LOBs in the same database. The parameter can be changed with an ALTER SYSTEM statement. Below is a listing of possible settings:

- never: disallows creation LOBs as securefiles
- ignore: ignores all securefile and securefile options are ignored
- always: attempts to create LOBs as securefiles but falls back to basicfiles if specified other
- force: enforces all LOBs to be created as securefiles
- permitted (DEFAULT): allows for securefile LOBs to be created

```
LUTZ AS SYSDBA @ orcl SQL> show parameter securefile

NAME                                  TYPE        VALUE
------------------------------------  ----------  -------------------
db_securefile                         string      PERMITTED
```

Securefile LOBs can only be stored in tablespaces that use Automatic Segment Space Management (ASSM). The encryption wallet must be opened to use TDE for LOBs:

```
LUTZ AS SYSDBA @ orcl SQL> ALTER SYSTEM SET ENCRYPTION WALLET OPEN
IDENTIFIED BY "lutz1234";
```

System altered.

The status of the wallet is visible through *v$encryption_wallet*.

```
LUTZ AS SYSDBA @ orcl SQL> SELECT * FROM v$encryption_wallet;

WRL_TYPE             WRL_PARAMETER                           STATUS
-------------------- --------------------------------------- -------
file                 /etc/ORACLE/WALLETS/oracle              OPEN
```

```
LUTZ AS SYSDBA @ orcl SQL> SELECT tablespace_name,
                           encrypted,
                           extent_management,
                           segment_space_management
                      FROM dba_tablespaces;
```

```
TABLESPACE_NAME                 ENC EXTENT_MAN SEGMEN
------------------------------- --- ---------- ------
SYSTEM                          NO  LOCAL      MANUAL
SYSAUX                          NO  LOCAL      AUTO
UNDOTBS1                        NO  LOCAL      MANUAL
TEMP                            NO  LOCAL      MANUAL
USERS                           NO  LOCAL      AUTO
ENCRYPT_TS                      NO  LOCAL      AUTO
```

```
SYTEM @ orcl SQL> ALTER USER lutz DEFAULT TABLESPACE encrypt_ts
QUOTA UNLIMITED ON encrypt_ts;
```

Create a table with an encrypted lob column:

```
LUTZ @ orcl SQL> SELECT CREATE TABLE encrypt_01(
    id NUMBER,
    resume_pdf CLOB ENCRYPT USING 'AES128' )
  LOB(resume_pdf) STORE AS SECUREFILE
  (DEDUPLICATE LOB CACHE NOLOGGING);
```

In the CREATE TABLE statement, the choice has been made to
use the 128-bit size Advanced Encryption Standard key for the
column RESUME_PDF which will use securefile lobs with de-
duplication.

If the STORE AS SECUREFILE clause is omitted, Oracle will
use basicfile LOB as the default for backward compatibility. Then
check for securefile LOB segments by using the view
dba_segments:

```
LUTZ AS SYSDBA @ orcl SQL> SELECT segment_name, segment_type,
segment_subtype
                  FROM dba_segments
```

```
                              WHERE tablespace_name='ENCRYPT_TS';


SEGMENT_NAME                           SEGMENT_TYPE         SEGMENT_SU
------------------------------------   ------------------   ----------
ENCRYPT_01                             TABLE                ASSM
SYS_IL0000060728C00002$$               LOBINDEX             ASSM
SYS_LOB0000060728C00002$$              LOBSEGMENT           SECUREFILE
```

The views *_encrypted_columns show the details about encrypted columns in the database:

```
LUTZ  @ orcl SQL> SELECT * FROM user_encrypted_columns;


TABLE_NAME      COLUMN_NAME        ENCRYPTION_ALG        SAL
-----------     -------------      ----------------      -----
ENCRYPT_01      RESUME_PDF         AES 128 bits key      YES
```

The properties of the lob segments are visible via the *_lobs views:

```
LUTZ  @ orcl SQL>  SELECT table_name,
                          securefile,
                          segment_name,
                          column_name,
                          encrypt,
                          compression,
                          deduplication
                   FROM user_lobs;

TABLE_NAME SEC SEGMENT_NAME                 COLUMN_NAM ENCR COMPRE
DEDUPLICATION
---------- --- ------------------------- ---------- ---- ------ ----
----------
ENCRYPT_01 YES SYS_LOB0000060728C00002$$ RESUME_PDF YES  NO     LOB
```

The overloaded procedure space_usage from the package *dbms_space* can be used to monitor the LOB segments. There is one procedure for basicfiles and one for securefile LOB segments:

```
LUTZ  @ orcl SQL> DESC dbms_space

PROCEDURE SPACE_USAGE
```

Intelligent LOB Encryption with Secure File LOBs **249**

```
Argument Name                   Type                  In/Out Default?
------------------------------  --------------------  ------ --------
SEGMENT_OWNER                   VARCHAR2              IN
SEGMENT_NAME                    VARCHAR2              IN
SEGMENT_TYPE                    VARCHAR2              IN
UNFORMATTED_BLOCKS              NUMBER                OUT
UNFORMATTED_BYTES               NUMBER                OUT
FS1_BLOCKS                      NUMBER                OUT
FS1_BYTES                       NUMBER                OUT
FS2_BLOCKS                      NUMBER                OUT
FS2_BYTES                       NUMBER                OUT
FS3_BLOCKS                      NUMBER                OUT
FS3_BYTES                       NUMBER                OUT
FS4_BLOCKS                      NUMBER                OUT
FS4_BYTES                       NUMBER                OUT
FULL_BLOCKS                     NUMBER                OUT
FULL_BYTES                      NUMBER                OUT
PARTITION_NAME                  VARCHAR2              IN     DEFAULT

PROCEDURE SPACE_USAGE
Argument Name                   Type                  In/Out Default?
------------------------------  --------------------  ------ --------
SEGMENT_OWNER                   VARCHAR2              IN
SEGMENT_NAME                    VARCHAR2              IN
SEGMENT_TYPE                    VARCHAR2              IN
SEGMENT_SIZE_BLOCKS             NUMBER                OUT
SEGMENT_SIZE_BYTES              NUMBER                OUT
USED_BLOCKS                     NUMBER                OUT
USED_BYTES                      NUMBER                OUT
EXPIRED_BLOCKS                  NUMBER                OUT
EXPIRED_BYTES                   NUMBER                OUT
UNEXPIRED_BLOCKS                NUMBER                OUT
UNEXPIRED_BYTES                 NUMBER                OUT
PARTITION_NAME                  VARCHAR2              IN     DEFAULT
```

This is the procedure to use for securefile LOB segments:

```
PROCEDURE UNUSED_SPACE
Argument Name                   Type                  In/Out Default?
------------------------------  --------------------  ------ --------
SEGMENT_OWNER                   VARCHAR2              IN
SEGMENT_NAME                    VARCHAR2              IN
SEGMENT_TYPE                    VARCHAR2              IN
TOTAL_BLOCKS                    NUMBER                OUT
TOTAL_BYTES                     NUMBER                OUT
UNUSED_BLOCKS                   NUMBER                OUT
UNUSED_BYTES                    NUMBER                OUT
LAST_USED_EXTENT_FILE_ID        NUMBER                OUT
LAST_USED_EXTENT_BLOCK_ID       NUMBER                OUT
LAST_USED_BLOCK                 NUMBER                OUT
PARTITION_NAME                  VARCHAR2              IN     DEFAULT
```

Here is an example of how to use the *dbms_space.space_usage*:

```
LUTZ   @ orcl SQL>

BEGIN
  dbms_space.space_usage
  (
    'LUTZ',
    SYS_LOB0000060728C00002$$',
    'LOB',
  segment_size_blocks  => :seg_size_blcks,
  segment_size_bytes   => :seg_size_bytes,
  used_blocks          => :u_blcks,
  used_bytes           => :u_bytes,
  expired_blocks       => :exp_blcks,
  expired_bytes        => :exp_bytes,
  unexpired_blocks     => :unexp_blcks,
  unexpired_bytes      => :unexp_bytes
  );
END;
/
```

PL/SQL procedure successfully completed.

```
LUTZ   @ orcl SQL> PRINT seg_size_bytes u_blcks u_bytes exp_blcks
exp_bytes unexp_blcks unexp_bytes;
```

```
SEG_SIZE_BYTES U_BLCKS U_BYTES EXP_BLCKS EXP_BYTES UNEXP_BLCKS
UNEXP_BYTES
-------------- ------- ------- --------- --------- ----------- -----
------

       131072       5   40960         0         0           0       0
```

Here are a few more examples for securefile LOB columns:

```
LUTZ   @ orcl SQL> CREATE TABLE encrypt_02 (
 id NUMBER, resume_xls  CLOB)
 LOB(resume_xls) STORE AS SECUREFILE            -- store as
securefiles
        (COMPRESS HIGH                          -- compress
          RETENTION MIN 3600                    -- keep undo for at
least 1 hour
                                                -- DEFAULT is
RETENTION AUTO
        KEEP_DUPLICATES                            -- do not de-
duplicate
        CACHE READS                             -- cache only when
reading
        NOLOGGING                               -- do not create redo
for DML
        );
```

```
LUTZ  @ orcl SQL> CREATE TABLE encrypt_03
 (id NUMBER, resume_doc  CLOB)                  -- store as
encrypted
 LOB(resume_doc) STORE AS SECUREFILE (ENCRYPT); -- securefiles
using default
                                                -- algorithm AES192


LUTZ  @ orcl SQL> CREATE TABLE encrypt_04
 (id NUMBER, resume_doc  CLOB ENCRYPT)          -- store as
encrypted
 LOB(resume_doc) STORE AS SECUREFILE;           -- securefiles
using default
                                                -- algorithm AES192
```

The second and third example have the same results, it is just different syntax.

The Cache Option defaults to NOCACHE. Possible values are as follows:

- CACHE: Oracle places LOB data into the buffer cache which provides fast access. CACHE is only supported in combination with the logging option.

- NOCACHE: LOB values are not placed into the buffer cache.

- CACHE READS: LOB values are placed into the buffer cache but only for read operations. Write operations are not cached.

- NOCACHE (default)

Oracle 11g uses a cache called SHARED I/O POOL for securefile LOBs operations if NOCACHE is used for the LOBs. Oracle can automatically adjust the size of this cache to up to 4% of the buffer cache. The default size of shared I/O pool is 0:

```
LUTZ AS SYSDBA @ orcl SQL>  SELECT * FROM v$sgainfo
```

```
NAME                                BYTES RES
-------------------------------- ---------- ---
Fixed SGA Size                     1300380 No
Redo Buffers                       6119424 No
Buffer Cache Size                213909504 Yes
Shared Pool Size                 201326592 Yes
Large Pool Size                    4194304 Yes
Java Pool Size                     4194304 Yes
Streams Pool Size                        0 Yes
Shared IO Pool Size                      0 Yes
Granule Size                       4194304 No
Maximum SGA Size                 431046656 No
Startup overhead in Shared Pool   46137344 No
Free SGA Memory Available                0

12 rows selected.
```

The shared I/O pool uses shared memory and, therefore, can be used by large concurrent operations of securefile LOBs. If the memory for the shared I/O pool is too small for a large securefile LOB operation, the server process will temporarily utilize PGA memory until enough shared memory is available again.

Securefile LOBs can be created with different LOGGING options. The default is LOGGING that creates redo records for the creation of the LOB segment as well as for the subsequent changes.

Another alternative is FILESYSTEM_LIKE_LOGGING. This only create redo for the metadata of the securefile LOB. This reduces the mean time to recover in case of an instance crash. At the same time, full data recoverability is ensured. The drawback here is that data can change during an online backup which would lead to inconsistency. This would be fatal in case of media recovery being necessary.

> Make sure that LOGGING is enforced for the lob storage during online backups!
> Make sure that all redo which was generated during the online backup is archived!

Here is the syntax to enforce logging and to disable it again:

```
LUTZ AS SYSDBA @ orcl SQL> ALTER DATABASE FORCE LOGGING;
...
LUTZ AS SYSDBA @ orcl SQL> ALTER DATABASE NO FORCE LOGGING;
```

It is also possible to use ALTER TABLE to modify the properties of securefile LOB columns:

```
ALTER TABLE encrypt_03 MODIFY LOB (resume_doc) (KEEP_DUPLICATES);
ALTER TABLE encrypt_03 MODIFY LOB (resume_doc) (DEDUPLICATE LOB);
ALTER TABLE encrypt_03 MODIFY PARTITION p1 LOB (resume_doc)
(DEDUPLICATE LOB);


ALTER TABLE encrypt_03 MODIFY LOB (resume_doc) (NOCOMPRESS);
ALTER TABLE encrypt_03 MODIFY LOB (resume_doc) (COMPRESS HIGH);
ALTER TABLE encrypt_03 MODIFY PARTITION p1 LOB (resume_doc)
(COMPRESS HIGH);


ALTER TABLE encrypt_03 MODIFY (resume_doc CLOB ENCRYPT USING
'3DES168');
ALTER TABLE encrypt_03 MODIFY PARTITION p1 LOB (resume_doc) (
ENCRYPT );
ALTER TABLE encrypt_03 MODIFY (resume_doc CLOB ENCRYPT IDENTIFIED BY
lutz1234);
```

Although it is possible to use the ALTER TABLE statement to enable encryption, compression or de-duplication of securefile LOBs after the creation, Oracle recommends using ONLINE REDEFINITION for such operations.

The ENCRYPT and DECRYPT keywords can only be used to encrypt not yet encrypted or decrypt already encrypted LOB columns.

> 💣 If one tries to encrypt an already encrypted column, Oracle will return an error ORA-28334.

```
LUTZ  @ orcl SQL> alter table encrypt_01 modify (resume_pdf CLOB
encrypt using 'AES192');
alter table encrypt_01 modify (resume_pdf CLOB encrypt using
'AES192')
                                 *
ERROR at line 1:
ORA-28334: column is already encrypted
```

```
[oracle@rhas4 ~]$ oerr ora 28334
28334, 0000, "column is already encrypted"
// *Cause: An attempt was made to encrypt an encrypted column.
//
// *Action:
//
```

Lobs can only be encrypted on a per column basis. Transparently Encrypted Exports of securefile LOBs are only possible with ORACLE datapump (expdp). The same is true for transportable tablespaces with securefile lobs.

> 🔔 **Table shrinking** is not supported for securefile LOBs in Oracle 11g.

Securefile Lobs at work with OEM

Oracle Enterprise Manager fully supports the creation of securefile LOB columns as shown in Figure 8.5.

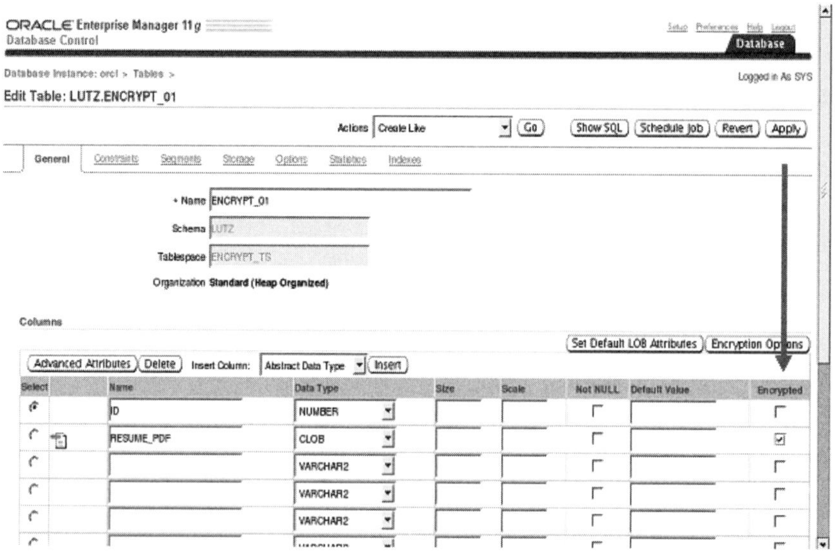

Figure 8.5: *Creating Securefile Lob Columns*

With the Encryption Options button, the page is reached where it can be specified as to which encryption algorithm is to be used for the column on the Encryption Options screen.

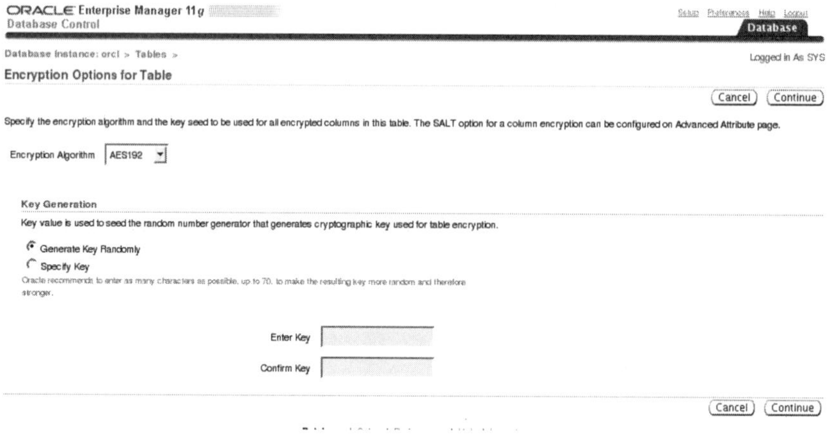

Figure 8.6: *Encryption Options Screen*

The Set Default LOB Attributes button leads to the place where the lob type securefile or basicfile can be specified and the tablespace to use for the log segment as well as caching options:

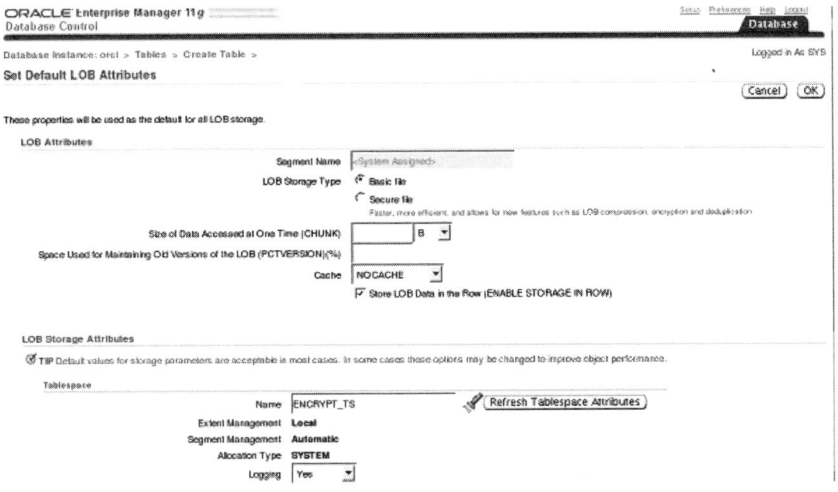

Figure 8.7: *Set Default LOB Attributes Screen*

Virtual Private Catalogues for RMAN

Previously, the recovery catalog owner had full access to all backup information in the recovery catalog. Before Oracle's version 11g, there was no way to restrict access to limited parts of the catalog for users who had the *recovery_catalog_owner* privileges. Either a user had full access or no access to the catalog.

Oracle 11g now comes with the possibility to create virtual private catalogs which makes it easy to limit access to backup information selectively for multiple users and thus, separate responsibilities by restrictive grants on clearly defined parts of the catalog. A virtual private catalog is a subset of the base recovery catalog.

The catalog owner is the master of the base catalog and has access to all the metadata of the catalog. This user has full control over the privileges on all backups for all registered databases.

The metadata in the catalog includes the following information:

- Backup sets and backup pieces containing datafiles and archived redo logfiles
- Datafile copies
- Archived redo logs and their copies
- Structure of the target database including historical information
- Stored scripts, which can be target specific or global scripts since 10g
- Persistent RMAN configurations

The owner of the base catalog can use the new RMAN commands *grant* and *revoke* to limit access on subsets of the catalog to certain users of the same recovery catalog database. These users are called virtual catalog owners. In their schemas, a set of views and synonyms is stored.

In the following section, this chapter demonstrates what virtual private catalogs are and how to use them. The example uses the following four databases:

- rcat11g   recovery catalog database
- prod11g1   single instance target
- prod11g2   single instance target
- rac11g   cluster database target

As a first step, the recovery catalog master and two virtual catalog owners are created:

```
LUTZ AS SYSDBA @rcat11g SQL> CREATE USER rcat_master IDENTIFIED BY
ORACLE1
  2   DEFAULT TABLESPACE rman_ts
  3   QUOTA UNLIMITED ON rman_ts;
User created.
LUTZ AS SYSDBA @rcat11g SQL> CREATE USER rac_vpc IDENTIFIED BY
oracle1
  2   DEFAULT TABLESPACE rman_vpcs
  3   QUOTA UNLIMITED ON  rman_vpcs;
User created.
LUTZ AS SYSDBA @rcat11g SQL> CREATE USER prod_vpc IDENTIFIED BY
oracle1
  2   DEFAULT TABLESPACE rman_vpcs
  3   QUOTA UNLIMITED ON  rman_vpcs;
User created.
LUTZ AS SYSDBA @rcat11g SQL> GRANT recovery_catalog_owner TO
rcat_master;
Grant succeeded.
LUTZ AS SYSDBA @rcat11g SQL> GRANT recovery_catalog_owner TO
rac_vpc;
Grant succeeded.
LUTZ AS SYSDBA @rcat11g SQL> GRANT recovery_catalog_owner TO
prod_vpc;
Grant succeeded.
```

Two different tablespaces have been used for the base catalog and the virtual catalog owners. The goal is to be independent for possible upgrading in the future and for export. Also, all the users have been granted full access to the base catalog at the beginning.

The owner of the base catalog as well as the owners of the virtual private catalogs needs the *recovery_catalog_owner* role. If the virtual catalog owner tries to create a virtual catalog and does not have the *recovery_catalog_owner* role, the following error is thrown by RMAN:

```
RMAN> create virtual catalog;
RMAN-00571:
============================================================
RMAN-00569: =============== ERROR MESSAGE STACK FOLLOWS
==============
RMAN-00571:
============================================================
RMAN-06426: RECOVERY_CATALOG_OWNER role must be granted to user LUTZ
```

```
[oracle@rac11b-pub ~]$ oerr rman 6426
6426, 1, "RECOVERY_CATALOG_OWNER role must be granted to user %s"
```

```
// *Cause:  The CREATE CATALOG or UPGRADE CATALOG command was used,
but the
//          USERID that was supplied in the CATALOG connect string
does not
//          have the RECOVERY_CATALOG_OWNER role granted as a
DEFAULT role.
// *Action: Grant the RECOVERY_CATALOG_OWNER role to the recovery
catalog
//          owner.
```

It is necessary for the next step that the master of the base catalog makes sure that no one but them can gain access to the full catalog by creating the catalog and grant access to parts of the catalog to the virtual catalog owners.

```
[oracle@rac11b-pub ~]$ rman target sys/oracle1@prod11g2 catalog
rcat_master/oracle1@rcat11g

Recovery Manager: Release 11.1.0.6.0 - Production on Sun Jan 27
01:33:44 2008
Copyright (c) 1982, 2007, Oracle.  All rights reserved.

connected to target database: PROD11G1 (DBID=1350648997)
connected to recovery catalog database

RMAN> CREATE CATALOG;

recovery catalog created
```

Then all other target databases are registered in the catalog:

```
RMAN> REGISTER DATABASE;

database registered in recovery catalog
starting full resync of recovery catalog
full resync complete

[oracle@rac11b-pub ~]$ rman target sys/oracle1@prod11g2 catalog
rcat_master/oracle1@rcat11g

Recovery Manager: Release 11.1.0.6.0 - Production on Sun Jan 27
01:35:26 2008
Copyright (c) 1982, 2007, Oracle.  All rights reserved.
connected to target database: PROD11G2 (DBID=1566175465)
connected to recovery catalog database

RMAN> REGISTER DATABASE;
database registered in recovery catalog
starting full resync of recovery catalog
full resync complete
```

```
[oracle@rac11b-pub ~]$ rman target sys/oracle1@rac11g1 catalog
rcat_master/oracle1@rcat11g
Recovery Manager: Release 11.1.0.6.0 - Production on Sun Jan 27
01:40:20 2008
Copyright (c) 1982, 2007, Oracle.  All rights reserved.

connected to target database: RAC11G1 (DBID=411270766)
connected to recovery catalog database
```

```
RMAN> REGISTER DATABASE;
database registered in recovery catalog
starting full resync of recovery catalog
full resync complete

RMAN> GRANT CATALOG FOR DATABASE prod11g1 TO prod_vpc;
Grant succeeded.
RMAN> GRANT CATALOG FOR DATABASE prod11g2 TO prod_vpc;
Grant succeeded.
```

Now the virtual catalogs can be created by the virtual catalog
owners:

```
[oracle@rac11b-pub ~]$ rman catalog prod_vpc/oracle1@rcat11g
connected to recovery catalog database

RMAN> CREATE VIRTUAL CATALOG;
found eligible base catalog owned by RCAT_MASTER
created virtual catalog against base catalog owned by RCAT_MASTER
```

The previous RMAN command only works with a catalog
database of version 11g and an RMAN client with version 11g. If
the RMAN client is a compatible client from a previous release,
run the procedure owned by the base catalog owner
dbms_rcvcat.create_virtual_catalog in SQL*Plus in order to create a
virtual catalog.

Here is the syntax to create a virtual catalog for pre-11g rman
clients:

```
SQL> CONNECT prod_vpc/oracle1@rcat11g
SQL> exec rcat_master.dbms_rcvcat.create_virtual_catalog;
```

Below shows what can be accessed in the catalog:

```
RMAN> LIST INCARNATION;
```

```
List of Database Incarnations
DB Key  Inc Key DB Name  DB ID          STATUS   Reset SCN  Reset Time
-------  ------- -------- -------------  -------  ---------- ----------
1        2       PROD11G1 1350648997     CURRENT  1          26-JAN-08
31       32      PROD11G2 1566175465     CURRENT  1          26-JAN-08
```

A user will not be allowed to create a virtual catalog a long as they have not been granted access to parts of the base.

```
[oracle@rac11b-pub ~]$ rman catalog rac_vpc/oracle1@rcat11g
Recovery Manager: Release 11.1.0.6.0 - Production on Sun Jan 27
02:34:14 2008
Copyright (c) 1982, 2007, Oracle.  All rights reserved.
connected to recovery catalog database
RMAN> CREATE VIRTUAL CATALOG;
found ineligible base catalog owned by RCAT_MASTER
RMAN-00571:
===========================================================
RMAN-00569: =============== ERROR MESSAGE STACK FOLLOWS
===============
RMAN-00571:
===========================================================
RMAN-06801: no base catalog found
```

After a grant, it works:

```
[oracle@rac11b-pub ~]$ rman catalog rcat_master/oracle1@rcat11g
Recovery Manager: Release 11.1.0.6.0 - Production on Sun Jan 27
02:34:14 2008
Copyright (c) 1982, 2007, Oracle.  All rights reserved.
connected to recovery catalog database

RMAN> GRANT CATALOG FOR DATABASE rac11g1 TO rac_vpc;
Grant succeeded.

 [oracle@rac11b-pub ~]$ rman catalog rac_vpc/oracle1@rcat11g
Recovery Manager: Release 11.1.0.6.0 - Production on Sun Jan 27
02:34:53 2008
Copyright (c) 1982, 2007, Oracle.  All rights reserved.
connected to recovery catalog database

RMAN> CREATE VIRTUAL CATALOG;
found eligible base catalog owned by RCAT_MASTER
created virtual catalog against base catalog owned by RCAT_MASTER

RMAN> LIST INCARNATION;
List of Database Incarnations
DB Key   Inc Key DB Name  DB ID              STATUS  Reset SCN  Reset
Time
-------  ------- -------- ----------------- --- ---------- ----------
```

```
61      62      RAC11G1  411270766      CURRENT 1          26-JAN-
08
```

The base catalog contains the entire metadata for all registered
targets:

```
RCAT_MASTER  @ rcat11g SQL>  SELECT COUNT(*), table_type
   2    FROM cat
   3    GROUP BY table_type;
  COUNT(*) TABLE_TYPE
---------- -----------
         1 SEQUENCE
        44 TABLE
        98 VIEW
```

Here is the information about the virtual catalog owners with the
table VPC_USERS.

```
RCAT_MASTER  @ rcat11g SQL> SELECT * FROM vpc_users;
FILTER_USER                          A VERSION
---------------------------- - ------------
PROD_VPC                             Y 11.01.00.06
RAC_VPC                              N 11.01.00.06
```

And the registered target databases via the table *vpc_databases:*

```
RCAT_MASTER  @ rcat11g SQL>  SELECT * FROM vpc_databases;

FILTER_USER                          DB_ID
---------------------------- ----------
PROD_VPC                        1350648997
PROD_VPC                        1566175465
RAC_VPC                          411270766
```

These two tables can only be directly read by the base catalog
owner. In the virtual catalog schema, *vpc_databases* is a synonym.

The virtual catalog consists of a number of views and synonyms:

```
RAC_VPC  @ rcat11g SQL>SELECT  COUNT(*)table_type


  COUNT(*) TABLE_TYPE
---------- -----------
        46 SYNONYM
```

Other security aspects about backup in 11g

There are two default archive destinations in an Oracle 11g database. *log_archive_dest_10* is set to *use_db_recovery_file_dest* by default if a flash recovery area exists, as it was in 10g.

But also, *log_archive_dest_1* is set by default, which may not be desired.

> 💣 Caution! By default, *log_archive_dest_1* points to *$ORACLE_HOME/dbs/arch/* in Oracle 11g

Here in Figure 8.8 is an example from database control:

Figure 8.8: *Recovery Settings Example*

Conclusion

This chapter has covered how Oracle has put a lot of effort into providing a more secure database environment. Many security risks have been addressed in 11g. However, this chapter does not make any claim to be complete about the new security features.

The problem is that they are not documented in one place and perhaps, as time goes by, other features will be addressed that are not mentioned here

Many of these features are only available with the Enterprise Edition in combination with extra cost options like the Advanced Security Option and the Advanced Compression Option. Some of the new security features can have a big impact on applications when upgrading and enabling them. It is up to the DBA to test thoroughly before implementing these features in production.

11g New Features Streams and Data Guard

CHAPTER

9

Data Guard

Data Guard has been around for the past few major releases and enables zero data loss disaster recovery. Data Guard is most often used for site failures, as opposed to storage failures, human errors, or corruption. As site failures do not happen on a regular occurrence, these disaster recovery (DR) servers can be sitting idle for long periods of time without any use or value being obtained. Prior to 11g, businesses were unable to benefit as greatly from their DR investment. Oracle's goal for 11g is to make DR cost effective, better utilize standby resources, and allow for easy testing of DR.

Data Guard is included with the Enterprise Edition of Oracle, but it should be noted that a named user or the purchase of a processor license may be needed for the database. It is always recommended to check with an Oracle sales representative when adding new options.

The DBA has several options available for configuring, implementing and managing a Data Guard configuration: Oracle Enterprise Manager, Data Guard broker command-line interface (DGMGRL), SQL*Plus commands, and initialization parameters. Oracle also has deprecated redundant SQL commands and initialization parameters to simplify the Data Guard configuration.

Physical Standby + Real-Time Query

Oracle Active Data Guard allows DBAs and users to run real-time queries on a physical standby system for reporting and other purposes while still seeing transactional consistent results. As opposed to previous versions where applying of logs had to stop while reporting was taking place, it now runs simultaneously. Oracle versions 9 and 10 could not have the physical standby in readable state. 11g has this and is fully synced. This ability makes an organization's DR investment much more valuable. This capability is known as Real-time Query.

> ⏰ While Data Guard is available as an integrated feature of the Oracle Database (Enterprise Edition) at no extra cost, a license must be purchased for Oracle Active Data Guard in order to take advantage of Real-time Query.

A common question about Physical Standby Database with Real-time Query is whether Oracle will denounce Logical Standby Database. While a Physical Standby Database can facilitate real-time reporting like Logical Standby, it does serve a different purpose. With Logical Standby, the DBA can add additional indexes, materialized views, global temporary tables and such to improve performance for reporting on the standby database. Also, while Physical Standby handles all data types, it is not as flexible as Logical Standby.

Use of Physical Standby Database for Rolling Upgrades

To further leverage the physical standby system with 11g, the DBA can perform rolling upgrades by temporarily converting the physical standby to a logical standby in order to perform the upgrade. While this was available in 10g, it was more of a manual process for the DBA. Another advantage this new feature provides is that there is no longer a need for a separate logical standby system to test the upgrade. The following command temporarily converts the physical standby to a logical standby:

```
SQL> ALTER DATABASE RECOVER TO LOGICAL STANDBY KEEP IDENTITY;
```

The KEEP IDENTITY clause retains the *db_name* and *dbid* of the primary database. Once completed, the database can be converted back to a physical standby database.

Snapshot Standby

Snapshot Standby is an 11g new feature that has some interesting applications. One beneficial way to apply this technology would be if the DBA needs to perform testing, even potentially destructive testing. Rather than ordering another server to perform this testing, the DBA could utilize Snapshot Standby. The DBA performs the test on the standby, rewinds in time to back out changes and then syncs to get the standby current again.

This is different than Flashback Database, which was added in 10g to provide Data Guard a method to correct user errors. Flashback Database can be used on both the production and standby database to easily revert the databases to a point in time before the user made the error.

The following steps will switch a standby database to snapshot mode:

```
alter database convert to snapshot standby;
```

Logs are still sent to standby but they are not applied. The DBA can now make changes and perform testing on the standby database.

NOTE: There will be zero data loss due to the logs still being received, but since they are not being applied, users will not have Real-Time Query while in Snapshot Standby mode.

Once the testing is completed, the database can be reverted back to a physical standby database to catch-up to production:

```
alter database convert to snapshot standby;
```

It has now come full circle as it is a standby database again with all changes backed out and the redo is applied from the main database.

Creation of Standby Database

Enterprise Manager is now able to create a standby database from existing RMAN backups. To access the Clone Database interface, click the Data Movement tab, and then click Clone Database. Figure 9.1 illustrates this improved interface for database cloning. Here, the DBA can create a standby database from an existing RMAN backup.

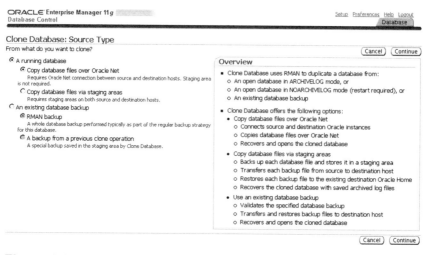

Figure 9.1: *Clone Database Interface*

RMAN can create a standby database by copying the files currently in use by the primary database without needing a backup. RMAN uses the DUPLICATE command to create the standby database.

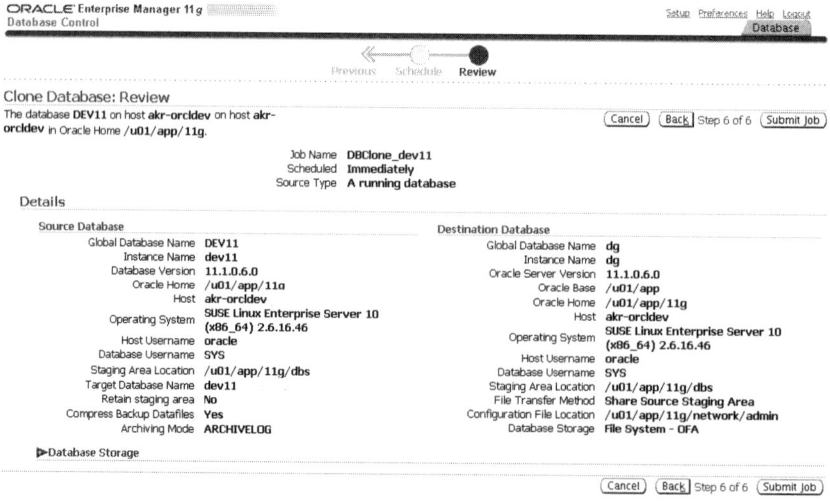

Figure 9.2: *Creating a Standby Database - Review*

Figure 9.3 shows the executions steps taken by OEM to create the standby database.

Name	Targets	Status	Started	Ended	Elapsed Time (seconds)
▼ Execution: akr-orcldev	akr-orcldev	Running	Nov 10, 2007 8:51:48 AM (UTC-05:00)		286
⊘ Previous					
Step: Source Preparation	akr-orcldev	Succeeded	Nov 10, 2007 8:51:57 AM (UTC-05:00)	Nov 10, 2007 8:51:58 AM (UTC-05:00)	1
Step: Create Control File	akr-orcldev	Succeeded	Nov 10, 2007 8:52:02 AM (UTC-05:00)	Nov 10, 2007 8:52:03 AM (UTC-05:00)	1
Step: Destination Directories Creation	akr-orcldev	Succeeded	Nov 10, 2007 8:52:07 AM (UTC-05:00)	Nov 10, 2007 8:52:08 AM (UTC-05:00)	1
Step: Copy Initialization and Password Files	akr-orcldev	Succeeded	Nov 10, 2007 8:52:12 AM (UTC-05:00)	Nov 10, 2007 8:52:12 AM (UTC-05:00)	0
Step: Copy Control File	akr-orcldev	Succeeded	Nov 10, 2007 8:52:17 AM (UTC-05:00)	Nov 10, 2007 8:52:18 AM (UTC-05:00)	1
Step: Destination Preparation	akr-orcldev	Succeeded	Nov 10, 2007 8:52:23 AM (UTC-05:00)	Nov 10, 2007 8:53:13 AM (UTC-05:00)	50
Step: Backup One Datafile	akr-orcldev	Succeeded	Nov 10, 2007 8:53:17 AM (UTC-05:00)	Nov 10, 2007 8:54:02 AM (UTC-05:00)	45
Step: Restore One Datafile	akr-orcldev	Succeeded	Nov 10, 2007 8:54:08 AM (UTC-05:00)	Nov 10, 2007 8:54:54 AM (UTC-05:00)	46
Step: Backup One Datafile	akr-orcldev	Succeeded	Nov 10, 2007 8:54:58 AM (UTC-05:00)	Nov 10, 2007 8:55:39 AM (UTC-05:00)	41
Step: Restore One Datafile	akr-orcldev	Succeeded	Nov 10, 2007 8:55:43 AM (UTC-05:00)	Nov 10, 2007 8:56:31 AM (UTC-05:00)	47
⊙ Next 11 - 11 of 11					

Figure 9.3: *Execution Steps for Creating a Standby Database*

Dynamic Setting of Oracle Data Guard SQL Apply Parameters

To improve manageability of a logical standby, it is now possible to configure specific SQL Apply parameters without requiring SQL Apply to be restarted. The *dbms_logstdby.apply_set* package is used to control nearly everything in a dynamic fashion.

One common use is to control the amount of SGA available to SQL Apply. By default, SQL Apply may use one quarter of the shared pool. To dynamically alter this:

```
execute dbms_logstdby.apply_set('max_sga', 20);
```

The *dbms_logstdby.apply_unset* package can be used to reset parameters back to their defaults.

Compression

Data Guard ships REDO to the standby system, either synchronously or asynchronously, as quickly as transactions are committed using either the Log Writer process or ARCH transport. 11g is able to compress these logs thereby improving performance. This is breakthrough watershed functionality. To enable compression, the following parameter can be changed:

```
log_archive_dest_x='service=bei sync compression=enable'
log_archive_dest_state_x=enable
```

> 🔔 Compression is a feature of the Oracle Advanced Compression option which is licensed separately.

Corruptions

11g also adds a new feature which prevents corruptions, or lost writes, from the master database from propagating over to the standby database. The storage industry seldom speaks of these lost writes. While it rarely happens, it causes many headaches for the DBA, especially if they do not have good backups. These lost writes occur when a storage subsystem acknowledges the completion of a block write in the database when, in fact, the write did not occur in the persistent storage. 11g can now detect these lost writes.

Security & Auditing Improvements

Maintaining security and auditing in a replicated environment is now easier. 11g adds new features to the database to enable Logical Standby to automatically replicate Virtual Private Database (VPD aka Row Level Security) and Fined Grained Auditing (FGA) policies from the primary DB to the standby DB.

For the replication of VPD and FGA to work, both the primary and standby need to be running a compatibility setting of 11.1:

```
SQL> alter system set compatible='11.1.0' scope=spfile;
```

When a VPD procedure is performed against an object on the primary, additional data is captured in the redo. This redo is then shipped to the Logical Standby where is it reconstructed and executed, thus saving the DBA from having to manually perform these steps.

Redo Transport Authentication

In previous versions, the DBA was required to keep an up-to-date password file on each physical and standby database. Anytime a user with the SYSDBA or SYSOPER changed their password, the DBA would have to update each physical and standby database.

11g gives administrators the option of using SSL authentication for REDO transport. In order to use the new SSL option for REDO transport, the databases must be members of the same (OID) enterprise domain. Then the DBA must enable current user database links between the databases within the common enterprise domain in OID. Additionally the *log_archive_dest_n, fal_server* (fetch archive log), and *fal_client* initialization parameters need to use Oracle Net connection descriptors configured for SSL and an Oracle wallet needs to be setup.

Streams

Oracle Streams is a high-speed messaging system that allows synchronization between Oracle databases and also to other varied databases. With 11g, Oracle Streams are expected to operate nearly twice as fast as in previous releases. Oracle Streams is an indispensable tool for companies with a heterogeneous application environment in which the business runs on applications from multiple different vendors. This type of application environment is very common and has its benefits (i.e. best of breed). However, this atmosphere brings with it integration challenges. Oracle Streams is a tool that can help DBAs integrate and replicate data among multiple systems and databases.

Previously with version 10g of the database, Oracle integrated Advanced Queuing (AQ) into Streams. Oracle Streams has three basic functions known as Capture, Stage and Consume. Capture works by extracting DML and DDL from the REDO log and pushes these updates to the Staging area. Once in the staging area, these changes are then consumed by an application or applied to the destination database. The Capture process runs in the source database and the Consume/Apply process runs in the destination database. Figure 9.shows this very high level architecture of how a stream functions.

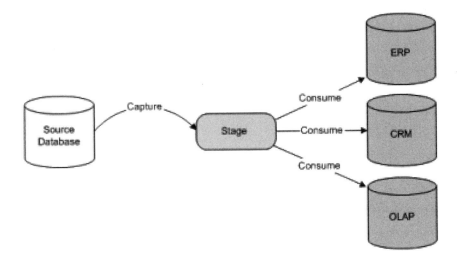

Figure 9.4: *Functions of Oracle Streams*

Just as in version 10, Oracle Streams is configurable via wizards in Oracle Enterprise Manager. In the following example, the schema SCOTT is replicated from the source database DEV11 to the destination database DG.

First, click the Data Movement tab in OEM and then click Setup under Streams. Since this is a new database, a wizard can be used to create the Streams Administrator as shown in Figure 9.

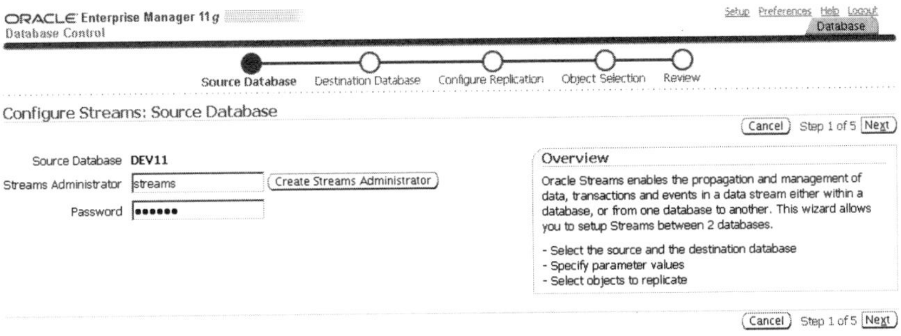

Figure 9.5: *Creating Streams Administrator in Enterprise Manager*

> 🔔 The username is case-sensitive because OEM uses quotes around the username when it generates scripts with the connect syntax (i.e. connect "STREAMS"/password@dev11)

The next step is to configure Streams to talk to the destination database:

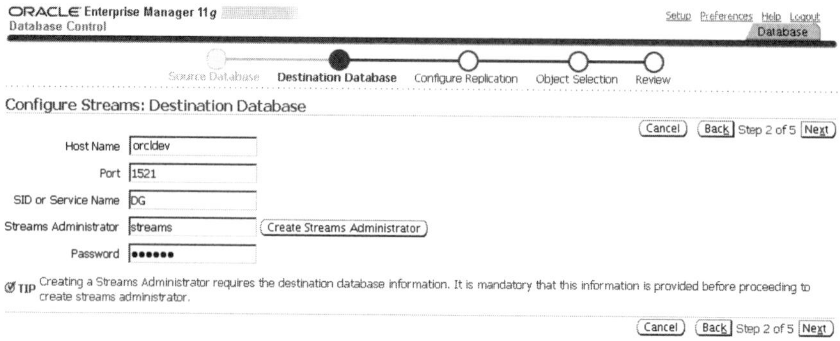

Figure 9.6: *Configure Streams*

The next screen is where the DBA configures a replication method, the Capture, Propogate and Apply processes, the directories to use and whether to replicate DDL, DML or both.

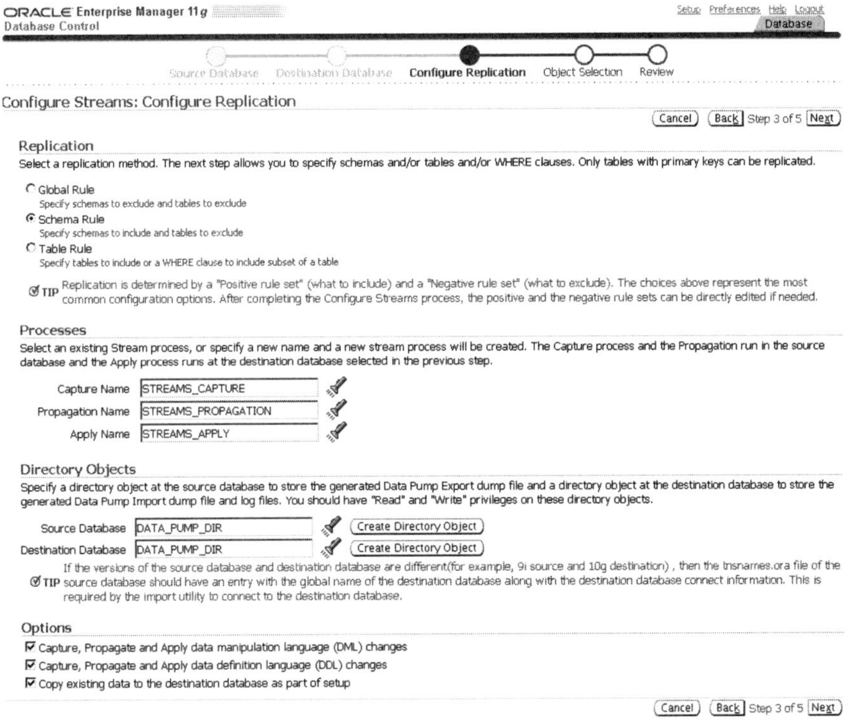

○————————○————————●————————○————————○
Source Database   Destination Database   **Configure Replication**   Object Selection   Review

Configure Streams: Configure Replication

(Cancel) (Back) Step 3 of 5 (Next)

Replication

Select a replication method. The next step allows you to specify schemas and/or tables and/or WHERE clauses. Only tables with primary keys can be replicated.

○ Global Rule
    Specify schemas to exclude and tables to exclude
● Schema Rule
    Specify schemas to include and tables to exclude
○ Table Rule
    Specify tables to include or a WHERE clause to include subset of a table

☑ TIP Replication is determined by a "Positive rule set" (what to include) and a "Negative rule set" (what to exclude). The choices above represent the most common configuration options. After completing the Configure Streams process, the positive and the negative rule sets can be directly edited if needed.

Processes

Select an existing Stream process, or specify a new name and a new stream process will be created. The Capture process and the Propagation run in the source database and the Apply process runs at the destination database selected in the previous step.

Capture Name	STREAMS_CAPTURE	✎
Propagation Name	STREAMS_PROPAGATION	✎
Apply Name	STREAMS_APPLY	✎

Directory Objects

Specify a directory object at the source database to store the generated Data Pump Export dump file and a directory object at the destination database to store the generated Data Pump Import dump file and log files. You should have "Read" and "Write" privileges on these directory objects.

| Source Database | DATA_PUMP_DIR | ✎ | (Create Directory Object) |
| Destination Database | DATA_PUMP_DIR | ✎ | (Create Directory Object) |

☑ TIP If the versions of the source database and destination database are different(for example, 9i source and 10g destination) , then the tnsnames.ora file of the source database should have an entry with the global name of the destination database along with the destination database connect information. This is required by the import utility to connect to the destination database.

Options

☑ Capture, Propagate and Apply data manipulation language (DML) changes
☑ Capture, Propagate and Apply data definition language (DDL) changes
☑ Copy existing data to the destination database as part of setup

(Cancel) (Back) Step 3 of 5 (Next)

Figure 9.7: *Configuration Replication screen*

Depending on the option taken for Replication in the previous step, the following screen is displayed for the DBA to choose objects to be replicated from the source to destination database.

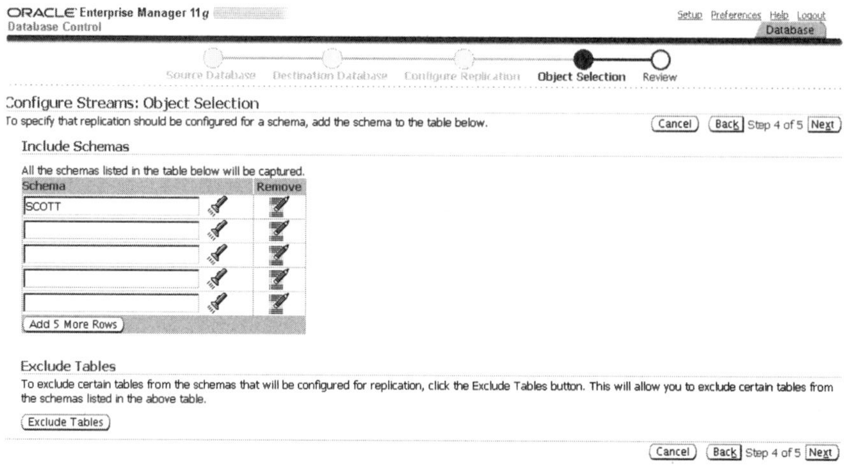

Figure 9.8: *Object Selection screen*

The final screen displayed before OEM creates the Streams job is the Review screen as shown below:

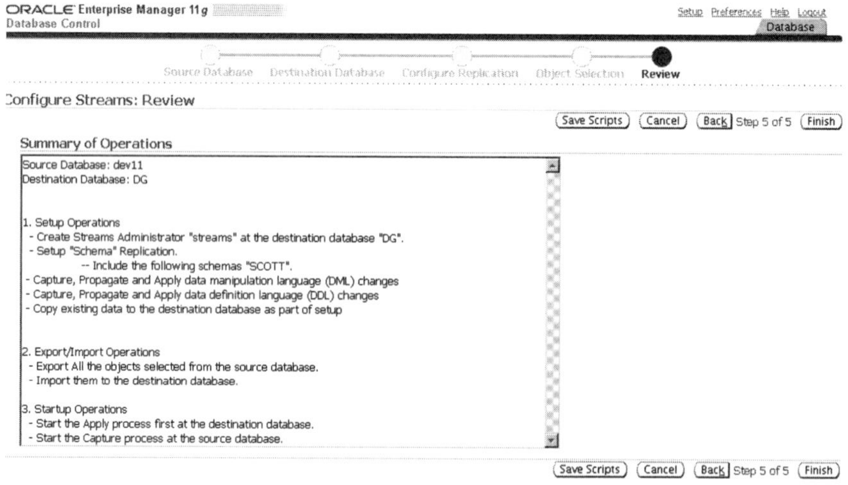

Figure 9.9: *Review screen for Configuration Replication*

The next step is for Oracle to create a job to setup the queue, export and import the data from source to destination, and startup the processes. OEM saves the DBA from creating tedious replication scripts. To achieve the same replication manually would require a script similar to the one below. Only a small portion of the 164 lines are included.

💾 Setup script (partial)

```
--**********************
--SETUP
--**********************
connect    streams/password@dev11;
BEGIN
  DBMS_STREAMS_ADM.SET_UP_QUEUE(
    queue_table => '"STREAMS_CAPTURE2_QT"',
    queue_name  => '"STREAMS_CAPTURE2_Q"',
    queue_user  => 'streams');
END;
/

BEGIN
  DBMS_STREAMS_ADM.ADD_SCHEMA_RULES(
    schema_name        => '"SCOTT"',
    streams_type       => 'capture',
    streams_name       => '"STREAMS_CAPTURE2"',
    queue_name         => 'streams."STREAMS_CAPTURE2_Q"',
    include_dml        => true,
    include_ddl        => true,
    include_tagged_lcr => false,
    inclusion_rule     => true);
END;
/
.
.
.
--**********************
--Export and Import
--**********************
connect
streams/password@"(DESCRIPTION=(ADDRESS_LIST=(ADDRESS=(PROTOCOL=TCP)
(HOST=ORCLDEV)(PORT=1521)))(CONNECT_DATA=(SID=DG)(SERVER=DEDICATED))
)";
set serverout on;
execute dbms_output.enable(50000);
DECLARE
  handle1 number;
  ind number;
  percent_done number;
  job_state VARCHAR2(30);
  le ku$_LogEntry;
  js ku$_JobStatus;
  jd ku$_JobDesc;
  sts ku$_Status;
BEGIN
  handle1 := DBMS_DATAPUMP.OPEN('IMPORT','SCHEMA', 'DEV11');
```

```
    DBMS_DATAPUMP.ADD_FILE(handle1, 'StreamImport_1194809001302.log',
'DATA_PUMP_DIR', '',  DBMS_DATAPUMP.KU$_FILE_TYPE_LOG_FILE);
    DBMS_DATAPUMP.METADATA_FILTER(handle1, 'SCHEMA_EXPR', 'IN
(''SCOTT'')');
    DBMS_DATAPUMP.SET_PARAMETER(handle1, 'INCLUDE_METADATA', 1);
    .
    .
    .
connect
streams/password@"(DESCRIPTION=(ADDRESS_LIST=(ADDRESS=(PROTOCOL=TCP)
(HOST=ORCLDEV)(PORT=1521)))(CONNECT_DATA=(SID=DG)(SERVER=DEDICATED))
)";
set serverout on;
--*************************************************************
--START CAPTURING AT SOURCE AND START APPLYING AT DESTINATION
--*************************************************************

BEGIN
DBMS_APPLY_ADM.SET_SCHEMA_INSTANTIATION_SCN(
    source_schema_name   => '"SCOTT"',
    source_database_name => 'DEV11',
    instantiation_scn    => 4669145,
    recursive            => true);
END;
/

DECLARE
    v_started number;
BEGIN
    .
    .
    .
```

11g adds a new feature with Streams for the DBA to quickly see the source databases and the direction they are being replicated. This can be very beneficial when several databases are being replicated. Figure 9.10 below shows a simple configuration:

Streams

Overview   Capture   Propagation   Apply   Messaging

Page Refreshed November 11, 2007 2:59:46 PM EST   (Refresh)

View Data Manual Refresh

Capture

Capture Processes   1
Capture Processes Having Errors ✓ 0

Propagation

Propagation Jobs   1
Propagation Errors ✓ 0

Apply

Apply Processes   2
Apply Processes Having Errors ✓ 0

Messaging

Queue Tables   12
Queues   17
Total Propagation Errors ✓ 0

Overview

Oracle Streams enables information sharing. Oracle Streams can share database changes and other information in a stream, which can propagate events within a database or from one database to another. The specified information is routed to specified destinations. The result is a feature that provides greater functionality and flexibility than traditional solutions for capturing and managing information, and sharing the information with other databases and applications.

- A capture process is an Oracle background process that scans the database redo log to capture DML and DDL changes made to database objects. It formats these changes into events called logical change records (LCRs) and enqueues them into a queue.

- Propagations send events from one queue to another, and these queues can be in the same database or in different databases.

- An apply process is an Oracle background process that dequeues events from a queue and applies each event directly to a database object or sends events to apply handlers for custom processing.

- Oracle Streams Messaging, also called as Oracle Streams Advanced Queuing, provides database integrated message queuing functionality.

The Streams Topology shows the current database and the databases to which it propagates messages. Also, it shows databases that propagate messages to the current database to be applied locally.

Figure 9.10: *Multiple Database Replication Configuration*

Streams Performance

11g adds new features for the DBA to view the topology and performance of Streams. Every Oracle database has at least one constraint and it may just be Streams. To aid in identifying bottlenecks in the Streams process, 11g has added some new views for the DBA which can be utilized via commands or AWR. First to be covered are the command line views for monitoring performance of Streams. Oracle has new advisors that allow a DBA to interrogate the performance of Streams:

VIEW	DESCRIPTION
dba_streams_tp_path_bottleneck	Displays components identified by Oracle as a bottleneck
dba_streams_tp_component_stat	Displays performance statistics for the components in an Oracle Streams topology
dba_streams_tp_path_stat	Displays path statistics for the stream paths

Table 9.1: *Command Line views for Monitoring Performance of Streams*

Before these views can be queried, the table must first be populated. To view the performance of Streams, first execute the *analyze_current_performance* procedure.

```
SQL> execute dbms_streams_advisor_adm.analyze_current_performance;
```

```
PL/SQL procedure successfully completed.
```

Running the above procedure updates the Oracle Streams performance tables. Execute the *analyze_current_performance* procedure at any time to gather the most current performance statistics.

Next, query the *dba_streams_tp_component_stat* table to identify the most recent ID.

```
SQL> select max(advisor_run_id) run_id from
dba_streams_tp_component_stat order by advisor_run_id;
```

```
   RUN_ID
----------
        3
```

Remember this number because it is used in the next query. The *dba_streams_tp_path_bottleneck* view identifies whether Oracle has flagged any components as a constraint. The following script exposes the bottlenecks. Pay attention to the

BOTTLENECK_IDENTIFIED field as it will indicate if the component has been flagged by Oracle as a constraint.

```
column c0 heading 'Component Id' format 999
column c1 heading 'Name' format a20
column c2 heading 'Type' format a20
column c3 heading 'Database' format a15
column c4 heading 'Bottleneck?' format a15

select component_id,
       component_name,
       component_type,
       component_db,
       bottleneck_identified
from dba_streams_tp_path_bottleneck
where advisor_run_id=3
order by path_id, component_id;
```

```
Component Id Name                     Type    Database       Bottleneck?
------------ --------------------     ------- -------------- -----------
           3 STREAMS_CAPTURE2         CAPTURE DEV11          YES
```

If the above query indicates any bottlenecks, check to see if the components are enabled. From there, dig into the streams environment to identify the cause of the constraint.

To drill into the statistics of each component in the Oracle Streams topology, use the following query:

💾 Component Statistics

```
column component_id heading 'Id' format 999
column component_name heading 'Name' format a15
column component_type heading 'Type' format a10
column statistic_name heading 'Statistics' format a25
column statistic_value heading 'Value' format 9999999.9
column statistic_unit heading 'Unit' format a24

select component_id,
       component_name,
       component_type,
       statistic_name,
       case when comp.statistic_unit='bytes' then
comp.statistic_value/1048576
           else comp.statistic_value end statistic_value,
       case when comp.statistic_unit='bytes' then 'megabytes'
           else comp.statistic_unit end statistic_unit
from dba_streams_tp_component_stat  comp
```

```
where advisor_run_id=3
  and session_id is null
  and session_serial# is null
order by component_id, component_name, component_type,
statistic_name;
```

```
 Id Name           Type       Statistics                Value Unit
---- -------------- ---------- ------------------------- ---------- ----------------------
--
  3 STREAMS_CAPTURE CAPTURE    BYTES SENT VIA SQL*NET TO    1.4 MEGABYTES
  2                            DBLINK

  3 STREAMS_CAPTURE CAPTURE    CAPTURE RATE                 1.2 MESSAGES PER SECOND
  2

  3 STREAMS_CAPTURE CAPTURE    ENQUEUE RATE                  .0 MESSAGES PER SECOND
  2

  3 STREAMS_CAPTURE CAPTURE    EVENT: ASM file metadata     1.0 PERCENT
  2                            operation

  3 STREAMS_CAPTURE CAPTURE    EVENT: CPU + Wait for CPU   14.0 PERCENT
  2

  3 STREAMS_CAPTURE CAPTURE    EVENT: log file sequentia    .3 PERCENT
  2                            l read

  3 STREAMS_CAPTURE CAPTURE    LATENCY                       .0 SECONDS
  2

  3 STREAMS_CAPTURE CAPTURE    SEND RATE TO APPLY            .0 BYTES PER SECOND
  2

  6 STREAMS_APPLY2  APPLY      EVENT: CPU + Wait for CPU     .7 PERCENT
  6 STREAMS_APPLY2  APPLY      LATENCY                     34.0 SECONDS
  6 STREAMS_APPLY2  APPLY      MESSAGE APPLY RATE            .0 MESSAGES PER SECOND
  6 STREAMS_APPLY2  APPLY      TRANSACTION APPLY RATE        .0 TRANSACTIONS PER
SECOND
```

Finally, to display path statistics for the stream paths, the DBA can run the following to query the *dba_streams_tp_path_stat* view:

💾 Path statistics

```
column path_id heading 'Path id' format 999
column statistic_name heading 'Statistic' format a25
column statistic_value heading 'Value' format 99999999.9
column statistic_unit heading 'Unit' format a25

select path_id,
       statistic_name,
       statistic_value,
       statistic_unit
from dba_streams_tp_path_stat
where advisor_run_id=2
order by path_id, statistic_name;
```

The output below shows the number of transactions and messages happening on the stream every second.

```
Path ID Statistic                    Value Unit
------- ----------------------    ----------- ------------------------
      2 MESSAGE RATE                      2.1 MESSAGES PER SECOND
      2 TRANSACTION RATE                   .2 TRANSACTIONS PER SECOND
```

As mentioned above, 11g also adds new views to the AWR report for monitoring Streams. This is just one more tool for the DBA of a replicated environment to use for identifying bottlenecks.

Persistent Queues

- Persistent Queue statistics ordered by enqueue rate

Queue Schema and Name	Incoming Msg per second	Outgoing Msg per second	Expired Msg per second	Ready Msg per second
SYSMAN.MGMT_TASK_Q	0	0	0	0
STREAMS.STREAMS_CAPTURE_Q	0	0	0	0
SYS.ALERT_QUE	0	0	0	0
SYSMAN.MGMT_NOTIFY_Q	0	0	0	0

Back to Streams Statistics
Back to Top

Persistent Subscribers

- Persistent Subscribers Statistics ordered by enqueue rate

Subscriber Name	Incoming Msg per second	Outgoing Msg per second	Expired Msg per second
AKR_ORCLDEV_G_1830_DEV11	0	0	0
DG	0	0	0
HAE_SUB	0	0	0

Figure 9.11: *Persistent Queues and Subscribers*

Streams Topology

Managing a replicated environment can be a challenge. Oracle 11g has new views that allow a view of the topology of Streams. If a situation occurs, such as taking over management of Streams from another DBA who has kept poor documentation, these new views can be of great assistance:

VIEW	DESCRIPTION
dba_streams_tp_database	Displays the databases in the Oracle Streams replication environment
dba_streams_tp_component	Displays the components in the Oracle Streams replication
dba_streams_tp_component_link	Displays the paths in the Oracle Streams topology for the components

Table 9.2: *Views That Allow a View of the Topology of Streams*

The following query shows the databases involved in an Oracle Streams replication environment:

🖫 **Databases Involved**

```
column global_name heading 'db name' format a15
column last_queried heading 'queried'
column version heading 'version' format a12
column compatibility heading 'compatible' format a12
column management_pack_access heading 'management pack' format a20

select
  global_name,
  last_queried,
  version,
  compatibility,
  management_pack_access
from dba_streams_tp_database;
```

```
db name         queried   version      compatible    management pack
--------------- --------- ------------ ------------ -----------------
----
DEV11           13-NOV-07 11.1.0.6.0   11.1.0.0.0
DIAGNOSTIC+TUNING
DG              13-NOV-07 11.1.0.6.0   11.1.0.0.0
DIAGNOSTIC+TUNING
```

The above query allows the DBA to quickly see the databases involved in the replication of data via Streams.

Another useful view is *dba_streams_tp_component* that shows each component in the Stream and the role it plays (ie. Capture, Queue, Propogation, Apply):

🖫 What is Happening in the Streams Environment

```
column component_id heading 'comp id' format 999999999
column component_name heading 'component' format a25
column component_name truncated
column component_db heading 'db of component' format a15
column component_type heading 'type' format a12
column component_changed_time heading 'last changed'

select
    *
from dba_streams_tp_component;
```

```
   comp id component                db of component type        last changed
---------- ------------------------ --------------- ----------- ------------
        6 STREAMS_APPLY2            DG              APPLY       11-NOV-07
        2 "STREAMS"."STREAMS_CAPTUR DEV11           PROPAGATION 11-NOV-07
                                                    SENDER

        5 DEV11=>"STREAMS"          DG              PROPAGATION 11-NOV-07
                                                    RECEIVER

        1 "STREAMS"."STREAMS_CAPTUR DEV11           QUEUE       11-NOV-07
        3 STREAMS_CAPTURE2          DEV11           CAPTURE     11-NOV-07
        4 "STREAMS"."STREAMS_APPLY2 DG              QUEUE       11-NOV-07
```

From this query, the DBA is able to quickly identify what is happening in this Streams environment. Data on the DEV11 database is being captured and then applied over to the DG database. The Last Changed column is useful when the replication suddenly stops working for no apparent reason. Especially if there are multiple DBAs on a team and they all swear they did not change anything.

The following query illustrates the flow of data between the Streams components:

🖫 Flow of data

```
select
  trim(source_component_db) || ' ' ||
  trim(source_component_type) || '-->' ||
  trim(destination_component_db)  || ' ' ||
  trim(destination_component_type) "Path of Streams"
from DBA_STREAMS_TP_COMPONENT_LINK
where active='YES'
order by position;
```

```
Path of Streams
-------------------------------------------------------------------
DEV11 CAPTURE-->DEV11 QUEUE
DEV11 QUEUE-->DEV11 PROPAGATION SENDER
DEV11 PROPAGATION SENDER-->DG PROPAGATION RECEIVER
DG PROPAGATION RECEIVER-->DG QUEUE
DG QUEUE-->DG APPLY
```

This query shows the DBA that DEV11 captures, queues and propagates the data to the DG database where it is received, queued and applied.

Other new features of Streams in 11g not covered in detail here include:

- Performance optimizations (2x faster)

- Hub & Spoke replication ability

- Compare and converge Source and Target data

- Ability to trace Streams messages from start to finish

- Synchronous change capture

Materialized Views

The focus of this chapter is on Streams, Replication and Data Guard. Materialized Views are a form of replication and can allow the DBA to maintain copies of data from remote databases on the local system. Materialized views are also used for the purposes of pre-aggregating data.

Oracle has been adding new features to ANSI SQL over the years. CUBE and ROLLUP were new in 8i, GROUPING SETS were added in 9i, enhancements to the MERGE statement in 10g. With 11g, Cube Organized Materialized Views are arguably the best yet. Additionally, Oracle's acquisition of Hyperion's OLAP software now gives Oracle access to the powerful Essbase engine, which will be integrated with the legacy Oracle Express technology that Oracle acquired from IRI software.

Cube Organized Materialized Views Have Extra Costs

Many extra-cost components have moved inside the 11g kernel software and are tightly integrated to the Oracle11g RDBMS engine. Because of their tightly coupled nature, they are installed by Oracle 11g by default - add-on tools such as the Automatic Workload Repository, components of the Oracle 11g BI Suite, Oracle Data Mining (ODM), and the Oracle warehouse builder (OWB).

Though these are now available by default, be aware that these are extra-cost features and their usage can be audited by Oracle Corporation.

> Oracle Database 11g Enterprise Edition Release 11.1.0.6.0 - Production
>
> With the Partitioning, Real Application Clusters, OLAP, Data Mining and Real Application Testing options

Using Cube Organized Materialized Views

Oracle has devised a way to use Oracle's materialized view construct to store OLAP cubes, much in the same fashion as materialized views are used to pre-join tables and pre-aggregate table data.

Today the DBA must basically know the SQL that users will throw at the database. Instead of dozens of Materialized Views, there could theoretically be just one Cube Organized Materialized View. This new feature in 11g also gives applications which normally would not be able to take advantage of cubes, i.e. 3rd-party ad-hoc query tools which cannot be rewritten to use this powerful feature. The new query rewrite with 11g automatically rewrites the SQL to take advantage of the cube.

Inside the Oracle 11g Cube Organized Materialized Views

Inside the 11g Business Intelligence Suite, these OLAP cubes are the underlying representation of Oracle's multidimensional star schema.

- Cube organized materialized views can be accessed by standard SQL queries (with the pivot syntax) with the base tables being accessed via the query re-write mechanism.

- Cube organized materialized views can also be accessed via the Oracle Express traditional dimensional queries.

- Cube-organized materialized views are supported within RAC/Grid.

- OLAP cubes are presented as cube organized materialized views and can be integrated into a star schema.

Note: Cube-organized materialized views cannot be used with transportable tablespaces.

Access to the cube organized materialized views is available directly within Oracle SQL. Cube organized materialized views do not replicate or store data, but instead are metadata objects that access data from the OLAP cube. It uses the same query re-write mechanism and has the same automatic update mechanism to keep the OLAP cube fresh as data changes within the underlying dimensions. The refresh mechanism offers several refresh mechanisms:

- Instant cube organized materialized view refreshing (on commit using *dbms_mview.refresh*)

- Refresh after a pre-defined threshold of tolerated staleness is exceeded.

- A scheduled refresh, often performed hourly, daily or weekly

As an example of a cube organized materialized view, consider the daily collection of sales summary data by region. This is a standard two-dimensional table with sales rows and distinct columns for each region. When the time dimensional is added in, the representation becomes cubic, or three dimensional. In practice, the third dimension of an OLAP cube is often a DATE datatype.

Creating a Cube Organized Materialized View

To test how a cube organized materialized view allows for transparent rewrite of queries against the source tables, create an example using the old standard GLOBAL Sales cube.

The DBA can use the 11g Analytic Workspace Manager to enable a cube for transparent rewrite capability. First, drill down to the cube that needs to have rewrite enabled. Then click on the Materialized View tab:

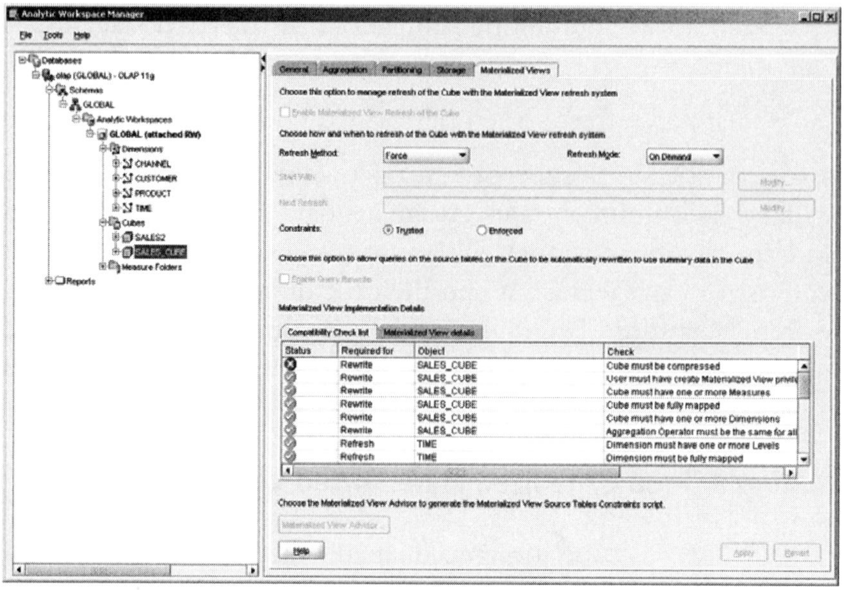

Figure 9.12: *Materials View Screen for Rewrite*

Notice the warning given by AWM. This is telling the DBA that the cube must be compressed in order to take advantage of query rewrite. The next figure shows what may be considered the right way.

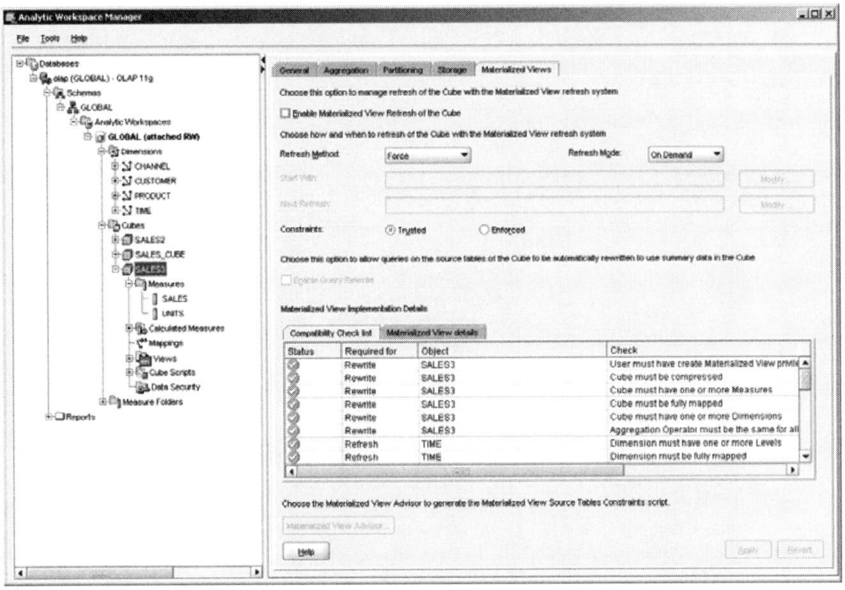

Figure 9.13: *Materials View Screen for Rewrite-the Right Way*

Once all the Compatibility Checklist warnings are resolved, the DBA will select Enable Materialized View Refresh of the Cube. Choose the desired refresh options, and then click the Enable Query Rewrite and then click Apply:

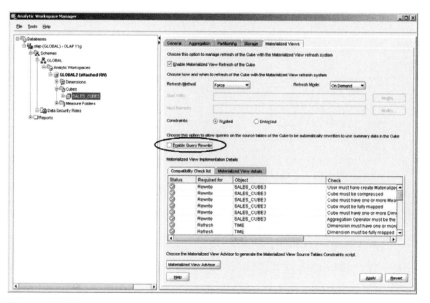

Figure 9.14: *Enable Query Rewrite screen*

To see the Cube Organized Materialized Views in the database the DBA can run the query:

🖫 Cube Organized Materialized Views

```
column object_name heading 'Object' format a30
column object_type heading 'Object Type' format a25

select object_name,object_type
from dba_objects
where object_name like 'CB$%';
```

```
Object                          Object Type
------------------------------  -----------------
CB$CHANNEL_PRIMARY              TABLE
CB$CHANNEL_PRIMARY              MATERIALIZED VIEW
CB$CUSTOMER_MARKET_SEGMENTS     TABLE
CB$CUSTOMER_MARKET_SEGMENTS     MATERIALIZED VIEW
CB$CUSTOMER_SHIPMENTS           TABLE
CB$CUSTOMER_SHIPMENTS           MATERIALIZED VIEW
CB$PRODUCT_PRIMARY              TABLE
CB$PRODUCT_PRIMARY              MATERIALIZED VIEW
CB$SALES_CUBE3                  TABLE
CB$SALES_CUBE3_1                TABLE
CB$SALES_CUBE3_1                MATERIALIZED VIEW
CB$TIME_CALENDAR_YEAR           TABLE
CB$TIME_CALENDAR_YEAR           MATERIALIZED VIEW
```

All Cube Organized Materialized Views are prefixed with CB$.

🖫 Before Enabling Query Rewrite on the Cube

```
--Run query against the base tables (with Query Rewrite disabled on
the cube)
ALTER MATERIALIZED VIEW GLOBAL.CB$SALES_CUBE3 DISABLE QUERY REWRITE;
set autotrace traceonly explain
select
ch.channel_id channel,
sum(CAST(SALES AS NUMBER))   SALES,
sum(CAST(UNITS AS NUMBER))   UNITS
from
GLOBAL.channel_dim ch,
GLOBAL.units_history_fact f
where ch.channel_id = f.channel_id
group by
ch.channel_id;
```

```
Execution Plan
----------------------------------------------------------
    0      SELECT STATEMENT Optimizer=ALL_ROWS (Cost=925 Card=3
Bytes=9
          6)

    1    0   SORT (GROUP BY NOSORT) (Cost=925 Card=3 Bytes=96)
    2    1     MERGE JOIN (Cost=925 Card=3 Bytes=96)
    3    2       SORT (JOIN) (Cost=921 Card=3 Bytes=87)
    4    3         VIEW OF 'VW_GBC_5' (VIEW) (Cost=921 Card=3
Bytes=87)
    5    4           HASH (GROUP BY) (Cost=921 Card=3 Bytes=45)
    6    5             TABLE ACCESS (FULL) OF 'UNITS_HISTORY_FACT'
(TAB
          LE) (Cost=882 Card=885988 Bytes=13289820)

    7    2       SORT (JOIN) (Cost=4 Card=3 Bytes=9)
    8    7         TABLE ACCESS (FULL) OF 'CHANNEL_DIM' (TABLE)
(Cost=3
          Card=3 Bytes=9)
```

Before the query against the base tables will rewrite the Materialized Views, it needs to be refreshed by executing the *dbms_mview.refresh* procedure similar to the following:

🖫 After Enabling Query Rewrite on the Cube

```
exec dbms_mview.refresh ('CB$CUSTOMER_MARKET_SEGMENTS','CF');
exec dbms_mview.refresh ('CB$CHANNEL_PRIMARY','CF');
exec dbms_mview.refresh ('CB$CUSTOMER_SHIPMENTS','CF');
```

```
exec dbms_mview.refresh ('CB$PRODUCT_PRIMARY','CF');
exec dbms_mview.refresh ('CB$TIME_CALENDAR_YEAR','CF');
exec dbms_mview.refresh ('CB$SALES_CUBE3','CF');
```

To test if queries against the base tables are rewritten against the Cube Organized Materialized Views, run an explain plan:

🖫 Explain plan

```
--Run query against the base tables (but with Query Rewrite enabled
on the cube)
ALTER MATERIALIZED VIEW GLOBAL.CB$SALES_CUBE3 ENABLE QUERY REWRITE;
set autotrace traceonly explain
select
ch.channel_id channel,
sum(CAST(SALES AS NUMBER))   SALES,
sum(CAST(UNITS AS NUMBER))   UNITS
from
GLOBAL.channel_dim ch,
GLOBAL.units_history_fact f
where ch.channel_id = f.channel_id
group by
ch.channel_id;
```

```
Execution Plan
-----------------------------------------------------------
   0      SELECT STATEMENT Optimizer=ALL_ROWS (Cost=34 Card=3
Bytes=30
         9)

   1   0   HASH (GROUP BY) (Cost=34 Card=3 Bytes=309)
   2   1     HASH JOIN (Cost=33 Card=60 Bytes=6180)
   3   2       TABLE ACCESS (FULL) OF 'CHANNEL_DIM' (TABLE) (Cost=3
C
         ard=3 Bytes=9)

   4   2       CUBE SCAN (PARTIAL OUTER) OF 'CB$SALES_CUBE3'
(Cost=29
         Card=2000 Bytes=200000)
```

The above SQL example was written to query the UNITS_HISTORY_FACT table, but due to Cube Organized Materialized Views, it was rewritten behind-the-scenes to query against the cube. The execution plan above is similar to the following SQL where the DBA wrote the SQL to specifically query against an OLAP cube.

```
set autotrace traceonly explain
SELECT *
FROM
TABLE(CUBE_TABLE('GLOBAL.SALES2'));
```

```
Execution Plan
-----------------------------------------------------------
    0       SELECT STATEMENT Optimizer=ALL_ROWS (Cost=29 Card=2000
Bytes
          =200000)

    1    0   CUBE SCAN (PARTIAL OUTER) OF 'SALES2' (Cost=29 Card=2000
B
          ytes=200000)
```

The advantage to Cube Organized Materialized Views is realized in the above examples where a query that normally would have queried against the relational table was seamlessly rewritten to access the OLAP cube without making any changes to the SQL. Thus, applications which are impossible or difficult to alter can take advantage of OLAP cubes without altering a single line of code.

To further expand the number of queries that can take advantage of materialized views, Oracle can now rewrite queries on remote tables.

Conclusion

11g has added many new enhancements (482 to be precise). However, to get the value from these improvements the DBA must first learn the new features and then understand how to employ them to meet the needs of the business. 11g enables the DBA to provide improved levels of service through the use of replication. For example, the standby database (with Real-Time query) can be up on the weekends while the DBA is patching or upgrading the primary database, thereby allowing the business to run reports. Replication such as Streams is up to two times faster with 11g, helping the DBA to meet service level objectives.

Another way 11g helps meet service level objectives is through the use of Enhanced Fast-Start Failover. The DBA can failover for user configurable health conditions. This chapter covered some of the ways 11g DataGuard, Streams and other replication options have been enhanced to provide better high availability.

Oracle 11g Change Management

RAT - Real Application Testing

Applying any change to a production system is the biggest challenge to administrators. This could be hardware changes, patches applied to the OS, adding nodes to a cluster, migrating from single instance to RAC or simply changed parameters in the instance or different behavior of the optimizer after the installation of Oracle Patches. It normally needs thorough testing for weeks or even months before going live can be considered. The three big "Ts" as Tom Kyte preaches are TESTING, TESTING, and TESTING! The testing must happen under conditions that are as close as possible to the real life conditions. If an application is needed to serve 100 concurrent sessions, then it is necessary to test with a concurrency of 100 and not with a scaled down workload but with a real life workload.

This is exactly where the problems come in real life. It is not that easy to create a realistic workload with all the real time waiting and locking, concurrency and all in the right sequence. There are workload simulators which are normally used for benchmark testing like Benchmark Factory[1] or even freeware like Swingbench[2]. The problem is that these tools run a fictive user defined workload in multiple sessions at the same time but not a realistic workload with all its concurrency and locking problems as they would occur on a production system. This issue is one of

---

[1] http://www.quest.com/benchmark-factory/
[2] http://www.dominicgiles.com/swingbench.html

the most important fields for improvement in Oracle's Database Release 11g. It is something that a lot of customers have been demanding for a long time.

The marketing expression for a number of new functionalities is Real Application Testing, or RAT. Under this name, Oracle has again subsumed two completely different technologies:

- Database Replay

- SQL Performance Analyzer. This feature was originally named SQL Replay in the Beta Version and was renamed for production.

Real Application Testing is only available with Enterprise Edition ($ 40'000/Processor). It requires an EXTRA COST LICENSE ($ 10'000/Processor). The Real Application Testing Suite includes:

- SQL Performance Analyzer - including the command line API DBMS_SPA

- Database Replay - including the command line APIs

  - *dbms_workload_capture*

  - *dbms_workload_replay*

- SQL Tuning Sets

- the package DBMS_SQLTUNE

> 💣 The Oracle Real Application Testing license is required on both capture and replay systems for Database Replay and is charged by the total number of CPUs on those systems[1].

In this chapter and the next these two features, as well as new possibilities for the maintenance of SQL plan stability by using

---

[1] Source: Oracle Licensing Information

SQL Plan Baselines, will be covered beginning with the command line and then taking a look at the graphical interface OEM.

Testing with a snapshot standby database

Before getting into the details with RAT, the focus should be on what is needed for Real Application Testing besides the licenses. The most important part is a testing system that has already been exposed to the changes to be tested.

Never use the production system for testing!

Oracle 11g offers a new possibility that is very convenient for real life testing. If there is a physical standby database, it can be converted to a snapshot standby database and use it as a testing environment, as shown in Figure 10.1.

NOTE: A snapshot standby database cannot be used for real-time query or fast-start failover.

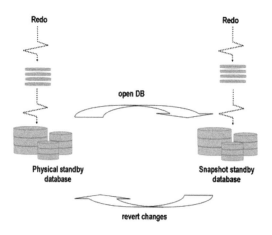

Figure 10.1: *Testing Environment Diagram*

Here is the syntax for activating a snapshot standby database:

```
Lutz as sysdba @ standby11 SQL> ALTER DATABASE CONVERT TO SNAPSHOT
STANDBY;
```

After testing, reconvert to the physical standby mode:

```
Lutz as sysdba @ standby11 SQL> ALTER DATABASE CONVERT TO PHYSICAL
STANDBY;
```

It is also possible to use **DGMGRL** commands for activating or deactivating a snapshot standby database:

```
DGMGRL> CONVERT DATABASE standby11 TO SNAPSHOT STANDBY;
DGMGRL> CONVERT DATABASE standby11 TO PHYSICAL STANDBY;
```

The role of a database can be retrieved from its control file:

```
Lutz as sysdba @ standby11 SQL> SELECT database_role FROM
v$database;
```

```
DATABASE_ROLE
----------------
SNAPSHOT STANDBY
```

A database that is a fast-start failover target cannot be converted to a snapshot standby database. Switchover or failover to a snapshot standby database is not possible. If the database is the only physical standby in a maximum protection Data Guard Configuration, it cannot be turned into a snapshot standby database.

Converting a physical standby database into a snapshot standby database puts it into a state that allows opening it for read/write. Now it can be used to run recorded workloads for testing. In the meantime, redo will still be received from the primary site but not applied yet.

Oracle creates an implicit guaranteed restore point to ensure that a flashback database operation can be performed in order to reset the database to the status before the activation of the snapshot standby state. After testing is finished, it is possible to discard the changes and re-enable redo apply by converting the snapshot standby database into a physical standby database again.

> Since redo is received but not applied on the snapshot standby database, a possibly corrupted shipped redo archive would only be discovered after re-enabling the redo apply!

SQL Performance Analyzer (SPA)

In this section of the chapter, SQL Performance Analyzer will be used to predict the impact of changes to the database system on SQL statements in a workload. This feature is useful for DBAs who want to foresee changes in performance of a workload caused by changes to their system as well as for developers who need to know what happens when they apply change to schemas, applications or database objects.

The following situations are good candidates for the SQL Performance Analyzer:

- Upgrades of the database
- Accepting recommendations for tuning
- Changes to schema
- Gathering of new statistics for the optimizer
- Parameter changes for the instance
- Changes to the hardware
- OS patches

These are the steps of a typical SQL Performance Analyzer workflow:

1. Capture the SQL workload on the production system for testing.

2. Ship the captured workload to a test system.

3. Gather performance statistics for the workload before changes are applied to the test system.

4. Apply changes to the test system.

5. Gather performance statistics for the workload after changes are applied to the test system.

6. Compare the performance results for the two test runs and identify regressing SQL statements.

7. Tune the regressing SQL statements.

SQL Performance Analyzer using PL/SQL

The built in packages *dbms_sqltune* and *dbms_sqlpa* contain all procedures and functions needed to perform an SPA tuning session. Following is a closer look at the steps of the workflow:

Step 1

To capture the workload for testing, a SQL Tuning Set (STS) must be created. The package *dbms_sqltune* is used for this. The STS is the unit that will be packed into a staging table and shipped to the testing system. An STS is a schema object owned by a user. It is possible to use the actual workload from the cursor cache or, as an alternative source, choose a historical workload retrieved from the Automatic Workload Repository by using an AWR snapshot or an AWR baseline. An ADW baseline is a preserved snapshot set in the AWR which does not automatically age out after the retention period is over but stays persistently in the AWR until it is dropped by the DBA.

A SQL Tuning Set contains:

- the text of the captured SQL statements

- the name of the parsing schema and used bind variable values

- performance statistics for the execution of the statements such as average elapsed time and execution count

- the execution plans the optimizer has created

- row source statistics (number of rows processed for each step of execution)

It is possible to filter out unwanted statements from a workload. Incremental capturing can be used to populate SQL statements over a period of time from the cursor cache into an STS.

First, create the STS with the built in package *dbms_sqltune*. *dbms_sqltune* is a package that was introduced in 10g and has been extended in 11g.

```
Lutz @ orcl11g SQL> EXEC DBMS_SQLTUNE.CREATE_SQLSET(-
  sqlset_name => 'my_workld_sts', -
  description => 'my test workload');
```

Then capture the workload into the STS. Here is a simple example for capturing SQL statements from the cursor cache into an STS:

```
Lutz @ orcl11g SQL> EXEC DBMS_SQLTUNE.CAPTURE_CURSOR_CACHE_SQLSET( -
                                      sqlset_name     =>
'my_workld_sts', -
                                      time_limit      =>   300); --
seconds
```

It is possible to specify a repeat interval and add filters for the capture process as well as options for how to handle repeating SQL.

Step 2

After creating the STS, which now contains the workload data, it must be loaded (packed) into a staging table that can then be shipped to the testing system using *expdp* / *impdp* or a database link.

Create the staging table:

```
Lutz @ orcl11g SQL> EXEC
DBMS_SQLTUNE.CREATE_STGTAB_SQLSET(table_name => 'MY_STAGETABLE'); --
the name of the table is case sensitive!
```

Then load the STS into the staging table:

```
Lutz @ orcl11g SQL> EXEC DBMS_SQLTUNE.PACK_STGTAB_SQLSET(-
                    sqlset_name - => 'my_workld_sts', -
                    staging_table_name => 'MY_STAGETABLE');
```

Now the workload is ready for shipping to the test system.

After importing the staging table with the STS into the test system, unload it from the imported staging table (unpack) and then perform the first test run of the workload. This unloads STS from the staging table into the data dictionary:

```
Lutz @ orcl_test SQL> EXEC DBMS_SQLTUNE.UNPACK_STGTAB_SQLSET(-
                       sqlset_name - => 'my_workld_sts', -
                       staging_table_name => 'MY_STAGETABLE');
```

Step 3

In this and the next steps, use the built-in 11g package dbms_sqlpa. Run the imported workload two times on the testing system. The before change run is used to capture the first set of performance statistics for the captured workload in the test environment. These can then be compared to the performance statistics which will be taken for the second run that will be called the after change run.

First, create a tuning task on the test system:

```
Lutz @ orcl_test SQL> var task_name varachar2(30)
                       exec :task_name:=
dbms_sqlpa.create_analysis_task ( -
                       sqlset_name=>'my_workld_sts', task_type
=> 'sqlpa');
```

Next, perform the before change run:

```
Lutz @ orcl_test SQL> exec dbms_sqlpa.execute_analysis_task
(:task_name, -
                     execution_type=>'test execute' -
                     execution_name=> 'before_changes');
```

> 🔔 The parameter *task_type* with value TEST EXECUTE puts all SQL texts into the report. This parameter also accepts the value EXPLAIN PLAN which creates a report that holds the explain plans for all statements of the workload.

This creates the first set of performance statistics for the test workload on the test system. Look at the performance report of the first test run. Here is the syntax:

```
Lutz @ orcl_test SQL> SELECT dbms_sqlpa.report_analysis_task (-
                            task_name=>:task_name,-
                            type=>'text',-
                            section=>'summary')
                     FROM dual;
```

The function *report_analysis_task* returns a CLOB (Character Large Object).

Step 4

Make the changes to the test system to see the impact on the workload.

Step 5

After changing the system, perform the after change run using exactly the same syntax as for the before change run. The overloaded procedure *set_analysis_task_parameter* can be used to adjust the analysis task.

```
DBMS_SQLPA.SET_ANALYSIS_TASK_PARAMETER(
  task_name       IN VARCHAR2,
  parameter       IN VARCHAR2,
  value           IN VARCHAR2);

DBMS_SQLPA.SET_ANALYSIS_TASK_PARAMETER(
  task_name       IN VARCHAR2,
  parameter       IN VARCHAR2,
  value           IN NUMBER);
```

This is a list of the parameters which can be adjusted:

- *apply_captured_compilenv*
- *comparison_metric*
- *days_to_expire*
- *default_execution_type*
- *execution_days_to_expire*

- *execution_name1*
- *execution_name2*
- *local_time_limit*
- *basic_filter*
- *plan_filter*
- *rank_measure1*
- *rank_measure2*
- *rank_measure3*
- *resume_filter*
- *basic_filter*
- *sql_impact_threshold*
- *sql_limit*
- *sql_percentage*
- *time_limit*
- *workload_impact_threshold*

Run the workload for the second time:

```
Lutz @ orcl_test SQL> exec dbms_sqlpa.execute_analysis_task
(:task_name, -
                 execution_type=>'test execute' -
                 Execution_name => 'after_changes');
```

Then review the task report summary:

```
Lutz @ orcl_test SQL> SELECT dbms_sqlpa.report_analysis_task (-
                           task_name=>:task_name,-
                           type=>'text',-
                           section=>'summary')
                 FROM dual;
```

Step 6

In the next step, analyze the performance for the two runs and compare the results:

```
Lutz @ orcl_test SQL> exec dbms_sqlpa.execute_analysis_task
(:task_name,
            execution_type => 'compare performance',
                            execution_name => 'analysis_results',
                            execution_params =>
dbms_advisor.arglist(-
                                        'execution_name1',
'before_changes',
                                        'execution_name2',
'after_changes',
                                        'comparison_metric',
'buffer_gets'));
```

```
Lutz @ orcl_test SQL> SELECT dbms_sqlpa.report_analysis_task (-
                        task_name=>:task_name,-
                        type=>'text',-
                        section=>'summary')
                FROM dual;
```

The value COMPARE PERFORMANCE for the parameter *excution_type* can only be used after two runs when either *test_execute* or *explain_plan* have been performed.

> ↻ By default, the *comparison_metric* parameter value *elapsed_time* is used for the comparison.
> It is also possible to choose one of the following metrics for the analysis task: *buffer_gets, cpu_time, direct_writes, optimizer_cost* or *disk_reads*.
> Use an arithmetic expression for the metric. An example is *cpu_time + buffer_gets * 1.5*

Step 7

Now it is possible to identify the SQL statements which have encountered performance regression after the changes have been made to the testing system. There are a number of data dictionary views which can be used to monitor the SQL Performance Analyzer:

- *dba{user}_advisor_sqlplans*: list of all user's SQL execution plans
- *dba{user}_advisor_sqlstats*: list of all users SQL compilation and execution statistics
- *dba{user}_advisor_tasks*: details about the advisor task
- *dba{user}_advisor_executions*: list of metadata for the execution of the task.
- *dba{user}_advisor_findings*: list of analysis findings.

Step 8:

In the last step, the regressing statements are handed over to the SQL Tuning Advisor or the SQL Access Advisor to see if it can find better execution plans. The output of this tuning task could be recommendations to implement SQL profiles for the regressing statements or other implementations.

The exact impact of the changes to the system on the original workload have been reviewed and after having tested for improvements and regressions, one could apply the tested changes to the production as well. The SQL profiles could be shipped back to the production system and imported there.

As a final step, feed these improved plans into the SQL Plan Baselines in the SQL Management Base (SMB) of the production system in its SYSAUX tablespace. These concepts will be covered in a later section of this chapter.

Next, force the optimizer in the production database to use the better execution plans that the SQL Performance Advisor has found on the testing system.

SQL Performance Analyzer using OEM

The SPA can be found through different links in the Enterprise
Manager. The workload capture can be managed from the page
where STSs can be created, exported, and imported. It can be
reached from the Performance Tuning page. In this case, it is a
cluster database:

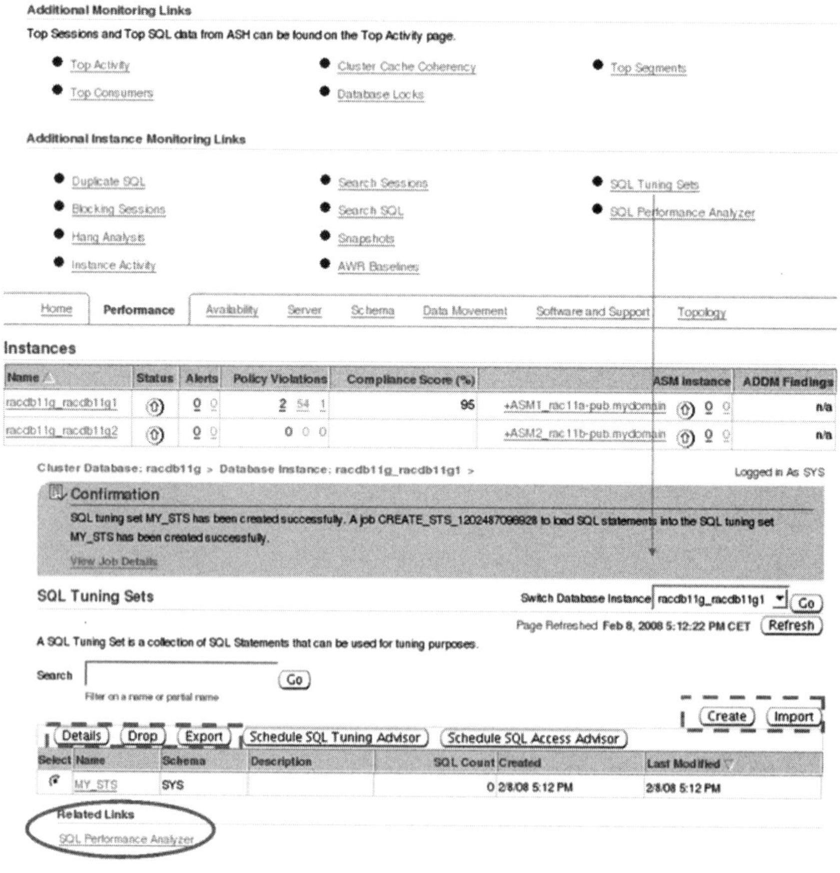

Figure 10.2: *Additional Links*

The SQL Performance Analyzer can be reached directly as well as by going to the Advisor Central page. OEM offers full control for the workload filtering:

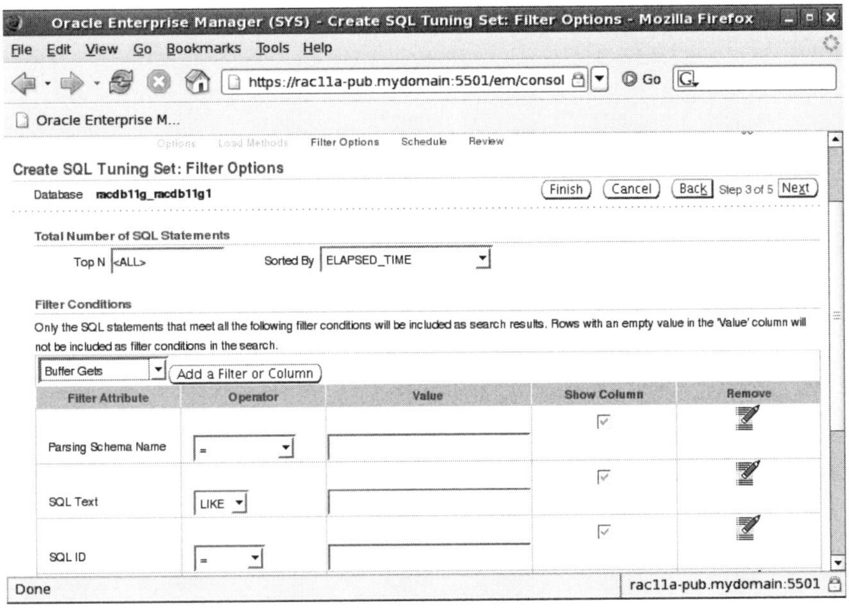

Figure 10.3: *Oracle Enterprise Manager Filter Options*

It is also possible to view the SQL for the workload capture:

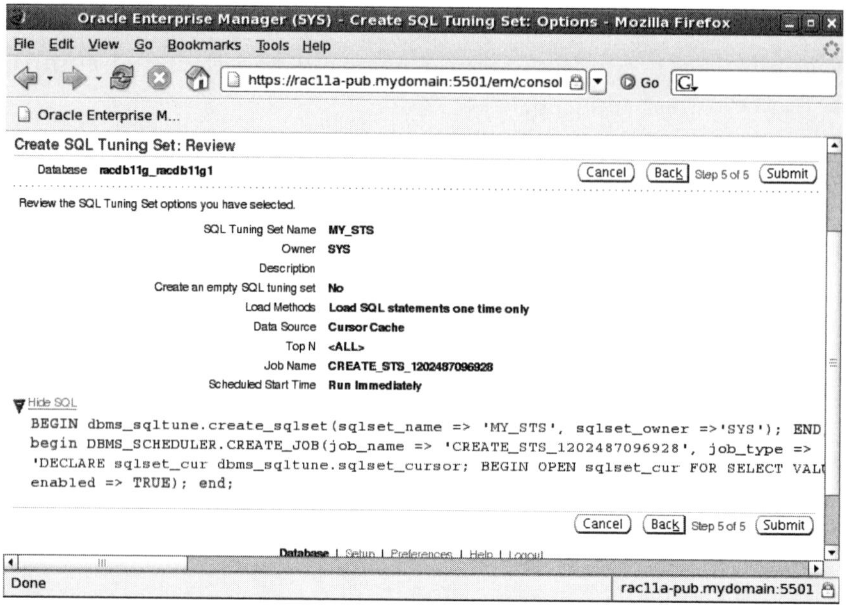

Figure 10.4: *SQL Tuning Set Options*

After capturing the workload by creating an STS, call the SPA on the testing system. SPA offers three different options in the OEM:

- Optimizer Upgrade Simulation

- Parameter Change

- Guided Workflow

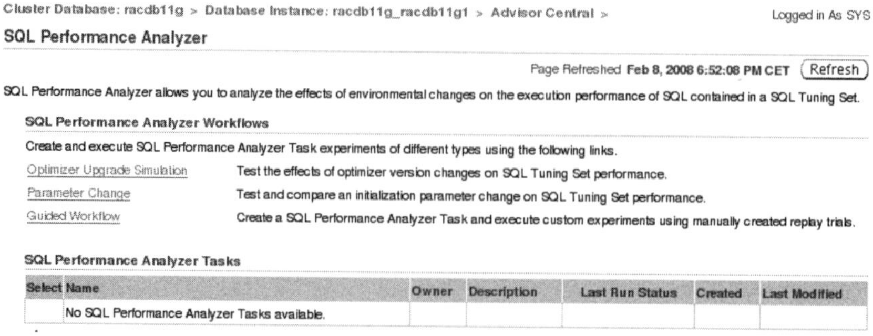

Figure 10.5: *SPA options*

Optimizer Upgrade Simulation makes two runs of the workload with different optimizer options enabled:

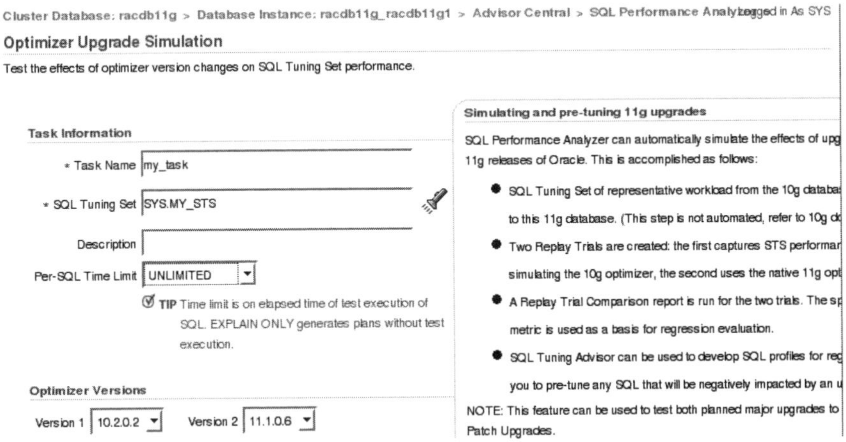

Optimizer Upgrade Simulation

Test the effects of optimizer version changes on SQL Tuning Set performance.

Task Information

* Task Name   my_task
* SQL Tuning Set   SYS.MY_STS
Description
Per-SQL Time Limit   UNLIMITED

TIP Time limit is on elapsed time of test execution of SQL. EXPLAIN ONLY generates plans without test execution.

Optimizer Versions

Version 1   10.2.0.2   Version 2   11.1.0.6

Simulating and pre-tuning 11g upgrades

SQL Performance Analyzer can automatically simulate the effects of upg 11g releases of Oracle. This is accomplished as follows:

- SQL Tuning Set of representative workload from the 10g database to this 11g database. (This step is not automated, refer to 10g do
- Two Replay Trials are created: the first captures STS performan simulating the 10g optimizer, the second uses the native 11g opt
- A Replay Trial Comparison report is run for the two trials. The sp metric is used as a basis for regression evaluation.
- SQL Tuning Advisor can be used to develop SQL profiles for reg you to pre-tune any SQL that will be negatively impacted by an u

NOTE: This feature can be used to test both planned major upgrades to Patch Upgrades.

Figure 10.6: *Optimizer Upgrade Simulation*

Parameter Change performs two runs of the workload with different parameter settings, as shown in Figure 7:

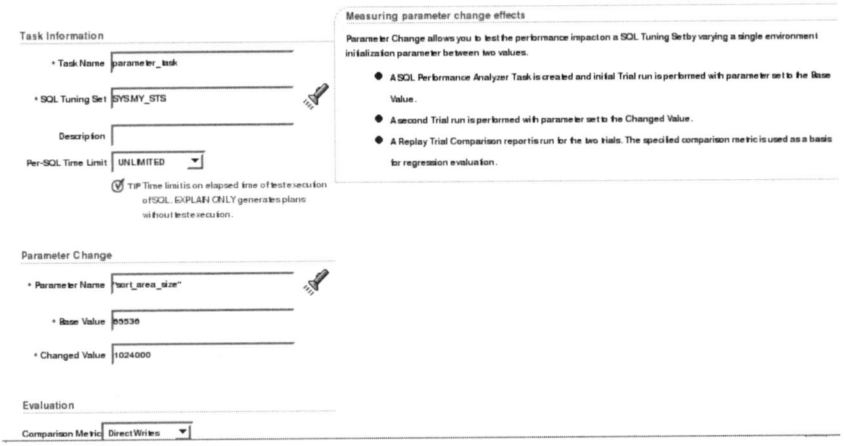

Task Information

* Task Name   parameter_task
* SQL Tuning Set   SYS.MY_STS
Description
Per-SQL Time Limit   UNLIMITED

TIP Time limit is on elapsed time of test execution of SQL. EXPLAIN ONLY generates plans without test execution.

Parameter Change

* Parameter Name   "sort_area_size"
* Base Value   65536
* Changed Value   1024000

Evaluation

Comparison Metric   Direct Writes

Measuring parameter change effects

Parameter Change allows you to test the performance impact on a SQL Tuning Set by varying a single environment initialization parameter between two values.

- A SQL Performance Analyzer Task is created and initial Trial run is performed with parameter set to the Base Value.
- A second Trial run is performed with parameter set to the Changed Value.
- A Replay Trial Comparison report is run for the two trials. The specified comparison metric is used as a basis for regression evaluation.

Figure 10.7: *Parameter Change screen*

Guided Workflow shows a step by step process through a user defined test:

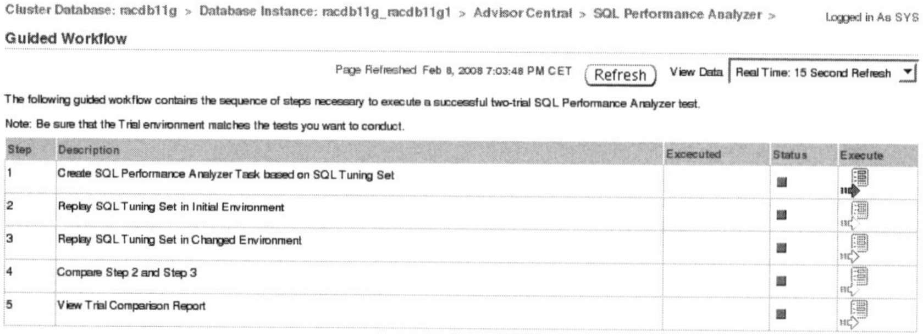
Cluster Database: racdb11g > Database Instance: racdb11g_racdb11g1 > Advisor Central > SQL Performance Analyzer >
Logged in As SYS
Guided Workflow
Page Refreshed Feb 8, 2008 7:03:48 PM CET
Refresh
View Data
Real Time: 15 Second Refresh
The following guided workflow contains the sequence of steps necessary to execute a successful two-trial SQL Performance Analyzer test.
Note: Be sure that the Trial environment matches the tests you want to conduct.
Step
Description
Executed
Status
Execute
1
Create SQL Performance Analyzer Task based on SQL Tuning Set
2
Replay SQL Tuning Set in Initial Environment
3
Replay SQL Tuning Set in Changed Environment
4
Compare Step 2 and Step 3
5
View Trial Comparison Report

Figure 10.8: *Guided Workflow screen*

After all steps of the guide workflow have been performed, view the comparison report for the two test runs. The report shows the list of regressing and improving SQL statements and from there the results can be analyzed:

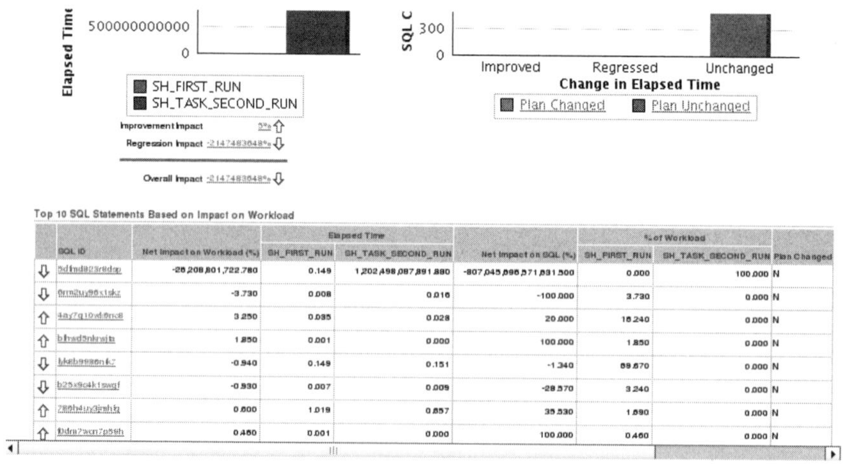
Elapsed Time
500000000000
0
SH_FIRST_RUN
SH_TASK_SECOND_RUN
Improvement Impact
Regression Impact
Overall Impact
SQL C
300
0
Improved
Regressed
Unchanged
Change in Elapsed Time
Plan Changed
Plan Unchanged
Top 10 SQL Statements Based on Impact on Workload
SQL ID
Net Impact on Workload (%)
Elapsed Time
SH_FIRST_RUN
SH_TASK_SECOND_RUN
Net Impact on SQL (%)
% of Workload
SH_FIRST_RUN
SH_TASK_SECOND_RUN
Plan Changed

Figure 10.9: *Comparison Report of Two Test Runs*

Examine the details of the execution results for the single statements and find out what the exact differences for the metrics collections are:

SQL Performance Analyzer Task Result: SYS.MY_SH_TASK

Task Name	MY_SH_TASK
Task Owner	SYS
Task Description	

SQL Tuning SetName	MY_STS
STS Owner	SYS
Total SQL Statements	659
SQL Statements With Errors	73

Replay Trial 1	SH_FIRST_RUN
Replay Trial 2	SH_TASK_SECOND_RUN
Comparison Metric	Elapsed Time

SQL Details: 5dfmd823r8dsp

Parsing Schema SYS   Execution Frequency 1   (Schedule SQL Tuning Advisor)

▶ SQL Text

Single Execution Statistics

	Execution Statistic Name	Net Impact on Workload (%)	Execution Statistic Collected		Net Impact on SQL (%)	% of Workload	
			SH_FIRST_RUN	SH_TASK_SECOND_RUN		SH_FIRST_RUN	SH_TASK_SECOND_RUN
⇩	Elapsed Time	-26,208,900,768.000	0.149	1,202,498,043,904.000	-907,045,895,537,152.000	0.000	100.000
⇨	Parse Time	0.000	0.018	0.021	-18.870	0.000	0.000
⇩	CPU Time	-4,519.780	0.131	188,864.328	-128,903,968.000	0.000	98.000
⇩	Buffer Gets	-0.170	204.000	90,823.000	-44,421.078	0.000	0.170
⇨	Optimizer Cost	0.000	3.000	3.000	0.000	0.000	0.000
⇩	Disk Reads	-3.840	0.000	932.000	-93,200.000	0.000	9.820
⇩	Direct Writes	-93,500.000	0.000	895.000	-93,500.000	0.000	7.300
⇨	Rows Processed	0.000	0.000	0.000	0.000	0.000	0.000

Figure 10.10: *Details of the Execution Results*

From here, call the SQL Performance Advisor and schedule a tuning task for the regressing statements. The result may be a recommendation to accept a SQL Profile because a potentially better execution plan was found by the advisor.

Recommendations for SQL ID:5dfmd823r8dsp

(Return)

Only one recommendation should be implemented.

SQL Text

insert into wrh$_memory_resize_ops (snap_id, dbid, instance_number, component, oper_type, start_time, end_time, target_size, oper_mode, parameter, initial_size, final_size, status) selects ...

Select Recommendation

(Original Explain Plan (Annotated))

(Implement)

Select	Type	Findings	Recommendations	Rationale	Benefit (%)	New Explain Plan	Compare Explain Plans
○	SQL Profile	A potentially better execution plan was found for this statement.	Consider accepting the recommended SQL profile.		99.88	👁🔍	👁🔍
⦿	Miscellaneous	The optimizer could not merge the view at line ID 3 of the execution plan.					

(Return)

Figure 10.11: *SQL Performance Advisor Recommendations, Part 1*

Alternatively, the recommendation could be to run the SQL Access Advisor to analyze the workload in order to find out if an additional index could be helpful. See Figure 10.12:

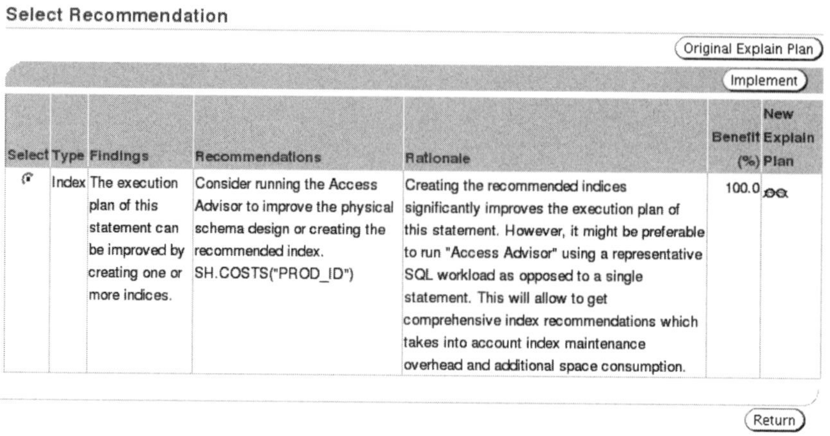

(Original Explain Plan)

(Implement)

Select	Type	Findings	Recommendations	Rationale	Benefit (%)	New Explain Plan
⦿	Index	The execution plan of this statement can be improved by creating one or more indices.	Consider running the Access Advisor to improve the physical schema design or creating the recommended index. SH.COSTS("PROD_ID")	Creating the recommended indices significantly improves the execution plan of this statement. However, it might be preferable to run "Access Advisor" using a representative SQL workload as opposed to a single statement. This will allow to get comprehensive index recommendations which takes into account index maintenance overhead and additional space consumption.	100.0	

(Return)

Figure 10.12: *SQL Performance Advisor Recommendations, Part 2*

Database Replay

After capturing SQL statements from the cursor cache or AWR snapshots in a production database, pack it into a staging table and run it for testing on another database to find out how the statements perform under changed conditions with the SQL Performance Analyzer feature. SPA runs every statement of the workload only one time, serially, and skips side effects of DDL and DML statements.

The next step will be to see how a realistic workload coming in from external clients with all its concurrency and contention problems and realistic timing relations can be tested on another database. This is the biggest highlight among the 11g New Features. Oracle has a new technology which uses external clients to replay a workload that has been recorded as multiple streams in special external files. The capture includes the following requests coming in to the database system from all external clients:

- SQL queries

- PL/SQL blocks

- remote procedure calls

- DML

- DDL

- Object Navigation requests

- OCI calls

The following activities cannot be captured:

- Direct path load of external files

- Shared Server requests

- Streams

- Advanced Replication streams

- Non PL/SQL AQ

- Flashback queries

- Flashback database operation

- OCI based object navigations

- Non SQL based object access

- Distributed transactions

- Remote describe/commit operations

Background processes and all internal activities of the instance and database are not captured.

Database replay using the command line

The technology behind database replay is a new executable plus two built in packages:

- *dbms_workload_capture* is the recording infrastructure used for the capturing. The EXECUTE privilege is needed on this package for capturing a workload. Run the capture with SYSDBA privileges.

- *dbms_workload_replay* is used by the replay clients to replay the captured workload. The EXECUTE privilege is also needed on this package for replaying a workload.

- Oracle uses the new executable $ORACLE_HOME/bin/wrc to start external clients reading the captured streams from the capture files.

The packages are created automatically if the database is created with DBCA. For a manually created database, run the script *$ORACLE_HOME/rdbms/admin/dbmswrr.sql* to create the two packages.

Preparing the system for capture

First, create a capture directory object in the database:

```
Lutz @ orcl11g as sysdba SQL> CREATE DIRECTORY workload_dir AS
'/home/oracle/my_workload_dir';
```

 The capture directory must be empty!

In a RAC configuration with local installations on each node, it is possible to capture the workload of each instance into local directories. The capture files in this case must be manually copied into one common location for processing and replay.

The testing system that will be used for the replay of the captured workload must be in a state that is as close as possible to the state of the system where the capture was made. Therefore, make sure that capturing is not started while user transactions are still ongoing.

If the application is using timestamps for DML, it is necessary to reset the system clock of the testing system to the same time when capture started.

Note the *current_scn* from *v$database* before capture starts. This would be the offset SCN for the replay.

If capturing is started without having restricted the database an error will be encountered:

```
ERROR at line 1:
ORA-15504: cannot start workload capture because instance 1 not
present in
RESTRICTED SESSION mode
ORA-06512: at "SYS.DBMS_WORKLOAD_CAPTURE", line 723
ORA-06512: at line 1
Database Replay
```

It is strongly recommended to start the database in restricted mode before workload capture starts. If restricted mode is not possible, use the argument *no_restart_mode=TRUE,* though this is not an ideal situation.

```
Lutz @ orcl11g as sysdba SQL> SHUTDOWN IMMEDIATE
Lutz @ orcl11g as sysdba SQL> STARTUP RESTRICT
```

Capturing the workload

The workload capture can be named in order to identify it later:

```
Lutz @ orcl11g as sysdba SQL> exec
dbms_workload_capture.start_capture -
('my_capture_1','WORKLOAD_DIR'); -- name of the directory must be
UPPER CASE!
```

After starting the capturing, Oracle automatically disables restricted session mode again. From now on, the workload

---

Database Replay

happening on the database will be recorded into capture files in the capture directory. It is possible to filter out parts of the workload by either specifying what to exclude or what to include in the capture. Here is a description of the *add_filter* procedure:

```
dbms_workload_capture.ADD_FILTER( fname        IN VARCHAR2,
                                  fattribute   IN VARCHAR2,
                                  fvalue       IN VARCHAR2)
```

And here is a code example:

```
Lutz @ orcl11g as sysdba SQL> exec dbms_workload_capture.ADD_FILTER
- ('hr_filter','USER','HR');
```

This would include only work done by HR into the workload capture:

```
Lutz @ orcl11g as sysdba SQL> exec
dbms_workload_capture.start_capture -
('my_capture_2','WORKLOAD_DIR',default_action='INCLUDE');
```

This would exclude all work done by HR from the capture:

```
Lutz @ orcl11g as sysdba SQL> exec
dbms_workload_capture.start_capture -
('my_capture_2','WORKLOAD_DIR',default_action='EXCLUDE');
```

> 💣 Caution! The default value for *default_action* is EXCLUDE!

Possible filter attributes are:

- SESSION_ID
- USER
- MODULE
- ACTION
- PROGRAM

- SERVICE

The *delete_filter* procedure can be used to remove filters again from the capture.

OMSs and agents are filters by default:

```
Lutz @ orcl11g as sysdba SQL>  SELECT * FROM dba_workload_filters

TYPE     ID STATUS NAME                                  ATTRIBUTE
VALUE
------- -- ------ ------------------------------------- --------------
- ---------
CAPTURE  1 USED   ORACLE MANAGEMENT SERVICE (DEFAULT) PROGRAM
OMS
CAPTURE  1 USED   ORACLE MANAGEMENT AGENT (DEFAULT)   PROGRAM
emagent%
```

The capture period should include a representative workload for testing.

This is the syntax for stopping the capturing after the representative workload is finished:

```
Lutz @ orcl11g as sysdba SQL> exec
dbms_workload_capture.finish_capture()
```

The data dictionary holds in detail information about the workload captures:

```
Lutz @ orcl11g as sysdba SQL> SELECT id,
                                     name,
                                     status,
                                     start_time,
                                     end_time,
                                     connects,
                                     user_calls,
                                     dir_path
                              FROM   dba_workload_captures
                              WHERE  id = (SELECT MAX(id)
                                           FROM
dba_workload_captures) ;
```

It is possible to review a report about the capture by using the report function from the *dbms_workload_capture* package:

```
Lutz @ orcl11g as sysdba SQL> SELECT
dbms_workload_capture.report(1,'TEXT')
                            FROM dual;
```

```
Database Capture Report For ORCL11G

DB Name         DB Id    Release      RAC Capture Name
Status
-----------  ----------- ----------   --- --------------------------
----------
ORCL11G         2825011450 11.1.0.6.0 NO  my_capture_2
COMPLETED


                     Start time: 07-Feb-08 13:18:19 (SCN = 1587787)
                       End time: 07-Feb-08 13:23:29 (SCN = 1685135)
                       Duration: 5 minutes 10 seconds
                   Capture size: 3.81 KB
               Directory object: WORKLOAD_DIR
                 Directory path: /home/oracle/my_workload_dir
         Directory shared in RAC: FALSE
                   Filters used: 0

Captured Workload Statistics                      DB: ORCL11G
Snaps: 125-126
-> 'Value' represents the corresponding statistic aggregated
      across the entire captured database workload.
-> '% Total' is the percentage of 'Value' over the corresponding
      system-wide aggregated total.

Statistic Name                               Value     % Total
-------------------------------------- ------------- ---------
DB time (secs)                               18.92      22.61
Average Active Sessions                       0.08
User calls captured                             15      17.65
User calls captured with Errors                  2
Session logins                                   2      11.00
Transactions                                    24     100.00
          ----------------------------------------------------------
---

Workload Filters                                  DB: ORCL11G
Snaps: 125-126

                 No data exists for this section of the report.
          ----------------------------------------------------------
---


oracle@rhas4 ~]$ ls -la /home/oracle/my_workload_dir
```

```
-rw-r--r--   1 oracle oinstall       1125 Feb 11 13:17
wcr_4gc1wu40025vf.rec
-rw-r-----   1 oracle oinstall       1182 Feb 11 13:17
wcr_4gc1wu40026k6.rec
-rw-r--r--   1 oracle oinstall       1181 Feb 11 13:17
wcr_4gc1wu80026k9.rec
-rw-r--r--   1 oracle oinstall       1111 Feb 11 13:17
wcr_4gc1wuc00268n.rec
-rw-r--r--   1 oracle oinstall        904 Feb 11 13:17
wcr_4gc1wuh0025vj.rec
-rw-r--r--   1 oracle oinstall       1114 Feb 11 13:17
wcr_4gc1wun0025vu.rec
-rw-r--r--   1 oracle oinstall       1114 Feb 11 13:17
wcr_4gc1wv0002688.rec
-rw-r--r--   1 oracle oinstall       4505 Feb 11 13:19
wcr_4gc1wv00026kj.rec
-rw-r--r--   1 oracle oinstall       1115 Feb 11 13:17
wcr_4gc1wvc0025vy.rec
-rw-r--r--   1 oracle oinstall       1111 Feb 11 13:17
wcr_4gc1wvn0025uy.rec
-rw-r--r--   1 oracle oinstall        899 Feb 11 13:17
wcr_4gc1wvn00269v.rec
-rw-r--r--   1 oracle oinstall        918 Feb 11 13:18
wcr_4gc1wzs00268x.rec
-rw-r--r--   1 oracle oinstall       1115 Feb 11 13:18
wcr_4gc1x3s0025wf.rec
-rw-r--r--   1 oracle oinstall       1114 Feb 11 13:18
wcr_4gc1x3s0025wj.rec
-rw-r--r--   1 oracle oinstall       1113 Feb 11 13:18
wcr_4gc1x3s0025x6.rec
-rw-r--r--   1 oracle oinstall       4034 Feb 11 13:20
wcr_4gc1xan0026mz.rec
-rw-r--r--   1 oracle oinstall       1115 Feb 11 13:19
wcr_4gc1xbh0025wm.rec
-rw-r--r--   1 oracle oinstall       1114 Feb 11 13:19
wcr_4gc1xbh0025yf.rec
-rw-r--r--   1 oracle oinstall       1114 Feb 11 13:19
wcr_4gc1xbh0025yh.rec
-rw-r--r--   1 oracle oinstall       1127 Feb 11 13:20
wcr_4gc1xp40025vw.rec
-rw-r--r--   1 oracle oinstall       1020 Feb 11 13:22
wcr_4gc1xxs0026q6.rec
-rw-r-----   1 oracle oinstall 11673600 Feb 11 13:25 wcr_ca.dmp
-rw-r--r--   1 oracle oinstall      16135 Feb 11 13:25 wcr_ca.log
-rw-r-----   1 oracle oinstall      12288 Feb 11 13:26
wcr_conn_data.extb
-rw-r--r--   1 oracle oinstall      52386 Feb 11 13:22 wcr_cr.html
-rw-r--r--   1 oracle oinstall      25536 Feb 11 13:22 wcr_cr.text
-rw-r--r--   1 oracle oinstall        272 Feb 11 13:22 wcr_fcapture.wmd
-rw-r-----   1 oracle oinstall        156 Feb 11 13:26 wcr_login.pp
-rw-r-----   1 oracle oinstall         35 Feb 11 13:26 wcr_process.wmd
```

During the capture, MMON has created a performance snapshot from the SGA and stored them into the Automatic Workload Repository (AWR).

The view *dba_workload_captures* shows which ones were created:

```
Lutz @ orcl11g as sysdba SQL> SELECT id,
                             AWR_BEGIN_SNAP,
                             AWR_END_SNAP
                  FROM dba_workload_captures;

        ID AWR_BEGIN_SNAP AWR_END_SNAP
---------- -------------- ------------
         1            125          126
```

To get a detailed report for the snapshot range, run the script *$ORACLE_HOME/rdbms/admin/awrrpt.sql*. These snapshots can be compared against the snapshots that will be created for the replay of the captured workload on the testing system.

How to capture a workload in a 10g database for replay in an 11g database (patchset 10.2.0.4)

At the end of February 2008, Oracle released the 10.2.0.4. patchset. This patchset not only contains bug fixes but also comes with a number of new features for 10gR2. The most important highlight here is the possibility to capture a workload in a 10g database and run it in an 11g database for testing. Look how this works in a 10g database.

With 10.2.0.4, Oracle has introduced a new parameter that can only be used in 10.2.0.4 to enable resp. disable workload capturing:

```
LUTZ AS SYSDBA @ orcl10g SQL> SELECT * FROM v$version;
```

```
BANNER
-------------------------------------------------------------------
Oracle Database 10g Enterprise Edition Release 10.2.0.4.0 - Prod
PL/SQL Release 10.2.0.4.0 - Production
CORE    10.2.0.4.0      Production
TNS for Linux: Version 10.2.0.4.0 - Production
NLSRTL Version 10.2.0.4.0 - Production
```

```
LUTZ AS SYSDBA @ orcl10g SQL> show parameter pre_11
NAME                                 TYPE        VALUE
------------------------------------ ----------- -------------------
-----------
pre_11g_enable_capture               boolean     FALSE
```

There are two scripts that can be used to modify the parameter:

- *$ORACLE_HOME/rdbms/admin/wrrenbl* for enabling

- *$ORACLE_HOME/rdbms/admin/wrrdsbl.sql* for disabling

> Note: The *pre_11g_enable_capture* initialization parameter can only be used with Oracle Database 10g Release 2 (10.2). This parameter is not valid in subsequent releases. After upgrading the database, remove the parameter from the server parameter file (*spfile*) or the initialization parameter file (*init.ora*); otherwise, the database will fail to start up.[1]

The package *dbms_workload_capture* has been added to the 10g RDBMS. This is the interface to workload capturing and filtering. Also, the data dictionary views *dba_workload_captures* and *dba_workload_filters* can be used to monitor the captures. The Enterprise Manager has a graphical interface for Replay Database integrated found in the Server Pane:

---

[1] From Oracle Online Documentation:
http://download.oracle.com/docs/cd/B19306_01/server.102/b14211/wcr.htm#BABI
ABIA

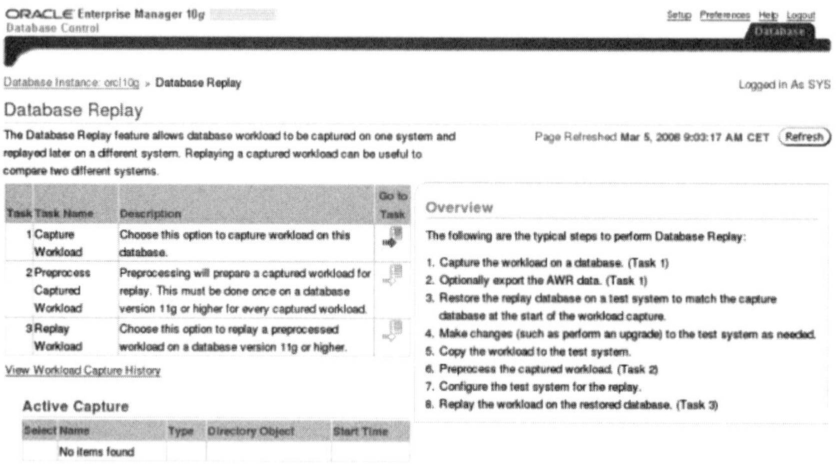

Figure 10.13: *Database Replay Screen*

A workload can only be captured on a 10g database system. The replay must be run on an 11g or higher version.

With this 10g New Feature, it is possible to test the impact of an upgrade to RDBMS Server 11g and the consensus is that this will boost Oracle's license sales dramatically.

Preparing the testing system for workload replay

After the workload has been recorded in external capture files, the testing system needs to be prepared. The testing system should be a logical copy of the original system, in detail depending of the type of captured workload. If the captured workload only contains SELECT statements, then the structure of the testing database must be the same as the structure of the original database.

If the captured workload contains DML, then the testing database must be in a logical state which allows running the DML statements for replay.

> 💣 Make sure that the testing system is totally isolated from any production system so that the workload replay cannot cause any damages!

Now ship all capture files from the capture directory of the original system to the testing server. Choose the host rhas4test as test server where the directory */home/oracle/replay_dir* is used for the capture files. For the replay of the workload, start external replay clients on the testing system. First of all, find out how many of these clients would suffice for the replay. This depends on the number of concurrent sessions which were captured into the capture files. For this, run the wrc executable in calibration mode:

```
oracle@rhas4test ~]$ wrc replaydir=/home/oracle/replay_dir
mode=calibrate
```

A calibration report for the workload and the replay system is received:

```
Workload Replay Client: Release 11.1.0.6.0 Production on Mon Feb 11
12:35:35

Copyright (c) 1982, 2007, Oracle.  All rights reserved.


Report for Workload in: /home/oracle/replay_dir
-----------------------

Recommendation:
Consider using at least 1 clients divided among 1 CPU(s).

Workload Characteristics:
- max concurrency: 1 sessions
- total number of sessions: 2

Assumptions:
- 1 client process per 50 concurrent sessions
- 4 client process per CPU
- think time scale = 100
- connect time scale = 100
- synchronization = TRUE
```

One replay client could handle up to 50 threats, one for each session in the workload. Since only two sessions have been captured all together, start one replay client for the replay. Next, look at which arguments the wrc executable accepts:

```
[oracle@rhas4test ~]$ wrc -help

Workload Replay Client: Release 11.1.0.6.0 - Production on Mon Feb
11 12:33:35 2008

Copyright (c) 1982, 2007, Oracle.  All rights reserved.


FORMAT:
=======
 wrc [user/password[@server]] [MODE=mode-value] KEYWORD=value

Example:
========
    wrc   REPLAYDIR=.
    wrc   scott/tiger@myserver REPLAYDIR=.
    wrc   MODE=calibrate REPLAYDIR=./capture
 The default privileged user is: SYSTEM

Mode:
=====
wrc can work in different modes to provide additional
functionalities.
The default MODE is REPLAY.

Mode        Description
----------------------------------------------------------------
REPLAY      Default mode that replays the workload in REPLAYDIR
CALIBRATE   Estimate the number of replay clients and CPUs
            needed to replay the workload in REPLAYDIR.
LIST_HOSTS  List all the hosts that participated in the capture
            or replay.

Options (listed by mode):
=========================

MODE=REPLAY (default)
---------------------

Keyword     Description
----------------------------------------------------------------
USERID      username (Default: SYSTEM)
PASSWORD    password (Default: default password of SYSTEM)
SERVER      server connection identifier (Default: empty string)
REPLAYDIR   replay directory (Default:.)
WORKDIR     work directory (Default:.)
DEBUG       FILES, STDOUT, NONE   (Default: NONE)
            FILES  (write debug data to files at WORKDIR)
```

```
            STDOUT  (print debug data to stdout)
            BOTH    (print to both files and stdout)
            NONE    (no debug data)
CONNECTION_OVERRIDE  TRUE, FALSE (Default: FALSE)
            TRUE    All replay threads connect using SERVER,
                    settings in DBA_WORKLOAD_CONNECTION_MAP will be
ignored!
            FALSE   Use settings from DBA_WORKLOAD_CONNECTION_MAP
SERIALIZE_CONNECTS   TRUE, FALSE (Default: FALSE)
            TRUE    All the replay threads will connect to
                    the database in a serial fashion one after
                    another. This setting is recommended when
                    the replay clients use the bequeath protocol
                    to communicate to the database server.
            FALSE   Replay threads will connect to the database
                    in a concurrent fashion mimicking the original
                    capture behavior.


MODE=CALIBRATE
--------------

Keyword     Description
----------------------------------------------------------------
REPLAYDIR   replay directory (Default:.)

Advanced parameters:
PROCESS_PER_CPU        Maximum number of client process than can be
run
                       per CPU (Default: 4)
THREADS_PER_PROCESS    Maximum number of threads than can be run
within
                       a client process (Default: 50)


MODE=LIST_HOSTS
--------------

Keyword     Description
----------------------------------------------------------------
REPLAYDIR   replay directory (Default:.)
```

In order to run the captured workload on the testing system, start the appropriate number of replay clients (in this case, one). This will be done in a later step after everything has been prepared for replay.

Before the replay can begin, the capture files must be preprocessed. This processing can happen on any server. It does not necessarily need to be the testing server. The only constraint is the version of the replay clients used to pre-process the capture

---

files. It must be the same version as the replay clients used for the workloads replay.

```
Lutz @ orcl11gtest as sysdba SQL exec
DBMS_WORKLOAD_REPLAY.PROCESS_CAPTURE - ('REPLAY_DIR');
```

> 💣 **The preprocessing significantly consumes system resources and should not be performed on the production system!**

The preprocessing is a one time action. It creates additional files in the replay directory to where the capture files have been shipped:

```
oracle@rhas4test ~]$ ls -la /home/oracle/replay_dir
```

```
-rw-r--r--  1 oracle oinstall    1125 Feb 11 13:17
wcr_4gc1wu40025vf.rec
-rw-r-----  1 oracle oinstall    1182 Feb 11 13:17
wcr_4gc1wu40026k6.rec
-rw-r--r--  1 oracle oinstall    1181 Feb 11 13:17
wcr_4gc1wu80026k9.rec
-rw-r--r--  1 oracle oinstall    1111 Feb 11 13:17
wcr_4gc1wuc00268n.rec
-rw-r--r--  1 oracle oinstall     904 Feb 11 13:17
wcr_4gc1wuh0025vj.rec
-rw-r--r--  1 oracle oinstall    1114 Feb 11 13:17
wcr_4gc1wun0025vu.rec
-rw-r--r--  1 oracle oinstall    1114 Feb 11 13:17
wcr_4gc1wv0002688.rec
-rw-r--r--  1 oracle oinstall    4505 Feb 11 13:19
wcr_4gc1wv00026kj.rec
-rw-r--r--  1 oracle oinstall    1115 Feb 11 13:17
wcr_4gc1wvc0025vy.rec
-rw-r--r--  1 oracle oinstall    1111 Feb 11 13:17
wcr_4gc1wvn0025uy.rec
-rw-r--r--  1 oracle oinstall     899 Feb 11 13:17
wcr_4gc1wvn00269v.rec
-rw-r--r--  1 oracle oinstall     918 Feb 11 13:18
wcr_4gc1wzs00268x.rec
-rw-r--r--  1 oracle oinstall    1115 Feb 11 13:18
wcr_4gc1x3s0025wf.rec
-rw-r--r--  1 oracle oinstall    1114 Feb 11 13:18
wcr_4gc1x3s0025wj.rec
-rw-r--r--  1 oracle oinstall    1113 Feb 11 13:18
wcr_4gc1x3s0025x6.rec
-rw-r--r--  1 oracle oinstall    4034 Feb 11 13:20
wcr_4gc1xan0026mz.rec
```

```
-rw-r--r--  1 oracle oinstall      1115 Feb 11 13:19
wcr_4gc1xbh0025wm.rec
-rw-r--r--  1 oracle oinstall      1114 Feb 11 13:19
wcr_4gc1xbh0025yf.rec
-rw-r--r--  1 oracle oinstall      1114 Feb 11 13:19
wcr_4gc1xbh0025yh.rec
-rw-r--r--  1 oracle oinstall      1127 Feb 11 13:20
wcr_4gc1xp40025vw.rec
-rw-r--r--  1 oracle oinstall      1020 Feb 11 13:22
wcr_4gc1xxs0026q6.rec
-rw-r-----  1 oracle oinstall  11673600 Feb 11 13:25 wcr_ca.dmp
-rw-r--r--  1 oracle oinstall     16135 Feb 11 13:25 wcr_ca.log
-rw-r-----  1 oracle oinstall     12288 Feb 11 13:26
wcr_conn_data.extb
-rw-r--r--  1 oracle oinstall     52386 Feb 11 13:22 wcr_cr.html
-rw-r--r--  1 oracle oinstall     25536 Feb 11 13:22 wcr_cr.text
-rw-r--r--  1 oracle oinstall       272 Feb 11 13:22 wcr_fcapture.wmd
-rw-r-----  1 oracle oinstall       156 Feb 11 13:26 wcr_login.pp
-rw-r-----  1 oracle oinstall        35 Feb 11 13:26 wcr_process.wmd
-rw-r-----  1 oracle oinstall  12394496 Feb 11 13:44
wcr_ra_1399125366.dmp
-rw-r--r--  1 oracle oinstall         0 Feb 11 13:44
wcr_ra_1399125366.log
-rw-r--r--  1 oracle oinstall       998 Feb 11 13:43 wcr_replay.wmd
-rw-r--r--  1 oracle oinstall     10124 Feb 11 13:43
wcr_rr_1399125366.xml
-rw-r-----  1 oracle oinstall       205 Feb 11 13:17 wcr_scapture.wmd
-rw-r-----  1 oracle oinstall     12288 Feb 11 13:26
wcr_scn_order.extb
-rw-r-----  1 oracle oinstall     12288 Feb 11 13:26
wcr_seq_data.extb
```

After calibration and preprocessing, perform a last preparatory step before replaying the workload. The database must be initialized for workload replay.

```
Lutz @ orcl11gtest as sysdba SQL exec
DBMS_WORKLOAD_REPLAY.INITIALIZE_REPLAY -
('my_test_replay_1','REPLAY_DIR');
```

Now the database can accept connections from the replay clients. This reads the connection maps. It is possible to remap connections. This is necessary because the network strings are different on the testing system. The mappings can be one-to-one mappings or many-to-one mappings.

> 🔔 Connection remapping comes in handy for load balancing in a RAC environment if the workload has been captured on a single instance database and needs to be replayed in a cluster database.

```
exec DBMS_WORKLOAD_REPLAY.REMAP_CONNECTION (connection_id,
replay_connection);
```

The re-mappings for connections are visible in the data dictionary:

```
Lutz @ orcl11gtest as sysdba SQL> desc dba_workload_connection_map

Name                    Null?     Type
-------------------     --------  ---------------
REPLAY_ID               NOT NULL  NUMBER
CONN_ID                 NOT NULL  NUMBER
CAPTURE_CONN            NOT NULL  VARCHAR2(4000)
REPLAY_CONN                       VARCHAR2(4000)
```

The replay of the workload is completely managed from outside the database through the replay clients.

Workload replay and analysis on the testing system

The last adjustment to be made before running the replay is about the replay itself. Here is where it can be specified as to whether the commit sequence should be respected during the replay or not.

> 🔔 The default for the *synchronization* parameter is TRUE which means that dependent commits must be completed before the next work can be performed.

Additionally, it is possible to adjust connect time and think time to a percentage value of the original workload capture time. For example, if the first session connected 12 minutes after the capture started and the second session connected 18 minutes after the capture started, this could be scaled down to six and nine minutes by setting *connect_time_scale* to 50. It is similar with think time which can be used to adjust the time between two calls of the same session. Adjusting connect time and think time can be useful if the testing system is significantly stronger or weaker than the original system.

Leaving *think_time_auto_correct* set to its default value or TRUE leaves the adjusting to the server.

```
Lutz @ orcl11gtest as sysdba SQL> exec
DBMS_WORKLOAD_REPLAY.PREPARE_REPLAY -
                    (synchronization =>TRUE,
                    connect_time_scale => 50,
                    think_time_scale =>50,
                    think_time_auto_correct => FALSE);
```

If the choice is to run the replay exactly as it was recorded, do this:

```
Lutz @ orcl11gtest as sysdba SQL>
DBMS_WORKLOAD_REPLAY.PREPARE_REPLAY()
```

Now the system is waiting for the actual start of the appropriate number of replay clients. Here is how to start a replay client:

```
oracle@rhas4test ~]$ wrc replaydir=/home/oracle/replay_dir

Workload Replay Client: Release 11.1.0.6.0 Production on Mon Feb 11
12:42:35 2008
Copyright (c) 1982, 2007, Oracle.  All rights reserved.
Wait for the replay to start (12:42:35)
```

Note: The replay client logs onto the testing system by default as user SYSTEM.

This is what is found in *v$session* on the testing instance:

```
Lutz @ orcl11gtest as sysdba SQL> SELECT username, program, event,
status
                              FROM v$session
                              WHERE event like '%WCR%';
```

```
USERNAME    PROGRAM                                  EVENT STATUS
----------  -------------------------------------    ---------------------
SYSTEM      wrc@rhas4.mydomain (TNS V1-V3)           WCR: replay client
notify ACTIVE
```

It is possible to start multiple replay clients on the same machine.
It is also possible to start replay clients on multiple machines in a
clustered environment to replay the workload. This is how to
actually start the replay:

```
Lutz @ orcl11gtest as sysdba SQL> DBMS_WORKLOAD_REPLAY.START_REPLAY
```

The replay clients will show this:

```
Replay started (13:23:27)
```

A number of data dictionary views can be used to monitor the
replay:

```
Lutz @ orcl11gtest as sysdba SQL> SELECT id,
                                         name,
                                         dbversion,
                                         status,
                                         elapsed_time_diff,
                                         awr_begin_snap,
                                         awr_end_snap
                              FROM dba_workload_replays;
```

```
ID NAME         DBVERSION     STATUS   ELAPSED_TIME_DIFF AWR_BEGIN_SNAP
AWR_END_SNAP
-- ------       ---------     -------  ---------------- --------------- -
----------
1 test_replay_1  11.1.0.6.0 COMPLETED    16423           89            90
```

A report can also be shown in text or html format from the
package:

```
Lutz @ orcl11gtest as sysdba SQL> SELECT
dbms_workload_replay.report(1,'TEXT')
                              FROM dual;
```

```
DB Replay Report for test_replay_1
--------------------------------------
| DB Name   | DB Id      | Release    | RAC | Replay Name   | Replay
Status |
----------------------------------------------------------------------
-------
| ORCL11GTEST | 2825011450 | 11.1.0.6.0 | NO  | test_replay_1 |
COMPLETED    |
----------------------------------------------------------------------
-------


Replay Information
----------------------------------------------------------------------
-----------|   Information   | Replay
| Capture                    |
----------------------------------------------------------------------
-----------| Name            | my_test_replay_1
| test_capture_2             |
----------------------------------------------------------------------
-----------
| Status        | COMPLETED                        |
COMPLETED      |
----------------------------------------------------------------------
-----------
| Database Name | ORCL11GTEST                          |
ORCL11G              |
----------------------------------------------------------------------
-----------| Database Version | 11.1.0.6.0
| 11.1.0.6.0              |
----------------------------------------------------------------------
-----------| Start Time      | 11-FEB-08 14:19:27
| 11-FEB-08 14:19:27         |
----------------------------------------------------------------------
-----------
| End Time       | 11-FEB-08 14:22:41              | 11-FEB-
08 14:25:35            |
----------------------------------------------------------------------
-----------
| Duration       | 3 minute 14 seconds              |5
minutes 8 seconds          |
----------------------------------------------------------------------
-----------
| Directory Object | CAPTURE_DIR                  | WORKLOAD_DIR
|
----------------------------------------------------------------------
-----------
| Directory Path  | /home/oracle/capture_dir |
/home/oracle/my_workload_dir |
----------------------------------------------------------------------
-----------
Replay Options
-----------------------------------------------------------------
|      Option Name    | Value                     |
-----------------------------------------------------------------
| Synchronization     | TRUE                      |
-----------------------------------------------------------------
| Connect Time        | 50%                       |
```

```
--------------------------------------------------------------
| Think Time                | 50%                           |
--------------------------------------------------------------
| Think Time Auto Correct | FALSE                           |
--------------------------------------------------------------
| Number of WRC Clients   | 1 (1 Completed, 0 Running ) |
--------------------------------------------------------------
```

Replay Statistics

```
--------------------------------------------------
|        Statistic        | Replay    | Capture  |
--------------------------------------------------
| DB Time                 | 96206     | 112629   |
--------------------------------------------------
| Average Active Sessions | .01       | .01      |
--------------------------------------------------
| User calls              | 15        | 15       |
--------------------------------------------------
| Network Time            | 2523      | .        |
--------------------------------------------------
| Think Time              | 19158449  | .        |
--------------------------------------------------
| Elapsed Time Difference | 16423     | .        |
--------------------------------------------------
| New Errors              | 0         | .        |
--------------------------------------------------
| Mutated Errors          | 0         | .        |
--------------------------------------------------
```

Workload Profile Top Events (+) Show (-) Hide
```
--------------------------------------------------
| No data exists for this section of the report. |
--------------------------------------------------
```

Top Service/Module/Action (+) Show (-) Hide
```
--------------------------------------------------
| No data exists for this section of the report. |
--------------------------------------------------
```

Top SQL with Top Events (+) Show (-) Hide
```
--------------------------------------------------
| No data exists for this section of the report. |
--------------------------------------------------
```

Top Sessions with Top Events (+) Show (-) Hide
```
--------------------------------------------------
| No data exists for this section of the report. |
--------------------------------------------------
```

Replay Divergence Session Failures By Application (+) Show (-) Hide
```
--------------------------------------------------
| No data exists for this section of the report. |
--------------------------------------------------
```

Error Divergence By Application (+) Show (-) Hide
```
--------------------------------------------------
| No data exists for this section of the report. |
--------------------------------------------------
```

By SQL (+) Show (-) Hide
```
--------------------------------------------------
| No data exists for this section of the report. |
--------------------------------------------------
```

By Session (+) Show (-) Hide

```
----------------------------------------------------
| No data exists for this section of the report. |
----------------------------------------------------
DML Data Divergence By Application (+) Show (-) Hide
----------------------------------------------------
| No data exists for this section of the report. |
----------------------------------------------------
By SQL (+) Show (-) Hide
----------------------------------------------------
| No data exists for this section of the report. |
----------------------------------------------------
SELECT Data Divergence By Application (+) Show (-) Hide
----------------------------------------------------
| No data exists for this section of the report. |
----------------------------------------------------

End of Report
```

```
Lutz @ orcl11gtest as sysdba SQL> desc
dba_workload_replay_divergence
```

```
 Name                                    Null?    Type
 --------------------------------------- -------- ------------------
 ---------
 REPLAY_ID                               NOT NULL NUMBER
 TIMESTAMP                                        TIMESTAMP(6) WITH
 TIME ZONE
 DIVERGENCE_TYPE                         NOT NULL NUMBER
 IS_QUERY_DATA_DIVERGENCE                         VARCHAR2(1)
 IS_DML_DATA_DIVERGENCE                           VARCHAR2(1)
 IS_ERROR_DIVERGENCE                              VARCHAR2(1)
 IS_THREAD_FAILURE                                VARCHAR2(1)
 EXPECTED_ROW_COUNT                               NUMBER
 OBSERVED_ROW_COUNT                               NUMBER
 EXPECTED_ERROR#                                  NUMBER
 OBSERVED_ERROR#                                  NUMBER
 STREAM_ID                                        NOT NULL NUMBER
 CALL_COUNTER                                     NOT NULL NUMBER
 SQL_ID                                           VARCHAR2(13)
 SESSION_ID                              NOT NULL NUMBER
 SESSION_SERIAL#                         NOT NULL NUMBER
 SERVICE                                          VARCHAR2(64)
 MODULE                                           VARCHAR2(48)
 ACTION                                           VARCHAR2(32)
```

In order to analyze the divergences between the capture run and
the replay of the workload, it would be best to use the
comparison report for the two snapshot ranges in the AWR and
use ADDM to get recommendations for improvement. This will
be shown with the graphical interface.

Database replay in the GUI

Real Application Testing is located in the Software and Support pane of the RAC instance. This is the location of the links for Database Replay as well as another link for SQL Performance Analyzer:

> 🔔 The enterprise manager provides a DBA with almost full control for workload capture, preprocessing the capture files and replay. Only the starting of the replay clients needs to be done manually from the shell.

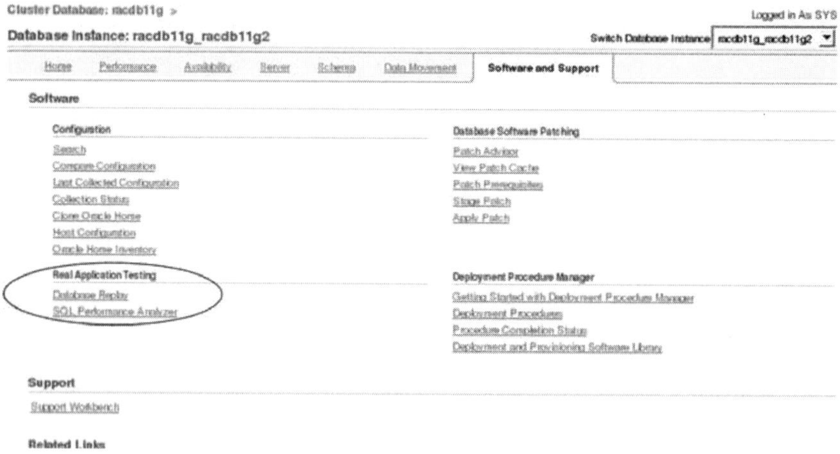

Figure 10.14: *Software and Support Screen*

Replay Database in the Enterprise Manager is a very straightforward procedure. OEM is a guide to workflow of workload capture and reply options step by step. For every step in detail, explanations are provided by the graphical interface:

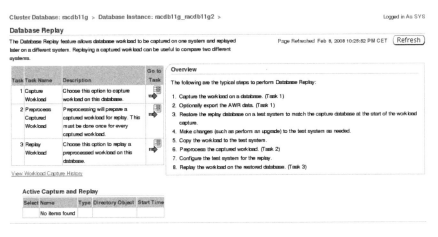

Database Replay

The Database Replay feature allows database workload to be captured on one system and replayed   Page Refreshed Feb 8, 2008 10:25:52 PM CET [Refresh]
later on a different system. Replaying a captured workload can be useful to compare two different
systems.

Task	Task Name	Description	Go to Task
1	Capture Workload	Choose this option to capture workload on this database.	→
2	Preprocess Captured Workload	Preprocessing will prepare a captured workload for replay. This must be done once for every captured workload.	→
3	Replay Workload	Choose this option to replay a preprocessed workload on this database.	→

View Workload Capture History

Overview

The following are the typical steps to perform Database Replay:

1. Capture the workload on a database. (Task 1)
2. Optionally export the AWR data. (Task 1)
3. Restore the replay database on a test system to match the capture database at the start of the workload capture.
4. Make changes (such as perform an upgrade) to the test system as needed.
5. Copy the workload to the test system.
6. Preprocess the captured workload. (Task 2)
7. Configure the test system for the replay.
8. Replay the workload on the restored database. (Task 3)

Active Capture and Replay

Select	Name	Type	Directory Object	Start Time
	No items found			

Figure 10.15: *Active Capture and Replay Screen*

Before capturing can begin, acknowledge the strongly recommended requirements in Figure 16:

Capture Workload: Plan Environment

Database   racdb11g_racdb11g2   [Cancel] Step 1 of 5 [Next]
Logged In As   SYS

The following prerequisites should be met before proceeding to capturing the workload to avoid potential problems.

It is highly recommended to meet and acknowledge each of the following prerequisites.

Prerequisite	Acknowledge
Restarting the database prior to workload capture is recommended for the best workload replay result. Consider scheduling the workload capture at a time when the database can be restarted.	☑
Make sure there is enough disk space to hold the captured workload. Consider doing a short duration workload capture and use it for estimating disk space requirement of a full workload capture.	☑
Make sure you can restore the replay database to match the capture database at the start of the workload capture. A successful workload replay depends on application transactions accessing application data identical to that on a capture system. Common ways to restore application data state include point-in-time recovery, flashback, and import/export.	☑

Figure 10.16: *Plan Environment Screen*

The next screen asks for confirmation for the restart of the database:

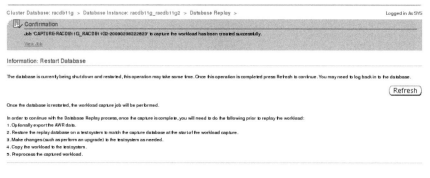

Confirmation

Job 'CAPTURE-RACDB11G_RACDB11G2-20080206222623' to capture the workload has been created successfully.

View Job

Information: Restart Database

The database is currently being shutdown and restarted, this operation may take some time. Once this operation is completed press Refresh to continue. You may need to log back in to the database.

[Refresh]

Once the database is restarted, the workload capture job will be performed.

In order to continue with the Database Replay process, once the capture is complete, you will need to do the following prior to replay the workload:
1. Optionally export the Database AWR data.
2. Restore the replay database on a test system to match the capture database at the start of the workload capture.
3. Make changes (such as perform an upgrade) to the test system as needed.
4. Copy the workload to the test system.
5. Preprocess the captured workload.

Figure 10.17: *Restart Database Screen*

Then capture directory can be created in the GUI:

Confirmation

Directory object created successfully.

Capture Workload: Parameters

Database   racdb11g_racdb11g2   [Cancel] [Back] Step 3 of 5 [Next]
Logged in As   SYS

Workload Capture Parameters

* Capture Name   [LUTZ_CAPTURE]

* Directory Object   [cap_dir   ▼] (Create Directory Object)
Select a directory object to hold the captured workload. The selected directory object cannot already contain a captured workload.

✓ TIP You must select a directory object that is valid for every instance of a cluster database.

Database Shutdown Parameters

⊙ Immediate
Rollback active transactions and disconnect all connected users.

Figure 10.18: *Creating Capture Directory*

A scheduler job will be created and the filter options can be set for the workload capture:

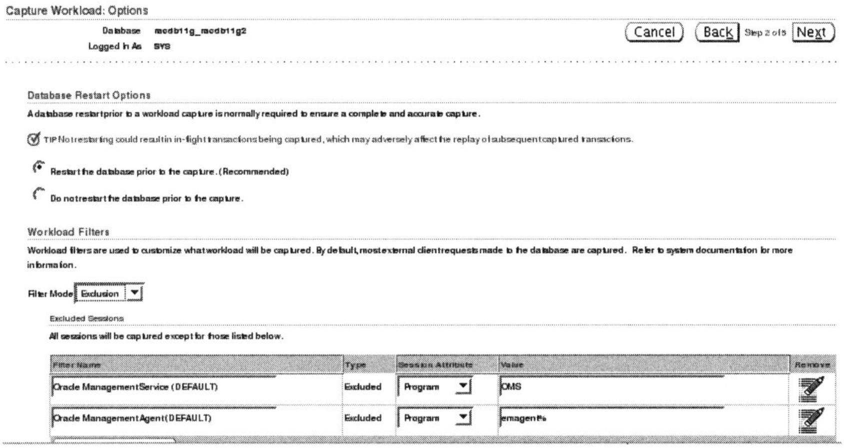

Figure 10.19: *Capture Workload Restart and Filter Options*

After the capture has been stopped, look at the capture report and perform the preprocessing of the capture files:

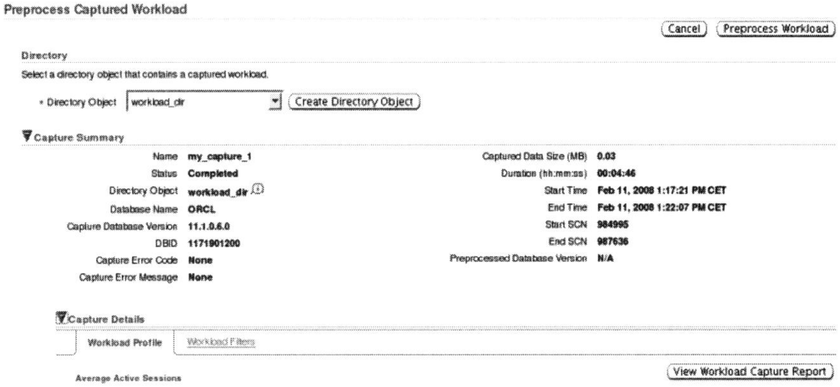

Figure 10.20: *Preprocess Captured Workload Screen*

After preprocessing has finished, the replay of the captured workload can be started. First acknowledge that this is located on the testing system and not in production:

Database Replay

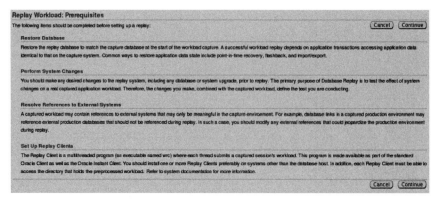

Figure 10.21: *Replay Workload Prerequisites*

The next screen shows the adjustment for the replay settings:

Replay Workload: Choose Initial Options

Database	**orcl**
Capture Name	**my_capture_1**
Logged In As	**SYS**

Cancel   Step 1 of 5   Next

* Replay Name   REPLAY-orcl-20080211133110

Initial Options

Choose the initial replay options.

- ⦿ Use the default replay options
- ⦾ Use replay options from a previous replay

Replay Name   [▾]

Cancel   Step 1 of 5   Next

Figure 10.22: *Initial Replay Options Screen*

After defining the replay parameters, start the replay clients. This must be done on the command line. The GUI will wait until at least one client is started:

Replay Workload: Prepare Replay Clients

Database	**orcl**
Capture Name	**my_capture_1**
Logged In As	**SYS**

Cancel   Back   Step 3 of 5   Next

The Replay Client is a multithreaded program (an executable named wrc) where each thread submits a captured session's workload. This program is made available as part of the standard Oracle Client as well as the Oracle Instant Client. Refer to system documentation on how to set up and start the Replay Clients.

When you are ready to start the Replay Clients, continue to the next step and then start the Replay Clients.

Cancel   Back   Step 3 of 5   Next

Figure 10.23: *Preparing Replay Client Screen*

Once the replay has started, navigate to the replay workload control page from where the replay can be monitored. Here is an overview of work done and this permits access to the connection mappings, replay parameters, and reports for divergences and compare periods in detail:

View Workload Replay: REPLAY-orcl-20080211133110

OK

Status **Completed**

▼ Summary

Replay Name	**REPLAY-orcl-20080211133110**
Directory Object	**workload_dir** ①
Database Name	**ORCL**
DBID	**1171901200**
Replay Error Code	**N/A**
Replay Error Message	**None**

Capture Name	**my_capture_1**
Duration (hh:mm:ss)	**00:02:52**
Prepare Time	**Feb 11, 2008 1:32:45 PM CET**
Start Time	**Feb 11, 2008 1:40:27 PM CET**
End Time	**Feb 11, 2008 1:43:19 PM CET**

Workload Profile | Connection Mappings | Replay Parameters | Report

Network Time (hh:mm:ss) **00:00:00**   Clients **1**
Think Time (hh:mm:ss) **00:02:12**   Clients Finished **1**

Elapsed Time Comparison

Capture

Replay

| 0.0 0.5 1.0 1.5 2.0 2.5 3.0 3.5 4.0 4.5 5.0 |
Elapsed Time (Minutes)

☐ Replay Elapsed
■ Capture Elapsed
☐ Not Yet Replayed

Assessing the Replay

The Elapsed Time Comparison chart shows how much time the replayed workload has taken to accomplish the same amount of work as captured.

When the Replay bar is shorter than the Capture bar then the replay environment is processing the workload faster than the capture environment.

The divergence table gives information about both the data and error discrepancies between the replay and capture environments, which can be used as a measure of the replay quality.

Figure 10.24: *Workload Profile et al Screen*

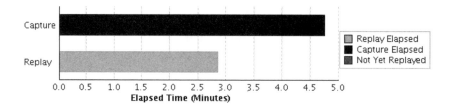

Divergence

	Number of Calls	Percentage of Total Calls
Error Divergence:		
Session Failures Seen During Replay	0	0.00
Errors No Longer Seen During Replay	0	0.00
Errors Mutated During Replay	0	0.00
New Errors Seen During Replay	0	0.00
Data Divergence:		
DMLs with Different Number of Rows Modified	0	0.00
SELECTs with Different Number of Rows Fetched	0	0.00

▷ Detailed Comparison

Figure 10.25: *Capture and Replay Comparison Screen*

From here, start investigating the divergences. Those could be errors which disappear in the replay or mutated, even new errors occurring on the testing system. Compare the number of processed rows for individual statements and use the advisors such as ADDM to compare and analyze the performance snapshots which were created during the capture and the replay run. This makes it easy for the DBA to predict pitfalls beforehand even in very complicated environments.

> 🔔 As of April, 2008, the Grid Control version for 11g is not available yet and Database Control is the limit for now.

Conclusion

There have been multiple techniques to control execution plans available for quite a while. These include hints, stored outlines and SQL profiles. What all of these methods have in common is that they need manual intervention since they are fixed remedies that do not adjust to changed demands automatically. Also, they can only be used after the problem has actually occurred, so they are reactive methods.

SQL Management

SQL Plan Management with SQL Plan Baselines

Among the biggest challenges for a DBA are changes in the execution plans for SQL statements which occur all of a sudden, sometimes for no visible reasons. This can be caused by changed behavior of the optimizer after a new patch was implemented or simply because an automatic job has gathered new optimizer statistics over night.

There was a situation a couple of years ago where hundreds of employees suddenly were queuing up in front of the main entrance of a large business bank without being able to access the building because the application which controlled the badges was so slow. This again led to manual access control like it was done ages ago. Investigations for the direct reasons took several weeks. This incident happened in times of terrorist threats with bomb alerts and an increasing need for security.

> 🔔 SQL Plan Management is only available with the Enterprise Edition and there are no extra cost options required for the package *dbms_spm*.

In this case, it would have been very handy to guarantee execution plan stability somehow. Oracle has taken care of such issues in 11g with a feature called SQL Plan Management (SPM) with SQL plan baselines. Plan baselines can be either maintained manually by feeding well tuned execution plans into the system or by enabling automatic SQL plan baseline capturing.

This final part of the change management chapter will cover how to achieve stability for a good execution plan by maintaining SQL plan baselines. This is a method to preventively guarantee plan stability and thus, preserve performance characteristics of SQL statements.

How Automatic SQL Plan Management works

In version 10g, Oracle has introduced the new mandatory SYSAUX tablespace. It is the default location for a number of tools which had their own tablespaces before 10g, such as Oracle Text, Ultra Search, and Statspack and some more. These tools' tablespaces have all been consolidated into the SYSAUX tablespace per default.

Also with version 10g, Oracle introduced the Automatic Workload Repository (AWR), which is a kind of data warehouse for historical performance statistics. Oracle 10g creates performance snapshots in memory statistics from the SGA per default every hour and retains them in the AWR for seven days if these settings are not adjusted. The built in package *dbms_workload_repository* can be used to adjust the snapshot interval and snapshot retention period.

There are historical statistics about waits and resource consumption in the database, even across shutdown and startup operations. This feature utilizes the wait interface, which was introduced in version 7, and is subject to permanent improvement. The Oracle kernel currently captures more than 800 statistics on the fly.

Beside the AWR in an 11g database, another structure is located in the SYSAUX tablespace. It is a special infrastructure which is called SQL Management Base (SMB). It holds the SQL Plan Baselines as well as SQL Profiles that are created by the SQL Performance Analyzer that is implemented with the package *dbms_sqltune*. SQL Profiles were introduced with Oracle 10gR1. In an Oracle 10g database, they are stored in the SYSTEM tablespace. There was no such thing as SMB in 10g. When upgrading a 10g database to 11g, the upgrade script moves SQL Profiles from the SYSTEM to the SYSAUX tablespace automatically. SQL profiles are a reactive method for fixing performance problems of SQL statements. In 10g this is always done manually by the DBA.

As of 11g, Automatic SQL Tuning happens every night via an automatic task job if the choice is to allow the server to not only create SQL Profiles but also implement them automatically. This will be covered more at the end of this chapter.

> 🔔 If the SYSAUX tablespace is offline in 11g, this can cause significant performance impact because needed SQL Profiles are not accessible. This could not happen in 10g!

Another reactive method to implement plan stability is the use of Stored Outlines. For backward compatibility, Oracle uses existing stored outlines. A plan generated using a stored outline is not stored in the SMB even if automatic plan capture is enabled for the session. Stored Outlines have been deprecated in 11g and have been replaced by SQL plan management features.

Also beginning in 11g, a SQL Log for all statements as well as a SQL Plan History for repeatable SQL is maintained in the SMB by the optimizer along with the SQL plan baselines.

By default, Oracle uses SQL plan baselines but does not automatically capture new plans.

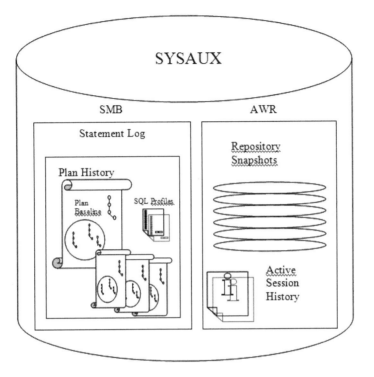

Figure 11.1: *Schematic of SYSAUX Tablespace*

The graphic shown above displays the AWR and the SMB in the SYSAUX tablespace. This tablespace must be created with Automatic Segment Space Management (ASSM) enabled to allow automatic purging tasks to maintain the SMB. If the SYSAUX tablespace is offline, the optimizer cannot maintain the SQL Log and the SQL Plan History and cannot use SQL Plan Baselines.

Oracle uses two new parameters to manage the SMB:

- *optimizer_capture_sql_plan_baselines*
- *optimizer_use_sql_plan_baselines*

```
LUTZ AS SYSDBA @ orcl11g SQL> show parameter plan_base

NAME                                 TYPE         VALUE
------------------------------------ ------------ --------------------
-----------
optimizer_capture_sql_plan_baselines boolean      FALSE
optimizer_use_sql_plan_baselines     boolean      TRUE
```

It is possible to feed SQL execution plans manually into the SQL plan baselines. By this, an execution plan can be fixed and thus force the optimizer to use it. The manual SQL plan maintenance will be reviewed later in this chapter.

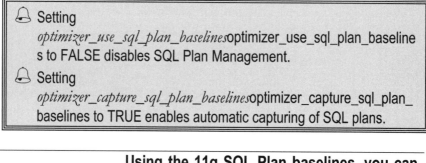

🔔 Setting *optimizer_use_sql_plan_baselines* optimizer_use_sql_plan_baseline s to FALSE disables SQL Plan Management.

🔔 Setting *optimizer_capture_sql_plan_baselines* optimizer_capture_sql_plan_ baselines to TRUE enables automatic capturing of SQL plans.

 **Using the 11g SQL Plan baselines, you can allow for the automatic capture of execution plans. You simply set the parameter *optimizer_capture_sql_plan_baselines*=true and Oracle will begin collecting your baselines automatically.**

Both parameters are dynamically changeable:

```
LUTZ AS SYSDBA @ racdb11g1 SQL> ALTER SYSTEM SET
optimizer_capture_sql_plan_baselines= TRUE;
```

From now on, the optimizer starts capturing SQL execution plans automatically. A list of SQL_IDs, or the SQL log, is used to check if a statement has been executed before. The SQL_ID is a unique identifier by which a statement can be found in the AWR and the SMB. It was introduced in 10g and is created using an algorithm which can create more unique values than the old hashing algorithm for HASH VALUEs which were used before 10g to identify a shared SQP area in the LIBRARY CACHE

If a statement is parsed for the first time, its SQL_ID gets inserted into the SQL log in the SMB. For each statement that is executed multiple times, the optimizer starts maintaining a SQL plan history. There is a plan history for every repeatable SQL statement in the SMB.

The plan history includes all relevant information the optimizer has used to produce an execution plan and thus makes it reproducible. The information in the plan history includes the following:

- SQL text
- outline
- bind variables
- compilation environment

When a statement is parsed, the optimizer creates a best cost plan using object statistics from the data dictionary for the new statement. If it is parsed the first time, a SQL plan baseline is also created in the SMB for the new statement. The next time, the same statement is reparsed for whatever reason, so again a best cost plan is created. Before this plan can be used, the optimizer first checks if the same plan has been created before and if it is in the statement's plan baseline. If this is the case, the statement is executed with this plan. Subsequently created differing plans for the same statement are added to the plan history and marked for verification. They have the status ENABLED but not ACCEPTED and cannot be used for execution as long it has not been checked if they do not cause performance regression.

The verification is a task which can be performed manually by the DBA. It is called SQL plan evolution. It will be shown later that this can also be made manually using *dbms_spm.evolve_sql_plan_baseline*. The plan baselines can also be loaded manually from the cursor cache or SQL Tuning Sets. Only plans with status ENABLED and ACCEPTED are part of the SQL plan baseline. All other plans are part of the plan history.

SQL plan evolution can also happen automatically via a new automatic maintenance task. Oracle runs an automatic SQL tuning job every night. It can create SQL Profiles automatically and implement them, therefore populating SQL plan baselines. This will be covered more at the end of this section.

The next graphic shows the evaluation workflow for SQL Plan Management:

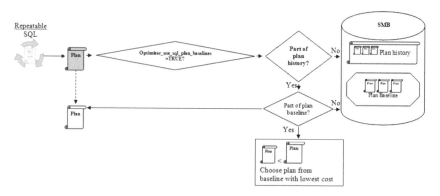

Figure 11.2: *Evaluation Workflow – SQL Plan Management*

The SMB can be monitored in the data dictionary:

```
LUTZ AS SYSDBA @ orcl11g SQL> SELECT * FROM
dba_sql_management_config;

PARAMETER_NAME         PARAMETER_VALUE LAST_MODIFIED   MODIFIED_BY
---------------------- --------------- -------------   -----------
SPACE_BUDGET_PERCENT   10
PLAN_RETENTION_WEEKS   53
```

The SMB consumes at least 1% and can use a maximum of 50% of the total size of the SYSAUX tablespace. By default, the space quota for the SMB is limited to 10% of the size of the SYSAUX tablespace. Unused execution plans are automatically purged from the SMB after 53 weeks by default with a weekly scheduled automatic task. The retention policy can be adjusted to any value between 5 and 523 week, which is more than 10 years!

The quota can be adjusted as well as the retention period for unused SQL execution plans with the built in package *dbms_spm*:

```
LUTZ AS SYSDBA @ orcl11g SQL> exec dbms_spm.configure -
                            ('space_budget_percent', 20 )
```

```
LUTZ AS SYSDBA @ orcl11g SQL> exec dbms_spm.configure -
                            ('plan_retention_weeks', 25)
```

```
LUTZ AS SYSDBA @ orcl11g SQL> SELECT * FROM
dba_sql_management_config;

PRAMETER_VALUE          LAST_MODIFIED                  MODIFIED_BY
--------------------    ---------------------------    -----------
-
SPACE_BUDGET_PERCENT  20  12-FEB-08 02.31.52.000000 PM   SYS
PLAN_RETENTION_WEEKS  25  12-FEB-08 02.34.04.000000 PM   SYS
```

The details can be viewed about existing SQL plan baselines with *dba_sql_plan_baselines*:

```
LUTZ AS SYSDBA @ racdb11g1 SQL> desc dba_sql_plan_baselines

 Name                                     Null?    Type
 ---------------------------------------- -------- ----------------
 -----------
 SIGNATURE                                NOT NULL NUMBER
 SQL_HANDLE                               NOT NULL VARCHAR2(30)
 SQL_TEXT                                 NOT NULL CLOB
 PLAN_NAME                                NOT NULL VARCHAR2(30)
 CREATOR                                           VARCHAR2(30)
 ORIGIN                                            VARCHAR2(14)
 PARSING_SCHEMA_NAME                               VARCHAR2(30)
 DESCRIPTION                                       VARCHAR2(500)
 VERSION                                           VARCHAR2(64)
```

```
CREATED                            NOT NULL TIMESTAMP(6)
LAST_MODIFIED                               TIMESTAMP(6)
LAST_EXECUTED                               TIMESTAMP(6)
LAST_VERIFIED                               TIMESTAMP(6)
ENABLED                                     VARCHAR2(3)
ACCEPTED                                    VARCHAR2(3)
FIXED                                       VARCHAR2(3)
AUTOPURGE                                   VARCHAR2(3)
OPTIMIZER_COST                              NUMBER
MODULE                                      VARCHAR2(48)
ACTION                                      VARCHAR2(32)
EXECUTIONS                                  NUMBER
ELAPSED_TIME                                NUMBER
CPU_TIME                                    NUMBER
BUFFER_GETS                                 NUMBER
DISK_READS                                  NUMBER
DIRECT_WRITES                               NUMBER
ROWS_PROCESSED                              NUMBER
FETCHES                                     NUMBER
END_OF_FETCH_COUNT                          NUMBER
```

```
LUTZ AS SYSDBA @ racdb11g1 SQL> SELECT count(*) FROM
dba_sql_plan_baselines;
```

```
  COUNT(*)
----------
         0                 -- Automatic capturing is now enabled
```

Oracle automatically handles changing execution plans with SQL plan baselines. A brand new database is being used so there are no parsed statements for any user tables yet. Run the first SELECT statement:

```
LUTZ AS SYSDBA @ racdb11g1 SQL> SELECT last_name, salary
                        FROM hr.employees
                        WHERE employee_id=100;
```

```
LAST_NAME                     SALARY
------------------------- ----------
King                           24000
```

Now find the 10 SQL plans that are in the SMB, the query plus recursive calls:

```
LUTZ AS SYSDBA @ racdb11g1 SQL> select SQL_TEXT, SQL_HANDLE from
dba_sql_plan_baselines;
```

```
SQL_TEXT
-------------------------------------------------------------
SQL_HANDLE
-------------------------------
delete from sdo_geor_ddl__table$$
SYS_SQL_02a86218930bbb20

 SELECT value
                        FROM gv$osstat
                        WHE
SYS_SQL_3a2aebd897c53743

SELECT INSTANTIABLE, supertype_owner, supertype_name,
LOCAL_ATTRIBUTES FROM all_
SYS_SQL_3b96046878c8878e

 SELECT inst_id, service_name,
             TO_CHAR(CAST(begin_time AS TIMES
SYS_SQL_3fb286c29fe007c1

 SELECT instance_name
                    FROM gv$instance

SYS_SQL_573300848514663d

select emd_url  from mgmt_targets where  target_name= :1 and
target_type=:2
SYS_SQL_7f900a3c2a229199

select last_name, salary from hr.employees where employee_id=100
SYS_SQL_818c1879b000a439

SELECT OWNER,JOB_NAME,COMMENTS FROM DBA_SCHEDULER_JOBS WHERE
JOB_NAME LIKE 'EM_I
SYS_SQL_82a5064ccbe7ec60

 SELECT s.inst_id, s.name, i.instance_name
                    FROM gv$active_se
SYS_SQL_bfae8140a25b2697

 SELECT value FROM gv$osstat
            WHERE SYS_SQL_e0292aa6e5e37835

10 rows selected.
```

This means that 10 SQL plan baselines have been selected in the SMB, one per captured statement. The optimizer has created a best cost plan for the SELECT and the plan for this execution is the only plan in the statement's SQL plan baseline now. The status of the plan is ENABLED and ACCEPTED but not FIXED. Fixed SQL Plan Baselines will be covered later on in the section about manual maintenance of SQL plan baselines.

ENABLED means that the plan was created as a best cost plan by the optimizer, ACCEPTED means that the plan has been verified as a good plan and is in the SQL plan baseline for this statement and can be used for execution. Obviously the first best cost plan which is created will always have the status ENABLED and ACCEPTED. It is the only plan which exists for the statement up to now.

Look at the SQL plan baseline for the following statement:

```
LUTZ AS SYSDBA @ racdb11g1 SQL> SELECT * FROM
table(dbms_xplan.display_sql_plan_baseline(sql_handle=>'SYS_SQL_818c
1879b000a439', format=> 'basic'));
```

```
PLAN_TABLE_OUTPUT
------------------------------------------------------------------
-----------

------------------------------------------------------------------
-----------
SQL handle: SYS_SQL_818c1879b000a439
SQL text: select last_name, salary from hr.employees where
employee_id=100
------------------------------------------------------------------
-----------

------------------------------------------------------------------
-----------
Plan name: SYS_SQL_PLAN_b000a439c0e983c6
Enabled: YES     Fixed: NO      Accepted: YES     Origin: AUTO-
CAPTURE
------------------------------------------------------------------
-----------

Plan hash value: 1833546154


-------------------------------------------------------
| Id  | Operation                   | Name         |
-------------------------------------------------------
|   0 | SELECT STATEMENT            |              |
|   1 |  TABLE ACCESS BY INDEX ROWID| EMPLOYEES    |
|   2 |   INDEX UNIQUE SCAN         | EMP_EMP_ID_PK |
-------------------------------------------------------

20 rows selected.
```

The 11g procedure *dbms_xplan.display_sql_plan_baseline* shows information based on the plan baseline. It would be better to say from the SQL Plan history because it also shows plans that are not ACCEPTED. The Oracle Documentation says SQL Plan Baseline.

The next time the statement gets executed, the optimizer will probably create a best cost plan for it. This time, it will add the new plan to plan history and mark it as NON-ACCEPTED. The optimizer looks in the execution history to determine if this statement has been executed before and verifies it by comparing the new best cost plan against those that already exist in the SQL plan baseline. If the new plan already exists in the baseline, the optimizer will use this plan. If the new plan does not exist in the baseline but is better in costs then the existing ones, it will be put into the plan baseline and marked as ACCEPTED and can then get used for further executions.

If the new plan is worse in cost than the ones already existing in the plan baseline, the optimizer will just add it the plan history. Plans marked as ENABLED only but not as ACCEPTED are plans which have been ACCEPTED once but are not accepted for execution currently or plans which were created as a best cost plan, though they have not been verified yet. This means that those plans are part of the baseline as plans that can be considered for execution.

Plans which are neither ENABLED nor ACCEPTED will only be part of the plan history for the statement as a plan which has been created as a best cost plan by the optimizer. The SQL plan baseline only consists of plans with status ACCEPTED plus ENABLED.

Now change something in the design. Drop the primary key of the table plus the index:

```
LUTZ AS SYSDBA @ racdb11g1 SQL> ALTER TABLE hr.employees DROP
PRIMARY KEY CASCADE;
Table altered.
```

```
LUTZ AS SYSDBA @ racdb11g1 SQL> DROP INDEX hr.emp_emp_id_pk;
Index dropped.
```

Run the statement again and look at the plan baseline. Now there are two plans in the baseline, the new one which is ENABLED and ACCEPTED for execution and the first one which is now ENABLED but not ACCEPTED any more:

```
LUTZ AS SYSDBA @ racdb11g1 SQL> SELECT *
                        FROM table
(dbms_xplan.display_sql_plan_baseline(sql_handle=>'SYS_SQL_818c1879b
000a439', format=> 'basic'));
```

```
PLAN_TABLE_OUTPUT
---------------------------------------------------
SQL handle: SYS_SQL_818c1879b000a439
SQL text: select last_name, salary from hr.employees where
employee_id=100
----------------------------------------------------------------------
----------

----------------------------------------------------------------------
-----------
Plan name: SYS_SQL_PLAN_b000a439c0e983c6
Enabled: YES     Fixed: NO      Accepted: YES     Origin: AUTO-
CAPTURE
----------------------------------------------------------------------
-----------

Plan hash value: 1445457117

----------------------------------------
| Id  | Operation          | Name      |
----------------------------------------
|   0 | SELECT STATEMENT   |           |
|   1 |   TABLE ACCESS FULL| EMPLOYEES |

----------------------------------------
SQL handle: SYS_SQL_818c1879b000a439
SQL text: select last_name, salary from hr.employees where
employee_id=100
----------------------------------------------------------------------
--------
Plan name: SYS_SQL_PLAN_b000a4397d478871
Enabled: YES     Fixed: NO      Accepted: NO      Origin: AUTO-
CAPTURE
```

```
------------------------------------------------------------------
--------
Plan hash value: 3640292141

------------------------------------------------------
| Id | Operation                    | Name         |
------------------------------------------------------
|  0 | SELECT STATEMENT             |              |
|  1 |  TABLE ACCESS BY INDEX ROWID| EMPLOYEES     |
|  2 |   INDEX UNIQUE SCAN          | EMPLOYEES_PK |
Source ------------------------------------------------------
```

So the optimizer has created a new best cost plan for the statement and now uses a full table scan instead of an index access. The original plan has been invalidated because it is non-reproducible since the index used is gone.

Add a primary key again and run the statements again. There are now three plans in the plan baseline, the new one that uses the new primary key and the two historical plans. Note that only one plan is ACCEPTED now the others are only ENABLED. The old plan with the index access was invalidated because it was not reproducible and now the server has remembered that there was a better plan sometime in the past, from the plan history, which used an index and performed much better. It puts this plan in place for further executions automatically:

```
LUTZ AS SYSDBA @ racdb11g1 SQL> ALTER TABLE hr.employees ADD
CONSTRAINT employees_pk PRIMARY KEY (employee_id);
Table altered.
```

```
LUTZ AS SYSDBA @ racdb11g1 SQL> SELECT last_name, salary FROM
hr.employees WHERE employee_id=100;
LAST_NAME                    SALARY
------------------------ ----------
King                          24000
```

```
LUTZ AS SYSDBA @ racdb11g1 SQL> SELECT *
                       FROM table
(dbms_xplan.display_sql_plan_baseline(sql_handle=>'SYS_SQL_818c1879b
000a439', format=> 'basic'));

PLAN_TABLE_OUTPUT
------------------------------------
SQL handle: SYS_SQL_818c1879b000a439
```

```
SQL text: select last_name, salary from hr.employees where
employee_id=100
----------------------------------------------------------------------
--------
Plan name: SYS_SQL_PLAN_b000a4397d478871
Enabled: YES      Fixed: NO      Accepted: NO      Origin: AUTO-
CAPTURE
----------------------------------------------------------------------
--------

Plan hash value: 3640292141

---------------------------------------------------
| Id  | Operation                   | Name        |
---------------------------------------------------
|   0 | SELECT STATEMENT            |             |
|   1 |  TABLE ACCESS BY INDEX ROWID| EMPLOYEES   |
|   2 |   INDEX UNIQUE SCAN         | EMPLOYEES_PK |
Source ---------------------------------------------------

----------------------------------------------------------------------
--
Plan name: SYS_SQL_PLAN_b000a439c0e983c6
Enabled: YES      Fixed: NO      Accepted: YES     Origin: AUTO-
CAPTURE
----------------------------------------------------------------------
--

Plan hash value: 3640292141

---------------------------------------------------
| Id  | Operation                   | Name        |
---------------------------------------------------
|   0 | SELECT STATEMENT            |             |
|   1 |  TABLE ACCESS BY INDEX ROWID| EMPLOYEES   |
|   2 |   INDEX UNIQUE SCAN         | EMPLOYEES_PK |
---------------------------------------------------

----------------------------------------------------------------------
--
Plan name: SYS_SQL_PLAN_b000a439cf314e9e
Enabled: YES      Fixed: NO      Accepted: NO      Origin: AUTO-
CAPTURE
----------------------------------------------------------------------
---

Plan hash value: 1445457117

-------------------------------------
| Id  | Operation        | Name      |
-------------------------------------
|   0 | SELECT STATEMENT |           |
|   1 |  TABLE ACCESS FULL| EMPLOYEES |
-------------------------------------

49 rows selected.
```

Here are the details from the data dictionary of the plan baseline:

```
LUTZ AS SYSDBA @ racdb11g1 SQL> SELECT sql_handle,
                                       plan_name,
                                       enabled,
                                       accepted,
                                       fixed
                                FROM   dba_sql_plan_baselines
                                WHERE  LOWER(sql_text) LIKE
'%hr.employees%';
```

```
SQL_HANDLE                PLAN_NAME                         ENA ACC FIX
------------------------- --------------------------------- --- --- ---
SYS_SQL_818c1879b000a439  SYS_SQL_PLAN_b000a4397d478871     YES NO  NO
SYS_SQL_818c1879b000a439  SYS_SQL_PLAN_b000a439c0e983c6     YES YES NO
SYS_SQL_818c1879b000a439  SYS_SQL_PLAN_b000a439cf314e9e     YES NO  NO
```

This example was not really fair because dropping an index forces the optimizer to come up with something new. So what happens if a plan cannot be reproduced?

If a SELECT has been parsed before an index ever existed and then reparsed after an index has been created, the optimizer would create a new best cost plan but leave it marked as NON ACCEPTED but ENABLED. This is because the original plan is still reproducible since an index is added and it also works without it. In the case of an index drop, the original plan which would use the index is not reproducible and cannot be used as such.

So in the case of an index creation after the SELECT was parsed the first time, the index will not be used for execution until the plan baseline is evolved manually. In this case, it is the DBA's job to manually evolve the plan baseline. A good way to deal with such a case would be to capture the full scan first and then stop auto capture in order not to get too many different plans. After adding the index, wait for the auto SQL tuning task job to run the next time or trigger SQL tuning manually and look at the

---

results and possibly load new plans manually into the plan baseline.

Also, new optimizer statistics gathered overnight would not lead to an automatic evolution of a SQL plan baseline unless the auto-task job starts evaluating the statement and permission has been given to automatically implement SQL Profiles. The SQL plan management with the SMB is a conservative method to guarantee plan stability in the first place.

So the next question to ask is what is it good for?

Use cases for Automatic SQL Plan Management

Good candidate situations would certainly be any upgrades of the Oracle 11g database system. Again, use a testing system with a changed environment, possibly a Snapshot Standby Database, and run the application for a representative period of time. During this period, Automatic SQL Plan Management would be enabled and Oracle would evolve the SQL Plan Baselines for the application.

After this evolution, it is possible to use *dbms_spm* to create a staging table and then *expdp* to EXPORT the captured baselines and import them into the production system directly after upgrading. This would guarantee stable execution plans from the very beginning. How this is done will be shown in detail shortly.

Another scenario would be the deployment of a new application. The application vendor would ship well tuned plans in the form of exported SQL plan baselines together with the application that could be imported after the application was added to the database system. This would guarantee that the good plans would be used right away from the very beginning. Oracle would use new plans only if they were verified to not cause performance degradation.

A variation of this case could be using an 11g database as a testing system and import SQL Tuning Sets using a staging table from a pre-11g database system. By setting *optimizer_features_enable* to a pre-11g value, Oracle finds the best execution plans for the workload on the 11g testing system. After this, use the SQL Tuning set packed into a staging table again and then import them back into the pre-11g database.

SQL Plan Management in OEM

The enterprise manager comes with an interface for SQL plan management and offers full control of SQL plan evolution.

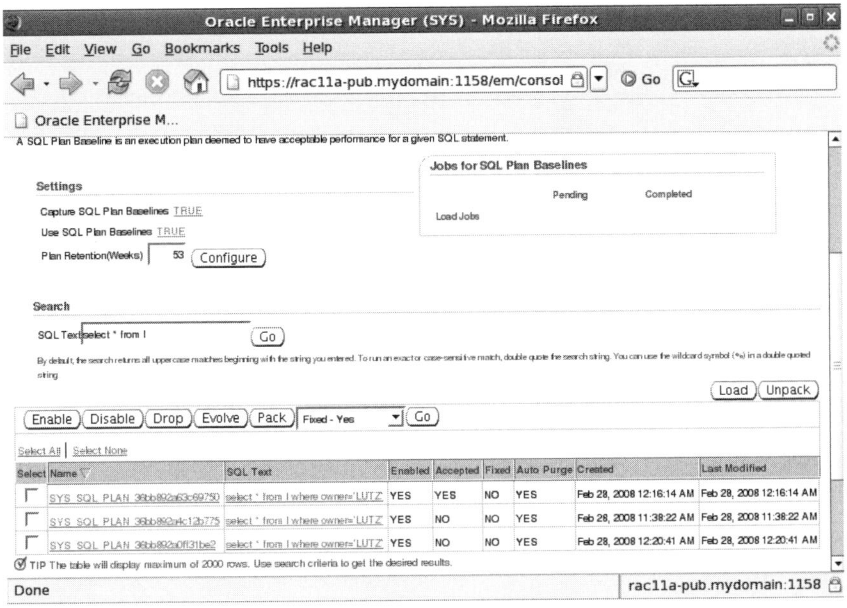

Figure 11.3: *SQL Plan Control for the SMB*

This shows the link to SQL Plan Control for the SMB in the Query Optimizer section of the SERVER pane. Also find the SQL Profiles and SQL Patches. SQL Patches can be created with the 11g SQL Repair Advisor. They are possibly stored in the SMB.

How Manual SQL Plan Loading works

By default, Automatic SQL Plan Capture is disabled in 11g. Therefore, feed the SQL Plan Baselines manually if this feature needs to be used. There are multiple ways to manage SQL Plan Baselines manually. All of them utilize the packages *dbms_spm* and possibly *dbms_sqltune*.

The SQL plans can be loaded manually into SQL Plan Baselines from three different sources:

- SQL tuning sets
- AWR snapshots
- Cursor cache

The CONFIGURE procedure of the package *dbms_spm* can be used to adjust the size and retention policy for the SMB. This package is the command line interface for the SMB and, thus the SQL plan Baselines, and it provides full control for Manual SQL Plan Management.

It contains procedures and functions for loading execution plans from the various sources and for packing them into staging tables as well unpacking them again. The package can be used to DROP and ALTER plan baselines.

> 🔔 The ADMINISTER SQL MANAGEMENT OBJECT system privilege is needed to use the package *dbms_spm*.

Until now, SQL plan baselines were shown that were not fixed. This means that the optimizer uses costing mechanisms to evaluate plans. With Manual SQL Management, plans can be fixed in baselines, thereby forcing the optimizer to consider only those plans from a plan baseline that have been manually marked as possible candidates.

There might be reasons why a guarantee may be desired that states the execution plans for certain SQL do not change, i.e. Plan Stability. For example, a new application has been developed using Oracle database 11g that has been tested thoroughly and is now ready to be deployed to the customers. Since it cannot be known how the application would behave in the environment at the customer's site, the baselines could be fixed for the SQL and ship them together with the application where the well-tuned plans could be fed into the customer's system. This way, encountering regression can be avoided in the well tuned application.

Now force the optimizer to use the one and only chosen plan:

```
LUTZ AS SYSDBA@racdb11g1 SQL>  var my_var number
LUTZ AS SYSDBA@racdb11g1 SQL>exec :my_var :=
dbms_spm.alter_sql_plan_baseline -
> (sql_handle => 'SYS_SQL_818c1879b000a439', -
> plan_name => ' SYS_SQL_PLAN_b000a4397d478871', -
> attribute_name => 'ACCEPTED', attribute_value => 'YES')
PL/SQL procedure successfully completed.
```

Using *dbms_spm.alter_sql_plan_baseline,* the plan has been changed to ACCEPTED and, therefore, added it to the plan baseline. So how is this achieved by looking at the baseline from above again?

```
LUTZ AS SYSDBA @ racdb11g1 SQL> SELECT sql_handle,
                                       plan_name,
                                       enabled,
                                       accepted,
                                       fixed
                                FROM   dba_sql_plan_baselines
                                WHERE  LOWER(sql_text) LIKE
'%hr.employees%';
```

```
SQL_HANDLE                    PLAN_NAME                              ENA
ACC FIX
------------------------      --------------------------------  ---  ---  ---
SYS_SQL_818c1879b000a439      SYS_SQL_PLAN_b000a4397d478871      YES  YES  NO
SYS_SQL_818c1879b000a439      SYS_SQL_PLAN_b000a439c0e983c6      YES  YES  NO
SYS_SQL_818c1879b000a439      SYS_SQL_PLAN_b000a439cf314e9e      YES  NO   NO
```

There are three plans in the statement history for the SQL handle SYS_SQL_818c1879b000a439. All three are ENABLED, two are ACCEPTED. Those two are part of the plan baseline for the statement. The optimizer will choose either of those two. None of the plans is FIXED. This means that the plan baseline is NOT FIXED as plans can still evolve.

This plan baseline can also be forced to be static by fixing a plan in it:

```
LUTZ AS SYSDBA@racdb11g1 SQL>  var my_var number
LUTZ AS SYSDBA@racdb11g1 SQL>exec :my_var :=
dbms_spm.alter_sql_plan_baseline -
> (sql_handle => 'SYS_SQL_818c1879b000a439', -
> plan_name => 'SYS_SQL_PLAN_b000a439c0e983c6', -
> attribute_name => 'FIXED', attribute_value => 'YES')
PL/SQL procedure successfully completed.
```

The function has changed one plan in the baseline:

```
LUTZ AS SYSDBA @ racdb11g1 SQL> print my_var
    MY_VAR
----------
         1
```

```
LUTZ AS SYSDBA @ racdb11g1 SQL>  SELECT  sql_handle,
                                         plan_name,
                                         enabled,
                                         accepted,
                                         fixed
                                 FROM dba_sql_plan_baselines
WHERE LOWER(sql_text) LIKE '%hr.employees%';
```

```
SQL_HANDLE                      PLAN_NAME                      ENA
ACC FIX
------------------------------- ------------------------------ --- --
- ---
SYS_SQL_818c1879b000a439        SYS_SQL_PLAN_b000a4397d478871  YES
YES NO
SYS_SQL_818c1879b000a439        SYS_SQL_PLAN_b000a439c0e983c6  YES
YES YES
SYS_SQL_818c1879b000a439        SYS_SQL_PLAN_b000a439cf314e9e  YES NO
NO
```

Now this plan is fixed and the baseline is fixed as well. If none of the ACCEPTED plans in the plan baseline are reproducible, the optimizer will pick the best cost plan from the list of the plans with status only ENABLED. The optimizer will now advance this one fixed plan for execution and only choose a non-fixed but ACCEPTED plan if none of the fixed plans are reproducible. Plan evolution does not apply for fixed plan baselines. A plan baseline is FIXED as soon as it contains at least one plan with the attribute FIXED=YES.

Now pack this one plan from the baseline into a staging table and ship it to another system with export. First, create a staging table MY_STG_TAB in the tablespace USERS owned by the user SYSTEM:

```
LUTZ AS SYSDBA @ racdb11g1 SQL> exec dbms_spm.create_stgtab_baseline
(-
> table_name => 'MY_STG_TAB', table_owner =>'SYSTEM' ,
tablespace_name => 'USERS')
PL/SQL procedure successfully completed.
```

Here is the information that will be packed into the staging table:

```
LUTZ AS SYSDBA @ racdb11g1 SQL> desc system.MY_STG_TAB

 Name                                      Null?    Type
 ----------------------------------------- -------- ----------------
 ------------
 VERSION                                            NUMBER
 SIGNATURE                                          NUMBER
 SQL_HANDLE                                         VARCHAR2(30)
 OBJ_NAME                                           VARCHAR2(30)
 OBJ_TYPE                                           VARCHAR2(30)
```

```
PLAN_ID                          NUMBER
SQL_TEXT                         CLOB
CREATOR                          VARCHAR2(30)
ORIGIN                           VARCHAR2(30)
DESCRIPTION                      VARCHAR2(500)
DB_VERSION                       VARCHAR2(64)
CREATED                          TIMESTAMP(6)
LAST_MODIFIED                    TIMESTAMP(6)
LAST_EXECUTED                    TIMESTAMP(6)
LAST_VERIFIED                    TIMESTAMP(6)
STATUS                           NUMBER
OPTIMIZER_COST                   NUMBER
MODULE                           VARCHAR2(48)
ACTION                           VARCHAR2(32)
EXECUTIONS                       NUMBER
ELAPSED_TIME                     NUMBER
CPU_TIME                         NUMBER
BUFFER_GETS                      NUMBER
DISK_READS                       NUMBER
DIRECT_WRITES                    NUMBER
ROWS_PROCESSED                   NUMBER
FETCHES                          NUMBER
END_OF_FETCH_COUNT               NUMBER
CATEGORY                         VARCHAR2(30)
SQLFLAGS                         NUMBER
TASK_ID                          NUMBER
TASK_EXEC_NAME                   VARCHAR2(30)
TASK_OBJ_ID                      NUMBER
TASK_FND_ID                      NUMBER
TASK_REC_ID                      NUMBER
INUSE_FEATURES                   NUMBER
PARSE_CPU_TIME                   NUMBER
PRIORITY                         NUMBER
OPTIMIZER_ENV                    RAW(2000)
BIND_DATA                        RAW(2000)
PARSING_SCHEMA_NAME              VARCHAR2(30)
COMP_DATA                        CLOB
```

Now pack the one and only plan into the staging table:

```
LUTZ AS SYSDBA @ racdb11g1 SQL> exec :my_var:=
dbms_spm.pack_stgtab_baseline (-
> table_name => 'MY_STG_TAB', table_owner =>'SYSTEM' , -
> sql_handle => 'SYS_SQL_818c1879b000a439' ,   -
> plan_name => 'SYS_SQL_PLAN_b000a439c0e983c6', fixed => 'YES')
PL/SQL procedure successfully completed.
```

```
LUTZ AS SYSDBA @ racdb11g1 SQL> print my_var
```

```
    MY_VAR
----------
         1
```

This is what is in the staging table now:

```
LUTZ AS SYSDBA @ racdb11g1 SQL> select SQL_HANDLE,  OBJ_NAME,
SQL_TEXT from  system.my_stg_tab;

SQL_HANDLE                  OBJ_NAME           SQL_TEXT
------------------------ ---------- ------------------ ------------
-----------
SYS_SQL_818c1879b000a439 SYS_SQL_PLAN_b000a439c0e983c6  select
last_name, salary from hr.employees where employee_id=100
```

Now import the staging table using a database link with *impdp* into another database where the SQL plan baseline is unloaded:

```
SYSTEM  @ prod11g1 SQL> CREATE DATABASE LINK imp_link
  2  CONNECT TO system IDENTIFIED BY oracle1
  3  USING 'racdb11g1';

[oracle@rac11a-pub ~]$ impdp system/oracle1 tables='MY_STG_TAB'
network_link=imp_link directory=imp_dir logfile=stg_imp.log
Import: Release 11.1.0.6.0 - Production on Wednesday, 13 February,
2008 0:47:57

Copyright (c) 2003, 2007, Oracle.  All rights reserved.

Connected to: Oracle Database 11g Enterprise Edition Release
11.1.0.6.0 - Production
With the Partitioning, Real Application Clusters, OLAP, Data Mining
and Real Application Testing options
Starting "SYSTEM"."SYS_IMPORT_TABLE_01":  system/********
tables=MY_STG_TAB network_link=imp_link directory=imp_dir
logfile=stg_imp.log
Estimate in progress using BLOCKS method...
Processing object type TABLE_EXPORT/TABLE/TABLE_DATA
Total estimation using BLOCKS method: 192 KB
Processing object type TABLE_EXPORT/TABLE/TABLE
. . imported "SYSTEM"."MY_STG_TAB"                          1 rows
Job "SYSTEM"."SYS_IMPORT_TABLE_01" successfully completed at
00:48:52
```

Look at the imported staging table now:

```
LUTZ AS SYSDBA @ prod11g1 SQL> SELECT sql_handle,
                               obj_name,
                               sql_text,
                               db_version,
                               origin
                        FROM  system.my_stg_tab;
```

```
SQL_HANDLE                    OBJ_NAME                      SQL_TEXT
DB_VERSION ORIGIN
----------------------        ----------------------        --------------
----  -----------   -----------
SYS_SQL_818c1879b000a439  SYS_SQL_PLAN_b000a439c0e983c6
select last_name, salary from hr.employees where employee_id=100
11.1.0.6.0 AUTO-CAPTURE
```

Check the SQL plan baseline in the target system:

```
LUTZ AS SYSDBA @ prod11g1 SQL> SELECT sql_handle,
                                      plan_name,
                                      enabled,
                                      accepted,
                                      fixed
                               FROM dba_sql_plan_baselines
                               WHERE LOWER(sql_text) LIKE
'%hr.employees%'
LUTZ AS SYSDBA @ prod11g1 SQL> /
no rows selected
```

Of course there is nothing yet, so unpack the staging table first:

```
LUTZ AS SYSDBA @ prod11g1 SQL> var new_var number

SYS AS SYSDBA@prod11g1 SQL> exec :new_var:=
dbms_spm.unpack_stgtab_baseline (-
>   table_name => 'MY_STG_TAB', table_owner =>'SYSTEM' , -
>            sql_handle => 'SYS_SQL_818c1879b000a439',-
>            plan_name => 'SYS_SQL_PLAN_b000a439c0e983c6', -
>            fixed => 'YES')
PL/SQL procedure successfully completed.
```

Check again and here it is!

```
LUTZ AS SYSDBA @ prod11g1 SQL> select  sql_handle, plan_name,
enabled, accepted, fixed
  2  FROM dba_sql_plan_baselines;
SQL_HANDLE                    PLAN_NAME                       ENA
ACC FIX
---------------------------   ------------------------------  --- --
- ---
SYS_SQL_818c1879b000a439      SYS_SQL_PLAN_b000a439c0e983c6   YES
YES YES
```

This has demonstrated how to export single plans from a SQL
plan baseline. It is also possible to pack all or selected plans

---

sourced from the cursor cache or SQL tuning sets into a staging table for export/import.

Integration of SQL Plan Management with Automatic SQL Tuning

Oracle 10g gave DBAs the ability to create SQL Profiles. This is a powerful tool, especially for database administrators who need to tune SQL that is outside of their control. For example, there is a third-party application where the queries it generates can not be modified. In this case, a DBA could generate a SQL Profile to tune poorly written SQL from this application.

The next step is also already implemented in Oracle database 11g. It is called Automatic SQL Tuning. With this feature enabled, Oracle runs an automatic task job every night in a maintenance window. These improvements may be through one of the following methods:

- SQL Profiles - supplementary statistics specific to a given statement; SQL profiles are particularly useful for packaged applications

- SQL Structure – these are problems that may be syntactic, semantic or just poorly written SQL

- Statistics – good statistics are generally always required for the optimizer

- Indexes - a data structure that improves the speed of operations in a table

Also referred to as Automatic SQL Tuning Advisor, it can search for high load SQL and start automatically tuning the worst statements. Output could be recommendations about missing indexes for instance. Automatic SQL Tuning utilizes the statistics from the Automatic Workload Repository (AWR) and churns through this data on a nightly basis. The administrator can decide to have these improvements automatically implemented. This is not enabled by default. The job would then feed the SQL plan baselines with the plans from the automatically created and implemented SQL profiles and mark the new plans as ENABLED and ACCEPTED.

The *sys_auto_sql_tuning_task* runs in the daily maintenance window and can be monitored with the data dictionary view *dba_advisor_executions*. The Automatic SQL Tuning job can be managed via the built in package *dbms_auto_task_admin*. The choice can also be made to not fix the plan in the new baseline and allow the optimizer from now on to evolve the plan baseline and use new best cost plans found for the statement, but only if it has been verified that they do not cause performance regression.

If the Automatic Tuning job finds a better plan and implements a SQL Profile automatically and automatic implementation of SQL Profiles has been allowed, it adds the new plan to the plan baseline but does not verify existing unaccepted plans. The criteria for automatic implementation of SQL profiles and feeding new plans into the plan baselines would be that the improvement of the new plan sums up to at least three times less cost (sum of CPU and I/O time). Only High Load Repeatable SQL is automatically tuned. Who cares about low load SQL?

The syntax to enable Automatic SQL Tuning is as follows:

```
LUTZ AS SYSDBA @ prod11g1 SQL> BEGIN
dbms_sqltune.set_tuning_task_parameter('SYS_AUTO_SQL_TUNING_TASK',
'ACCEPT_SQL_PROFILES', 'TRUE');
END;
```

> 🔔 The default value for *accept_sql_profiles* is FALSE!

Automatic SQL Tuning can be managed from the 11g OEM Database Control by clicking on the Server tab and then on Automated Maintenance Tasks. Figure 11.4 below shows that Automatic SQL Tuning is a schedulable maintenance task.

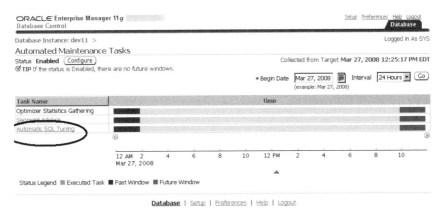

Figure 11.4: *Automated Maintenance Tasks*

Drilling into Automatic SQL Tuning is shown below:

Figure 11.5: *Tuning Result Summary*

In Figure 11.5, SQL Profiles would not be automatically implemented on this particular database since this is the default for 11g. This is usually the way Oracle introduces new options in their products. In the initial release, it is disabled by default. In release plus one or release plus two, it is enabled by default.

In order to enable the automatic implementation of SQL Profiles, the DBA would click the Configure button. The next screen is the task configuration screen.

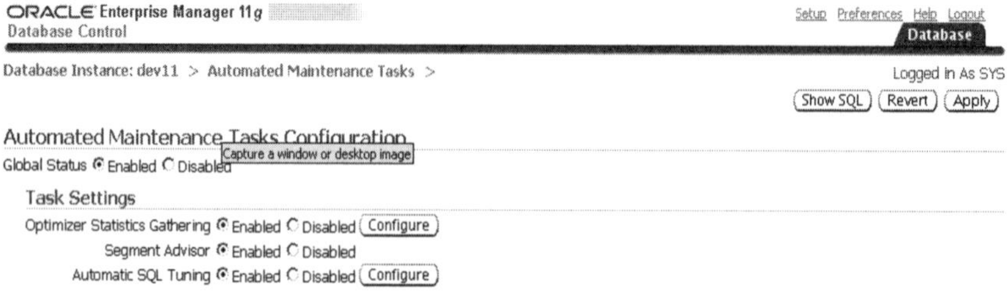

Figure 11.6: *Task Configuration Screen*

Clicking the Configure button allows the administrator to enable the Automatic Implementation of SQL Profiles as shown below.

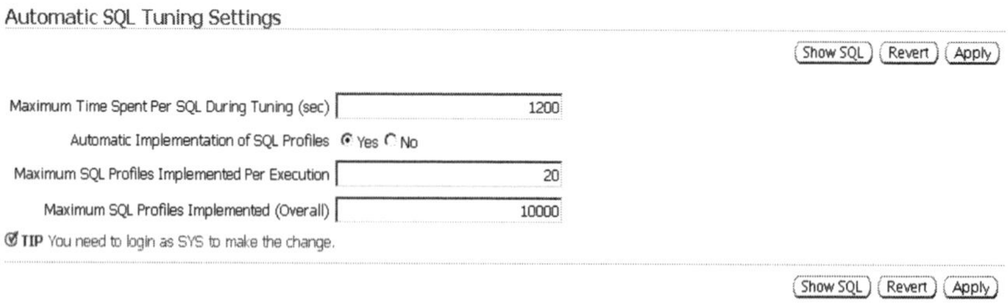

Figure 11.7: *SQL Automatic Implementation*

Any good DBA is going to be very cautious of this new feature. One way to ease into this new feature would be to enable this on the test instance. Once enabled, it can be checked periodically to see what SQL Profiles have been implemented as well as other recommendations the tool is making. To see these recommendations log into the 11g OEM Database Control. Click on the Server tab, then on Automated Maintenance Tasks, and then on Automatic SQL Tuning. For example, Automatic SQL Tuning has looked at 237 SQL statements over a period of 31 runs (nightly by default). It can also be seen from Figure 11.8

that the database most likely has missing or old statistics. Additionally, it has found some SQL that could use restructuring as well as several SQL Profiles that would improve performance.

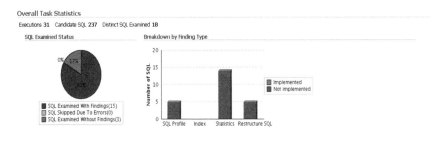

Figure 11.8: *Automatic SQL Tuning Overall Task Statistics*

The administrator can view the recommendations made in even greater detail than is shown above, as seen in Figure 11.9. This screen also gives the ability to implement all recommendations which may include gathering of statistics, creation of SQL Profiles, index creation, and the restructuring of SQL.

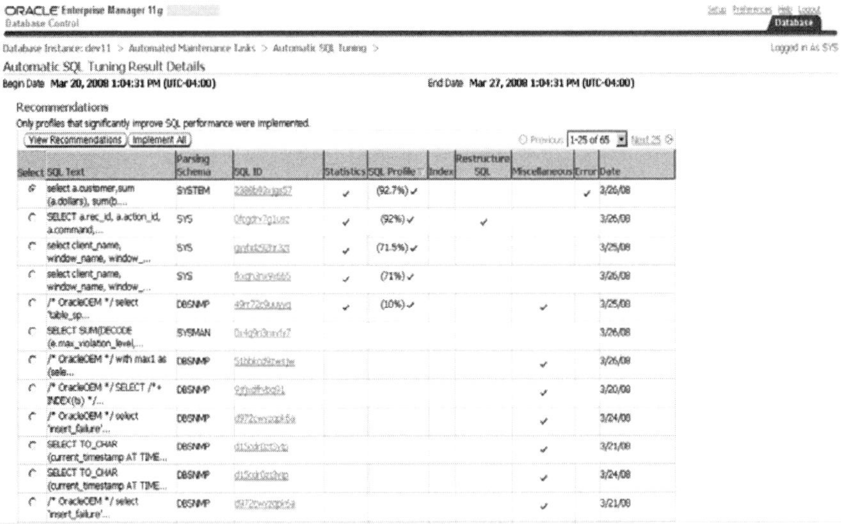

Figure 11.9: *Implementing Recommendations Screen*

Finally, to view the expected benefits gained by implementing the recommendations, Automatic SQL Tuning provides the pre-calculated time savings in the form of a column chart as shown in Figure 11.10.

Figure 11.10: *Precalculated Time Savings Chart*

One may read about Automatic SQL Tuning and take away that DBAs are no longer needed to tune a database. However, further inspection would show that Automatic SQL Tuning will free-up a DBA to focus on higher value tasks, at the very least.

<table>
<tr>
<td></td>
<td>This is a huge improvement over the hit-and-miss SQL tuning techniques of the past, but it's not a truly "fully-automated" approach either. We must remember that there will always be "outlier" SQL statements that must be tuned manually.</td>
</tr>
</table>

Conclusion

SQL Plan management is a proactive approach to possible upcoming problems and can help to ensure that performance regression is prevented and only execution plans which are significantly better than the well tuned and well known plans can be used by the optimizer.

Oracle 11g Flashback

A brief history of FLASHBACK functionalities

The first flashback functionalities came with the *dbms_flashback* packages within the release of Oracle 9.0. Flashback functionalities enabled the DBA to specify a consistent point in time for the session. By using *dbms_flashback.enable_at_time(my_timestamp)*, a session could be put into a state which read the consistent image of the database as it was at a point in time in the past.

This was enhanced in version 9.2 when Oracle introduced the Flashback Query functionality. The Flashback Query enabled users to query data as it appeared in the past, using normal SQL:

```
SELECT ...
   FROM...
      AS OF TIMESTAMP|SCN
   WHERE...
...;
```

Reading data by specifying a timestamp or a system change number (SCN) was also common at the time. Internally, every SELECT is a SELECT AS OF TIMESTAMP SYSDATE. Only as of version 9.2 was the normal user able to specify a timestamp to read the consistent data.

This concept was extended in Oracle's first 10g release on a row level. Consequently, the Flashback Versions Query functionality could be used to view all versions of a given row between two timestamps and two SCNs.

Once the transactions had been identified, it was also possible to look at the UNDO_SQL column of a view called *flashback_transaction_query*. The transaction's ID, using the pseudo column VERSIONS_XID, could also be found. The following pseudo columns are available with Flashback Versions Query:

- VERSIONS_XID
- VERSIONS_STARTSCN
- VERSIONS_STARTSCN
- VERSIONS_ENDSCN
- VERSIONS_STARTTIME
- VERSIONS_ENDTIME
- VERSIONS_OPERATION

Here, changes that were made by the same transaction could be found, per the appropriate SELECT ANY TRANSACTION system privilege.

```
SELECT UNDO_SQL
  FROM flashback_transaction_query
    WHERE XID=HEXTORAW('my_transaction-id');
```

This gave the principal option to spool the *undo_sql* from the *flashback_transaction_query* view and execute it to undo changes. However, this was not practical because of dependencies in transactions and applications that made it difficult to undo things in the correct sequence. Luckily, this has been addressed in Oracle 11g. This functionality will be examined shortly.

All flashback functionalities covered so far have utilized information from the Undo Segments in order to read the consistent image of data in the past. These types of functionalities do not change anything in the database, but instead read data as it was in the past. UNDO data is the logical information needed to undo a change. This being, if the logical information needed to undo a change is overwritten in between, then an error message appears explaining that it is not possible to reconstruct the consistent data in the past. However, 10gR1 introduced a number of other extensively new functionalities under the name FLASHBACK.

An example of the unique 10gR1 functionalities is the Flashback Drop. The Flashback Drop utilized the so-called recycle bin that could be disabled with the *recyclebin* parameter in Oracle 10gR2. The *recyclebin* had been enabled by default in prior releases, and in 10gR1 this parameter was the hidden parameter *_recyclebin.*. If a DBA dropped a table in 10g, it would be internally renamed and the segment would stay where it was. These extents were available for reuse or review in *dba_free_space*, but the server tries not to use them as long as possible. Oracle starts reusing these extents before auto extending a datafile. Once the server has reused the extents it is not possible to flashback to before drop. This process enabled the user to flashback the drop and simply rename the object back to its original name. Indexes and triggers are also flashed back.

> Foreign key constraints are not flashed back with the table. They must be manually recreated!

Since the object remained the same as before the drop operation, it also became possible for the DBA to read from it using the new name. The Flashback Query also offered the ability to read the object as it was in the past by using the new name and SELECT.

Another new feature in Oracle Database 10gR1 was Flashback Table. This provided the ability to put a table back into the state it was in at a previous point by applying undo data. FLASHBACK had previously only been possible in a tablespace with Automatic Segment Space Management (ASSM) and enabled ROW MOVEMENT on the table intended to use flashback. Until 10gR2, ASSM had been the default for tablespaces. ALTER TABLE *my_table* ENABLE ROW MOVEMENT allows the server to change the physical address of a row exceptionally. The ROWID is normally assigned with insertion and valid for the life time of a row.

```
FLASHBACK TABLE my_table
  TO TIMESTAMP|SCN;
```

The DBA was limited in the inability to flashback to a time before a DDL statement because if the definition of the table changed in between the flashback operation, it would error out.

Last but not least is Flashback Database, which was also introduced in 10gR1, with completely different technology. FLASHBACK DATABASE was not enabled by default and could only be enabled if the database was in ARCHIVELOG mode with the FLASH RECOVERY AREA defined. The parameters *db_recovery_file_dest* and *db_recovery_file_dest_size* are used to define a flash recovery area. In order to enable Flashback Database, DBAs had to shutdown and startup the database and make an entry into the controlfile with:

```
ALTER DATABASE FLASHBACK ON;
```

This would then start the recovery writer, *rvwr,* background process and allocate the flashback buffer in shared memory. Keep in mind that the size of the flashback buffer is dependent on the size of the redo log buffer. It reaches its full size of 16M if the redo log buffer has a size of at least 8M.

The *rvwr* creates the copies of buffers of the buffer cache before they are modified into the flashback buffer and flushes them to disk based on a complex algorithm. Once enabled, Oracle copied before images of buffers that had been modified in the buffer cache to the flashback buffer. From there, the *rvwr* would flush them to disk into the flashback logs of the flash recovery area. These copies could then be used to restore blocks directly in the datafiles during a flashback database operation. This was done using SQL*Plus, *rman* , or the OEM interface that would call *rman*.

Via the *flashback_retention_target* parameter, users were able to specify when flashback logs would age out from the flashback logs automatically. This determines how far into the past the database could be recovered. Also, a restore point was introduced as a named point in time to remember a timestamp or SCN that may be used for a flashback.

Since Oracle Database 10gR2, it has been possible to create guaranteed restore points. This provides the ability to use FLASHBACK for exactly one point in time in the past. As opposed to the normal restore points, these restore points are reliable. They do not age out unless the DBA deletes them, and can be used even if FLASHBACK is not enabled for the database. The flashback logs then hold all block copies which need to flash the database back to the particular point in time. This can be used for situations such as application upgrades. An ideal situation for using the flashback functionality is establishing a guaranteed restore point before an upgrade so that if results are unsatisfactory, the whole upgrade can easily be undone.

TRANSACTION BACKOUT in Oracle 11g

Transaction backout without OEM using PL/SQL

As of 10g, data could be read as a point in time in the past, and *undo sql* was viewed and manually applied to a segment level using flashback tables. Undoing all changes to a point in time in the past consisted of using OEM, Grid Control or Database control to flashback on a database level. However, it was not possible to apply undo for an entire transaction, including all dependent transactions. As of 11g however, flashing back transactions is now possible. This includes all dependencies and writing after write operations.

The functionality used to flashback transactions is called Transaction Backout.Transaction Backout utilizes LOGMINER functionalities. There are two interfaces for this feature:

- the new built in package *dbms_flashback*

- Oracle Enterprise Manager, including OEM, Grid Control and Database Control

Before this feature can be used, the database has to be prepared. Because the LogMiner functionality is being used to flashback transactions, all necessary information should be recorded in the redo log files. In other words, supplemental logging should be enabled, and it should be ensured that Oracle adds additional information into the redo stream. This warrants two important considerations:

- Oracle must be able to group and merge information for DML operations for objects like Index Organized Tables (OITs), clustered tables, and chained blocks. This is enabled by adding minimal supplemental logging data to the redo logs. Oracle will then be able to store the before image of the modified columns into the redo log files necessary for transaction recovery or instance recovery. Furthermore, Oracle will also store additional information about other columns in the row used as examples to reconstruct a full row from the redo independent of the physical address of the row.

The before image consists of all the logical information needed to undo a change applied to a block. This is used to perform any kind of recovery, transaction recovery, or instance recovery. It is stored in the undo segments and redo logs. In other words, redo is needed for the undo, in case an instance crash occurs in order to reconstruct undo information that was lost in the cache and was not on disk. Logging must be enabled for a transaction backout operation, and can be done using the following statement:

```
SYS AS SYSDBA @ orcl SQL> ALTER DATABASE ADD SUPPLEMENTAL LOG
DATA;
```

- When a row with a primary key is updated, all the columns of primary keys should be placed into the redo logs. The updated row can then be identified by the primary key as well as the ROWID.

It is also possible that SUPPLEMENTAL uses other information to reconstruct and identify a row. For example, if a table has no primary key but one or more non-nullable columns with unique constraints, one of the unique index keys is used to identify a row by adding this value to the redo logs for a DML operation. Also, if a table does not have a non-null unique constraint, all of the row data, except for LONG and LOB datatypes, are logged as a function of SUPPLEMENTAL.

This process of updating the primary key and updating a row to have the primary key and ROWID identification is called identification key logging at database level. There are more supplemental logging levels that can be used. The two described here are the minimum needed for Transaction Backout. For more information, refer to the LogMiner section in the UTILITIES volume of the Oracle Online Documentation. Identification key logging can be enabled with the following command:

```
SYS AS SYSDBA @ orcl SQL> ALTER DATABASE ADD SUPPLEMENTAL LOG
DATA (PRIMARY KEY) COLUMNS;
```

To see if supplemental logging is enabled, the following query can be used:

```
SYS AS SYSDBA @ orcl SQL> SELECT supplemental_log_data_pk AS
pk_sup,
                                supplemental_log_data_min AS
min_sup
                        FROM v$database;

PK_SUP MIN_SUP
------ --------
YES    YES
```

Only after making these two changes to the database can the LogMiner functionality be used to backout transactions.

The interface for flashback transaction is a new procedure in the *dbms_flashback* package. Flashback transaction can be directly called from PL/SQL, or indirectly through the OEM interface. The latter calls the overloaded procedure, *transaction_backout,* from the built in package. Using flashback transaction without supplemental logging enabled will throw error ORA-55510. Note that if OEM is being used to perform a transaction backout, *minimal supplemental logging* and *identification key logging* must be enabled, whereas ORA-55510 only requests *minimal supplemental logging*.

Using transaction backouts will be covered next. First of all, the transaction(s) which need to back out must be found. The 10g functionality Flashback Versions Query can be used to find the transaction id. The view *flashback_transaction_query*, also introduced in 10G, can be used next to find what the transaction has done.

```
LUTZ  @ orcl SQL> select versions_xid , col1 from t
   versions between scn minvalue and maxvalue;
```

```
VERSIONS_XID            COL1
----------------   ----------
07002000F2010000        2004
07002000F2010000        1004
01001F0002020000        2002
01001F0002020000        1002
0A000800200020000       2000
05000A00FA010000        1000
```

```
SQL> desc flashback_transaction_query
```

```
Name                                     Null?    Type
---------------------------------------- -------- ----------------
-----------
XID                                               RAW(8)
START_SCN                                         NUMBER
START_TIMESTAMP                                   DATE
COMMIT_SCN                                        NUMBER
COMMIT_TIMESTAMP                                  DATE
LOGON_USER                                        VARCHAR2(30)
UNDO_CHANGE#                                      NUMBER
OPERATION                                         VARCHAR2(32)
TABLE_NAME                                        VARCHAR2(256)
TABLE_OWNER                                       VARCHAR2(32)
ROW_ID                                            VARCHAR2(19)
UNDO_SQL                                          VARCHAR2(4000)
```

Remember that the SELECT ANY TRANSACTION system privilege is needed in order to use this view.

The *transaction_backout* procedure is overloaded with four different versions in the package *dbms_flashback*.

```
SYS AS SYSDBA @ orcl SQL> desc dbms_flashback
```

```
PROCEDURE DISABLE
PROCEDURE ENABLE_AT_SYSTEM_CHANGE_NUMBER
 Argument Name                    Type                    In/Out
Default?
 ------------------------------ ---------------------- ------ -----
---
 QUERY_SCN                        NUMBER                  IN
PROCEDURE ENABLE_AT_TIME
 Argument Name                    Type                    In/Out
Default?
 ------------------------------ ---------------------- ------ -----
---
 QUERY_TIME                       TIMESTAMP               IN
FUNCTION GET_SYSTEM_CHANGE_NUMBER RETURNS NUMBER
PROCEDURE TRANSACTION_BACKOUT
 Argument Name                    Type                    In/Out
Default?
 ------------------------------ ---------------------- ------ -----
---
 NUMTXNS                          NUMBER                  IN
 XIDS                             XID_ARRAY               IN
 OPTIONS                          BINARY_INTEGER          IN
DEFAULT
 SCNHINT                          NUMBER                  IN
DEFAULT
PROCEDURE TRANSACTION_BACKOUT
 Argument Name                    Type                    In/Out
Default?
 ------------------------------ ---------------------- ------ -----
---
 NUMTXNS                          NUMBER                  IN
 XIDS                             XID_ARRAY               IN
 OPTIONS                          BINARY_INTEGER          IN
DEFAULT
 TIMEHINT                         TIMESTAMP               IN
PROCEDURE TRANSACTION_BACKOUT
 Argument Name                    Type                    In/Out
Default?
 ------------------------------ ---------------------- ------ -----
---
 NUMTXNS                          NUMBER                  IN
 NAMES                            TXNAME_ARRAY            IN
 OPTIONS                          BINARY_INTEGER          IN
DEFAULT
 SCNHINT                          NUMBER                  IN
DEFAULT
PROCEDURE TRANSACTION_BACKOUT
 Argument Name                    Type                    In/Out
Default?
 ------------------------------ ---------------------- ------ -----
---
 NUMTXNS                          NUMBER                  IN
 NAMES                            TXNAME_ARRAY            IN
 OPTIONS                          BINARY_INTEGER          IN
DEFAULT
 TIMEHINT                         TIMESTAMP               IN
```

Once the DBA has decided which transaction(s) to back out, an array containing their transaction ids can be built. Progressively, the 11g database comes with a ready-made array datatypem *sys.xid_array*. In the PL/SQL block below, a SQL*Plus exchange variable has been used to hand over the transaction id as a string at the prompt asking for the specification of a value for the variable during runtime of the block.

```
DECLARE
        trans_arr SYS.XID_ARRAY :=  sys.xid_array();
        BEGIN
         trans_arr.extend;
         DBMS_OUTPUT.PUT_LINE(trans_arr.LAST);
          trans_arr(1) := '&tx_id';
         DBMS_FLASHBACK.TRANSACTION_BACKOUT (
             numtxns => 1,
             xids    => trans_arr,
             options => dbms_flashback.cascade);
END;
/
```

Using a loop, multiple rows of the array should be filled to back out multiple transactions. Then, the parameter *numtxns* can be adjusted to the number of transactions assigned to rows in the array. If something is not prepared properly, the procedure throws an error:

```
TRANSACTION BACKOUT requires the database to be in ARCHIVELOG mode

ERROR at line 1:
ORA-55510: Mining could not start
ORA-06512: at "SYS.DBMS_FLASHBACK", line 37
ORA-06512: at "SYS.DBMS_FLASHBACK", line 70
ORA-06512: at line 7
```

Oerr offers this information about the error:

```
> $ oerr ora 55510
55510, 0000, "Mining could not start"
// *Cause: Mining could not start for the following reasons.
//         1. A logminer session was processing
//         2. The database was not mounted or not opened for read
and write
```

```
//          3. Minimum supplemental logging was not enabled
//          4. Archiving was not enabled
// *Action: Fix the mentioned problems and try again. Note that if
//          you enable supplemental logging now, you will not be
able to
//          remove a transaction that has committed without
supplemental
//          logging.
```

When the procedure completes successfully, it has created a compensating transaction, having backed out the original transaction(s). This compensating transaction does not include a commit.

Here is an example in which two tables, t and t_d, have been used. Table t has a primary key on col1 and table t_d has a foreign key on col1 which references table t (col1):

```
LUTZ  @ orcl SQL> SELECT versions_xid , versions_operation , col1
                  FROM t
                  VERSIONS BETWEEN SCN MINVALUE AND MAXVALUE;


VERSIONS_XID        V       COL1
----------------    -    ----------
020017004B020000 I         4
020017004B020000 I         5
020017004B020000 I         6
020017004B020000 I         7
020017004B020000 I         8
020017004B020000 I         9
020017004B020000 I        10
03001300F8010000 D        10
03001300F8010000 D         9
03001300F8010000 D         8
03001300F8010000 D         7
   03001300F8010000 D            6
03001300F8010000 D         5
03001300F8010000 D         4
                           1
                           2
                           3
                           4
                           5
                           6
                           7
                           8
                           9
                          10

24 rows selected.
```

```
LUTZ   @ orcl SQL> SELECT versions_xid , versions_operation , col2
                FROM t_d
                VERSIONS BETWEEN SCN MINVALUE AND MAXVALUE;


VERSIONS_XID      V     COL2
---------------- - ----------
020017004B020000 U       11
03001300F8010000 U       14
090007005B020000 U       11
                         10
```

With id 03001300F8010000, one row has updated (the only row in the table) in table *t_d*, and deleted 7 rows in table t. One could even have a look at the SQL statements that would undo the transaction:

```
LUTZ   @ orcl SQL> SELECT undo_sql
                FROM flashback_transaction_query
                WHERE xid=HEXTORAW('03001300F8010000');


UNDO_SQL
--------------------------------------------------------------------
-----------insert into "LUTZ"."T"("COL1") values ('10');
insert into "LUTZ"."T"("COL1") values ('9');
insert into "LUTZ"."T"("COL1") values ('8');
insert into "LUTZ"."T"("COL1") values ('7');
insert into "LUTZ"."T"("COL1") values ('6');
insert into "LUTZ"."T"("COL1") values ('5');
insert into "LUTZ"."T"("COL1") values ('4');
update "LUTZ"."T_D" set "COL2" = '11' where ROWID =
'AAAO2xAAEAAAAAXAAA';
```

Next, the PL/SQL block is called with the value 03001300F8010000 for the exchange variable at the prompt. After a while, a message is received with the information that the procedure has successfully completed. The status of the transaction and the dependent and compensating transactions can be reviewed with the *_flashback_txn_state* views

```
LUTZ   @ orcl SQL> SELECT * FROM user_flashback_txn_state;
```

```
COMPENSATING_XID XID                    DEPENDENT_XID     BACKOUT_MODE
---------------- ----------------       ----------------- ----------------
03001300F7010000 09000C0058020000                         CASCADE
03001300F7010000 0100180013020000       09000C0058020000  CASCADE
020017004B020000 03001300F8010000                         CASCADE
0400140049020000 05001E001D020000                         CASCADE
```

> 💣 **The compensating transaction is not committed automatically and rows are locked by the compensating transaction.**

Here it is possible to see multiple rows for the same transaction; one for each dependent transaction.

At this point, it is possible to check the results of the compensating transaction to see if they are satisfactory. The DBA can also choose to commit, or respectively rollback, the compensating transaction if the results are unsatisfactory.

The results of executed but not yet committed or rolled back compensating transactions can be viewed in two dynamic performance views:

- *v$flashback_txn_mods* shows all modifications of all compensating transactions in memory:

```
SYS AS SYSDBA @ orcl SQL> desc V$FLASHBACK_TXN_MODS
 Name                        Null?    Type
 --------------------------- -----    ------
 COMPENSATING_XID                     RAW(8)
 COMPENSATING_TXN_NAME                VARCHAR2(255)
 XID                                  RAW(8)
 TXN_NAME                             VARCHAR2(255)
 PARENT_XID                           RAW(8)
 INTERESTING                          NUMBER
 ORIGINAL                             NUMBER
 BACKOUT_SEQ                          NUMBER
 UNDO_SQL                             VARCHAR2(4000)
 UNDO_SQL_SQN                         NUMBER
 UNDO_SQL_SUB_SQN                     NUMBER
 BACKOUT_SQL_ID                       NUMBER
 OPERATION                            VARCHAR2(30)
 BACKEDOUT                            NUMBER
 CONFLICT_MOD                         NUMBER
 MODS_PER_LCR                         NUMBER
```

- *v$flashback_txn_graph* shows the dependencies and conflicting operations after a compensating transaction has been started but are neither committed or rolled back yet:

```
SYS AS SYSDBA @ orcl SQL> desc V$FLASHBACK_TXN_GRAPH
 Name                     Null?    Type
 -------------------- -------- -------------
 COMPENSATING_XID              RAW(8)
 COMPENSATING_TXN_NAME         VARCHAR2(255)
 XID                           RAW(8)
 TXN_NAME                      VARCHAR2(255)
 PARENT_XID                    RAW(8)
 INTERESTING                   NUMBER
 ORIGINAL                      NUMBER
 BACKOUT_SEQ                   NUMBER
 NUM_PREDS                     NUMBER
 NUM_SUCCS                     NUMBER
 DEP_XID                       RAW(8)
 DEP_TXN_NAME                  VARCHAR2(255)
 TXN_CONF_SQL_ID               NUMBER
 DEP_TXN_CONF_SQL_ID           NUMBER
```

Detailed information about all compensating transactions in the database, including all dependencies, can be read from the data dictionary with the following data dictionary views:

- *_flashback_txn_report* - committed transactions report

- *_flashback_txn_state* - current state with dependency report

```
LUTZ  @ orcl SQL> desc  user_flashback_txn_report;
 Name                        Null?   Type
 ----------------------- ------ ----
 COMPENSATING_XID            NOT NULL RAW(8)
 COMPENSATING_TXN_NAME                VARCHAR2(256)
 COMMIT_TIME                          DATE
 XID_REPORT                           CLOB
```

```
LUTZ  @ orcl SQL>   SELECT xid_report
                      FROM user_flashback_txn_report
                        WHERE
COMPENSATING_XID=HEXTORAW('020017004B020000');
```

```
XID_REPORT
---------------------------------------------
<?xml version="1.0" encoding="ISO-8859-1"?>
<COMP_XID_REPORT XID="020017004B0200
```

Internally, the server has used LogMiner functionality and retrieved all information needed for the backout operation from

---

the redo log files. The server has also found all dependencies and created a list of statements. After this, it has applied the compensating statements ordered in the correct sequence.

The dependency handling can be managed with the *options* parameter of the *transcation_backout* procedure. There are several possibilities:

- NOCASCADE (default)- fails if there are dependencies.

- NONCONFLICTING_ONLY - flashes back only those rows which do not have any conflicting rows.

- NOCASCADE_FORCE - only the given particular transactions from the array are flashed back with no respect to any other dependent transaction. Note that the transactions are flashed back in reverse order of their commit times

- CASCADE- all dependent transactions are flashed back in reversed order.

There are a few important details to remember when using this feature:

- It is possible to back out not only the specified transaction but also all dependent transactions with CASCADE option

- DEFAULT for the OPTIONS parameter is NOCASCADE

- Using NOCASCADE throws an ORA-55504 if there are dependent transactions

- The *transaction_backout* procedure automatically checks the following dependencies:

  - dependencies produced by write after write operations

  - dependencies of primary key foreign key relationships

- The privileges needed for a transaction backout are:

  - EXECUTE on *dbms_flashback*

- SELECT ANY TRANSACTION (in OEM and for *flashback_transcation_query* view)
- SELECT, FLASHBACK and DML privileges on all tables involved in the transactions need to be backed out.

- The limitations for transaction backout are:

  - Only committed transactions can be flashed back.

  - Transactions that have dependent transactions can only be flashed back with either the CASCADE, NONCONFLICT_ONLY, or NOCASCADE_FORCE options.

  - DDL statements are not allowed to be flashed back in transactions.

  - Only transactions that do not make any changes that are not supported by the LogMiner can be flashed back.

  - All dependent transactions must be committed before the backout operation.

  - There cannot be any dependent transactions that have been aborted more than one minute after the beginning of the backout operation.

  - A backout operation can only be started if there is no active ongoing LogMiner session.

Best practices for transaction backout:

- Run *dbms_flashback.transaction_backout* as soon as possible after once it has been determined to be necessary.

- Back out performance will be worse that longer the wait.

Transaction backout with OEM

In the new 11g availability pane of the enterprise manager, the View and Manage Transactions link leads directly to the LogMiner page:

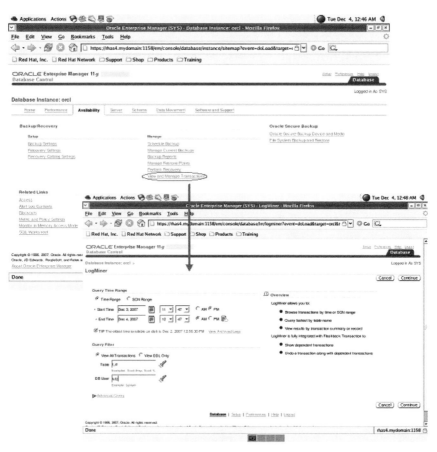

Figure 12.1: *Availability Pane of the Enterprise Manager*

Here, an interval between two timestamps or two SCNs can be chosen, and the Redo SQL for the transaction can be viewed by looking at the results of the mining operation.

From the LogMiner Results page, it is possible to drill down into a Transaction's Details and view exactly what would flashback this particular transaction chosen for back out.

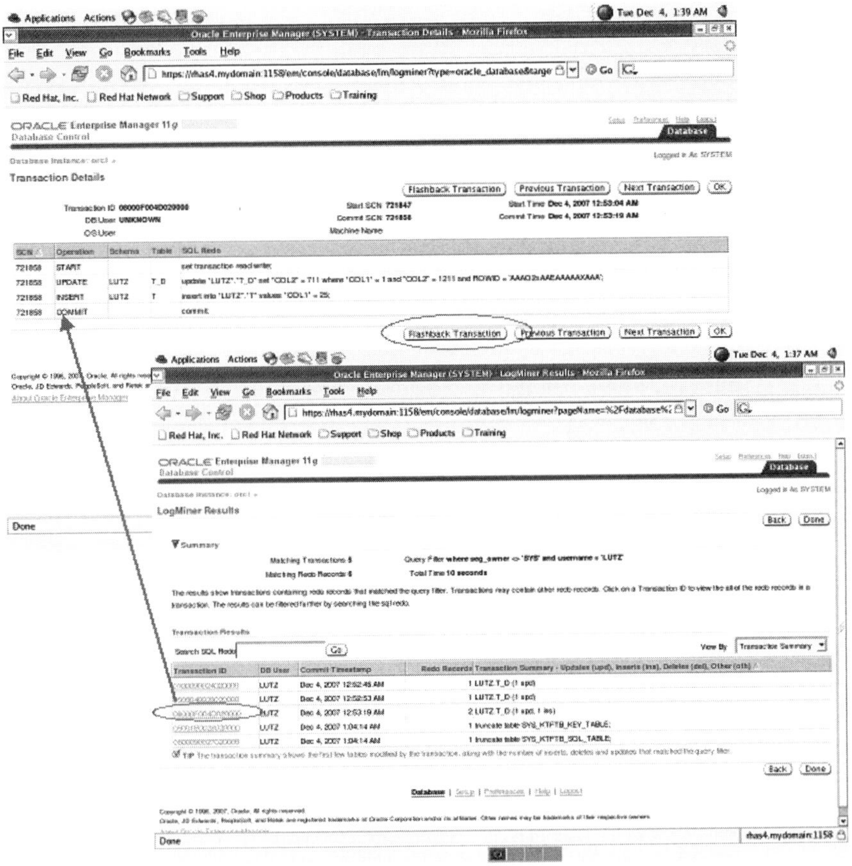

Figure 12.2: *Transaction Details*

After clicking the Flashback Transaction link, the results of the flashback operation can be viewed. This can be done by looking at the created Undo SQL Script, containing the SQL statements of the compensating transaction.

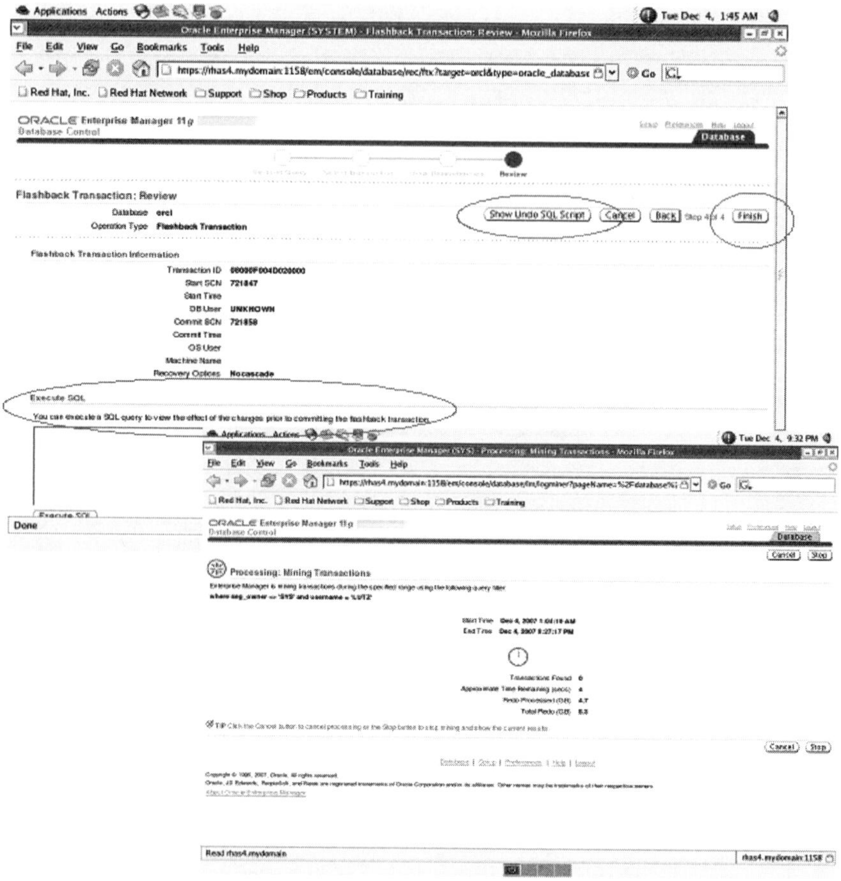

Figure 12.3: *Results of the Flashback Operation*

Notice that the compensating transaction has not committed yet. Clicking FINISH will complete the commit. It is also possible to view UNDO SQL of the flashback operation by clicking at the VIEW UNDO Script link before committing the compensating transaction. A query can also be run to see the results of the not yet committed compensating transaction

Oracle Total Recall

Oracle Total Recall can track transactional changes on tables over their lifetime by using the Flashback Data Archive. More and more, legal regulations such as Sarbanes Oxley and Basel II are enforcing strict change control of customer data. These obligations demand that a history of all changes to customer data must be maintained. Companies are commonly required to retain their data for periods of 5 or more years and must be able to review historical data almost in real time.

One common approach to this problem is the implementation of essentially home grown data management systems that integrate the maintenance of the history and archiving in business logic. The application has to keep track of data changes that can make applications terribly complex and create difficulties in applying upgrades to the application.

The approach of using PL/SQL triggers for tracking changes can have a massive impact on the performance of an application. This is because PL/SQL is compiled source code stored in the data dictionary that needs to execute again and again. Another drawback of such a solution is that there is no central interface for the management of those triggers.

Most of the flashback functionalities rely on UNDO data that will error out with an ORA-1555 Snapshot too Old if the required before image cannot be read any more. ORA-1555 occurs because it has already been overwritten in the undo tablespace. Furthermore, it is very unlikely that the old values can be reconstructed over a longer period of time, like months or even years, from data stored in the undo segments.

Luckily, this UNDO data time issue can now be remedied. With the Flashback Data Archive functionality of 11g, the Oracle database is capable of automatically tracking transactional changes to data over very long periods. Oracle achieves this by storing UNDO information in special segments within dedicated tablespaces.

Use of this feature is completely transparent for the application and the end user, who can view historical data from the flashback archive seamlessly with regular SQL statements. This is done by utilizing traditional flashback functionalities, such as flashback query, flashback versions query, flashback transaction query, etc.

The historical information in the flashback data archive ages out automatically and Oracle automatically purges it after the specified retention period has exceeded. However, the flashback data archive provides the DBA with a central interface for the management of historical data and change tracking.

> 🔔 With a flashback data archive it is possible to view data as any point in time since the flashback data archive was created. However, attempting to view data as a timestamp before the data archive is created causes the following error: ORA-01466: unable to read data - table definition has changed

The Technology Behind It

With every Oracle 11g database startup, the new flashback data archiver background process, FBDA, is automatically started. This is what generates and archives the historical data.

Transactions encounter very little performance impact from flashback data archiving because Oracle only marks DML operations as candidates for archiving. A special background process then generates and archives the history information asynchronously for tables enabled for flashback archival.

Oracle also automatically compresses the internally used history tables and partitions them based on a range partitioning scheme. The partitioning and compression of the history tables is fully transparent and does not require any additional administrative intervention.

A flashback data archive consists of at least one tablespace, and can span multiple tablespaces. It is possible to add a new tablespace to a flashback archive at any time.

Enabling Flashback Data Archive

The first thing that needs to be done to enable the flashback data archive is to create a flashback archive.

A user needs the FLASHBACK ARCHIVE ADMINISTER system privilege to create and manage flashback archives including:

- creating
- modifying; making default, setting retention time, purging
- manually, adding and removing tablespaces
- disabling tracking
- dropping

A user needs the FLASHBACK ARCHIVE object privilege for enabling tracking of history data for a table

```
LUTZ  @ orcl SQL> CREATE FLASHBACK ARCHIVE my_5_year_archive
  TABLESPACE fba_5_years_01
    QUOTA 10G
      RETENTION 5 YEARS;
```

This statement creates an object in the data dictionary, which is a logical container for the storage of history data.

```
SYS AS SYSDBA @ orcl SQL> SELECT * FROM dba_flashback_archive;

FLASHBACK_ARCHIVE_NAME FLASHBACK_ARCHIVE# RETENTION_IN_DAYS
CREATE_TIME LAST_PURGE_TIME  STATUS
---------------------- ------------------ -----------------  -------
--- ------------ ------------------------------------
MY_5_YEAR_ARCHIVE              1                  1825              05-DEC-
07   11.11.23.000000000 PM 05-DEC-07     11.11.23.000000000 PM
```

There are a number of restrictions for flashback archives:

- The tablespaces used for a flashback archive must use local extent management and automatic segment space management.

- The database must use automatic undo management.

With the QUOTA clause, the amount of disk space consumed by data archive in a tablespace is limited.

```
SYS AS SYSDBA @ orcl SQL> SELECT * FROM DBA_FLASHBACK_ARCHIVE_TS;

FLASHBACK_ARCHIVE_NAME   FLASHBACK_ARCHIVE# TABLESPACE_NAME
QUOTA_IN_MB
----------------- ----------------------- ---------------- --------
----
MY_5_YEAR_ARCHIVE              1                FBA_5_YEAR_01        50
```

The QUOTA can be adjusted dynamically at any time by adding more tablespaces to the flashback archive or by modifying the quota on a tablespace that is already part of the flashback archive.

```
SYS AS SYSDBA @ orcl SQL> ALTER FLASHBACK ARCHIVE my_5_year_archive
                ADD TABLESPACE fba_5_year_02 QUOTA 20M;


SYS AS SYSDBA @ orcl SQL> ALTER FLASHBACK ARCHIVE my_5_year_archive
                MODIFY TABLESPACE fba_5_year_02 QUOTA
30M;
```

Here are the quotas in the data dictionary again:

```
SYS AS SYSDBA @ orcl SQL> SELECT * FROM dba_flashback_archive_ts;
```

```
FLASHBACK_ARCHIVE_NAME FLASHBACK_ARCHIVE# TABLESPACE_NAME
QUOTA_IN_MB
---------------------- ------------------ ---------------  -----
-----------MY_5_YEAR_ARCHIVE           1                FBA_5_YEAR_01
50

MY_5_YEAR_ARCHIVE           1                FBA_5_YEAR_02
30
```

```
LUTZ  @ orcl SQL> ALTER FLASHBACK DATA ARCHIVE my_5_year_archive
      MODIFY RETENTION 10 YEARS;
```

```
SYS AS SYSDBA @ orcl SQL> SELECT * FROM dba_flashback_archive;
```

```
FLASHBACK_ARCHIVE_NAME FLASHBACK_ARCHIVE# RETENTION_IN_DAYS
CREATE_TIME LAST_PURGE_TIME   STATUS
---------------------- ------------------ ----------------- -------
--- ------------- ------------------------------------
MY_5_YEAR_ARCHIVE           1                3650             05-DEC-
07    11.11.23.000000000 PM 05-DEC-07    11.11.23.000000000 PM
```

To remove history data from the flashback archive ad hoc, and
before the RETENTION time has exceeded, the PURGE clause
has to be used:

```
LUTZ  @ orcl SQL> ALTER FLASHBACK ARCHIVE my_5_year_archive
                  PURGE BEFORE TIMESTAMP (SYSTIMESTAMP - INTERVAL
'5' MINUTE);
```

The RETENTION clause defines a purging policy for the
historical data of all tables associated with the flashback archive.
It is also possible to change the RETENTION policy of a
flashback data archive any time afterwards. The history data
automatically ages out with the RETENTION period and is
purged from the flashback archive.

It is possible to define a DEFAULT FLASHBACK ARCHIVE
for a database. However, note that there can only be one default
flashback archive.

```
LUTZ  @ orcl SQL> ALTER FLASHBACK DATA ARCHIVE my_5_year_archive
      SET DEFAULT;
```

```
SYS AS SYSDBA @ orcl SQL> SELECT flashback_archive_name, status
                              FROM dba_flashback_archive;
```

```
FLASHBACK_ARCHIVE_NAME   STATUS
---------------------    --------
MY_5_YEAR_ARCHIVE        DEFAULT
```

The DEFAULT key word can be specified in the following statements:

- CREATE FLASHBACK ARCHIVE
- ALTER FLASHBACK ARCHIVE

The next step after creating the flashback archive is to associate it with a table. In other words, flashback archiving should be enabled for a table, and the flashback archive to be used must be enabled.

```
SYS AS SYSDBA @ orcl SQL> ALTER TABLE lutz.t_d
                              FLASHBACK ARCHIVE my_5_year_archive;
```

Now the server will track DMLs on the table *lutz.t_d*.

What is in the Flashback Data Archive?

Directly after the creation of the flashback archive there are no objects in it.

```
SYS AS SYSDBA @ orcl SQL> SELECT segment_name, segment_type FROM
dba_segments WHERE tablespace_name='FBA_5_YEAR_01';
```

```
No rows selected
```

The next step is for the DBA to apply some changes to the data in the table:

```
SYS AS SYSDBA @ orcl SQL> UPDATE lutz.t_d SET col2=col2+1234;
SYS AS SYSDBA @ orcl SQL> COMMIT;
```

```
128 rows updated.
Commit complete.
```

In the data dictionary, information about an "archive table" can now be seen. This is the table which is used to hold the historical data:

```
SYS AS SYSDBA @ orcl SQL> SELECT * FROM
dba_flashback_archive_tables;


TABLE_NAME OWNER_NAME FLASHBACK_ARCHIVE_NAME ARCHIVE_TABLE_NAME
---------- ---------- ---------------------- ------------------
T_D        LUTZ       MY_5_YEAR_ARCHIVE      SYS_FBA_HIST_60849
```

```
SYS AS SYSDBA @ orcl SQL> desc lutz.SYS_FBA_HIST_60849

Name                 Null?     Type
-------------------- --------- ----------------
RID                            VARCHAR2(4000)    -- this is the rowid
STARTSCN                       NUMBER
ENDSCN                         NUMBER
XID                            RAW(8)
OPERATION                      VARCHAR2(1)
COL1                           NUMBER     -- here we find the column data
COL2                           NUMBER     -- here we find the column data
```

Directly after a DML operation, the history data in the archive table of the flashback archive is not seen. It takes some time until the undo information is moved by FBDA from the undo tablespace to the history table. Archive table and history table are used synonymously here. In the data dictionary it is *archive_table* and its name is *sys_fba_hist_xxx*.

```
SYS AS SYSDBA @ orcl SQL> SELECT * FROM  lutz.SYS_FBA_HIST_60849;

no rows selected
```

After some time, the information about the DMLs can be seen in the flashback archive.

```
SYS AS SYSDBA @ orcl SQL> SELECT * FROM lutz.SYS_FBA_HIST_60849;
```

```
RID                STARTSCN    ENDSCN XID              O      COL1
COL2
----------------- ---------    ----- ---------------- -      ------
----
AAAO4YAAEAAAAAWAAB            9505692                               2
1120 AAAO4YAAEAAAAAXAA+  950440     950569 040006008B020000 I
2      1120
AAAO4YAAEAAAAAXAA/  950440     950569 040006008B020000 I        2
1120
AAAO4YAAEAAAAAXAA0  950440     950569 040006008B020000 I        2
1120
AAAO4YAAEAAAAAXAA1  950440     950569 040006008B020000 I        2
1120
AAAO4YAAEAAAAAXAA2  950440     950569 040006008B020000 I        2
1120
AAAO4YAAEAAAAAXAA3  950440     950569 040006008B020000 I        2
1120
AAAO4YAAEAAAAAXAA4  950440     950569 040006008B020000 I        2
1120
AAAO4YAAEAAAAAXAA5  950440     950569 040006008B020000 I        2
1120
AAAO4YAAEAAAAAXAA6  950440     950569 040006008B020000 I        2
1120
   . . .
      . . .
AAAO4YAAEAAAAAXABs  950440     950569 040006008B020000 I        2
1120
AAAO4YAAEAAAAAXABt  950440     950569 040006008B020000 I        2
1120
AAAO4YAAEAAAAAXABu  950440     950569 040006008B020000 I        2
1120
AAAO4YAAEAAAAAXABv  950440     950569 040006008B020000 I        2
1120
AAAO4YAAEAAAAAXABw  950440     950569 040006008B020000 I        2
1120
AAAO4YAAEAAAAAXABx  950440     950569 040006008B020000 I        2
1120
AAAO4YAAEAAAAAXABy  950440     950569 040006008B020000 I        2
1120
AAAO4YAAEAAAAAXABz  950440     950569 040006008B020000 I        2
1120
128 rows selected.
```

There are also more objects in the tablespace contents of the flashback archive:

```
SYS AS SYSDBA @ orcl SQL> SELECT segment_name, segment_type FROM
dba_segments WHERE tablespace_name='FBA_5_YEAR_01';
```

```
SEGMENT_NAME                SEGMENT_TYPE
----------------------      ----------------------
SYS_FBA_DDL_COLMAP_60849    TABLE
SYS_FBA_HIST_60849          TABLE PARTITION
SYS_FBA_TCRV_60849          TABLE
SYS_FBA_TCRV_IDX_60849      INDEX
```

Note that the history table is partitioned. It has the same structure as the tracked table, plus a few additional columns needed for the transaction information. The data in the history table is automatically compressed with a new table compression algorithm. Oracle 11g can now use table compression for normal DML operations. Before 11g, table compression could only be used with bulk load operations such as DIRECT INSERTs.

```
SYS AS SYSDBA @ orcl SQL>  SELECT table_name, table_owner,
partition_name,
                              compression, compress_for
               FROM DBA_TAB_PARTITIONS
               WHERE tablespace_name='FBA_5_YEAR_01';
```

```
TABLE_NAME          TABLE_OWNER    PARTITION_NAME    COMPRESS
COMPRESS_FOR
---------------     -----------    ---------------   -------- --------
----------
SYS_FBA_HIST_60849  LUTZ           HIGH_PART         ENABLED  FOR ALL
OPERATIONS
```

Here is a look at the other table available in the flashback archive tablespace. This one contains not only the history of the INSERTs but also the history of the UPDATEs:

```
SYS AS SYSDBA @ orcl SQL> desc lutz.SYS_FBA_TCRV_60849;

 Name          Null?    Type
 -----------   -------- --------------------------------------------
 RID           VARCHAR2(4000)
 STARTSCN      NUMBER
 ENDSCN        NUMBER
 XID           RAW(8)
 OP            VARCHAR2(1)
```

```
SYS AS SYSDBA @ orcl SQL> SELECT * FROM  lutz.SYS_FBA_TCRV_60849;

 RID                                STARTSCN    ENDSCN XID
 O
 ---------------------------------  ---------- ---------- ---------------
 - -
 AAAO4YAAEAAAAAWAAB                  950569
 09000D00AF020000 U
 AAAO4YAAEAAAAAXAA+                  950569
 09000D00AF020000 U
```

```
AAAO4YAAEAAAAAXAA+          950440      950569
040006008B020000 I
AAAO4YAAEAAAAAXAA/          950569
09000D00AF020000 U
AAAO4YAAEAAAAAXAA/          950440      950569
040006008B020000 I
AAAO4YAAEAAAAAXAA0          950569
09000D00AF020000 U
AAAO4YAAEAAAAAXAA0          950440      950569
040006008B020000 I
AAAO4YAAEAAAAAXAA1          950569
09000D00AF020000 U
AAAO4YAAEAAAAAXAA1          950440      950569
040006008B020000 I
AAAO4YAAEAAAAAXAA2          950569
09000D00AF020000 U
AAAO4YAAEAAAAAXAA2          950440      950569
040006008B020000 I
AAAO4YAAEAAAAAXAA3          950569
09000D00AF020000 U
AAAO4YAAEAAAAAXAA3          950440      950569
040006008B020000 I
AAAO4YAAEAAAAAXAA4          950569
09000D00AF020000 U
AAAO4YAAEAAAAAXAA4          950440      950569
040006008B020000 I
AAAO4YAAEAAAAAXAA5          950569
09000D00AF020000 U
  .   .   .
      .   .   .
  .   .   .
AAAO4YAAEAAAAAXABr          950569
09000D00AF020000 U
AAAO4YAAEAAAAAXABr          950440      950569
040006008B020000 I
AAAO4YAAEAAAAAXABs          950569
09000D00AF020000 U
AAAO4YAAEAAAAAXABs          950440      950569
040006008B020000 I
AAAO4YAAEAAAAAXABt          950569
09000D00AF020000 U
AAAO4YAAEAAAAAXABt          950440      950569
040006008B020000 I
AAAO4YAAEAAAAAXABu          950569
09000D00AF020000 U
AAAO4YAAEAAAAAXABu          950440      950569
040006008B020000 I
AAAO4YAAEAAAAAXABv          950569
09000D00AF020000 U
AAAO4YAAEAAAAAXABv          950440      950569
040006008B020000 I
AAAO4YAAEAAAAAXABw          950569
09000D00AF020000 U
AAAO4YAAEAAAAAXABw          950440      950569
040006008B020000 I
AAAO4YAAEAAAAAXABx          950569
09000D00AF020000 U
```

```
AAAO4YAAEAAAAAXABx          950440        950569
040006008B020000 I
AAAO4YAAEAAAAAXABy          950569
09000D00AF020000 U

255 rows selected.
```

Applications and users do not need to query the history data directly from the history table. In fact, normal SQL can be used with flashback functionalities. This means that the history data is used seamlessly.

Here is what the execution plan for a flashback query on the flashback data archive looks like:

```
SYS AS SYSDBA @ orcl SQL> set autotrace trace explain
SYS AS SYSDBA @ orcl SQL> SELECT * FROM lutz.t_d AS OF TIMESTAMP
sysdate-1;
```

```
Execution Plan
----------------------------------------------------------
Plan hash value: 3381664885

| Id  | Operation                  | Name                  | Rows  |
Bytes | Cost (% CPU)| Time        | Pstart| Pstop |
-----------------------------------------------------------------------
-----------
|   0 | SELECT STATEMENT           |                       |     2 |
52 |    13 (8)| 00:00:01  |        |        |
|   1 |  VIEW                      |                       |     2 |
52 |    13 (8)| 00:00:01  |        |        |
|   2 |   UNION-ALL                |                       |       |
|     |              |        |        |
|*  3 |    FILTER                  |                       |       |
|     |              |        |        |
|   4 |     PARTITION RANGE SINGLE|                        |     1 |
17 |     3 (0)| 00:00:01  |  KEY  |     1 |
|*  5 |      TABLE ACCESS FULL     | SYS_FBA_HIST_60849 |     1 |
17 |     3 (0)| 00:00:01  |  KEY  |     1 |
|*  6 |    FILTER                  |                       |       |
|     |              |        |        |
|*  7 |     HASH JOIN OUTER        |                       |     1 |
34 |    10 ( 10)| 00:00:01  |        |        |
|*  8 |      TABLE ACCESS FULL     | T_D                   |     6 |
42 |     6 (0)| 00:00:01  |        |        |
|   9 |      VIEW                  |                       |   128 |
3456 |     3 (0)| 00:00:01  |        |        |
|* 10 |       TABLE ACCESS FULL    | SYS_FBA_TCRV_60849 |   128 |
3456 |     3 (0)| 00:00:01  |        |        |
```

```
----------------------------------------------------------------
-----------
Predicate Information (identified by operation id):
------------------------------------------------

3 - filter("TIMESTAMP_TO_SCN"(SYSDATE@!-1)<979993)
5 - filter("ENDSCN">"TIMESTAMP_TO_SCN"(SYSDATE@!-1) AND ("STARTSCN"
IS NULL O R
        "STARTSCN"<="TIMESTAMP_TO_SCN"(SYSDATE@!-1)) AND
"ENDSCN"<=979993)
6 - filter("F"."STARTSCN"<="TIMESTAMP_TO_SCN"(SYSDATE@!-1) OR
"F"."STARTSCN" IS NULL)
7 - access("T".ROWID=CHARTOROWID("F"."RID"(+)))
8 - filter("T"."VERSIONS_STARTSCN" IS NULL)
10 - filter(("ENDSCN" IS NULL OR "ENDSCN">979993) AND
("STARTSCN"<979993 OR "S TARTSCN" IS NULL))
```

DDL limitations for Flashback Data Archive

A flashback archive guarantees the capture of all changes to customer data. Therefore, all DDL operations that would invalidate the history data are not allowed for tables with flashback archiving enabled. These operations include:

- Dropping the table
- Truncating the table
- Renaming the table
- Dropping or removing columns of the table

In the flashback archive, there is a column mapping table that is used to map columns in the history table to columns in the original table.

```
SYS AS SYSDBA @ orcl SQL> SELECT * FROM
lutz.SYS_FBA_DDL_COLMAP_60849;

STARTSCN      ENDSCN XID   O COLUMN_NAME TYPE  HISTORICAL_COLUMN_NAME
----------    ------ ---   - ----------- ----- ---------------------
-----
    910480                              COL1    NUMBER COL1
    910480                              COL2    NUMBER COL2
```

The internal tables in the flashback archive cannot be dropped directly. They are automatically dropped with a DROP

FLASHBACK ARCHIVE statement. Dropping a flashback archive does not drop the tablespaces used by it. They could also contain other data!

What's new about UNDO and transactions in 11g?

Optimized UNDO BACKUP with RMAN

Prior to Oracle database 11g, RMAN always backed up all UNDO with a full backup, including UNDO for committed transactions. However, in 11g, RMAN is able to skip UNDO information for transactions that have already committed and for which the *undo_retention* time has exceeded. RMAN can do this because the committed UNDO is not needed for a recovery operation. This makes backups of the UNDO tablespace a lot faster, though it does not have any impact on flashback operations.

> 🔔 BACKUP UNDO OPTIMIZATION is an RMAN feature which is enabled by DEFAULT and cannot be switched off

Conclusion

As of Oracle 10g, DBAs were unable to apply UNDO on a whole transaction, despite advances in reading data from past points, and manually viewing undo SQL with flashback table. 11g does bring the DBA the ability to flashback transaction. Furthermore, using flashback data archive allows for UNDO data to no longer be time consuming by using dedicated tablespaces.

Due to increasing regulation of customer data in various organizations, flashback data archive offers automated transaction tracking over large spans of time. To ensure a seamless process in 11g startup, FBDA is used automatically as a background process for flashback data archiver. Furthermore in 11g, RMAN has also been improved when it comes to backing up and UNDO commands.

New 11g features covered in this chapter:

- Transaction Backouts using PL/SQL
- Transaction Backouts using OEM
- Using Flashback Data Archive
- UNDO and other 11g transactions

Oracle 11g ASM Enhancements

ASM Security Enhancements

Before looking at the 11g New Features for ASM in this chapter, a quick look at the history of ASM will be provided and a short outlook on the possible new features of upcoming releases will be covered. Automatic Storage management is certainly one of Oracle's most important projects. Oracle puts a lot of marketing energy into the promotion of ASM. For example, they included a two node RAC license in the standard edition license of the database software as of version 10gR1, but only in combination with the use of ASM for the shared storage.

ASM is one of Oracle's key Grid Computing Features next to RAC, STREAMS and GRID CONTROL. It is a logical volume manager not only for RAC, it also represents Oracle's solution for the SAME (stripe and mirror everything) demand for database storage. ASM offers a good means for storage consolidation.

It is part of Oracle's strategy to integrate more and more operation system functionalities into the database. Some day Oracle will probably be an OS itself. Today there is an Oracle proprietary logical volume manager (ASM) and Oracle can copy files on the same host to and from other hosts, which is implemented by the 10gR1 built in package *dbms_file_transfer*. This package was improved in 10gR2 to support OS to ASM and ASM to OS file transfer. In 10gR1, only ASM to ASM and OS to OS were possible.

Another 10gR2 feature for shifting large amounts of data around between databases is *dbms_streams_tablespace_adm*, a package that can be used for cloning tablespaces and tablespace versioning.

Furthermore, Oracle version 10gR2 Oracle ships its own media management server called Oracle Secure Backup (OSB) which cannot only backup Oracle files but entire file systems, NAS storage as well as SAN. It can handle tape libraries and barcode readers and is strongly integrated with Recovery Manager (RMAN). Oracle ships OSB with a Media Management Library (MML). This needs to be provided by the third party vendor of the media management software and is normally very expensive. Oracle's licensing policy is base on a per tape drive concept. Oracle Corporation puts a lot of effort into the development of the ASM functionality and it is still undergoing change. This will most likely continue in the next future releases.

In Oracle 10g as well as in 11g, it is only possible to store files that belong directly to the database, such as datafiles, online redo log files, and controlfiles. It is also possible to store spfiles, export data pump dump file sets and everything that has to do with backup and recovery, namely RMAN backupsets, datafile image copies and archived redo log files.

What Oracle is still working on with maximum effort is the possibility to store binary files; for example, an ORACLE_HOME, in ASM storage. It is even thinkable that any kind of file could be stored in ASM storage someday. Right now, *dbms_file_transfer* can be used to move files into and out of the ASM storage as well as from one ASM disk group to another one. It is also possible to simply use the FTP API of Oracle version 10gR2 called ASM FTP which utilizes the XML DB virtual folder functionality to move files into and out of ASM storage.

In future releases it will probably also be possible to use ASM disk groups to hold the Voting Disk and the Oracle Cluster Registry (OCR). In theory, it is already possible today - ASM could hold an OCR or a voting disk, but the problem here is the chicken-egg-story; in order to store the voting disk into ASM, there needs to be a clustered ASM which again would need the clusterware in place before it has been installed. Next to be covered are the ASM New Features in Oracle version 11gR1.

The first feature to be covered is the new volume for ASM in the Online Documentation. The documentation for ASM is now placed in its own volume in the Oracle® Database Storage Administrator's Guide 11g Release 1(11.1)Part Number B31107-02

SYSASM role in 11g

The Oracle release 11gR1 is the last version which supports logon to an ASM instance with SYSDBA privileges. In coming future releases, SYSASM privileges will need to be used in order to logon to an ASM instance using operation system authentication. This is a security enhancement that is used to cleanly separate ASM storage administrators from database administrators.

In 10gR2, Oracle had introduced the *asmcmd* tool to provide a storage administrator with an interface for managing ASM storage.

In the first 11g release, it is still possible to logon as SYSDBA as well as SYSASM. This will definitely be changed with the next coming release 11gR2. When Oracle 11g is installed, a question will come up about the operating system group which is allowed to logon to an ASM instance without needing a password in addition to the OS groups for logon as SYSDBA respectively as SYSOPER. The access to remote ASM instances is managed through the password file of the ASM instance. This password is case sensitive as all passwords are in an 11g database. For more information on secure passwords, refer to chapter 8.

There is a new column in *v$pwfile_users* for the SYSASM privilege. A user can be added to the password file by granting SYSASM privileges

```
SYS AS SYSDBA @ orcl11 SQL> select * from v$pwfile_users;

USERNAME                       SYSDB SYSOP SYSAS
------------------------------ ----- ----- -----
SYS                            TRUE  TRUE  FALSE
```

Oracle Enterprise Manager for 11g also provides an interface that allows creating and managing ASM users. This functionality can only be accessed when the user is logged on to OEM with SYSASM privileges. In Oracle version 11.1, a user logged on with SYSDBA privileges is also able to manage ASM users in OEM. This will be changed already with Oracle version, 11.2.

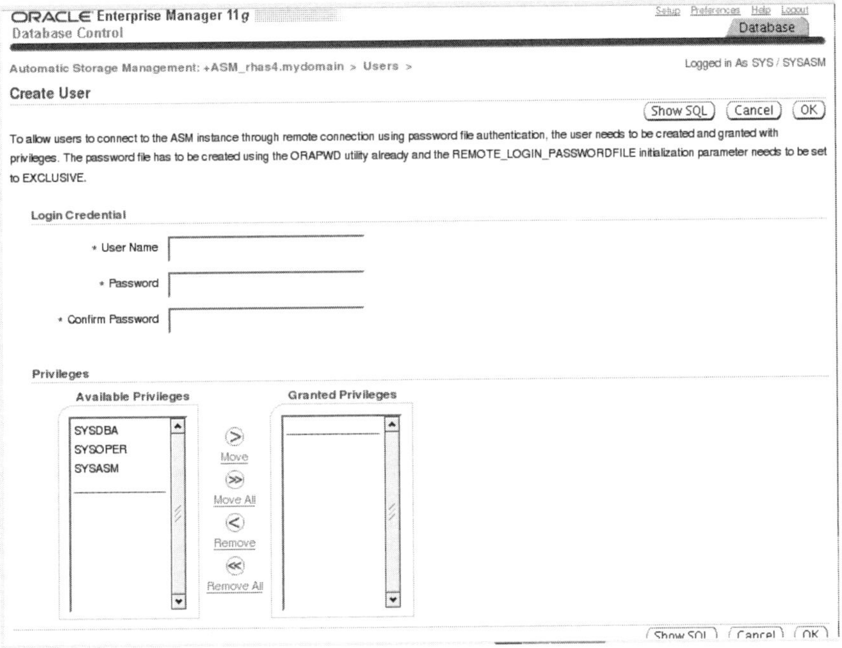

Create User

To allow users to connect to the ASM instance through remote connection using password file authentication, the user needs to be created and granted with privileges. The password file has to be created using the ORAPWD utility already and the REMOTE_LOGIN_PASSWORDFILE initialization parameter needs to be set to EXCLUSIVE.

Login Credential

* User Name

* Password

* Confirm Password

Privileges

Available Privileges

SYSDBA
SYSOPER
SYSASM

Granted Privileges

Figure 13.1: *Creating and Managing ASM-Users*

Separating storage management responsibilities from database administration duties is a very good idea. There should not be a need to explain what the difference between a database instance and an ASM instance is to the storage administrators and how to logon to it. Also, DBAs might not really be interested in how a database works and what a tablespace is. All a DBA wants from the storage administration side are enough LUNs in place in time.

On the other side, the storage administrator might only be interested if there is still enough free disk space left in the ASM disk groups. This is possible now. With *asmcmd,* a storage administrator can use UNIX-like commands to find out about the space utilization in the ASM storage. And by using the SYSASM operating system privileges, it is possible to limit the access to instances without needing a password for logon only to ASM instances.

UPGRADING ASM to 11g

When upgrading from Oracle database 10g to 11g, it comes in very handy to have installed the 10g Oracle software two times in two different ORACLE_HOME directories, an ASM_HOME and a DB_HOME. This is the recommended best practice if ASM is being used because it makes one independent when it comes to upgrading and because it is possible to have an 11g database use ASM disk groups that are managed by a 10g ASM instance and vice versa.

Therefore, just those 10g databases can be upgraded to 11g which are running applications that have already been certified for 11g and the others can remain on 10g until their applications are certified as well while still using the same ASM disk groups as before. In this case, it would be sensible to upgrade the ASM_HOME to 11g, which would cause downtime for all instances depending on the ASM instances running from this home.

After this, all database instances including the 10g and 11g, could use the ASM disk groups managed by the now upgraded Oracle 11g ASM instance. It would then be possible to convert the managed disk groups to 11g compatibility as soon as all databases using them have been upgraded to 11g. From this moment on, all databases could benefit from the 11g new features for ASM.

The difference between the relationships of database instances with ASM instances in 10g and 11g is the format of the messages sent between them and the format of the metadata that describe the disk groups. The format of these messages determines which ASM features can be used by a database. The format of the metadata determines which features a disk group can handle. A third factor that needs to match is the value of the initialization parameter *compatible* of the DB instance as well the ASM instance.

This is something that cannot be worked around when upgrading the ASM version in a single instance environment.

ASM disk group attributes

When an instance of a database that uses ASM storage starts up, it needs to negotiate the minimum compatibility of the ASM disk groups with the corresponding ASM instance. This minimum compatibility of ASM disk groups is determined by disk group attributes as well as by the value of the *compatible* parameter of both instances.

The two most important of these attributes of an ASM disk group are *compatible.asm* and *compatible.rdbms*. Both of them can be specified at creation of the ASM disk group.

```
SYS AS SYSDBA @ +ASM SQL> CREATE DISK GROUP data_new3
  2  DISK '/dev/raw/raw1', '/dev/raw/raw2' ATTRIBUTE
'compatible.asm'='11.1', 'compatible.rdbms'='11.1';
```

They can also be changed later with an ALTER DISKGROUP statement:

```
SYS AS SYSDBA @ +ASM SQL> ALTER DISK GROUP fra SET ATTRIBUTE
'compatible.rdbms'='11.1';
```

> 💣 By omitting these parameters, a disk group is created with both compatible attributes set to 10.1. This means that there is no benefit from the 11g New Features for ASM!

> 💣 It is only possible to advance these attribute settings dynamically. There is no way back.

An attempt to downgrade them results in an error:

```
SYS AS SYSDBA @ +ASM SQL> alter disk group fra set attribute
'compatible.rdbms'='10.1';
alter disk group fra set attribute 'compatible.rdbms'='10.1'
*
ERROR at line 1:
ORA-15032: not all alterations performed
ORA-15242: could not set attribute compatible.rdbms
ORA-15244: new compatibility setting less than current [11.1.0.0.0]
```

```
SYS AS SYSDBA @ +ASM SQL> alter disk group fra set attribute
'compatible.asm'='10.1';
alter disk group fra set attribute 'compatible.asm'='10.1'
*
ERROR at line 1:
ORA-15032: not all alterations performed
ORA-15242: could not set attribute compatible.asm
ORA-15244: new compatibility setting less than current [11.1.0.0.0]
```

This is what the *oerr* interface for Linux returns as an explanation for the error:

```
[oracle@rhas4 ~]$ oerr ora 15244
15244, 00000, "new compatibility setting less than current [%s]"
// *Cause:   The compatibility setting was invalid. The compatibility
//           setting can only be advanced.
// *Action: Check the version number.
//
```

The dynamic performance view *v$asm_attribute* shows the attributes of ASM disk groups and shows only information on those diskgroups that have *compatible.asm* of at least 11.1:

```
SYS AS SYSDBA @ +ASM SQL>    SELECT name, value, group_number FROM
v$asm_attribute;

NAME                  VALUE                 GROUP_NUMBER
-------------------   -------------------   ------------
disk_repair_time      3.6h                             1
au_size               1048576                          1
compatible.asm        11.1.0.0.0                       1
compatible.rdbms      10.1.0.0.0                       1
disk_repair_time      3.6h                             2
au_size               1048576                          2
compatible.asm        11.1.0.0.0                       2
compatible.rdbms      10.1.0.0.0                       2
```

There are two ASM disk groups and, as can be seen from the results of the query, there are more disk attributes. These will be covered in more depth a little bit later in this chapter.

The attributes *compatible.asm* and *compatible.rdbms* apply to both ASM and database instances. They determine which features can be used by a disk group and which ASM clients (database instances) can use the disk group. Since the attributes of different disk groups are independent from each other, it is possible to maintain heterogeneous environments with disk groups of different compatibility attributes managed by one ASM instance. They are furthermore determined by the initialization parameter *compatible*.

The dependency is as follows:

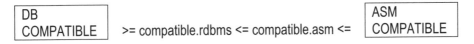

```
┌──────────────┐                                              ┌──────────────┐
│ DB           │                                              │ ASM          │
│ COMPATIBLE   │  >= compatible.rdbms <= compatible.asm <=    │ COMPATIBLE   │
└──────────────┘                                              └──────────────┘
```

compatible.rdbms limits the minimum compatibility of a database instance that can mount the ASM disk group. It determines the format of messages sent between the ASM instance and the DB instance which is a client for ASM. An ASM instance can manage disk groups of different compatibility attributes and its *compatible* parameter must be at least the version of the highest *compatible.asm* attribute of any disk group it manages.

A DB instance must have its *compatible* parameter set to at least the highest value of *compatible.rdbms* of all the disk groups which its database uses. A DB instance communicates at first startup time with the ASM instance at about the highest version of compatibility that both of them can support.

The compatibility information about the databases can be seen and their instances that use the ASM storage in *v$asm_client* both on the database side and on the ASM side. The code listing below shows the view from an 11g ASM instance serving both 10g and 11g clients:

```
SYS AS SYSDBA @ +ASM SQL> select * from v$asm_client;

GROUP_NUMBER INSTANCE_N DB_NAME  STATUS      SOFTWARE_VERSION
COMPATIBLE_VERSION
------------ ---------- -------- ---------- ---------------- -------
-------
           1 asm11      asm11     CONNECTED   11.1.0.5.0
11.1.0.0.0
           1 asm10gR2   asm10gR2 CONNECTED   10.2.0.1.0
10.2.0.1.0
```

The next listing shows the view from a 10g DB instance using an 11g ASM instance:

```
SYS AS SYSDBA @ asm10gR2 SQL> SELECT * FROM v$asm_client;

GROUP_NUMBER INSTANCE_N DB_NAME  STATUS     SOFTWARE_VERSION
COMPATIBLE_VERSION
------------ ---------- -------- -------- ------------------ -------
-----------
           1 +ASM       asm10gR2 CONNECTED   11.1.0.5.0
11.0.0.0.0
```

compatible.asm only determines the format of the persistent metadata that describes an ASM disk group. It must at least have the same value as the *compatible.rdbms* attribute of the disk group. It does not influence the format of files in the disk group. This is managed by the database itself.

> 🔔 It is only necessary to advance the compatible attribute of an ASM disk group if 11g New Features is to be used for an ASM disk group.

These features include variable extent sizes, fast mirror resyncing and the capability to take a disk group offline¦online as well as others that will be looked at shortly in this chapter. As has already been seen earlier, there are a few more attributes for ASM disk groups. Here they are, one by one:

- *au_size:* With this attribute, it is possible to influence the performance of ASM disk management. It is an automatic feature and does not need any manual adjusting. For more information, look at the Performance Enhancements section of this chapter

- *disk_repair_time:* specifies the amount of time before an ASM disk is dropped automatically from the disk group after offlining it. This attribute comes into play with FAST MIRROR RESYNC. For more information on this feature, refer to the respective section in this chapter.

- *template.<template_name>.redundancy:* redundancy level of template (HIGH ¦ MIRROR ¦ UNPROTECTED)

- *template.<template_name>.stripe:* striping unit size of template (COARSE ¦ FINE)

If creating a 10g database with *dbca* and using ASM disk groups with the attribute *compatible.rdbms*=11.1, an error is encountered.

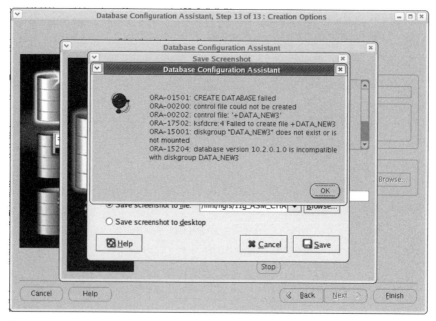

Figure 13.2: *Error with Creating 10g Database*

Resetting the CSSd

It is known that part of Oracle's Clusterware is needed, namely the Cluster Synchronization Service daemon (CSSd), in a single instance installation to communicate between a DB instance and an ASM instance. It is necessary to perform some operations as *root user* before creating an 11g ASM instance under Linux and Unix. In a cluster environment, this daemon is started with different start options than in a single instance installation in order to reboot the node in case of failure of the daemon.

When using the Oracle 11g *dbca*, it asks that *$ORACLE_HOME/bin/localconfig reset* be run in order to upgrade the version of the cluster synchronization services (CSS) if necessary. This is the case if creating a new 11g database is desired. There is no 11g ASM instance up and running and the CSSd is scheduled to start from a 10g ORACLE_HOME.

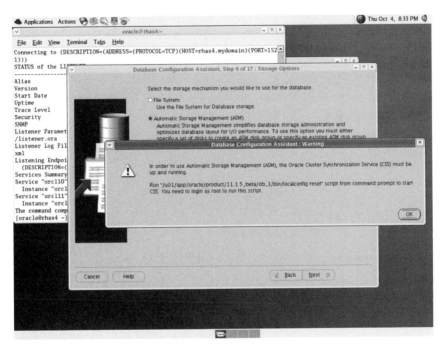

Figure 13.3: *Upgrading CCS in 11g dbca*

ASM Rolling Upgrade

An UPGRADE of ASM in a clustered environment is very different from a single instance installation. If there are multiple ASM instances with the parameter *cluster_database*=TRUE that are protected by the clusterware, the 11g ASM ROLLING UPGRADES New Feature can be used. This allows the ASM software to be upgraded in a rolling fashion, which means node by node in the cluster. As a result, it was not possible to test it; however, it is already documented in the Oracle® Database Storage Administrator's Guide 11g Release 1 (11.1) Part Number B31107-02. This can be done with the new syntax:

```
ALTER SYSTEM START ROLLING MIGRATION TO 11.2.0.0.0;
```

> ⚠ Rolling Upgrade for ASM only works from 11g upwards. So this cannot be used to upgrade from 10g to 11g!

This puts the entire ASM cluster into the rolling upgrade mode. This enables the ASM cluster software to be run in a multiversion mode. In order to do this, first upgrade the Oracle Clusterware on all nodes of the cluster to the new version before the upgrade of the ASM software can be started. During the rolling upgrade, only very limited operations are allowed in the cluster such as:

- Disk group mount and dismount

- Database file open, close, resize, and delete

- Limited access to fixed views and fixed packages

After the rolling upgrade process has been started, it is possible to shutdown one ASM instance after the other in order to upgrade the software installation.

ASM Fast Mirror Resync

This feature utilizes the disk group attribute *disk_repair_time* to determine how long to wait before an ASM disk is permanently dropped from an ASM disk group after it was taken offline for whatever reason. The default of *disk_repair_time* is 3.6 hours, which is 190 minutes. It is unknown where this strange default value comes from. The time can be specified in minutes, hours and days (M¦H¦D). If a unit is not specified, hours is used by default. This means that if a disk of an ASM disk group becomes unavailable for only a short period of time, the server waits for the disk to become available again instead of forcibly removing it at once from the disk group as was the case with Oracle 10g. This can be very handy if a disk is temporarily inaccessible possibly because of a temporary cable disconnect.

> Note: Fast mirror resynchronization of a disk group can be switched off by changing its attribute *disk_repair_time* to 0.

In 10g, such a disk would be dropped from the disk group right away. This could cause unnecessary re-balancing operations with lots of I/O load and need to be fixed twice. The first time, ASM would rebalance the disk group after dropping the disk. Oracle would then re-stripe everything within the disk group which was striped across *n* disks before the drop of the disk across now *n-1* disks. This re-balancing would have to take place a second time in order to re-stripe everything across again (n-1)+1 disks after re-adding the disk to the disk group later on. All these expensive I/Os can be prevented with the fast mirror resynchronization feature in 11g.

In the 11g scenario with fast mirror resync, the time that is needed to resynchronize a failure is reduced dramatically if the failure is only a transient failure and can be fixed within *disk_repair_time*. Only those extents that have been marked as modified in between need to be rebalanced after the failed disk has re-joined the disk group.

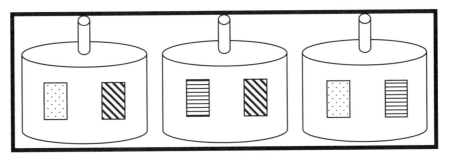

Figure 13.4: *ASM disk group with normal redundancy in 10g*

Figure 13.5: *Disk Two cannot be accessed temporarily*

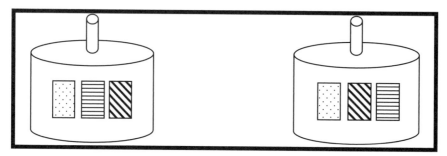

Figure 13.6: *Disk is dropped right away, all extents directly recreated on remaining disks*

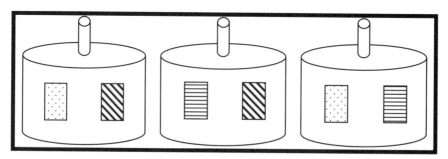

Figure 13.7: *Disk re-added to the disk group, extents rebalanced again*

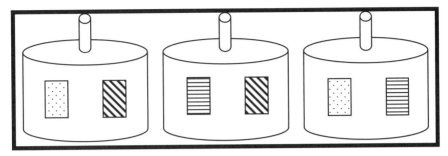

Figure 13.8: *ASM disk group with normal redundancy in 11g with disk_repair_time=3.6 hours*

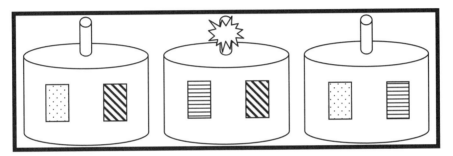

Figure 13.9: *Disk Two cannot be accessed temporarily*

Figure 13.10: *Failure time < disk_repair_time, modified extents are flagged as dirty*

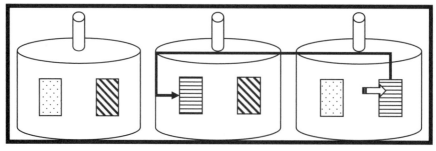

Figure 13.11: Modified Extents being Resynced

The view *v$asm_disk* has a column REPAIR_TIMER that shows the number of seconds remaining until the disk is automatically dropped and 0 if not failed.

> 🔔 Fast mirror resynchronization can dramatically reduce the time needed to rebalance a disk group when a disk becomes available again in time after a temporary disconnect.

The drawback of fast mirror resync is that in the time between the failure and the return of the disk, there is only one mirror of those extents left which are on the failed disk if the disk group uses normal redundancy. This is a dangerous situation. Keep this in mind when creating ASM disk groups with normal redundancy.

> 💣 The use of ASM disk groups with normal redundancy in combination with fast mirror resynchronization is risky. In case of disconnect of a second disk in the disk group, all mirrors of extents might be lost at the same time. This effectively could mean permanent loss of data. By default, there is vulnerability for the duration of 3.6 hours (190 minutes),

The view *v$asm_file* has the column REDUNDANCY_LOWERED as of 10gR2 which shows whether an ASM file has extents without the appropriate number of mirrors for some reason:

```
SYS AS SYSDBA @ +ASM SQL> SELECT group_number, file_number,
REDUNDANCY_LOWERED FROM  v$asm_file;

GROUP_NUMBER FILE_NUMBER REDUNDANCY_LOWERED
------------ ----------- -------------------
           1         256 Y
           1         257 N
           1         258 N
           1         259 N
           1         260 N
           1         261 N
           1         262 N
           1         263 N
           1         264 N
           1         265 N
           1         266 Y
```

A possible reason for a lowered redundancy could, among others, be an inaccessible disk in the disk group. Another reason for lowered redundancy of extents could be a lack of sufficient disk space in the disk group or an insufficient number of fail groups required for the redundancy level. ASM files showing LOWERED_REDUNDANCY in *v$asm_file* are an indicator for vulnerability. Check to see if the disks are accessible and have enough fail groups for the redundancy level and if the ASM disk group is running out disk space.

ASM Performance Enhancements

Variable size of Allocation Units

ASM uses allocation units (AU) as the basic units of allocation within a disk group. By default, the size of these AUs is 1MB in Oracle 10g. ASM extents are the raw storage used to hold the content of an ASM file. ASM mirrors ASM files on an extent basis. In Oracle Database 10g, each data extent is a single Allocation Unit.

The metadata for these extents are stored in bitmaps which describe the structure of an ASM file. These extent maps consume disk space as well as shared memory. The memory part is sent from the ASM instance to the ASMB background process of the DB instance. In Oracle 10g, ASM uses two different sizes for the AUs, 1MB for course striping and 128KB for fine striping.

Because of the one to one mapping of an extent to an AU in Oracle 10g, an ASM file extent map can grow to gigabytes in size in a very large database that can cause problems when an ASM file must be opened. It also creates inefficiencies in memory usage.

Oracle was aware of this problem already in 10g and addressed it with a workaround. In 10g, it is possible to increase the size for AUs for course striping to 16MB and for fine stripes to 1MB by adjusting the two hidden underscore-parameters:

- *_asm_ausize*=16777216

- *_asm_stripesize*=104857

It is not possible to change these parameters after disk groups have already been created. In other words, the parameters must be adjusted in the init file of the ASM instance and the instance restarted to make the changes effective before creating disk groups. It is necessary to adjust all templates for ASM disk groups additionally. This feature provides the possibility to reduce the size of the extent maps to 1/16 in an Oracle 10g environment which allows managing the database with 10TB upwards to PB in ASM. For more information about this feature in 10g, see Metalink Note:368055.1

In order to find out how much shared memory is needed to handle the extent maps, it is necessary to first find out how much ASM disk space the database utilizes:

```
SELECT SUM(bytes) / (1024*1024*1024)
FROM v$datafile;
SELECT SUM(bytes) / (1024*1024*1024)
FROM v$logfile a, v$log b
WHERE a.group#=b.group#;
SELECT SUM(bytes) / (1024*1024*1024)
FROM v$tempfile
WHERE status='ONLINE';
```

There is a formula to calculate this additional Shared Pool memory for an Oracle 10g database that uses ASM storage depending on the redundancy level (number of mirrors) of the ASM disk groups used by the instance:

- 1MB of additional shared pool for every 100GB of disk space + an additional 2MB for external redundancy (no mirroring),

- 1MB of additional shared pool for every 50GB of disk space + an additional 4MB for normal redundancy (two mirrors),

- 1MB of additional shared pool for every 33GB of disk space + an additional 6MB for high redundancy (three mirrors)

Beginning with Oracle 11g, it is possible to have AUs of different sizes within the same ASM disk group, even within the same ASM file. With this variable size extent support, the amount of shared memory needed for ASM can be reduced dramatically for very large databases (VLDB). By this, large files can be opened much faster because the amount of administrative shared memory structures is much less than with the old 1MB AUs. This feature is enabled by default and it does not need any additional administrative actions to use.

In 11g, an extent can be composed of multiple AUs and Oracle uses a special algorithm to automatically adjust the size of AUs as soon as the size of an ASM datafile exceeds a certain threshold. This means that the size of the extent maps can be reduced to 1/8 and even 1/64 with Oracle 11g ASM, thereby making the opening of very large ASM files much faster. An ASM file can

---

ASM Performance Enhancements

grow to a size of up to 140 PB! Oracle 11g Database supports datafile sizes up to 128 TB (only for bigfile tablespaces). ASM supports files with even greater sizes in any redundancy mode. The ASM file size limits are as follows:

- External redundancy - 140 PB

- Normal redundancy - 42 PB

- High redundancy - 15 PB

Here is how it works. By DEFAULT for the first 20000 extents (0-19999), the AU size is 1MB for Oracle 11g, as it was the default for all extents in Oracle 10g ASM. This one to one mapping of extents to AUs for a datafile is used until the ASM file reaches the size of 20GB. As of the 20001st extent, 8 AUs form an extent set which means that the size of the unit which is represented by one pointer in the extent map (an extent) is automatically increased to a set of 8 AUs. This reduces the size of the extent map to describe the ASM file to one eighth starting from here up to a size of 40GB for the datafile.

As of AU number 40000 in an ASM file, the number of AUs used to form one extent set is again automatically incremented by a factor of eight. In other words, 64 AUs of 1MB size make up one extent set as soon as the file gets larger than 40 gigabytes.

💣 Variable size extent support only works for disk groups with compatible attributes adjusted to at least 11g!

So far, just the DEFAULT behavior of ASM in Oracle 11g has been reviewed. It is also possible to manually fix the size of all AUs within an ASM disk group to a uniform size by adjusting the disk group attribute *au_size*. This must be done directly when the disk group is created and cannot be changed later on. The AU for fine striping is always 128KB, as it was in 10g ASM. The AU for an ASM disk group can be adjusted at creation time with the disk group attribute *au_size* to 1, 2, 4, 8, 16, 32 or 64 MB.

By using fine grained striping for redo log files, a lower latency is reached because smaller units get distributed across all disk members of an ASM disk group. Oracle uses AUs as stripes for files in ASM storage and spreads a file in an ASM disk group across all disks in a fail group. So now there is striping within a fail group and mirroring across the fail groups within a disk group. By using coarse striping for datafiles, Oracle achieves load balancing of read write operations across all disks within a disk group.

ASM Fast Rebalance

If there has ever been the need to remove a disk from an ASM disk group or add a disk, it should be known that the rebalancing which occurs after such an action can be significant and this should not be done unless absolutely needed. Especially in a clustered ASM configuration, the rebalancing can cause the sending of lots of extent map lock and extent map unlock messages between ASM instances.

In order to prevent this, it is possible with Oracle ASM 11g, where the ALTER DISKGROUP *<dg_name>* MOUNT *command* has been enhanced, to mount ASM disk groups in restricted mode. If a diskgroup is mounted in restricted mode by one ASM instance in a cluster, no other instance can mount the ASM disk group and access any files there. This eliminates the overhead of sending locking messages, which improves the performance of the rebalancing operation.

An ASM disk group that is mounted in restricted mode on one node of the cluster can be maintained fully like a disk group that is mounted in non-restricted mode, noting that now the maintenance procedure can be finished much faster. After the maintenance operation is finished, it is necessary to unmount the disk group explicitly and then re-mount it in normal mode.

The below code listing shows the commands:

```
SYS AS SYSDBA @ +ASM SQL> ALTER DISKGROUP data DISMOUNT;
SYS AS SYSDBA @ +ASM SQL> ALTER DISKGROUP data MOUNT RESTRICTED;

- - Perform maintenance now

SYS AS SYSDBA @ +ASM SQL> ALTER DISKGROUP data DISMOUNT;
SYS AS SYSDBA @ +ASM SQL> ALTER DISKGROUP data MOUNT;
```

It is also possible to start up an ASM in restricted session mode as the first ASM instance in a cluster. This causes all disk groups to be mounted by this particular instance in restricted mode for maintenance:

```
SYS AS SYSDBA @ +ASM SQL> STARTUP RESTRICT
```

Disk groups cannot be mounted in restricted mode while the ASM cluster is performing a rolling upgrade operation.

Stretched ASM cluster configuration with ASM Preferred Mirror Read in 11g

Preferred mirror read is a feature that is particularly relevant for extended cluster environments. Such configurations are also called stretched clusters. They are typically used to mirror entire data centers across distances longer than 6 miles. Assume that there are data centers which are located 40 miles from each other and the goal is to mirror the two sites. For this, use ASM shared storage for an Oracle cluster that has member nodes with active instances in each site that is to be mirrored. For the ASM storage, define one ASM disk group with multiple failure groups. The hardware requirements for such a configuration will not be covered here. It is a special technology called Dark Fiber that allows for the transmission of light signals across long distances with an acceptable low latency for a round trip of a message in a cluster configuration. The limitations that are confronted in such an environment are caused by the speed of light, which cannot travel over a distance less than 200 miles per millisecond and requirements of the cluster software, which cannot accept long latencies for network pings and pings to the voting disk and for a normal disk read. If the cluster software considers a remote disk to be down, it will attempt to reconfigure the cluster.

In 10g, an instance in an Oracle Real Application Cluster must always use the primary copy of an extent in order to read it, even if the secondary copy is located in the local fail group and the primary copy is on the remote site. This has the negative effect that the primary copy of an extent needs to be read from the remote disks into the other instance and would be shipped through the interconnect to the requesting instance.

This problem is addressed in 11g with the preferred mirror read feature. It is possible now to define preferred read fail groups within an ASM disk group for each instance in a clustered ASM configuration, which allows for a preferred read of the local to the instance copy of an extent no matter if it is the primary or the secondary copy. This configuration is shown in the graphic below.

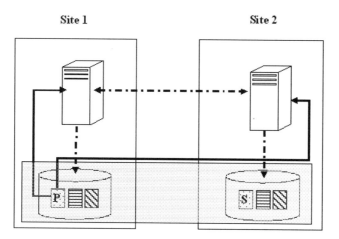

Figure 13.12: *Stretched Oracle 10g Cluster with Two ASM Fail Groups*

The graphic shows the situation in a 10g extended cluster configuration with two mirrored sites that both use the same ASM diskgroup with normal redundancy and two fail groups. Each fail group holds either the primary or the secondary copy of every ASM extent.

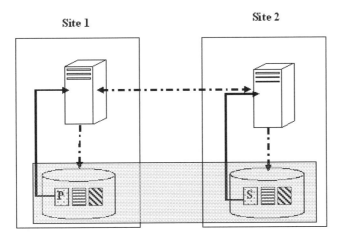

Figure 13.13: *Stretched Oracle 11g Cluster with Two ASM Fail Groups and Preferred Mirror Read*

The preferred fail group can be configured to use for an instance in a cluster by adjusting the *asm_preferred_read_failure_groups* initialization parameter for ASM instances. This parameter is dynamically changeable with the need for restart with an ALTER SYSTEM statement. It is not valid for DB instances - only for ASM instances.

> 💣 It is important to make sure that the failure groups specified in the *asm_preferred_read_failure_groups* parameter contain only disks that are local to the corresponding ASM instance.

There is a new column in *v$asm_disk* that shows the character Y if a disk belongs to a preferred read fail group for the ASM instance:

```
SELECT preferred_read FROM v$asm_disk;
```

The column PREFERRED_READ displays the status of the preferred read failure group:

- U - Disk group has no preferred read failure group
- Y - Disk is a preferred read disk
- N - Disk is not a preferred read disk

For a disk group with one or more preferred read failure groups, if the disk is in one of the preferred read failure groups, the value of this column is Y; otherwise it is N.

The view *v$asm_disk_iostat* can be queried from both an ASM instance as well as a DB instance for the disk I/O statistics. Queried on a DB instance, it only shows the statistics for this ASM client. If it is queried from an ASM instance, information will be shown for the I/O behavior of each ASM client.

```
SELECT * FROM v$asm_disk_iostat;
```

Now look at how to setup preferred mirror read. Assume that there are two sites which need to be mirrored with ASM using normal redundancy with two failure groups and preferred mirror read. Here are the *pfiles* of the two ASM instances.

init+ASM1.ora on site1:

```
instance_type='asm'
cluster_database=true
asm_diskgroups='DATA', 'FRA'
+ASM2.instance_number=2
+ASM1.instance_number=1
+ASM1.ASM_PREFERRED_READ_FAILURE_GROUPS=DATA.SITE1
. . .
```

init+ASM2.ora on site2:

```
instance_type='asm'
cluster_database=true
asm_diskgroups='DATA', 'FRA'
```

```
+ASM2.instance_number=2
+ASM1.instance_number=1
+ASM2.ASM_PREFERRED_READ_FAILURE_GROUPS=DATA.SITE2
. . .
```

How many fail groups for which redundancy level?

As a best practice, Oracle recommends for a two site stretched cluster with preferred mirror read and normal redundancy to configure two fail groups – one for each site – with the local disks as members of the same fail group. Only the local fail group should be configured as the preferred read fail group.

> 💣 Do not configure three fail groups in a two site stretched ASM cluster with a normal redundancy level because, in this case, it is not guaranteed that ASM would create one mirror on each site.

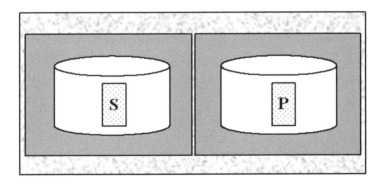

Figure 13.14: *Two Site Stretch Cluster with Normal Redundancy and Two Fail Groups*

If a high redundancy is to be used for a stretched cluster with two sites, a maximum of four fail groups is recommended – two for each site. Here, both local fail groups should be configured as preferred read fail groups for each local ASM instance. All the member disks for the fail groups should be local to the respective

---

ASM instance. The configuration of a disk group with three way mirroring (high redundancy) and two sites with preferred mirror read fail groups is tricky. It is best to define a maximum of four fail groups here and never define three fail groups. Either use two or four (one or two local on each site). Otherwise, it might happen that ASM does not really create mirrors of all extents on every site. This could then again affect the latency for reading an extent because all of them could be located remotely. Also, there would not be protection against the failure of an entire site. The figure below shows a two site stretch cluster with high redundancy disk group which has four fail groups, two on each site.

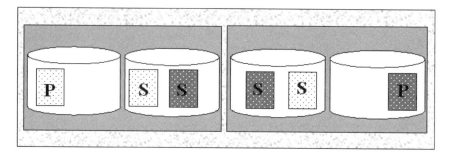

Figure 13.15: *Two Site Stretch Cluster with Four Fail Groups*

If mirroring three data centers is desired as a stretched cluster with three sites, then configure one ASM disk group with three fail groups – one on each site. ASM would subsequently create one local mirror copy for every extent in each site. This fully protects against the complete failure of any of the sites.

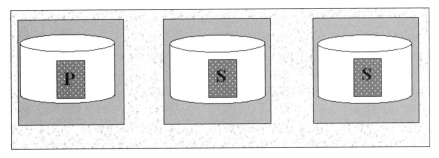

Figure 13.16: *Three Site Stretch Cluster with High Redundancy and Three Fail Groups*

ASMCMD new features

With the version 10gR2, Oracle has introduced the ASM command line interface *asmcmd*. This makes it easy to find out how much space is left in the disk groups and which files are inside the ASM storage. It is not necessary to know what an Oracle ASM instance is and how to start an Oracle Container for Java (OC4J) in order to use the enterprise manager interface for ASM. All that needs to be in place is a shell with the proper environment ($ORACLE_SID and $ORACLE_HOME).

Oracle 11g ships with an enhanced version of *asmcmd*. There are a number of additional functionalities and new commands in 11g. Here is a listing of the help function in *asmcmd* 11g:

```
[oracle@rhas4 ~]$ export ORACLE_SID=+ASM
[oracle@rhas4 ~]$ asmcmd
ASMCMD> help
...

        Type "help [command]" to get help on a specific ASMCMD
command.

        commands:
        --------
        help

        cd
        cp
        du
```

```
find
ls
lsct
lsdg
mkalias
mkdir
pwd
rm
rmalias

md_backup
md_restore

lsdsk
remap
```

The *lsdsk* command can be used to display the disk paths for all ASM disks. It utilizes the dynamic performance view *v$asm_disk* and *gv$asm_disk* in a clustered environment if the ASM instance is up and running. If it is down, then *asmcmd* can only run in non-connected mode. In this case, *lsdsk* reads the headers of the ASM disks. This command comes in very handy for storage administrators. They can use it to obtain and maintain lists of disks used by ASM.

```
ASMCMD> lsdsk
Path
/dev/raw/raw1
/dev/raw/raw2
/dev/raw/raw3
/dev/raw/raw
[oracle@rhas4 ~]$ asmcmd
ASMCMD-08103: failed to connect to ASM; ASMCMD running in non-
connected mode
ASMCMD> lsdsk
Path
/dev/raw/raw1
/dev/raw/raw2
/dev/raw/raw3
/dev/raw/raw4
```

The *cp* command can be used to copy files from one ASM diskgroup to another one regardless of whether it is a local disk group or one which is located remotely. The most interesting new commands are *md_backup* and *md_restore*. With these commands, the metadata of ASM disk groups can be dumped into a flat file and this data can be used to restore the metadata in case the diskgroup needs to be rebuilt even if a new diskgroup is created.

```
ASMCMD> help md_backup
        md_backup [-b <backup_file>]
                  [-g '<diskgroup_name>,<diskgroup_name>,...']

        Perform ASM metadata backup for disk groups.
        Back up into backup file disk group metadata information
including
        fail groups, disks, attributes, aliases, and templates.
        -b Store information into <backup_file>. If not specified,
it will
            be stored into the file ambr_backup_intermediate_file.
        -g Disk groups to backup. All diskgroups are backed up by
default.

ASMCMD> help md_restore
        md_restore -b <backup_file> [-li]
                   [-t (full)|nodg|newdg] [-f <sql_script_file>]
                   [-g '<diskgroup_name>,<diskgroup_name>,...']
                   [-o
'<old_diskgroup_name>:<new_diskgroup_name>,...']

        Perform ASM Metadata restore for disk groups.
        -b Read metadata information from <backup_file>.
        -l Print messages to a file (Not implemented).
        -i Ignore errors. Normally if md_restore encounters an
error, it
            will stop. Specifying this flag ignores that.
        -t Specify diskgroup creation.
            full - create disk group and restore metadata.
            nodg - restore metadata only.
            newdg - create disk group with a different name and
restore
                    metadata; -o is required.
        -f Write SQL commands to <sql_script_file> instead of
executing them.
        -g Select the disk groups to be restored. If no disk groups
defined,
            all of them will be restored.
        -o Rename disk group <old_diskgroup_name> to
<new_diskgroup_name>.

ASMCMD> md_backup -b my_diskgroup_metadata.lst
Disk group to be backed up: DATA
Disk group to be backed up: FRA
```

The metadata contain information about the disk path, disk name, failure groups, attributes, templates and user created directory structure of disk groups. The following listing shows the exported metadata from the dumpfile which was created in the local directory with the name that is specified. The default file name for the metadata dump is *ambr_backup_intermediate_file*.

```
[oracle@rhas4 ~]$ cat my_diskgroup_metadata.lst
@diskgroup_set =    (
  {
    'ATTRINFO' => {
'AU_SIZE' => '1048576',
'DISK_REPAIR_TIME' => '3.6h',
'COMPATIBLE.ASM' => '11.1.0.0.0',
'COMPATIBLE.RDBMS' => '10.1.0.0.0'
},
'DISKSINFO' => {
'DATA_0001' => {
'DATA_0001' => {
'TOTAL_MB' => '2047',
'FAILGROUP' => 'DATA_0001',
'NAME' => 'DATA_0001',
'DGNAME' => 'DATA',
'PATH' => '/dev/raw/raw2'
}
},
'DATA_0000' => {
'DATA_0000' => {
'TOTAL_MB' => '2047',
'FAILGROUP' => 'DATA_0000',
'NAME' => 'DATA_0000',
'DGNAME' => 'DATA',
'PATH' => '/dev/raw/raw1'
}
}
},
'DGINFO' => {
'DGTORESTORE' => 0,
'DGCOMPAT' => '11.1.0.0.0',
'DGNAME' => 'DATA',
'DGDBCOMPAT' => '10.1.0.0.0',
'DGTYPE' => 'NORMAL',
'DGAUSZ' => '1048576'
},
'ALIASINFO' => {},
'TEMPLATEINFO' => {
'6' => {
'DGNAME' => 'DATA',
'STRIPE' => 'COARSE',
'TEMPNAME' => 'XTRANSPORT',
'REDUNDANCY' => 'MIRROR',
'SYSTEM' => 'Y'
},
'11' => {
'DGNAME' => 'DATA',
```

```
'STRIPE' => 'FINE',
'TEMPNAME' => 'ONLINELOG',
'REDUNDANCY' => 'MIRROR',
'SYSTEM' => 'Y'
},
'3' => {
'DGNAME' => 'DATA',
'STRIPE' => 'COARSE',
'TEMPNAME' => 'DATAGUARDCONFIG',
'REDUNDANCY' => 'MIRROR',
'SYSTEM' => 'Y'
},
'7' => {
'DGNAME' => 'DATA',
'STRIPE' => 'COARSE',
'TEMPNAME' => 'AUTOBACKUP',
'REDUNDANCY' => 'MIRROR',
'SYSTEM' => 'Y'
},
'9' => {
'DGNAME' => 'DATA',
'STRIPE' => 'COARSE',
'TEMPNAME' => 'TEMPFILE',
'REDUNDANCY' => 'MIRROR',
'SYSTEM' => 'Y'
},
'2' => {
'DGNAME' => 'DATA',
'STRIPE' => 'COARSE',
'TEMPNAME' => 'ASM_STALE',
'REDUNDANCY' => 'HIGH',
'SYSTEM' => 'Y'
},
'12' => {
'DGNAME' => 'DATA',
'STRIPE' => 'COARSE',
'TEMPNAME' => 'ARCHIVELOG',
'REDUNDANCY' => 'MIRROR',
'SYSTEM' => 'Y'
},
'8' => {
'DGNAME' => 'DATA',
'STRIPE' => 'COARSE',
'TEMPNAME' => 'BACKUPSET',
'REDUNDANCY' => 'MIRROR',
'SYSTEM' => 'Y'
},
'4' => {
'DGNAME' => 'DATA',
'STRIPE' => 'FINE',
'TEMPNAME' => 'FLASHBACK',
'REDUNDANCY' => 'MIRROR',
'SYSTEM' => 'Y'
},
'1' => {
'DGNAME' => 'DATA',
'STRIPE' => 'COARSE',
```

```
'TEMPNAME' => 'DUMPSET',
'REDUNDANCY' => 'MIRROR',
'SYSTEM' => 'Y'
},
'0' => {
'DGNAME' => 'DATA',
'STRIPE' => 'COARSE',
'TEMPNAME' =>'PARAMETERFILE',
'REDUNDANCY' => 'MIRROR',
'SYSTEM' => 'Y'
},
'10' => {
'DGNAME' => 'DATA',
'STRIPE' => 'COARSE',
'TEMPNAME' => 'DATAFILE',
'REDUNDANCY' => 'MIRROR',
'SYSTEM' => 'Y'
},
'13' => {
'DGNAME' => 'DATA',
'STRIPE' => 'FINE',
'TEMPNAME' => 'CONTROLFILE',
'REDUNDANCY' => 'HIGH',
'SYSTEM' => 'Y'
},
'5' => {
'DGNAME' => 'DATA',
'STRIPE' => 'COARSE',
'TEMPNAME'=> CHANGETRACKING',
'REDUNDANCY' => 'MIRROR',
'SYSTEM' => 'Y'
}
}
                              },
{
'DISKSINFO' => {
'FAIL1' => {
'FRA_0001' => {
'TOTAL_MB' => '2047',
'FAILGROUP' => 'FAIL1',
'NAME' => 'FRA_0001',
'DGNAME' => 'FRA',
'PATH' => '/dev/raw/raw3'
}
},
'FAIL2' => {
'FRA_0000' => {
'TOTAL_MB' => '2047',
'FAILGROUP' => 'FAIL2',
'NAME' => 'FRA_0000',
'DGNAME' => 'FRA',
'PATH' => '/dev/raw/raw4'
}
}
},
'DGINFO' => {
'DGTORESTORE' => 0,
```

```
'DGCOMPAT' => '10.1.0.0.0',
'DGNAME' => 'FRA',
'DGDBCOMPAT' => '10.1.0.0.0',
'DGTYPE' => 'NORMAL',
'DGAUSZ' => '1048576'
},
'ALIASINFO' => {},
'TEMPLATEINFO' => {
'6' => {
'DGNAME' => 'FRA',
'STRIPE' => 'COARSE',
'TEMPNAME' => 'ASM_STALE',
'REDUNDANCY' => 'HIGH',
'SYSTEM' => 'Y'
},
'11' => {
'DGNAME' => 'FRA',
'STRIPE' => 'FINE',
'TEMPNAME' => 'CONTROLFILE',
 => 'HIGH',
'SYSTEM' => 'Y'
},
'3' => {
'DGNAME' => 'FRA',
'STRIPE' => 'COARSE',
'TEMPNAME' => 'CHANGETRACKING',
'REDUNDANCY' => 'MIRROR',
'SYSTEM' => 'Y'
},
'7' => {
'DGNAME' => 'FRA',
'STRIPE' => 'COARSE',
'TEMPNAME' => 'TEMPFILE',
'REDUNDANCY' => 'MIRROR',
'SYSTEM' => 'Y'
},
'9' => {
'DGNAME' => 'FRA',
'STRIPE' => 'FINE',
'TEMPNAME' => 'ONLINELOG',
'REDUNDANCY' => 'MIRROR',
'SYSTEM' => 'Y'
},
'2' => {
'DGNAME' => 'FRA',
'STRIPE' => 'FINE',
'TEMPNAME' => 'FLASHBACK',
'REDUNDANCY' => 'MIRROR',
'SYSTEM' => 'Y'
},
'12' => {
'DGNAME' => 'FRA',
'STRIPE' => 'COARSE',
'TEMPNAME' => 'DUMPSET',
'REDUNDANCY' => 'MIRROR',
'SYSTEM' => 'Y'
},
```

```
'8' => {
'DGNAME' => 'FRA',
STRIPE' => 'COARSE',
'TEMPNAME' => 'DATAFILE',
'REDUNDANCY' => 'MIRROR',
'SYSTEM' => 'Y'
},
'1' => {
'DGNAME' => 'FRA',
'STRIPE' => 'COARSE',
'TEMPNAME'=> 'DATAGUARDCONFIG',
'REDUNDANCY' => 'MIRROR',
'SYSTEM' => 'Y'
},
'4' => {
'DGNAME' => 'FRA',
'STRIPE' => 'COARSE',
'TEMPNAME' => 'XTRANSPORT',
'REDUNDANCY' => 'MIRROR',
'SYSTEM' => 'Y'
},
'0' => {
'DGNAME' => 'FRA',
'STRIPE' => 'COARSE',
'TEMPNAME' =>'PARAMETERFILE',
'REDUNDANCY' => 'MIRROR',
'SYSTEM' => 'Y'
},
'10' => {
'DGNAME' => 'FRA',
'STRIPE' => 'COARSE',
'TEMPNAME' => 'ARCHIVELOG',
'REDUNDANCY' => 'MIRROR',
'SYSTEM' => 'Y'
},
'13' => {
'DGNAME' => 'FRA',
'STRIPE' => 'COARSE',
'TEMPNAME' => 'BACKUPSET',
'REDUNDANCY' => 'MIRROR',
'SYSTEM' => 'Y'
},
'5' => {
'DGNAME' => 'FRA',
'STRIPE' => 'COARSE',
'TEMPNAME' => 'AUTOBACKUP',
'REDUNDANCY' => 'MIRROR',
'SYSTEM' => 'Y'
}
}
}
);
```

Automatic and manual ASM disk repair in 11g

Oracle 11g ASM is capable of repairing broken blocks on the fly when reading them. When Oracle finds a broken block, it attempts to read it from the mirror copy of the respective extent and repairs the broken version automatically. This can only happen on disk groups with at least normal redundancy and it only happens for those blocks which are read.

The new *remap* command of *asmcmd* can be used to recover a range of unreadable blocks. ASM would read a bad block from the good copy and restore it to a new location on the disk. This can also be run from the enterprise manager interface.

ASM Disk Group Checks Enhanced

The check command was already available in Oracle ASM 10g. It was necessary there to specify what to check with the check command. In 10g it was possible to specify the following values for the check command:

- FILE
- DISKS IN FAILGROUP
- DISK
- ALL

As of Oracle ASM 11g, this command has been simplified. It is no longer necessary to specify what to check because the command makes all available checks in one go. The CHECK keyword performs the following operations without the need for specifications:

- Checks if the disk is consistent
- Cross checks the file extent maps and allocation tables for consistency

- Checks if the metadata of the directories for alias and files are linked correctly

- Checks if the directory tree of the aliases is linked correctly.

- Checks that ASM metadata directories do not have unreadable allocated blocks.

The following two commands issued in an ASM instance would check all disks in the disk group and add a message to the ASM instance's alert log file with information about the successful run of the check and about found broken blocks. In addition, these commands would also recover the bad blocks. The repair option is the DEFAULT for the check command.

```
SYS AS SYSDBA @ +ASM SQL> ALTER DISKGROUP data CHECK;
```

```
SYS AS SYSDBA @ +ASM SQL> ALTER DISKGROUP data CHECK REPAIR;
```

The next command would only check for bad blocks but not recover them.

```
SYS AS SYSDBA @ +ASM SQL> ALTER DISKGROUP data CHECK NOREPAIR;

[oracle@rhas4 ~]$ tail -f
/u01/app/oracle/diag/asm/+asm/+ASM/alert/log.xml
```

The listing below shows the message in the xml version of the alter log of the ASM instance:

```
<txt>SUCCESS: check of diskgroup DATA found no errors
</txt>
</msg>
<msg time='2007-10-22T10:26:33.700+02:00' org_id='oracle'
comp_id='asm'
 client_id='' type='UNKNOWN' level='16'
 host_id='rhas4.mydomain' host_addr='192.168.1.1' module='OMS'
pid='12810'>
<txt>SUCCESS: ALTER DISKGROUP DATA CHECK
</txt>
</msg>
```

The full check for all metadata packages into one single command makes the checks easier, but the drawback is the additional overhead which is burdening the I/O subsystem now and might slow down performance. Additional information on the metadata of ASM in provided in the next section.

ASM metadata

ASM storage is described in a number of so called fixed tables. It is possible to view important parts of this metadata via *(g)v$views* which, in fact, read the information from these *x$tables*. In 11gR1, there are 28 *x$tables* which fully describe the ASM storage and there are 22 *v$views* which show information about ASM.

Some important *x$tables* are:

- *x$kffxpi:* mapping between files and allocation units

- *x$kfdpartner:* disk-to-partner   relationship of two disks of a given ASM diskgroup which hold a mirror copy of the same extent

- *x$kfdat:* details of all free and used allocation units

List of Dynamic Performance Views related to ASM:

```
SYS AS SYSDBA @ +ASM SQL> select view_name from
v$fixed_view_definition
  2  where view_name like '%ASM%';
```

```
VIEW_NAME
----------------------------
GV$ASM_TEMPLATE
V$ASM_TEMPLATE
GV$ASM_ALIAS
V$ASM_ALIAS
GV$ASM_FILE
V$ASM_FILE
GV$ASM_CLIENT
V$ASM_CLIENT
GV$ASM_DISKGROUP
V$ASM_DISKGROUP
GV$ASM_DISKGROUP_STAT
V$ASM_DISKGROUP_STAT
```

```
GV$ASM_DISK
V$ASM_DISK
GV$ASM_DISK_STAT
V$ASM_DISK_STAT
GV$ASM_DISK_IOSTAT
V$ASM_DISK_IOSTAT
GV$ASM_OPERATION
V$ASM_OPERATION
GV$ASM_ATTRIBUTE
V$ASM_ATTRIBUTE

22 rows selected.
```

List of Fixed Tables related to ASM:

```
SYS AS SYSDBA @ +ASM SQL> select name from v$fixed_table where name
like 'X$KF%';
```

```
NAME
-----------------------------
X$KFALS
X$KFCBH
X$KFCCE
X$KFBH
X$KFDSK
X$KFDSK_STAT
X$KFDAT
X$KFDFS
X$KFDDD
X$KFGRP
X$KFGRP_STAT
X$KFGMG
X$KFGBRB
X$KFKID
X$KFKLIB
X$KFMDGRP
X$KFNCL
X$KFNSDSKIOST
X$KFTMTA
X$KFFIL
X$KFFXP
X$KFDPARTNER
X$KFCLLE
X$KFENV
X$KFVOL
X$KFVOLSTAT
X$KFVOFS
X$KFVOFSV

28 rows selected.
```

Conclusion

This chapter covered many of the enhancement to ASM offered in Oracle 11g.

- One of the security enhancements is the ability to more effectively grant permission levels between ASM storage administrators and database administrators. There will be a clearer distinction between what access is granted with *sysdba* privileges and *sysasm* privileges.

- The new Rolling Upgrade feature allows the ASM software to be upgraded in a rolling fashion, which means node by node in the cluster.

- Oracle 11g offers the ability to establish a *disk_repair_time* that determines how long the ASM waits in the event an ASM disk group becomes unavailable. The benefit is that if a disk of an ASM disk group becomes unavailable for only a short period of time, the server waits for the disk to become available again instead of forcibly removing it at once from the disk group.

- 11g provides the ability to have allocation units of different sizes within the same ASM disk group, even within the same ASM file.

- ASM disk groups can be mounted in restricted mode on 11g. If a diskgroup is mounted in restricted mode by one ASM instance in a cluster, no other instance can mount the ASM disk group and access any files there. This eliminates the overhead of sending locking messages, which improves the performance of the rebalancing operation.

- Oracle 11g ships with an enhanced version of *asmcmd*.

- ASM capability is enhanced with the capability of repairing broken blocks on the fly. When Oracle finds a broken block, it attempts to read it from the mirror copy of the respective extent and repairs the broken version automatically.

Oracle has put a lot of marketing energy into the promotion of ASM and these enhancements certainly show the fruits of their labor.

Index

About the Authors

John Garmany

John Garmany is a Senior Oracle DBA with Burleson Consulting. A graduate of West Point, an Airborne Ranger and a retired Lt. Colonel with 20+ years of IT experience. John is an OCP Certified Oracle DBA with a Master Degree in Information Systems, a Graduate Certificate in Software Engineering, and a BS degree (Electrical Engineering) from West Point. A respected Oracle expert and author, John serves as a writer for Oracle Internals, DBAZine and SearchOracle and SELECT Magazine. John is also the author of four bestselling Oracle books by Rampant TechPress, Oracle Press and CRC Press and hosts a popular Oracle Application Server Newsletter.

Steve Karam

 Steve Karam is one of less than 20 DBA's worldwide to achieve the coveted Oracle 10g Certified Master status and the world's youngest OCM and Oracle ACE. A former senior instructor for Oracle University, Steve has a proven track record in performance and troubleshooting on dozens of high profile Oracle systems, and complex Oracle 10g RAC environments. Additionally, Steve has been developing against Oracle databases for ten years in a variety of platforms including PHP, Java, and Application Express.

Lutz Hartmann

Lutz Hartmann is a senior instructor specializing in Oracle trainings for DBAs and developers. Lutz has been an Oracle employee for more than 6 years. After leaving Oracle Corporation, Lutz has raised his own company sysdba database consulting GmbH in Switzerland which provides advanced Oracle consulting and support services as well as custom courses for DBAs and developers.

Lutz was one of the first trainers worldwide to deliver 11g New Features courses for Oracle University and Oracle Support Services. He has delivered Oracle trainings in more than 10 countries and three continents.

Lutz has published a great number of articles on Oracle new features in American, Swiss and German tech magazines and speaks at Oracle User Group meetings from time to time. His blog http://sysdba.wordpress.com is well recognized in the Oracle community and registers more than 100'000 hits per year.

For his outstanding contributions to the oracle communities he was awarded ORACLE ACE in 2006

V.J. Jain

V.J. Jain is an Oracle Database and Applications consultant with over 12 years of experience in database and ERP systems. He specializes in database performance, development, interfaces and high-performance solutions. V.J. actively evaluates Oracle's newest technologies and is a member of the Oracle Partner Network and Beta program. He has published articles on SearchOracle, OraFaq, OTN and is the owner of www.oracle-developer.com.

V.J. received his B.S. in Information and Computer Science from the University of California Irvine and is a veteran of the U.S. Army National Guard who was in military intelligence and held a TS/SCI security clearance. V.J. is the owner of Varun Jain, Inc., a Southern California based consulting firm.

Brian Carr

Brian Carr works as a Senior Oracle DBA and is an Oracle Certified Professional and Oracle ACE. His articles have appeared in SELECT Journal, OTN, Database Trends and Applications, JavaWorld, and DevX. He co-wrote a multithreaded Web crawler and search engine in Perl, as well as an anonymous web browsing service in C#. Brian also wrote a server monitoring solution that has been commercially released. Brian is currently pursuing a Master's degree.